Learning Microsoft Office 2007

Ramesh Bangia
B.Sc., Dip. Comp. Sc.
Formerly: Managing Editor, Software Today
Formerly: Incharge Computer Centre, Hindustan Copper Ltd., New Delhi

KHANNA BOOK PUBLISHING CO. (P) LTD.
Publisher of Engineering and Computer Books
4C/4344, Ansari Road, Darya Ganj, New Delhi-110002
Phone: 011-23244447-48 **Mobile:** +91-99109 09320
E-mail: contact@khannabooks.com, sales@khannapublishers.com
Website: www.khannabooks.com, www.khannapublishers.com

LEARNING MS OFFICE 2007
RAMESH BANGIA

ISBN: 978-81-906116-71

Reprint : 2007, 2008, 2009, 2010, 2011
Revised & Enlarged Edition : 2012
Repeat 2015

Published by:
Khanna Book Publishing Co. (P) Ltd.
Head Off.: 4C/4344, Ansari Road, Darya Ganj, New Delhi-02
Phone: 011-23244448 Telefax: 011-23244447
E-mail: contact@khannabooks.com
Website: www.khannabooks.com

Printed in India by:
S.P.S. Printers & Binders, Delhi

Preface

Learning of a software is both easy and difficult. It depends upto what level you are planning to learn. If you are learning only for the working use, then it is very easy. But, when you try to go deep into it, then you realise how difficult it is to master it.

Microsoft Office 2007 is such a vast subject that it will take a lot of time to understand it fully. This book has been written in mind to make you aware of the options available in the software and how they can be used. It is like telling the child about the steps and stairs. You are the one who is to climb the stair. This book will just guide you how to use the stairs.

I am indeed debited to my publishers Khanna Book Publishing Co. Pvt. Ltd., specially Sheetal Khanna for their suggestions and encouragement given in producing this book.

I would like to thank my family specially my wife Sadhna, kids Mayank and Samarth, for without their criticism this book would not have seen the day.

Suggestions for improvement of the book are indeed welcome.

Ramesh Bangia

CONTENTS

1 Introduction to Windows Vista

Introduction

Windows Vista is the new version of ever popular operating system called Windows. It is an enhancement of the different released till now, i.e., Windows 95, Windows 98, Windows NT, Windows 2000, Windows ME and Windows XP.

Windows Vista comes in five different versions: Home Basic, Home Premium, Business, Enterprise, and Ultimate.

Let us first see what is new in Windows Vista.

What's new in Windows Vista

Explore new features for searching, staying connected, networking, syncing devices, and managing files on your computer. Find things fast, get down to business, and focus on what matters to you.

Searching and organizing

In every folder in Windows, the Search box appears in the upper right corner. When you type in the Search box, Windows filters the view based on what you're typing. Windows looks for words in the file name, tags that you've applied to the file, or other file properties. To find a file in a folder, type any part of a file name in the Search box to find what you're looking for. You can also use Search folders when you don't know where a file is located or when you want to do an advanced search using more than just a single file name or property.

Security

Features such as Windows Firewall and Windows Defender can help keep your computer more secure. Windows Security Center has links for checking your computer's firewall, antivirus software, and update status. BitLocker Drive Encryption allows you to encrypt the entire system partition, which can improve security by preventing hackers from accessing important system files. User Account Control (UAC) can help prevent unauthorized changes to your computer by requiring permission before performing actions that could potentially affect your computer's operation or that change settings that affect other users.

Internet Explorer

Web feeds, tabbed browsing, and always-available search are just a few of the new features

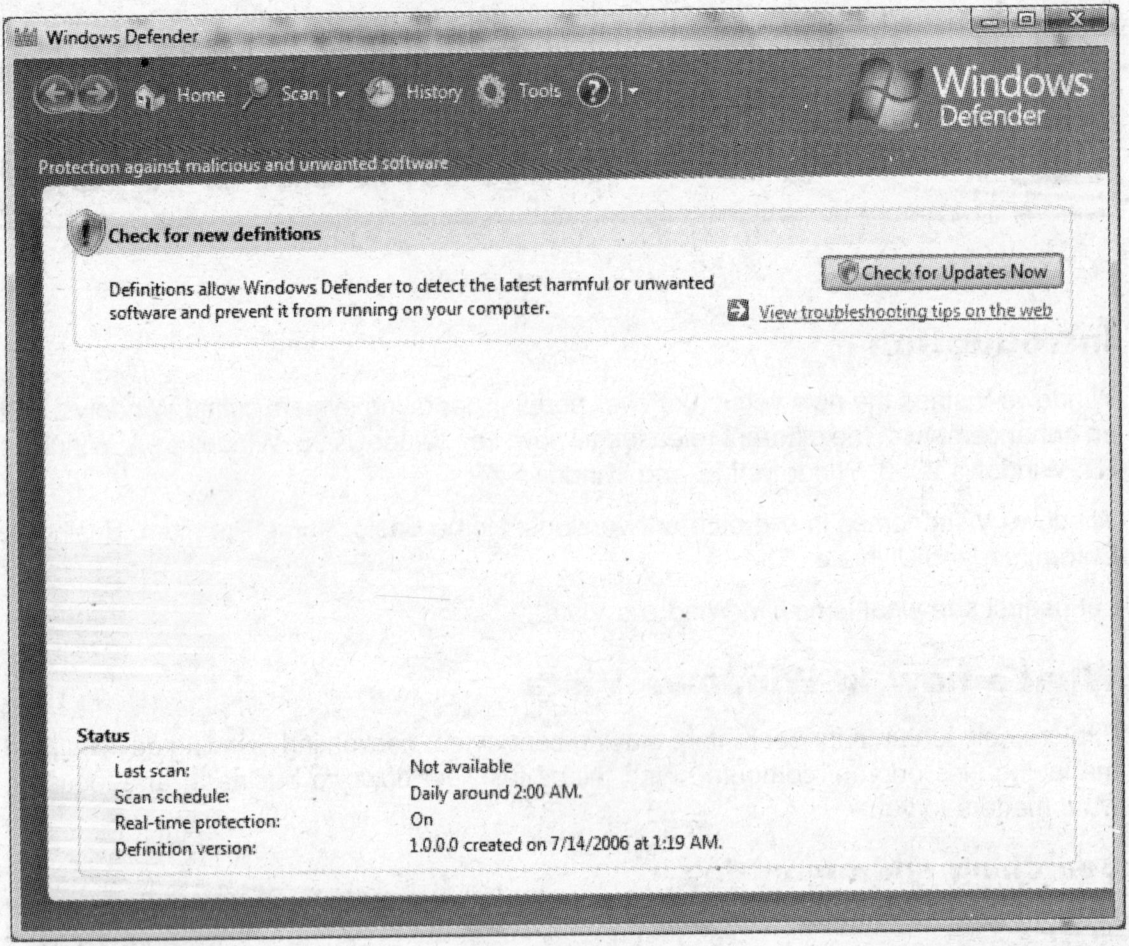

available in Internet Explorer. Web feeds provide frequently updated content published by a website that you can subscribe to for automatic delivery to your web browser. With a feed, you can get content such as breaking news or updates to a blog without having to go

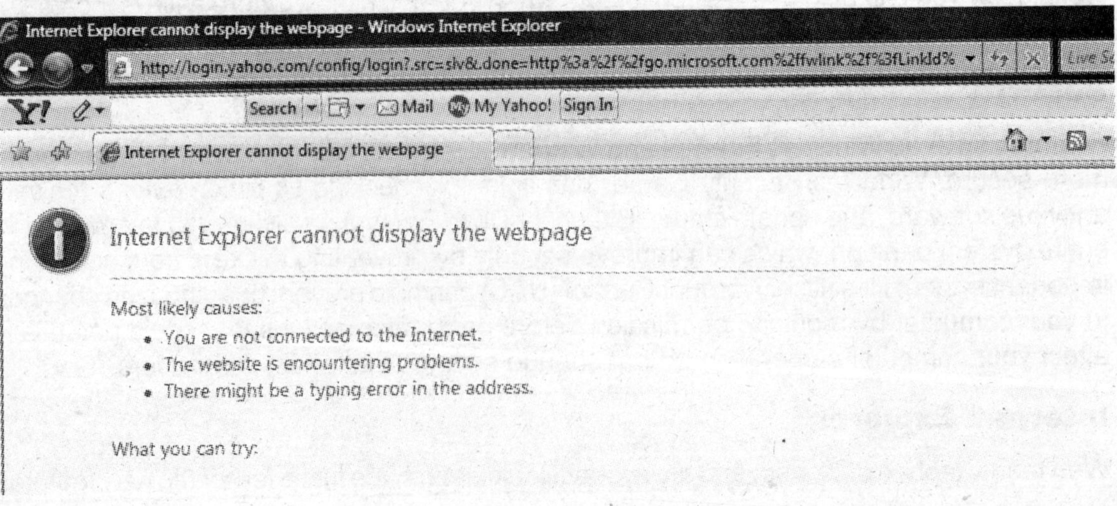

to the website. Tabbed browsing allows you to open multiple websites in a single browser window. You can open webpages or links on new tabs and then switch among them by clicking the tabs.

Sync and sharing

Sync with other devices such as portable music players and Windows Mobile devices. With Sync Center, you can keep devices in sync, manage how your devices sync, start a manual sync, see the status of current sync activities, and check for conflicts.

You can also share files and folders with people on your network, even if they use a computer that's not running Windows. When you share files and folders, other people can open and view the files and folders just as if they were stored on their own computer. And they can make changes, if you allow that.

Ease of Access Center

The new Ease of Access Center replaces Accessibility Options in earlier versions of Windows. The Ease of Access Center comes with several improvements and new features, including centralized access to accessibility settings and a new questionnaire that you can use to get suggestions for accessibility features that you might find useful.

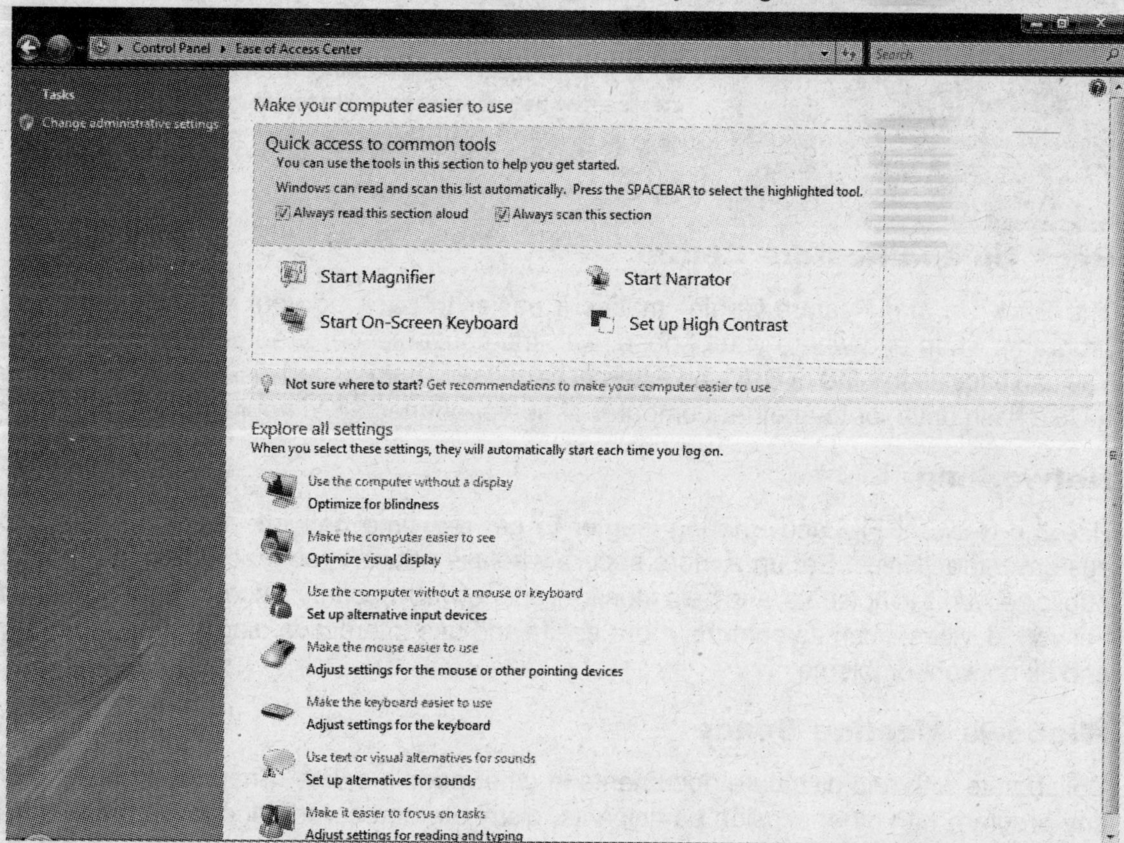

Parental Controls

Parental Controls makes it easy for parents to designate which games their children are allowed to play. Parents can allow or restrict specific game titles, limit their children's play to games that are rated at or below a certain age level, or block games with certain types of content that they don't want their children to see or hear.

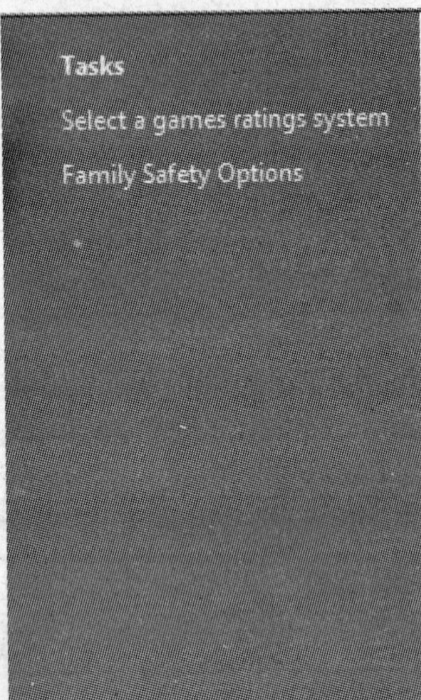

Choose a user and set up Parental Controls

What can I do with Parental Controls?

 One or more administrator accounts do not have a password
turn off parental controls. Click here to add a password for th

sun
Computer administrator
No Password

If you want to apply Parental Controls to someone who isn't in this
create a new user account for them to use.

Why do I need an account for this?

 Create a new user account

Back Up and Restore Center

The Back Up and Restore Center makes it easier to back up your settings, files, and programs when and where you choose, with the convenience of automated scheduling. You can back up to a CD or DVD, an external hard disk, another hard disk on your computer, a USB flash drive, or to another computer or server connected to your network.

Networking

Use the Network File and Sharing Center to get real-time network status and links to customized activities. Set up a more secure wireless network, connect more securely to public networks in hotspots, and help monitor your network security. Access files and shared network devices, such as printers, more easily and use interactive diagnostics to identify and fix network problems.

Windows Meeting Space

Collaborate with and distribute documents to other people online. Share your desktop or any program with other session participants, distribute and co-edit documents, and pass notes to others. Windows Meeting Space works in a meeting room, a favorite hotspot, or where no network exists.

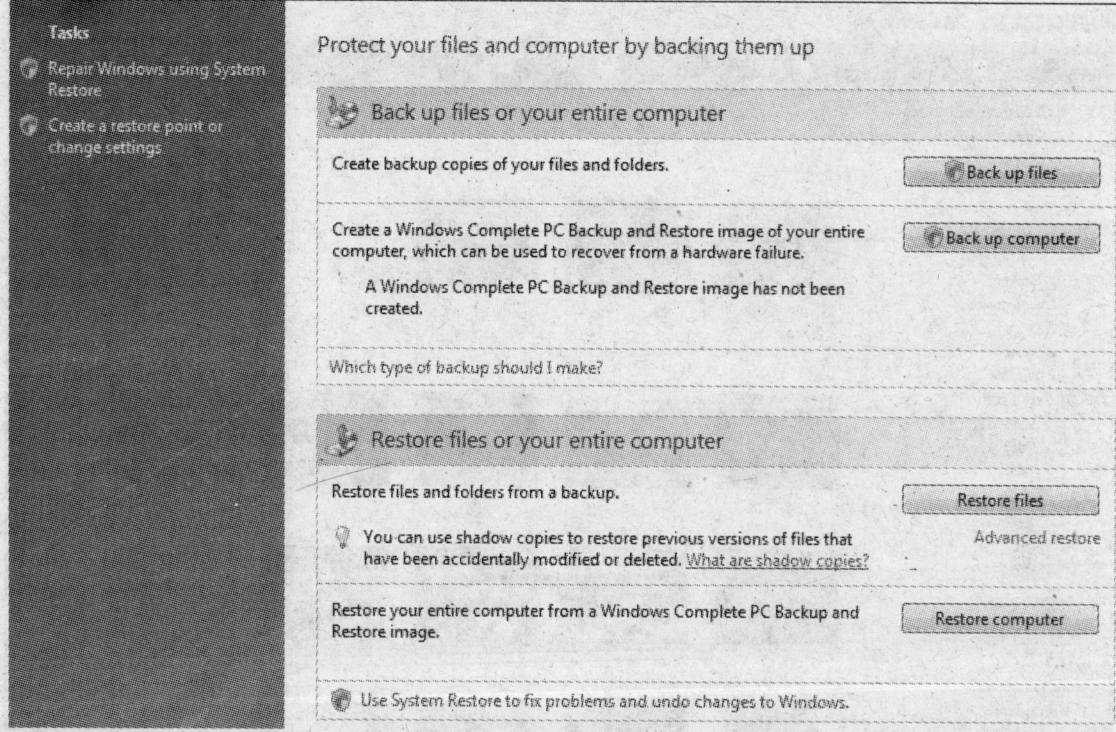

Windows Media Center

Enjoy all your favorite digital entertainment—including live and recorded TV, movies, music, and pictures—in one place with the Windows Media Center menu system and remote control. Windows Media Center in Windows Vista includes enhancements for expanded support of digital and high-definition cable TV, an improved menu system, and the ability to create a consumer-electronics-quality living-room experience, as well as new options for multi-room access to your entertainment through Media Center Extenders, including Microsoft Xbox 360.

Pictures

The Pictures folder and Windows Photo Gallery make it easy to view, organize, edit, share, and print digital pictures. When you plug your digital camera into your computer you can automatically transfer your photos to the Pictures folder. From there, you can use Windows Photo Gallery to crop photos, remove red eye, and make color and exposure corrections.

Mobile PC features

Use the Mobility Center to adjust settings you regularly change when you move from place to place (such as volume and screen brightness) and to check your connectivity status. Use a secondary, or auxiliary, display to check for your next meeting, read e mail, listen to music, or scan news without opening your mobile PC. You can also have an auxiliary display on a device, such as a cell phone or TV.

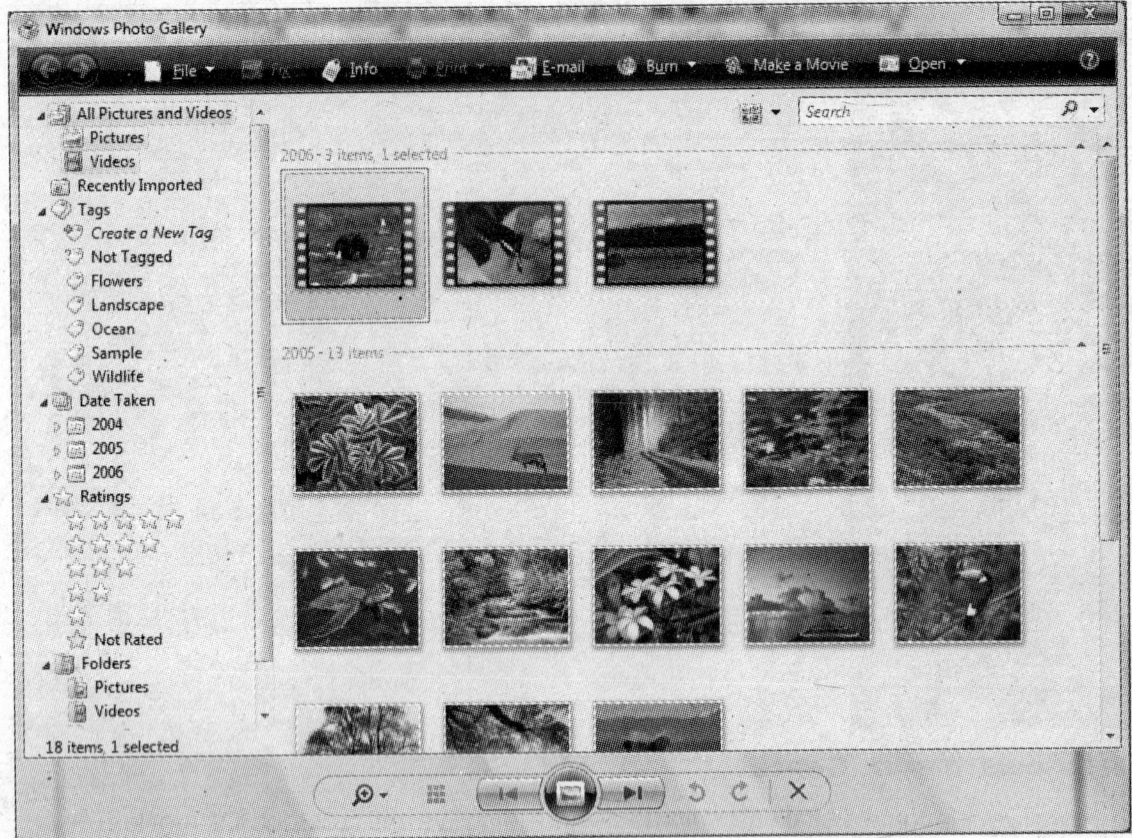

Tablet PC features

Improve handwriting recognition by personalizing the handwriting recognizer. Use flicks to navigate and perform shortcuts with your pen. See pen actions more clearly with optimized cursors. Use the Input Panel to handwrite, or use the soft keyboard anywhere on your screen. Use the touch screen to perform actions with your finger (the touch screen is only available if you have a touch-enabled Tablet PC).

Desktop of Windows Vista

As was in the earlier versions of Windows, Windows Vista too has a familiar desktop from where you can launch your programs using their shortcuts. A Windows Vista desktop is shown below, with all the relative icons. You may or may not have the same desktop on computer. But, it will be quite similar.

On the desktop, there are few icons, most of them are by choice, i.e., you can have them or not, the choice is yours only. But, the ones that you should have are: **Computer**, **Recycle Bin**, etc.

However, the most unfamiliar object on the desktop is the Start button, which used to be there since Windows 95, well, it has been replaced by a real button and does not have a name since by now everybody knows what that button means.

Another different feature is the presence of Gadgets on the right hand side of the desktop. There are few available and you can choose which one to have on the screen.

On pressing the Start button, as usual you would see the various programs which can be used by just clicking at them. It is in 2 cols. The first column gives the recently used programs at the bottom and favourite programs at the top.

The favourite ones are:

Internet : It opens up Internet Explorer version 7.0 for you to access Internet.

e-mail : If opens up Outlook Express for you to send and receive e-mail.

Next we have a list of the various programs which have been recently used. So you may have something different from this.

Exploring the Taskbar

It the bottom key line on the desktop. Starting with the right most corner, we see the following:

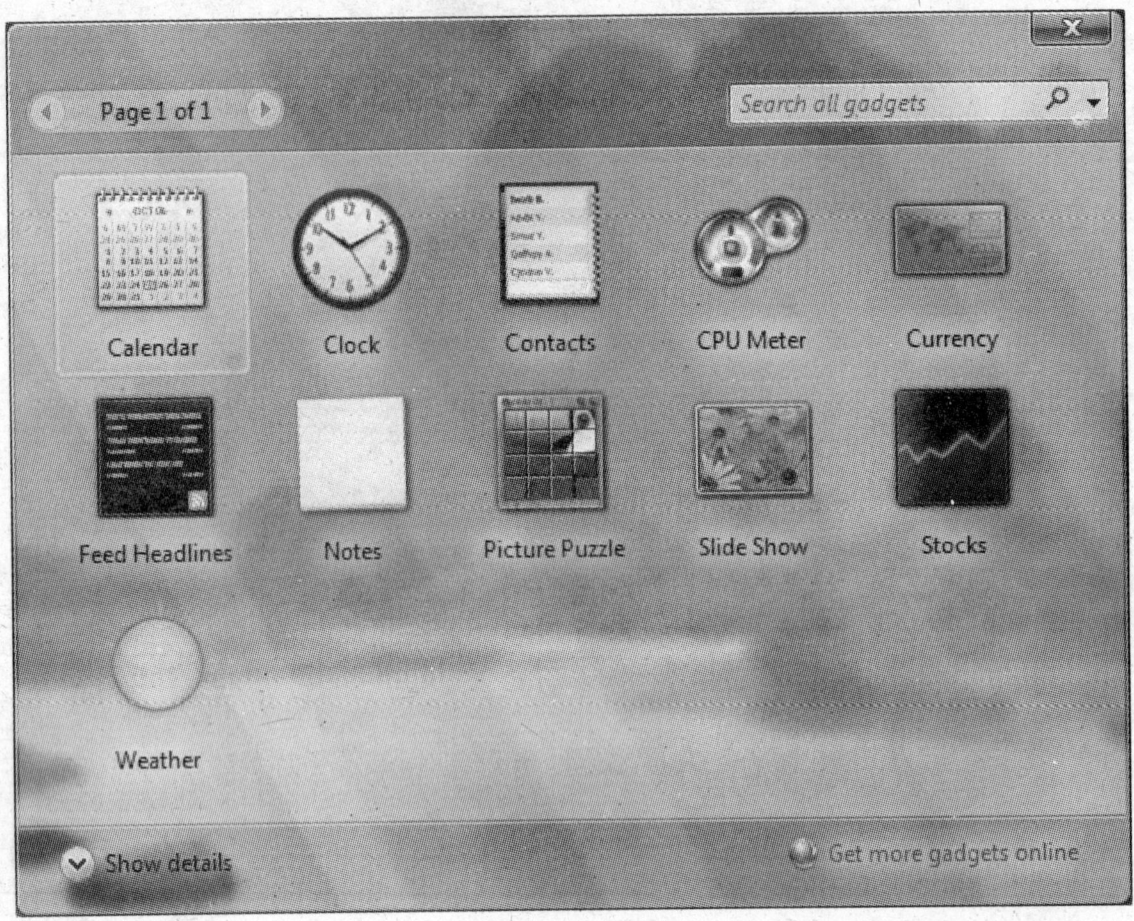

Date and Time : It shows you the date and time of the system.

Sound : It shows you the volume level which has been set.

Network : If your system is connected to a network, it shows.

WinZip Quick Pack : You can launch WinZip quickly from here.

Windows Defender : You will read more about it when we study Control Panel.

Windows Security Alerts : This alerts you when your system is at a security risk of being attacked by a virus.

Quick Launch Toolbar : Various icons here are the ones used for launching different programs. You have an option to put these icons here for the programs which you often use.

Running Tasks : When you have a program running in your system, its name will be reflected here on this taskbar to show that this program is open.

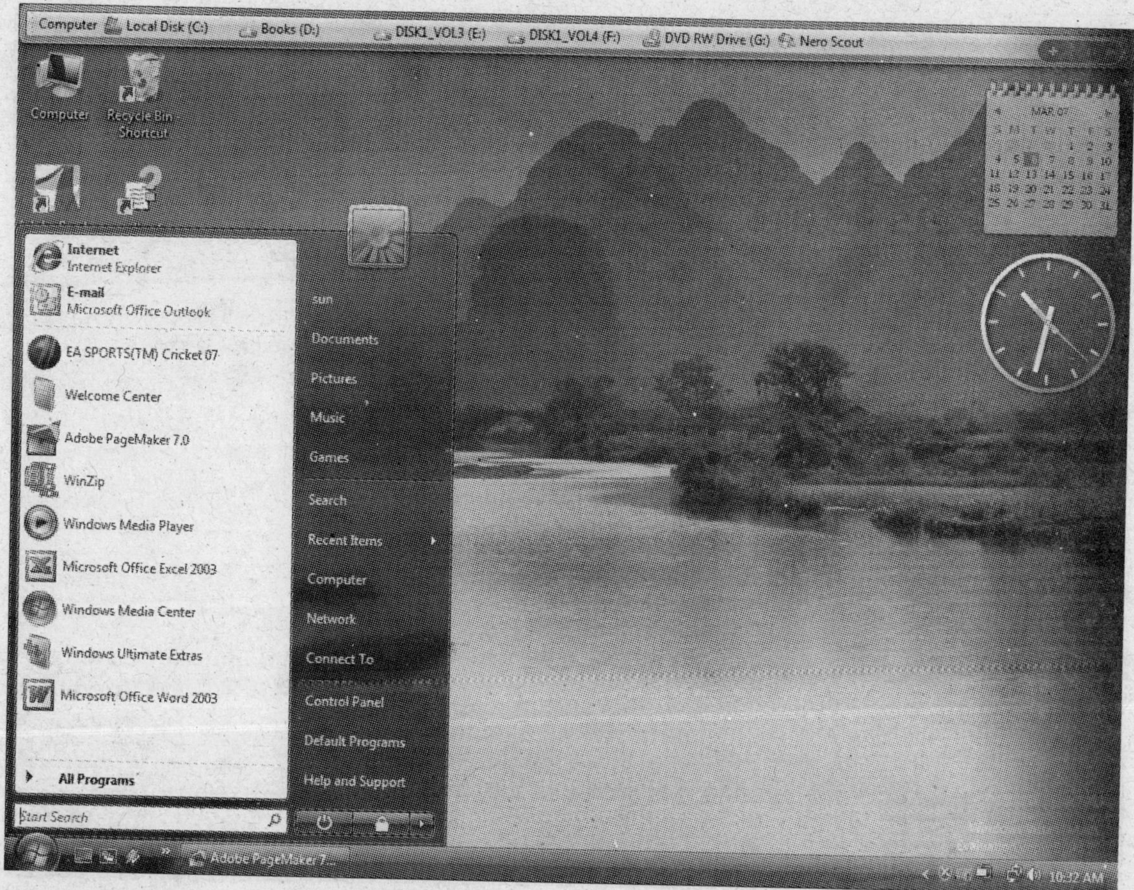

Computer

It helps you browse the contents of your computer, open folders, open documents and run your favourite applications. As shown here, it is divided into 2 sections, Favorite Links and Details. You click at any icon on the right hand side of the dialog box and then choose the option on the left hand side.

Details will give you the detail of the item selected. You can access other places by clicking at any one of them.

On the right hand side, you have the options of the followings:

Name: It gives you the option of sorting the icons by Name or by from A to H and I to Z.

Type: You can choose the type from CD Drive, Local Disk and System Folder and then Stack by Type.

Total Size: You can set the drives according to their size.

Free Space: You can set the drive to show how much space is available in them and list them according to the size, as shown below.

On the top there are buttons like this:

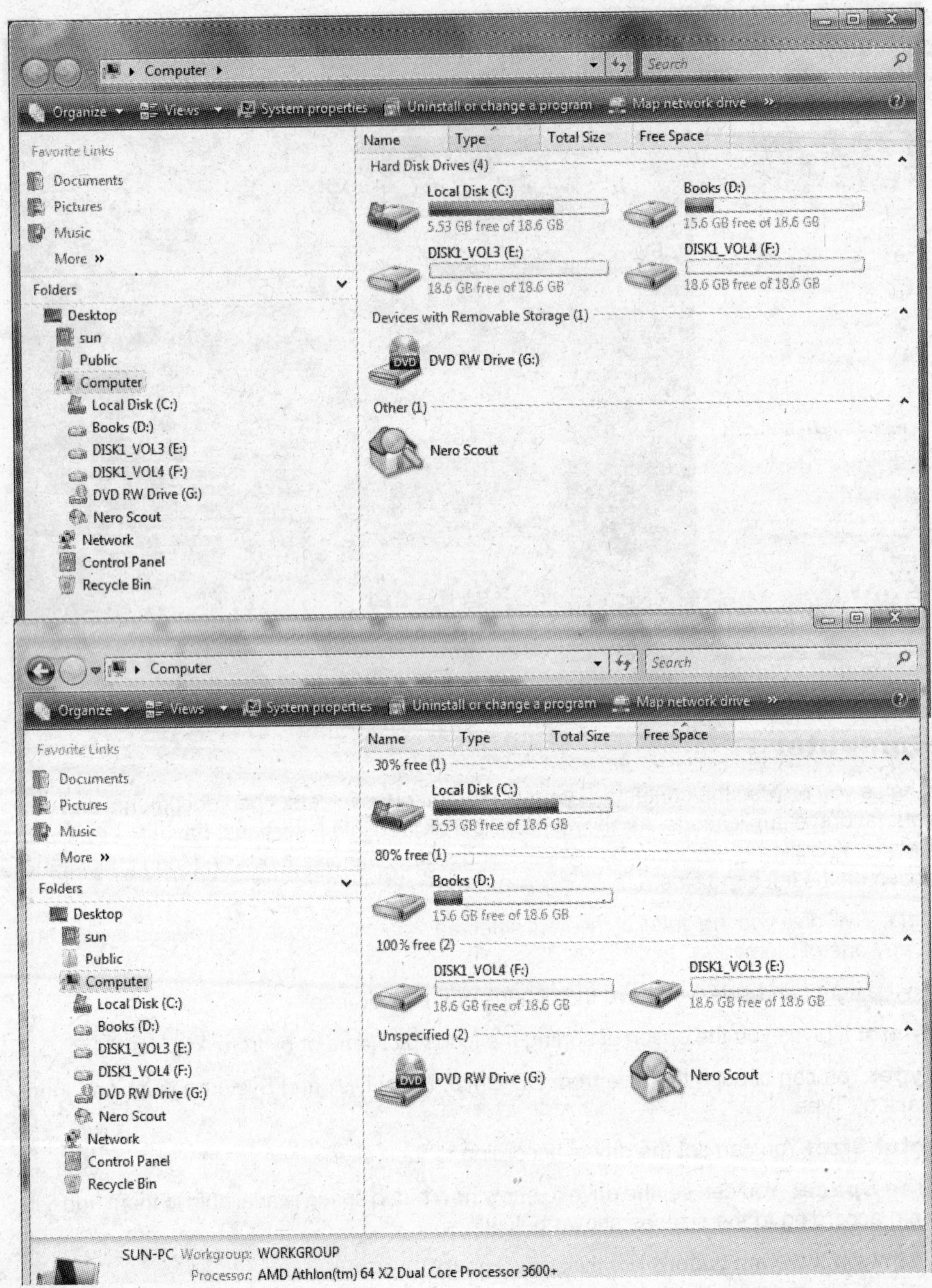
Computer
Search
Organize
Views
System properties
Uninstall or change a program
Map network drive
Favorite Links
Documents
Pictures
Music
More »
Folders
Desktop
sun
Public
Computer
Local Disk (C:)
Books (D:)
DISK1_VOL3 (E:)
DISK1_VOL4 (F:)
DVD RW Drive (G:)
Nero Scout
Network
Control Panel
Recycle Bin
Name
Type
Total Size
Free Space
Hard Disk Drives (4)
Local Disk (C:)
5.53 GB free of 18.6 GB
Books (D:)
15.6 GB free of 18.6 GB
DISK1_VOL3 (E:)
18.6 GB free of 18.6 GB
DISK1_VOL4 (F:)
18.6 GB free of 18.6 GB
Devices with Removable Storage (1)
DVD RW Drive (G:)
Other (1)
Nero Scout
Computer
Search
Organize
Views
System properties
Uninstall or change a program
Map network drive
Favorite Links
Documents
Pictures
Music
More »
Folders
Desktop
sun
Public
Computer
Local Disk (C:)
Books (D:)
DISK1_VOL3 (E:)
DISK1_VOL4 (F:)
DVD RW Drive (G:)
Nero Scout
Network
Control Panel
Recycle Bin
Name
Type
Total Size
Free Space
30% free (1)
Local Disk (C:)
5.53 GB free of 18.6 GB
80% free (1)
Books (D:)
15.6 GB free of 18.6 GB
100% free (2)
DISK1_VOL4 (F:)
18.6 GB free of 18.6 GB
DISK1_VOL3 (E:)
18.6 GB free of 18.6 GB
Unspecified (2)
DVD RW Drive (G:)
Nero Scout
SUN-PC Workgroup: WORKGROUP
Processor: AMD Athlon(tm) 64 X2 Dual Core Processor 3600+

Organize: This allows you to organize the folders and files according to your liking. Like creating a New Folder, Cutting, copying, pasting of folders/files. Other options are shown here.

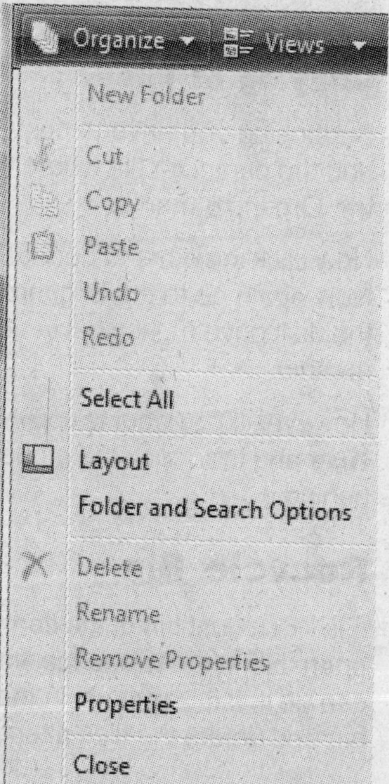

Views: It gives the option of viewing the folders/files in different views.

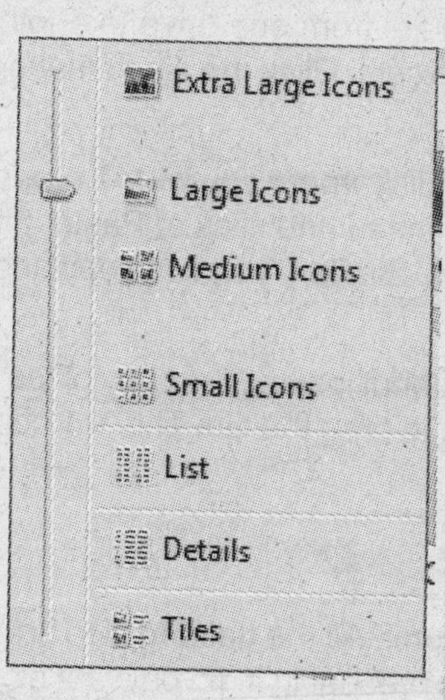

System properties: Shows information about your computer, such as the processor speed and the amount of installed memory.

Uninstall or change a program: Allows you to uninstall or change any program in the fixed drive.

Map network drive: It allows you to map a network drive.

Details of the folders available in the hard disk drive C: are shown here.

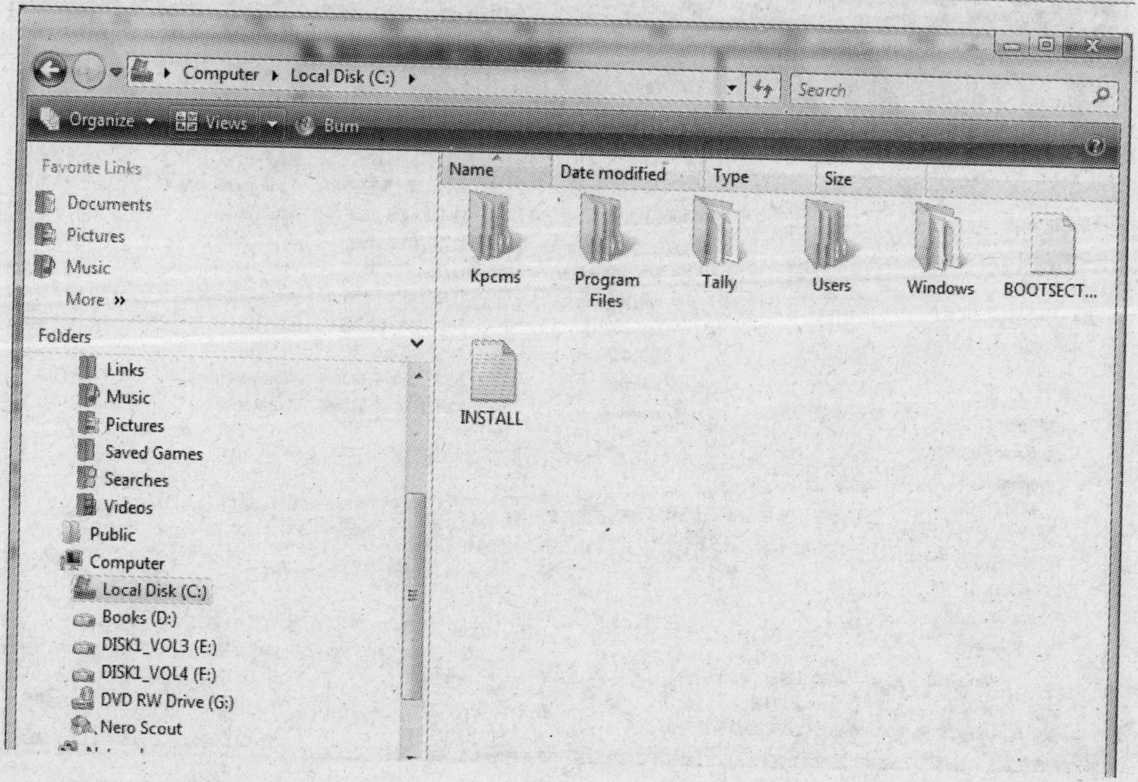

Now let us see how **Computer** is used for working with files.

Copying of Files

Supposing you have to copy a file from one drive to another. Open the folder of hard disk and the particular file where it exists. Click the file to make it selected. Now click at Copy in the Organize menu.

Now click the other folder/hard disk where you want to copy the file. Let us say disk drive F:. Now again go to the Organize menu and click at Paste, this time. The file will be pasted in the disk drive F:, as shown next. Similary you can copy and paste folders from one place to another.

However, if you want to copy without leaving the copy of the file in the source, press **Control Key** and then click the mouse to drag the file. This will copy the file and not leave the copy behind.

Recycle Bin

It is like a dust bin of the computer. All the deleted files are transferred here. You can in fact open this folder to see the files present in it. If you want at any stage to retrace any file, you can do it, if it is present in the **Recycle Bin**. However, if you choose to empty the recycle bin and delete the files altogether, then you cannot restore any of the file.

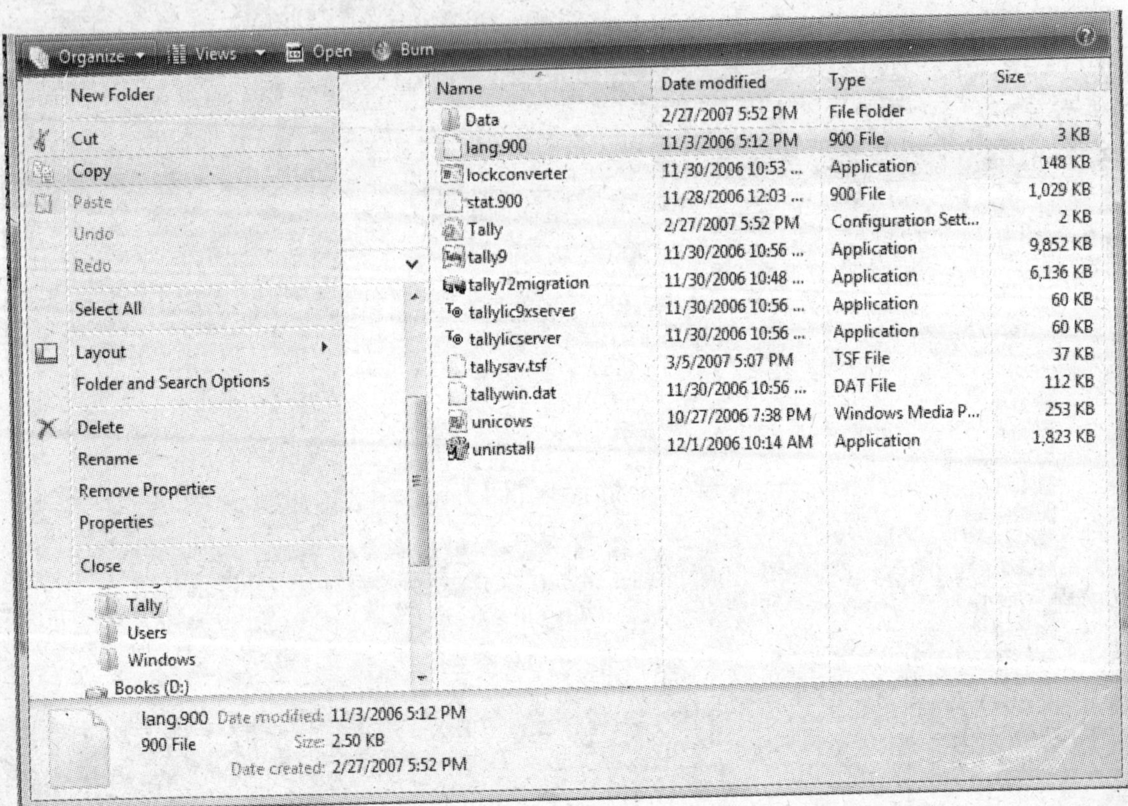

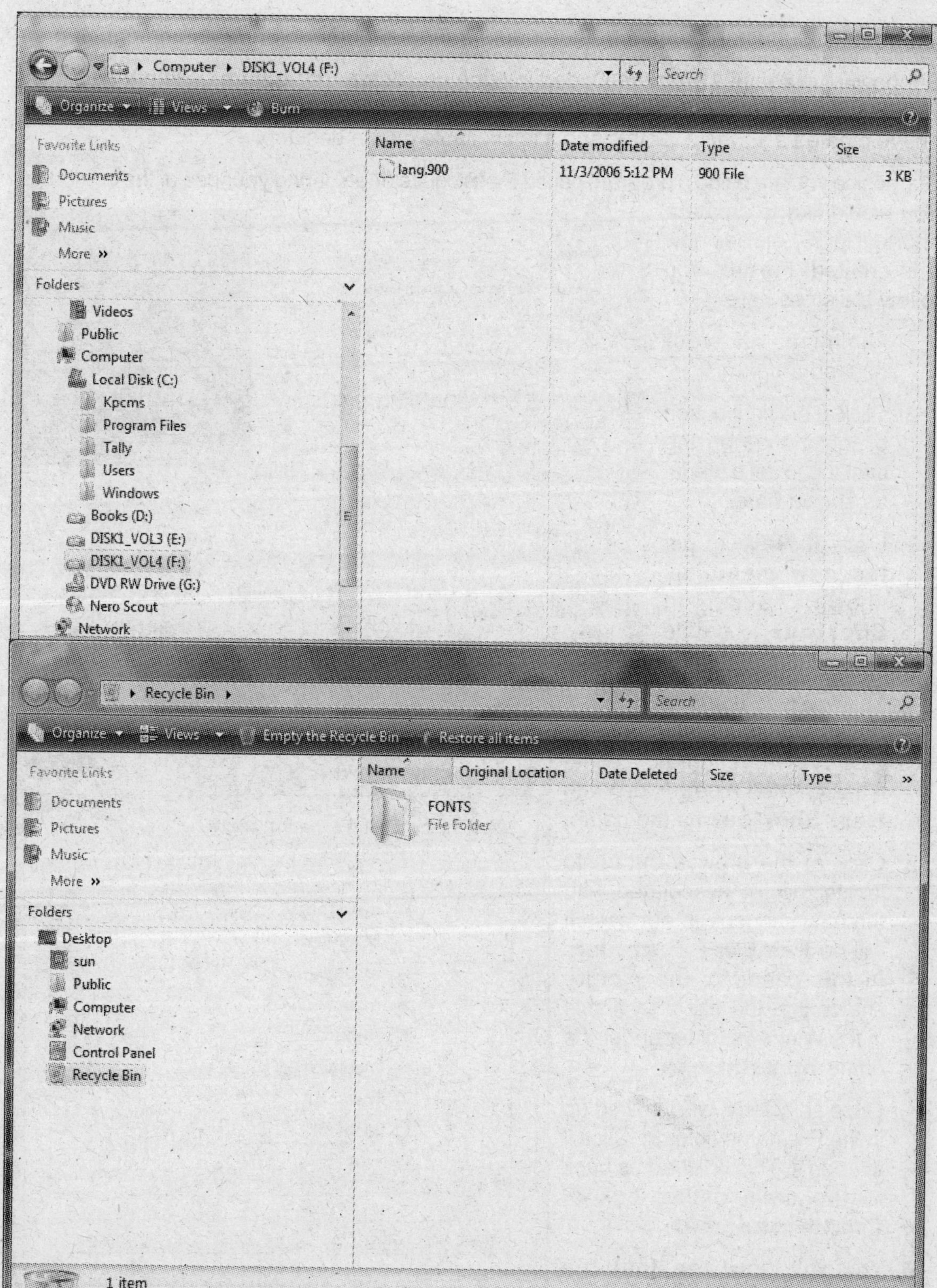
Computer
DISK1_VOL4 (F:)
Search
Organize
Views
Burn
Favorite Links
Documents
Pictures
Music
More »
Folders
Videos
Public
Computer
Local Disk (C:)
Kpcms
Program Files
Tally
Users
Windows
Books (D:)
DISK1_VOL3 (E:)
DISK1_VOL4 (F:)
DVD RW Drive (G:)
Nero Scout
Network
Name
Date modified
Type
Size
lang.900
11/3/2006 5:12 PM
900 File
3 KB
Recycle Bin
Search
Organize
Views
Empty the Recycle Bin
Restore all items
Favorite Links
Documents
Pictures
Music
More »
Folders
Desktop
sun
Public
Computer
Network
Control Panel
Recycle Bin
Name
Original Location
Date Deleted
Size
Type
FONTS
File Folder
1 item

Creating Shortcuts

Supposing you have a program loaded into the computer and you are quite often using it. So you would like to have a shortcut for it. For example, I use **PageMaker**, quite often, so I have created a shortcut for this and it is available on the desktop.

Supposing you are using a program called **Paint** quite often during your use of the computer. You would like to create a shortcut for it. Lets see how it is created. For this you follow the steps here.

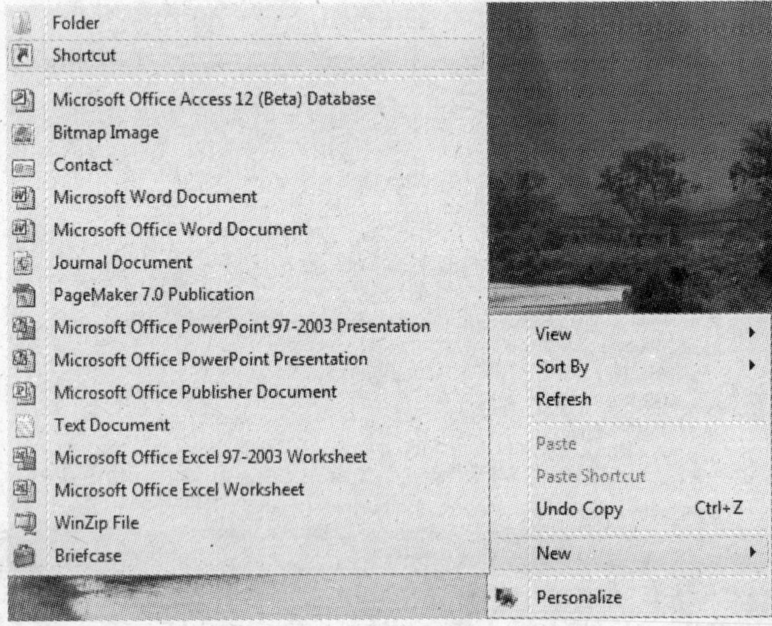

1. Minimize all your opened programs.
2. Click at the right button of the mouse on the desktop to get a menu, as shown here.
3. Click at **New** to get the new menu, as shown. Click at **Shortcut** to create one.
4. This will give rise to a dialog box, as shown. Side by side, you will notice that it has created a new folder with **New Shortcut** as the name.
5. Click at the browse button to locate the file associated with the new shortcut. In our case it will be **Paint** or **Paintbrush**. In this case, as the picture shows that the file is available in the Windows folder under the name **mspaint.exe**.

   Once selected it will be filled up in the File name column. Click it to open it. This will lead us back to the main dialog box of **Create Shortcut**.
6. You will now see that the

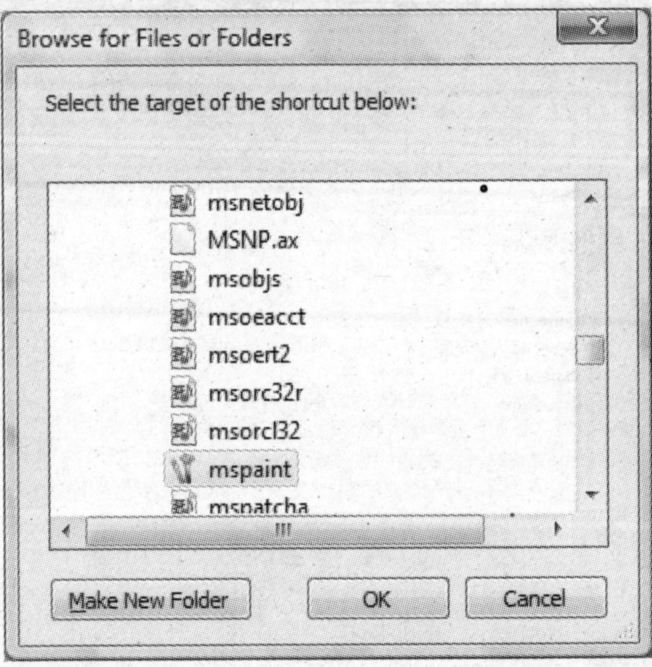

command line has been filled up with the exact location of the file which is to be Run for launching of this shortcut from the desktop.

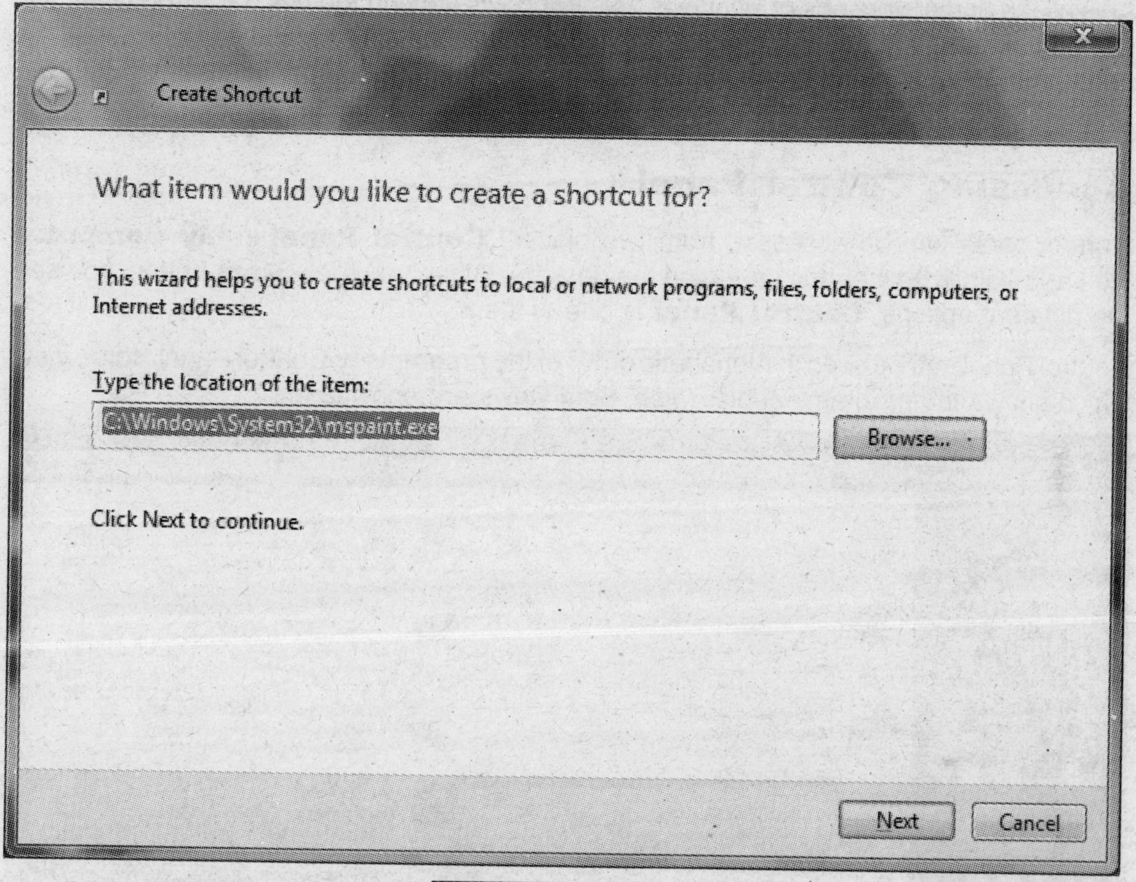

Create Shortcut
What item would you like to create a shortcut for?
This wizard helps you to create shortcuts to local or network programs, files, folders, computers, or Internet addresses.
Type the location of the item:
C:\Windows\System32\mspaint.exe
Browse...
Click Next to continue.
Next
Cancel

7. Click at **Next** to get the next dialog box. This will ask you fill up the name you want to give to the shortcut. Here we have given it as **PAINT**.
8. Clicking at **Finish** will end the procedure to create the shortcut. Once done, it will create a new shortcut named **PAINT**on the desktop. You can now use it to launch Paint.
9. This can be seen on the desktop.

Create Shortcut
What would you like to name the shortcut?
Type a name for this shortcut:
Paint
Click Finish to create the shortcut.

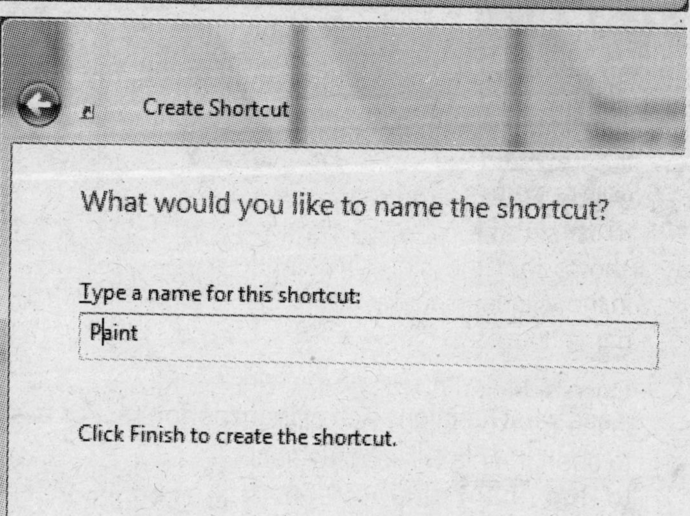

Introduction to Control Panel of Windows Vista

Like all the earlier versions of Windows, this Windows version too has a control panel. It is a group of icons which when selected invoke applications which allow you to change the settings of the Windows. Now, we will study about the various options available in the control panel.

Accessing Control Panel

Control panel can be accessed from two places: **Control Panel** in **My Computer** icon and from **Start** button on the on the desktop. When you click **Start** button, you see the different options. **Control Panel** is one of them.

Control Panel can be seen in Alphabetic order of the programs or Control Panel Home view which shows the programs subjec wise. Both views are shown here.

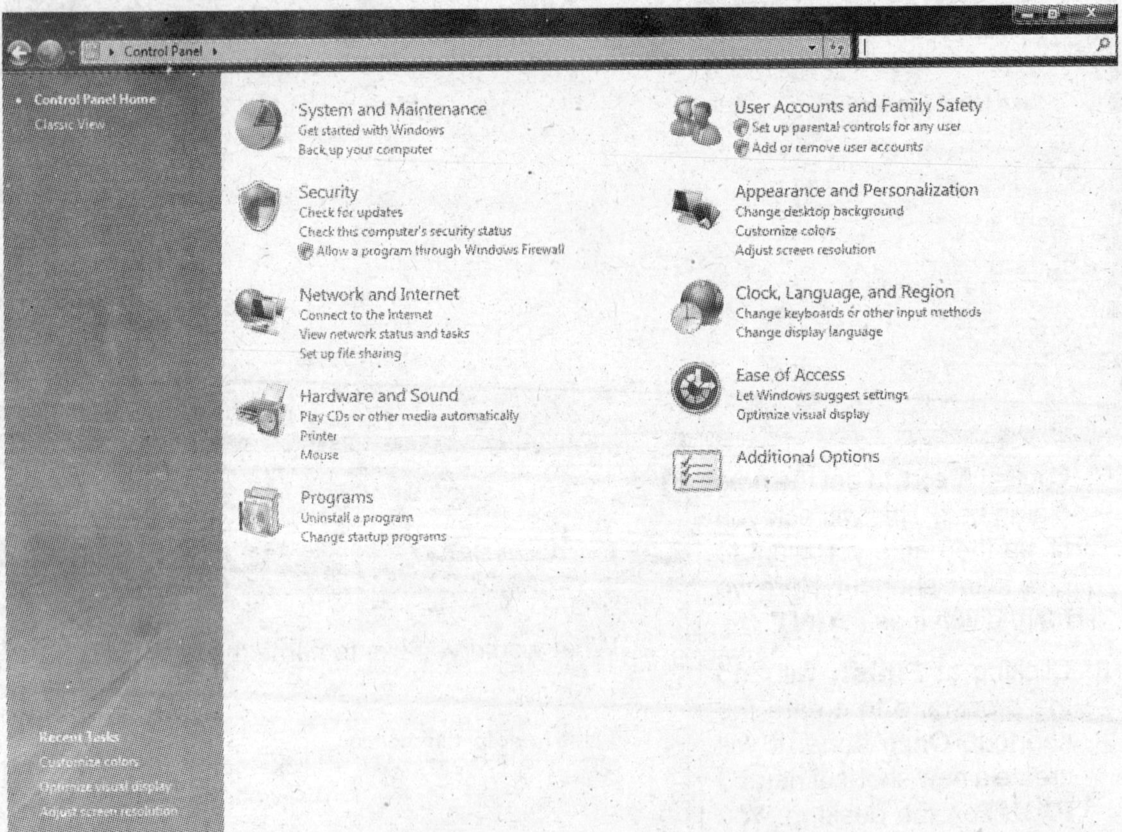

Let us see what function each of them performs. For this I am going through it alphabetically.

Add Hardware

You can install most hardware or portable devices by plugging them into your computer. Windows will automatically install the appropriate driver software if it's available, or prompt you to insert the disc that came with your hardware device if it's not.

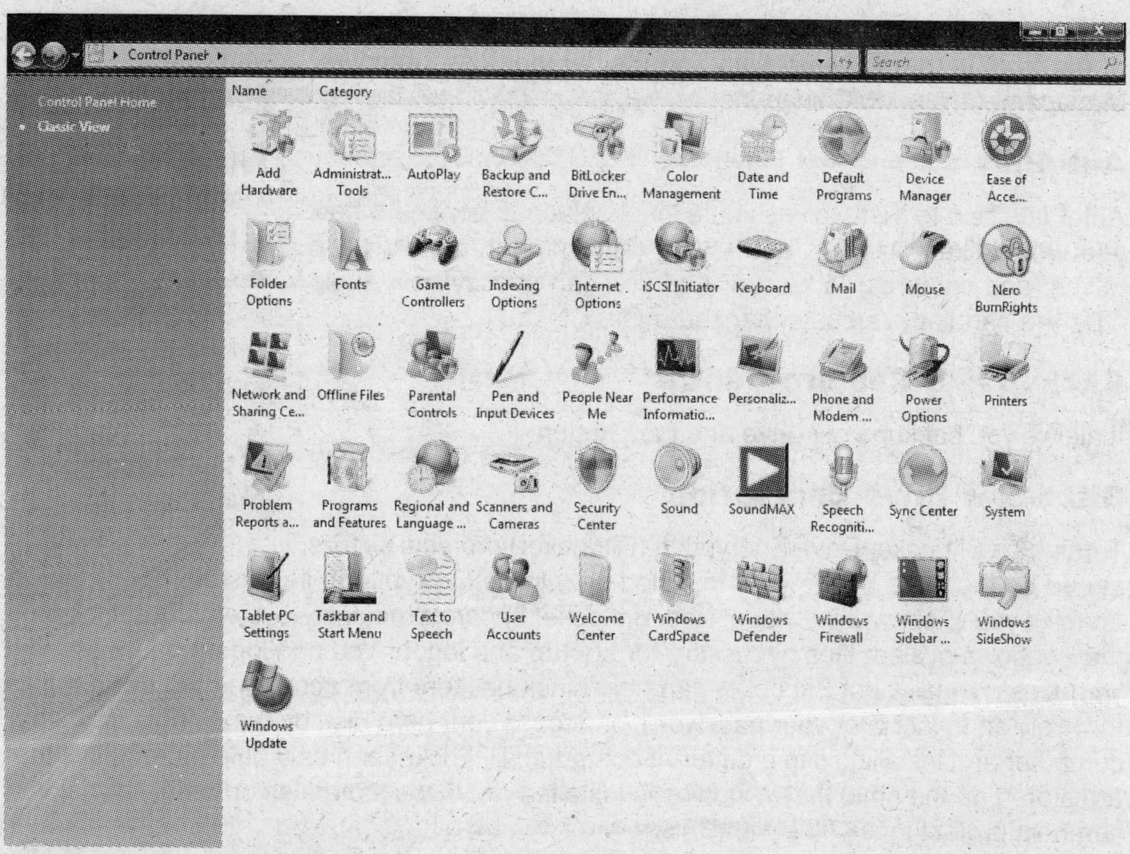

Adminstrative Tools

It has the different tools under it, they are: Computer Management, Data Sources (ODBC), Event Viewer, iSCSI Initiator, Local Security Policy, Memory Diagnostics Tool, Print Management, Reliability and Performance, Services, System Configuration, Task Scheduler and Windows Firewall with Advanced Security.

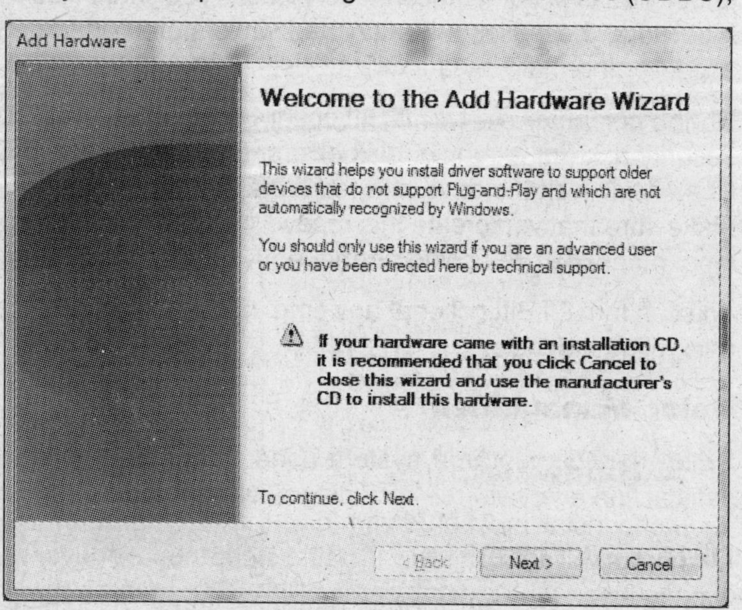

Microsoft Management Console (MMC) hosts and displays administrative tools created by Microsoft and other software vendors. These tools are called snap-ins, and they are used for managing the hardware, software, and network components of Windows. Several of the tools in the Administrative Tools folder, such as Computer Management, are MMC snap-ins.

Name
Computer Manageme
Data Sources (ODBC)
Event Viewer
iSCSI Initiator
Local Security Policy
Memory Diagnostics T
Print Management
Reliability and Perform
Services
System Configuration
Task Scheduler
Windows Firewall with

AutoPlay

AutoPlay, new to Vista, gives you a single place to configure how you would like your CDs and DVDs (and memory cards, flash drives, and cameras) to be run. And you can specify how audio CDs are handled, versus enhanced audio CDs.

Backup and Restore Centre

It allows you backup your drive and then restore it.

BitLocker Drive Encryption

Turning on BitLocker Drive Encryption (BitLocker) protects all files stored on the drive Windows is installed on. Unlike Encrypting File System (EFS), which enables you to encrypt individual files, BitLocker encrypts the entire system drive, including the Windows system files necessary for startup and logon. You can log on and work with your files normally, but BitLocker can help block hackers from accessing the system files they rely on to discover your password, or access your hard disk by removing it from your computer and installing it in a different computer. BitLocker can only help protect files that are stored on the drive that Windows is installed on. If you store files on other drives, you can help protect those files with EFS.

When you add new files to the drive with BitLocker, BitLocker encrypts them automatically. Files remain encrypted only while they are stored in the encrypted drive. Files copied to another drive or computer are decrypted. If you share files with other users, such as through a network, these files are encrypted while stored on the encrypted drive, but they can be accessed normally by authorized users.

During computer startup, if BitLocker detects a system condition that could represent a security risk (for example, disk errors, a change to the BIOS , or changes to any startup files), it will lock the drive and require a special BitLocker recovery password to unlock it. Make sure that you create this recovery password when you turn on BitLocker for the first time; otherwise, you could permanently lose access to your files.

You can turn off BitLocker at any time, either temporarily by disabling it, or permanently by decrypting the drive.

Color Management

Color management is a system used to ensure that color content is rendered to your satisfaction everywhere—including devices such as your display and your printer.

Date and Time

You can change the format Windows uses to display dates, times, currency, and measurements. You can also change the sorting order of text to match sorting rules used in a specific country or region.

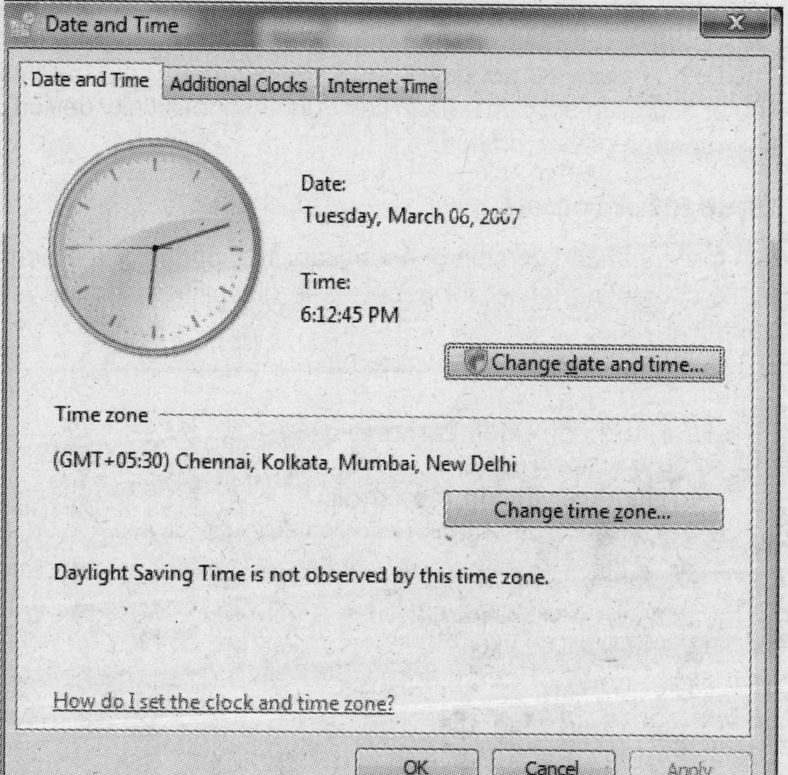

1. Click to open Regional and Language Options.
2. Click the Formats tab, and then, in the Current format list, select the locale to use for the display of the date, time, currency, and measurements.
3. You can see how these items will appear in the area below the list.
4. To customize how the date, time, currency, and measurements are displayed, click Customize this format, and then do one of the following:

- To change the way your computer displays numbers, click the Numbers tab. Items you might want to change based on the format language you chose are the decimal symbol and list separator, the format used for negative numbers and leading zeros, and the measurement system used (U.S. or metric).
- To change the way your computer displays currency values, click the Currency tab. Items you might want to change based on the format language you chose are the currency symbol, the formats used for positive or negative amounts, and the punctuation used to separate numbers.
- To change the way your computer displays the time, click the Time tab.
- To change the way your computer displays the date, click the Date tab.

Default Programs

Set Program Access and Computer Defaults makes it easy for you to change the default program used for certain activities, such as web browsing, sending e mail, playing audio and video files, and using instant messaging.

You can also specify which of these default programs are displayed on the Start menu, on the desktop, and in other locations.

Device Manager

The device manager console shows you where all your hardware money was spent. Here, you or your tech-support person can troubleshoot a flaky device, disable and enable devices, and manage device drivers.

Ease of Access

It is the enhanced version of Accessability Options of the earlier version. It is designed to make computing easier for people with disabilities, though some of the options here can benefit anyone.

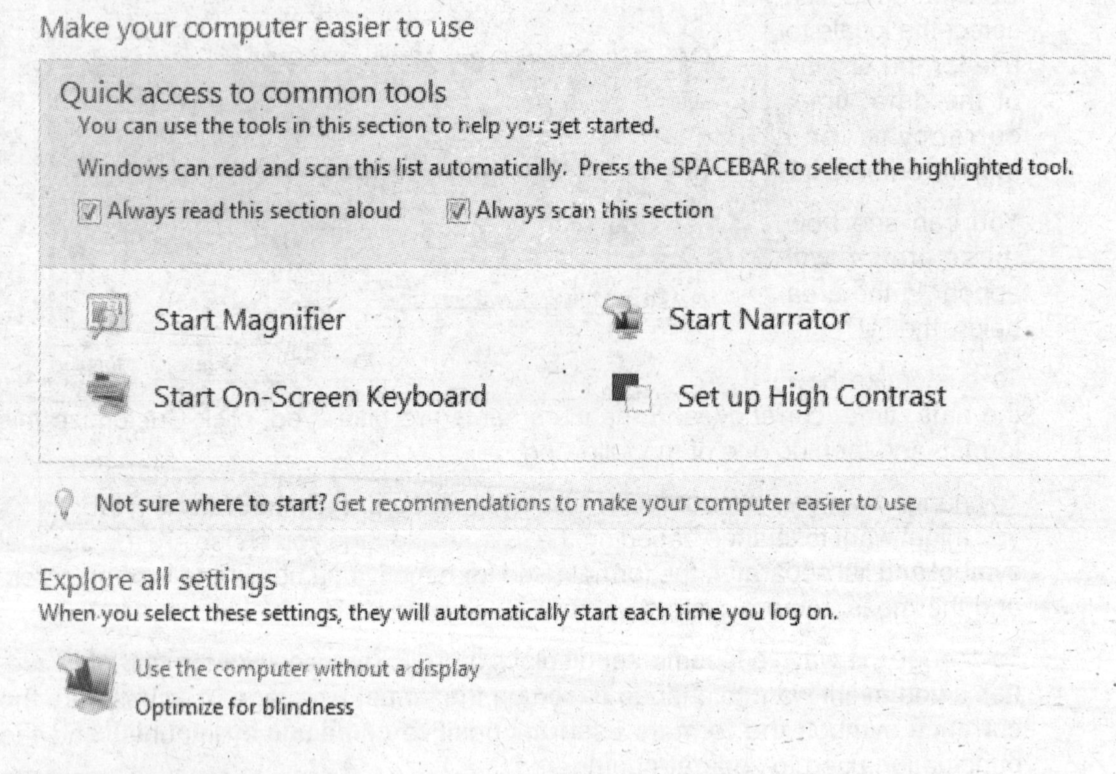

Folder Options

Using Folder Options in Control Panel, you can change the way your files and folders function, as well as how the content in your folders is displayed.

Click to open Folder Options.

Change the way folders are displayed

You can change the way your folders look and work to suit your needs. For example, you can open all files and folders with one click (like links in a webpage) instead of the usual double-click. Here is an overview of the settings you can change:

To	*Do this*
Turn off the Details pane and the Preview pane in all folders. This setting gives you more room to display files by hiding panes you might not need.	Click the General tab, and then click Use Windows classic folders. (To turn the panes back on, click Show preview and filters.)
Open every new folder in its own folder window. This can be convenient if you want to keep all the folders you are working with on the screen at the same time.	Click the General tab, and then click Open each folder in its own window. (To make each new folder replace the previous folder window, click Open each folder in the same window.)
Open an item with a single click. Use this setting if you want files and folders to open with one click, just like links in a webpage.	Click the General tab, and then click Single-click to open an item. (To switch back to the standard double-click, click Double-click to open an item.)

Change advanced file and folder settings

You can make additional changes to the appearance and behavior of your files and folders by using the advanced settings of Folder Options in Control Panel. Here is an overview of the advanced settings that you can change:

To	*Do this*
Always show static icons of files and never show thumbnail previews of files. Use this setting if the thumbnail previews are slowing down your computer. You'll get better performance by using static icons.	Click the View tab, and then select the Always show icons, never thumbnails check box.
Always show the menus above the toolbar. Use this setting if you prefer to have access to the Classic menus, which are hidden by default.	Click the View tab, and then select the Always show menus check box.
See the size of a folder in a tooltip when you rest your mouse pointer over the folder. Use this setting if you frequently need to know the total size of the contents of a folder and would like to see this information by resting the mouse pointer over the folder.	Click the View tab, and then select the Display file size information in folder tips check box.
See files and folders marked as hidden. Use this setting if you need to work with files that are usually hidden from view, such as user files that have been marked as hidden.	Click the View tab, and then click Show hidden files and folders.
See folders with lines that connect folders and subfolders.	Click the View tab, and then clear the Display simple folder view in Navigation pane check box.
See file name extensions as a part of file names. This is a good way to ensure that files are not malicious software disguised as common files.	Click the View tab, and then clear the Hide extensions for known file types check box.

See all system files that are usually hidden from view.	Click the View tab, and then clear the Hide protected operating system files check box.
Increase the stability of Windows by opening every folder in a separate part of memory. Use this setting if your computer frequently crashes, and you are trying to minimize problems or troubleshoot. Be aware, however, that doing this could slow down the performance of your computer.	Click the View tab, and then select the Launch folder windows in a separate process check box.
Ignore custom view settings for every folder and have every folder open using default settings instead. Use this setting to force all folders to stop using display settings you have specified.	Click the View tab, and then clear the Remember each folder's view settings check box.
Automatically open the folders that you were using when you last shut down Windows whenever you start your computer. Use this setting to help you preserve your work from session to session.	Click the View tab, and then select the Restore previous folder windows at logon check box.

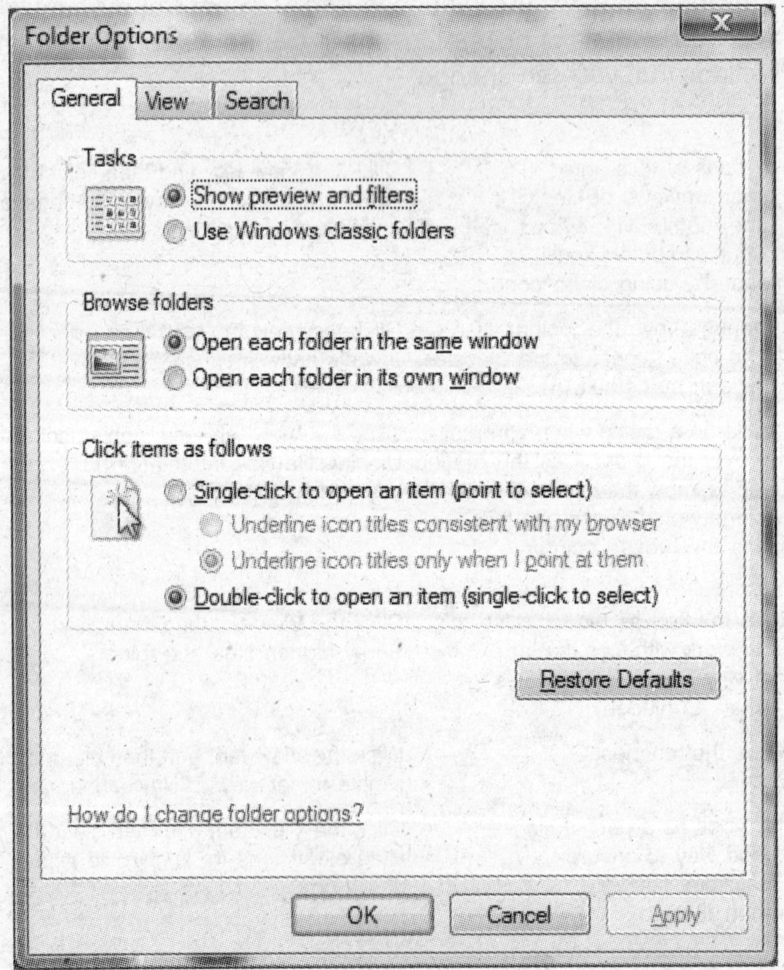

Hide the drive letter of each drive or device in the Computer folder. Use this setting if you don't want to see drive letters displayed on your computer and prefer to see only the friendly name of each drive.	Click the View tab, and then clear the Show drive letters check box.
Display encrypted or compressed NTFS files as ordinary files, without any unique color coding to identify them. Use this setting if you have encrypted or compressed NTFS files and do not want to see them represented differently than other files on your computer.	Click the View tab, and then clear the Show encrypted or compressed NTFS files in color check box.
Turn off the tooltips that appear when you rest your mouse pointer over files. Use this setting if you don't want to see the file information that appears in tooltips when you rest the pointer over files and folders.	Click the View tab, and then clear the Show pop-up descriptions for folder and desktop items check box.
Never show the contents of files in the Preview pane. Use this setting to improve the performance of your computer, or if you don't want to use the Preview pane.	Click the View tab, and then clear the Show preview handlers in preview pane check box.
Add check boxes to file views to make it easier to select several files at once, which can be useful if it is difficult for you to hold the CTRL key while clicking to select multiple files.	Click the View tab, and then select the Use check boxes to select items check box.

Fonts

It shows all the fonts available in the hard disk.

Game Controllers

If you are a serious gamer, this would interest you. You use it to configure and control the joysticks, steering wheels, game pads, flight yokes, and other controllers you have attached to your PC. Afterall, if your joysticks and controllers are not installed and confgured properly, you can't pulverize alients to full capacity.

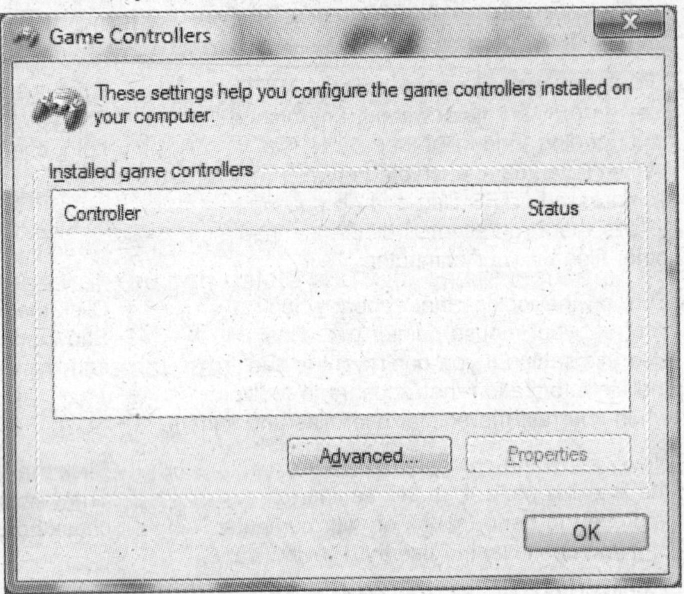

To get started, install the driver software that came you gaming device. If it's a modern, USB, Vista-compatible gadget, you may not even need to do that much. Just plug the device and watch the notifification area for a message that Vista has detected it and installed the correct driver.

Indexing Options

Similar to the way the index in a book helps you to keep track of its contents, the index in Windows keeps track of the files on your computer. The index stores information about files, including the file name, date modified, and properties like author, tags, and rating. You will never see the index, but it is used by Windows to perform very fast searches of the most common files on your computer.

The index is used to make searching for files much faster. Instead of looking through your entire hard disk for a file name or file property, Windows scans the index, which allows most results to appear in a small fraction of the time that a search without the index would take.

By default, all of the most common files on your computer are indexed. Indexed locations include all of the files in your personal folder (such as Documents, Pictures, Music, and Videos), as well as e mail and offline files. Files that are not indexed include program files and system files. The locations that contain those files are not indexed because you rarely need to search those files, and so not including them in the index makes your searches perform faster.

Internet Options

As can be seen from the figure here, it has the following tabs:

General, Security, Private and Content: These tabs control your home page, cache files, search field defaults, and history list. They also let you define certain Web pages as off-limits for your kids and manage RSS feeds, as well as block pop-up windows.

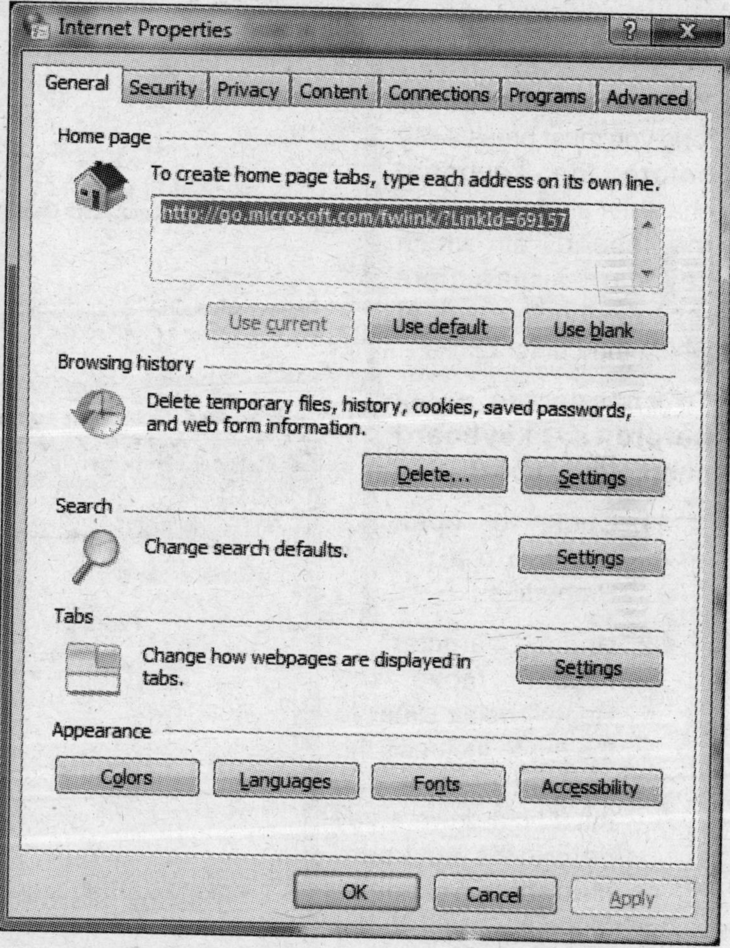

Connections: Controls when your PC modem dials.

Programs: Use this tab to manage browser add-ons, decide whether or not Internet Explorer should warn you whenever it is not the default browser (for your protection, of course), or choose the default programs that open, should you click a link to email someone, open a media file, or view the HTML source of a Web page.

Advanced: On this tab, you will find dozens of checkboxes, most of which are useful only in rare circumstances and affect your Web experience only in mirror ways. For example, "Enable personalized favorites menu" shortens your list of bookmarks over time, as Internet Explorer hides the names of Web sites you haven't visited in a while.

iSCSI Initiator

iSCSI is a way of connecting storage devices over a network using TCP/IP. It can be used over a local area network (LAN), a wide area network (WAN), or the Internet. iSCSI devices are disks, tapes, CDs, and other storage devices on another networked computer that you can connect to. Sometimes these storage devices are part of a network called a storage area network (SAN). In the relationship between your computer and the storage device, your computer is called an initiator because it initiates the connection to the device, which is called a target.

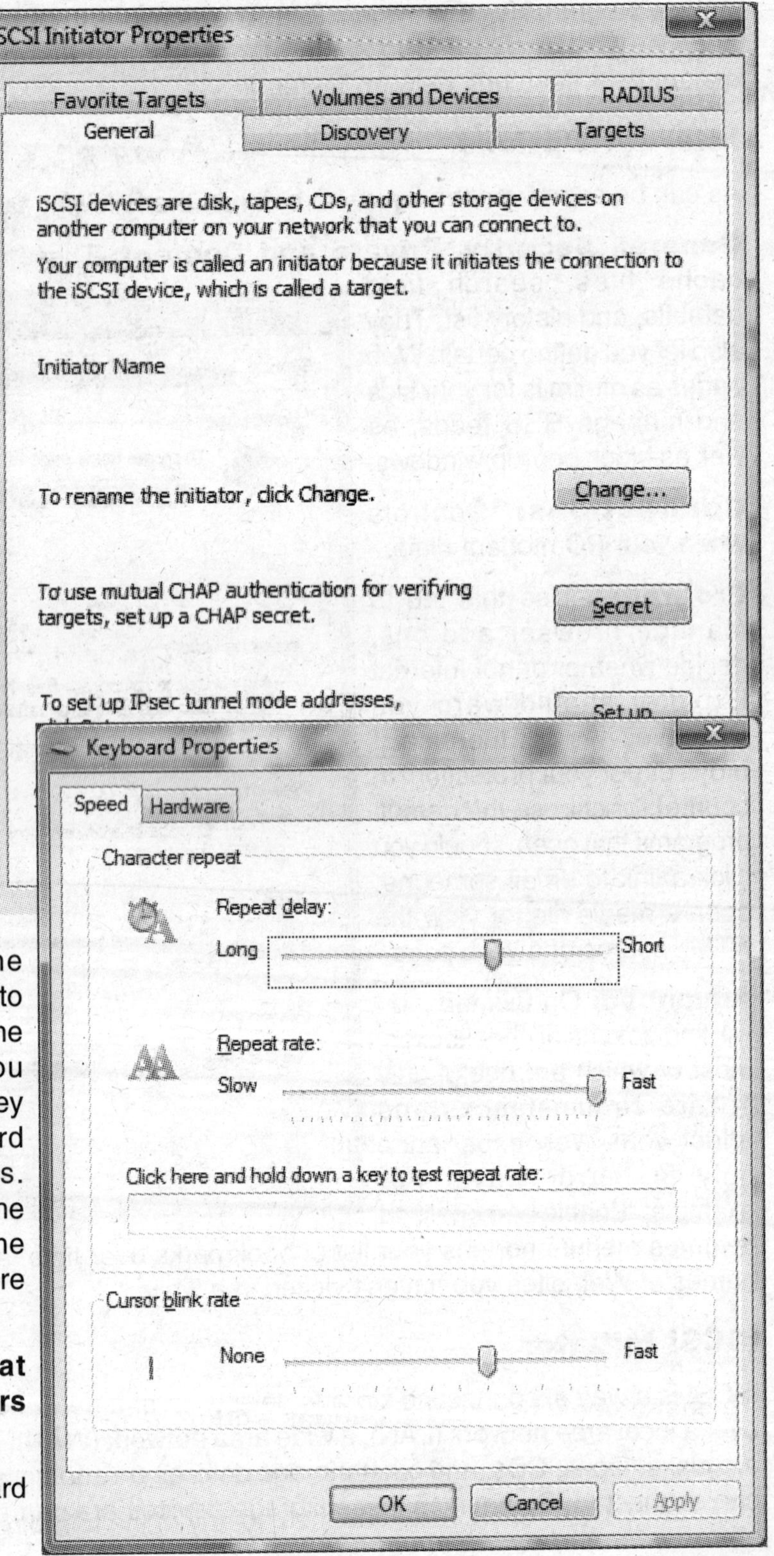

Keyboard

You can customize how long you must press a key before the keyboard character starts repeating, the speed at which keyboard characters repeat, and the rate at which the cursor blinks.

To change the delay before keyboard characters repeat

1. Click to open Keyboard Properties.
2. Under Character repeat, move the Repeat delay slider to the left to increase the amount of time you must hold down a key before the keyboard character repeats. Move the slider to the right to decrease the amount of time before characters repeat.

To change the speed at which keyboard characters repeat

1. Click to open Keyboard Properties.

2. Under Character repeat, move the Repeat rate slider to the left to make keyboard characters repeat more slowly, or to the right to make them repeat faster.

To change the cursor blink rate

1. Click to open Keyboard Properties.
2. Move the Cursor blink rate slider to the right to increase the cursor blink speed. If you move the slider all the way to the left, the cursor will stop blinking.

Mail

Windows Mail has the tools you need to exchange e mail with colleagues and friends, or join newsgroups to trade ideas and information.

Add or remove a Windows Mail account

You can set up a variety of different accounts using Windows Mail. You can set up a single personal e mail account, or you might also add your work e mail account and some newsgroups as well. Windows Mail makes managing multiple accounts easy by putting each account in its own folder.

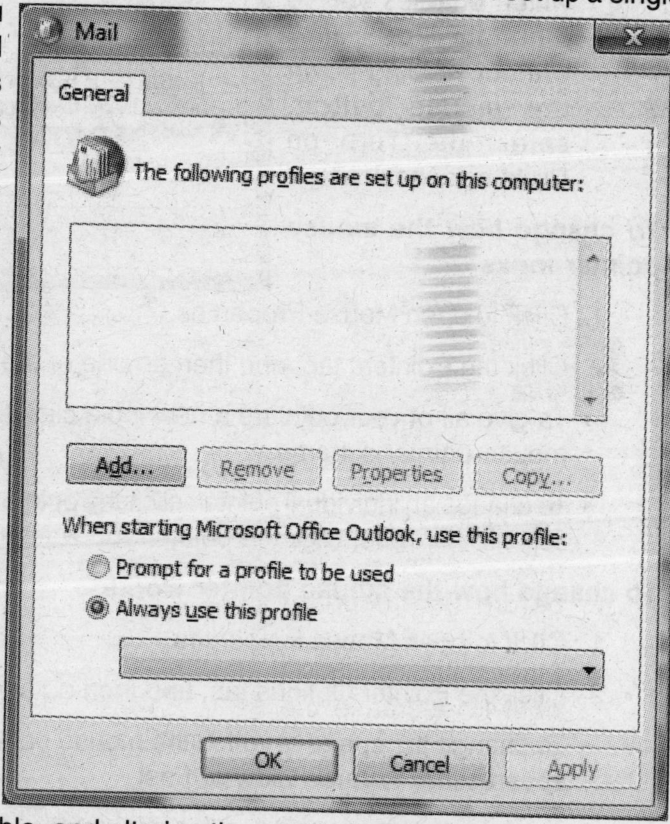

Windows Mail supports three types of accounts: mail, news (newsgroups), and directory services. Directory services are online address books that are typically offered by organizations such as colleges and businesses.

Before you add an account, be sure that you have the logon and server information for your e mail account.

Mouse

You can customize your mouse in a variety of ways, such as swapping the functions of your mouse buttons, making the mouse pointer more visible, and altering the scroll wheel speed.

To change how the mouse buttons work

1. Click to open Mouse Properties.
2. Click the Buttons tab, and then do any of the following:

- To swap the functions of the right and left mouse buttons, select the Switch primary and secondary buttons check box.
- To change how quickly you must click the buttons to perform a double-click, move the Double-click speed slider towards Slow or Fast.
- To turn on ClickLock, which enables you to highlight or drag without holding down the mouse button, select the Turn on ClickLock check box.

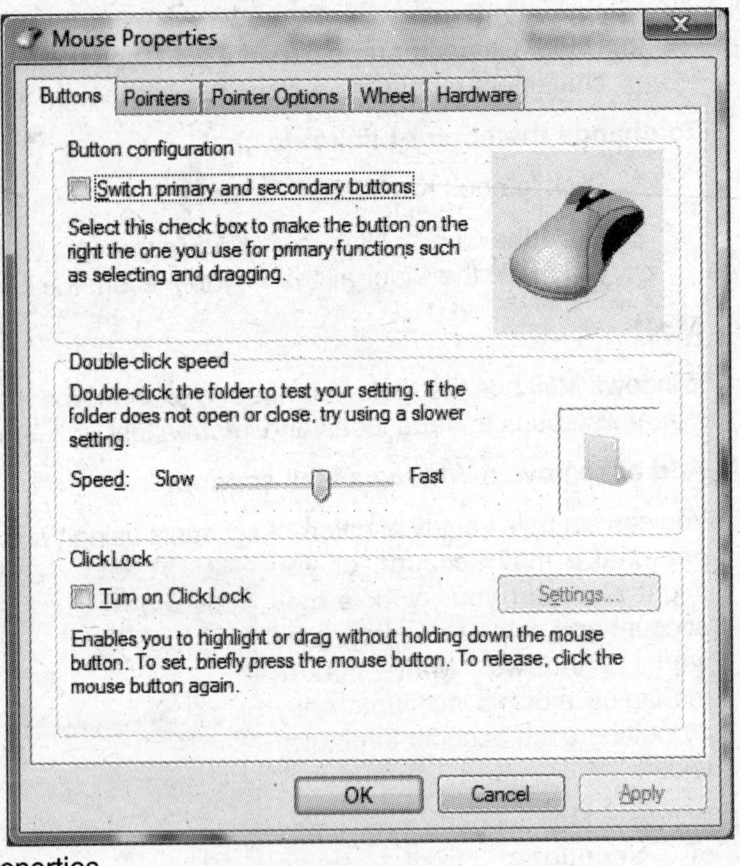

To change how the mouse pointer looks

1. Click to open Mouse Properties.
2. Click the Pointers tab, and then do one of the following:
   - To give all of your pointers a new look, click the Scheme list, and then click a new mouse pointer scheme.
   - To change an individual pointer, click the pointer you want to change in the Customize list, click Browse, click the pointer you want to use, and then click Open.

To change how the mouse pointer works

1. Click to open Mouse Properties.
2. Click the Pointer Options tab, and then do any of the following:
   - To change the speed at which the mouse pointer moves, move the Select a pointer speed slider towards Slow or Fast.
   - To make the pointer work more accurately when you're moving the mouse slowly, select the Enhance pointer precision check box.
   - To speed the process of selecting a choice when a dialog box appears, select the Automatically move pointer to the default button in a dialog box check box .

- To make the pointer easier to find when you move it, select the Display pointer trails check box, and then move the slider towards Short or Long to decrease or increase the length of the pointer trail.
- To ensure that the pointer doesn't block your view of the text you're typing, select the Hide pointer while typing check box.
- To find a misplaced pointer by pressing the CTRL key, select the Show location of pointer when I press the CTRL key check box.

To change how the mouse wheel works

1. Click to open Mouse Properties.
2. Click the Wheel tab, and then do one of the following:

- To set the number of lines the screen will scroll for each notch of mouse wheel movement, click The following number of lines at a time, and then enter the number of lines you want to scroll in the box.
- To scroll an entire screen of text for each click of the mouse wheel, click One screen at a time.
- If your mouse has a wheel that supports horizontal scrolling, in the Tilt the wheel to scroll the following number of characters at a time box, enter the number of characters you want to scroll horizontally when you tilt the wheel to the left or right.

Network and Sharing Centre

Windows provides two methods for sharing files directly from your computer. You can share files from any folder on your computer, or from the Public folder. Either method allows you to share files or folders with someone using your computer or another computer on the same network. Which method you use to share files with someone depends on where you want to store the shared files, who you want to share them with, and how much control you want to have over the files.

Share files from any folder on your computer

Follow these steps to share files from their current location without copying them to another location. Using this method, you can choose with whom you want to share files, regardless of whether they use this computer or another computer on the network.

1. Locate the folder with the files you want to share.
2. Click one or more files or folders that you want to share, and then, on the toolbar, click Share.
3. In the File Sharing dialog box, do one of the following:

- Type the name of the person you want to share files with, and then click Add.
- Click the arrow to the right of the text box, click the person's name in the list, and then click Add.

- If you don't see the name of the person you want to share files with in the list, click the arrow to the right of the text box, and then click Create a new user to create a new user account so that you can share files with the person using this account.

4. The name of the person or group that you selected appears in the list of people you want to share files with.

5. Under Permission Level, click the arrow next to the permission level for that person or group, and then do one of the following to set sharing permissions:

   - Click Reader to restrict the person or group to viewing files in the shared folder.
   - Click Contributor to allow the person or group to view all files, add files, and change or delete the files that they add.
   - Click Co-owner to allow the person or group to view, change, add, and delete files in the shared folder.
   - If you are sharing a file instead of a folder, there is no option to set the permission level to Contributor.

6. When you are finished choosing the people or groups you want to share files with, click Share. If you are prompted for an administrator password or confirmation, type the password or provide confirmation.

7. After you receive confirmation that your folder is shared, you should send a link to your shared files to the people you are sharing them with, so they know the files are shared and how to access them. Do one of the following:

   - Click E mail Link to automatically open a Windows Mail e mail message with the link to your shared files.
   - Manually copy and paste the link displayed on this screen into an e mail message. Right-click the link and click Copy Link. Then open a new e mail message and paste in the link. You might want to do this if you don't use Windows Mail as your e mail program.

8. If you don't want to send an e mail message to the person you are sharing files with, click Done. They won't be able to find the shared files, however, until you give them the network location of the files.

   - You can give a shared folder a share name that makes it easier for someone else to find it on your computer. You can do this by using the Advanced Sharing dialog box for the folder. To access this dialog box, right-click a folder you have already shared, click Properties, click the Sharing tab, and then click Advanced Sharing. If you are prompted for an administrator password or confirmation, type the password or provide confirmation.

Share files from the Public folder

When you share files from the Public folder, you don't share them with specific people.

Anyone with a user account on this computer can access the Public folder, but you decide whether to allow access to people on your network. You can only grant access to everyone or no one on the network.

You can also turn on password-protected sharing. This limits network access to the Public folder to only those people with a user account and password on your computer. By default, network access to the Public folder is turned off unless you enable it.

To share files from the public folder:

1. Copy or move whichever files you want to share to the Public folder or one of its subfolders, such as Public Documents or Public Music.
2. Your files in the Public folder are now shared with anyone who has access to the Public folder.

- You can't restrict access to some individual files and folders within the Public Folder but allow access to other files and folders there. If users have access to the Public folder, they will have access to everything in it.
- When you share files and folders with people using other computers, they can open and view those files and folders just as if they were stored on their own computers. Any changes you allow them to make to a shared file or folder will change the file or folder on your computer. However, you can restrict people to just viewing your shared files, without the ability to change them.

Offline Files

You can access files stored in a network folder even when that network folder is unavailable. You can do this by making the folder available offline. When you make a network folder available offline, Windows copies all the files from that folder to your computer. These copies of network files that are stored on your computer are called offline files. Windows automatically uses your offline files any time the network files are not available. This way you can keep working on the network files without interruption, even if you lose your connection to the network folder. When you connect to the network folder again, Windows will automatically sync the files on your computer with the files in the network folder.

To make files and folders available offline

To be able to work with a file offline, you first need to make it available offline.

1. Locate the network file or folder that you want to make available offline.
2. Right-click the file or folder, and then click Always Available Offline.
3. The next time you try to access this file or folder, you will be able to open it even if the network version is unavailable.

- To confirm that the file or folder is now available offline, right-click the file or folder again, and make sure that a check mark appears next to Always Available Offline.
- If you don't want a network file or folder to be available offline any longer, right-click

the file or folder, and then click Always Available Offline to clear the check mark next to the command.

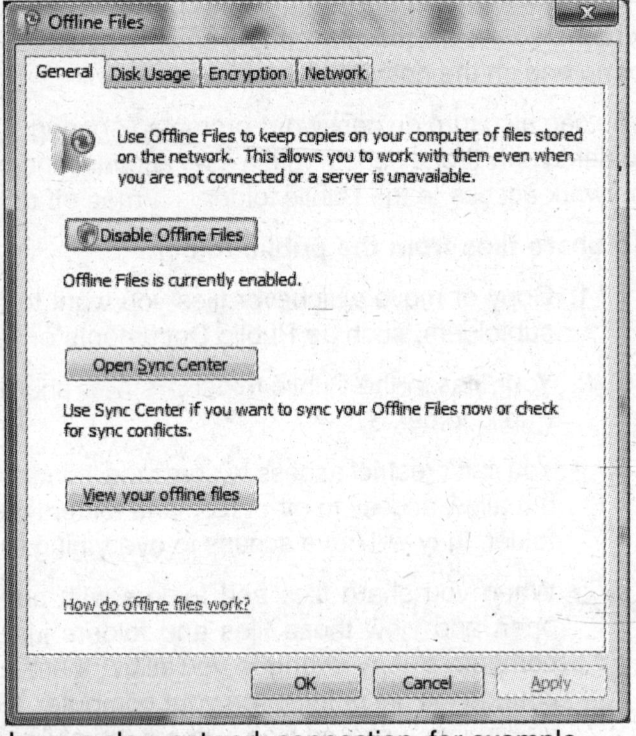

To enable offline files

Enable offline files if you want to work with files that are in a network folder. A copy of the file on your hard drive will be synchronized with the network copy as soon as you are back at work or you regain your network connection.

1. Click to open Offline Files.
2. Click the General tab, and then click Enable Offline Files.

To work offline

Sometimes you might want to work with the offline files stored on your computer rather than the files stored on the network. This can be a good idea if you have a slow network connection, for example.

1. Open the network folder that contains the files you have made available offline, and then, on the toolbar, click Work offline. This button appears only if you have already made this folder available offline.
2. When you are finished working with the files offline and want to begin working with the files in the network folder again, click Work online on the toolbar. This will sync any changes you have made offline with the files on the network.

To find out whether you're working offline

Offline files turn on automatically if you lose your network connection. A copy of your file is copied to your computer, and once your network connection is re-established, the two copies will be synchronized. To find out if you're working offline, do the following.

1. Open the network folder that contains the file you are working on.
2. Check the Details pane at the bottom of the window for the status. If the status is offline, you are working with a copy of the file on your computer. If the status in online, you are working with the file on the network.

To view all your offline files

If you work with offline files in many different folders, you may want to view all of them without opening each folder individually. Here's how to view all your offline files at once.

1. Click to open Offline Files.

2. Click the General tab, and then click View your offline files.

To sync all of your offline files immediately

Windows syncs your offline files for you automatically, so that when a network file is changed, the offline copy stored on your computer is also updated, and vice versa. But Windows does not sync your files continuously. Sometimes it is helpful to sync your offline files right away, such as if you are about to disconnect from a network and want to be sure you have the latest versions of files stored on the network.

1. Click to open Sync Center.
2. Click the Offline Files sync partnership, and then, on the toolbar, click Sync.
   - If you only want to sync the contents of a specific folder, open the folder that contains the files that you want to sync, and then, on the toolbar, click Sync. To sync an individual file, right-click the file, and then click Sync.

Parental Controls

You can use Parental Controls to help manage how your children use the computer. For example, you can set limits on your children's access to the web, the hours that they can log on to the computer, and which games they can play and programs they can run.

When Parental Controls blocks access to a webpage or game, a notification is displayed that the webpage or program has been blocked. Your child can click a link in the notification to request permission for access to that webpage or program. You can allow access by entering your account information.

Before you get started, make sure that each child that you want to set up Parental Controls for has a standard user account because Parental Controls can only be applied to standard user accounts. To set up Parental Controls for your child, you'll need an Administrator user account. Parental Controls cannot be applied to an Administrator user account.

To turn on Parental Controls for a standard user account

1. Click to open Parental Controls. If you are prompted for an administrator password or confirmation, type the password or provide confirmation.
2. Click the standard user account for which you want to set Parental Controls.
3. Under Parental Controls, click On.
4. Once you've turned on Parental Controls for your child's standard user account, you can adjust the individual settings that you want to control. You can control the following areas:
   - Web restrictions. You can restrict the websites that children can visit, make sure children only visit age-appropriate websites, indicate whether you want to allow file downloads, and set up which content you want the content filters to block and allow. You can also block or allow specific websites.

Choose a user and set up Parental Controls

What can I do with Parental Controls?

 One or more administrator accounts do not have a password. As long as an administrator account turn off parental controls. Click here to add a password for these accounts.

sun
Computer administrator
No Password

If you want to apply Parental Controls to someone who isn't in this list, create a new user account for them to use.

Why do I need an account for this?

 Create a new user account

- Time limits. You can set time limits to control when children are allowed to log on to the computer. Time limits prevent children from logging on during the specified hours and, if they are already logged on, they will be automatically logged off. You can set different logon hours for every day of the week.
- Games. You can control access to games, choose an age rating level, choose the types of content you want to block, and decide whether you want to allow or block unrated or specific games.
- Allow or block specific programs. You can prevent children from running programs that you don't want them to run.

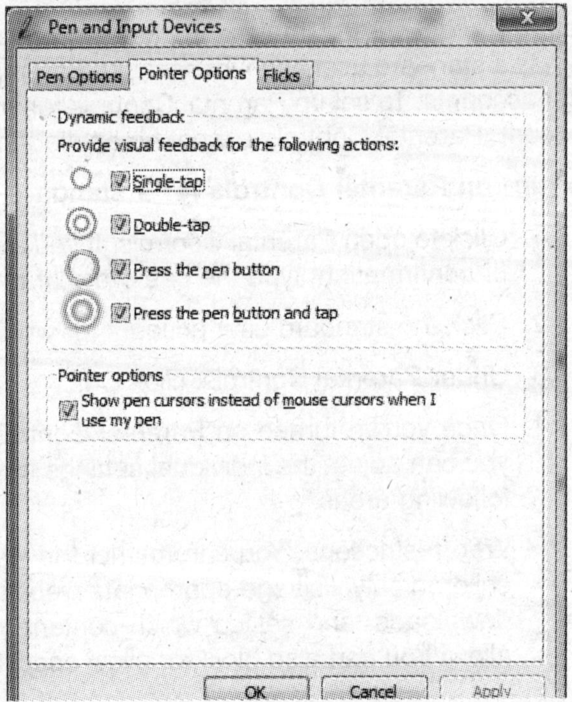

Pen and Input Devices

This applet opens up a dialog box where you can configure how your stylus (pen) interacts with the desktop and windows.

People Near Me

People Near Me is a service that identifies people nearby who are using computers and allows those people to send you invitations for programs such as Windows Meeting Space. They can only invite you to participate in programs that are installed on your computer. To use People Near Me, you have to sign in to the service.

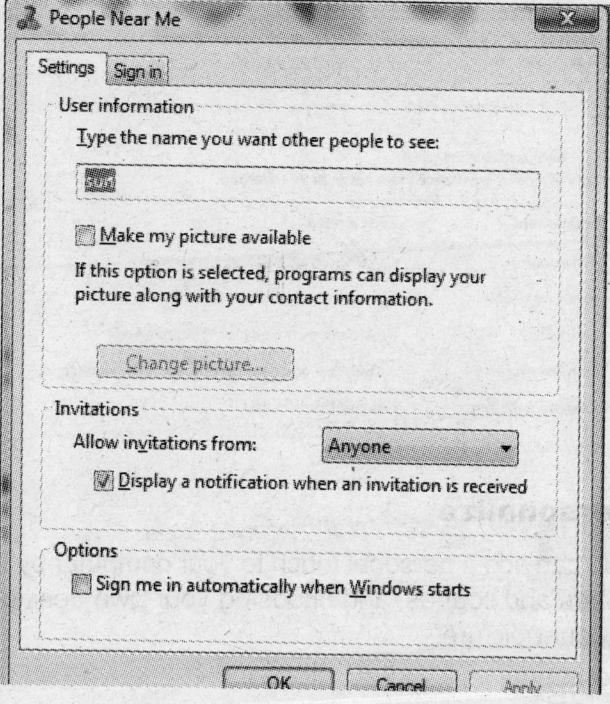

How to sign in to People Near Me?

1. Click to open People Near Me.
2. Click the Sign in tab, click Sign in to People Near Me, and then click OK. If you are prompted for an administrator password or confirmation, type the password or provide confirmation.
3. If this is the first time that you are signing in to People Near Me, you'll see an additional dialog box. In that dialog box, click OK.

- If you want to change your display name (the name that other people will see), type a new name on the Settings tab before signing in.

Performance Information

Performance Information and Tools lists your computer's Windows Experience Index base score, which indicates the performance and overall capability of your computer's hardware.

Click to open Performance Information and Tools.

The base score can help you buy programs that match your computer's performance level. The base score only pertains to the performance aspects of the computer that affect how well features in Windows and other programs will run on this computer, and does not reflect the overall quality of your computer.

Individual hardware components, such as your computer's central processing unit (CPU) and random access memory (RAM), are tested and receive a subscore. Your computer's base score is determined by the lowest subscore. For example, if the lowest subscore of an individual hardware component is 2.6, then the base score is 2.6. The base score is not an average of the various subscores.

If you install new hardware and want to see if your score has changed, click Update my score. To view additional details about your computer's hardware, click View and print details.

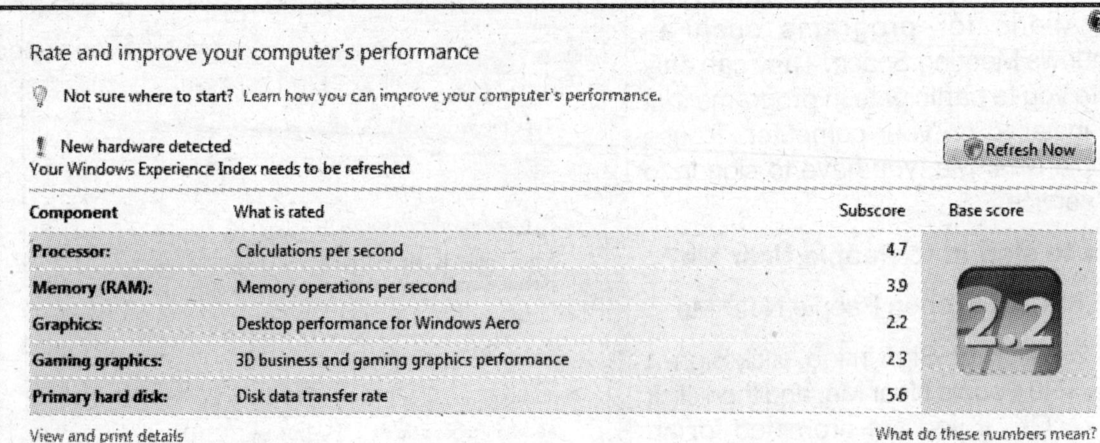
Rate and improve your computer's performance

Not sure where to start? Learn how you can improve your computer's performance.

New hardware detected
Your Windows Experience Index needs to be refreshed

Refresh Now

Component	What is rated	Subscore	Base score
Processor:	Calculations per second	4.7	2.2
Memory (RAM):	Memory operations per second	3.9	
Graphics:	Desktop performance for Windows Aero	2.2	
Gaming graphics:	3D business and gaming graphics performance	2.3	
Primary hard disk:	Disk data transfer rate	5.6	

View and print details

What do these numbers mean?

Personalize

You can add a personal touch to your computer by using themes, changing the computer's colors and sounds, and choosing your own desktop background, screen saver, and user account picture.

Themes

A theme is a collection of visual elements that can affect the style of windows, icons, fonts, colors, and sometime sounds. For example, a nature-based theme might include a desktop background with plants, a pointer that looks like a leaf, and system sounds that mimic bird chirps.

Color

Windows Aero is the premium visual experience of this version of Windows. It features a transparent glass design with subtle window animations and new window colors. Click the Start button, click Control Panel, click Appearance and Personalization, click Personalization, and then click Window Color and Appearance.

- If you see the Appearance Settings dialog box instead of the Window Color and Appearance window, the theme might not be set to Windows Vista, the color scheme might not be set to Windows Aero, or the computer might not meet the minimum hardware requirements for running Windows Aero.

Sound

You can change the sound your computer makes when you receive e mail, start Windows, or shut down your computer.

Desktop background

The desktop background, also called wallpaper, is a picture or design on the desktop. It provides a backdrop to your open windows.

Screen saver

A screen saver is a picture or animation that appears on the screen when you haven't used the mouse or keyboard for a set period of time. Windows includes a variety of screen savers to choose from.

You can create a personalized screen saver by displaying selected pictures and videos as a slide show.

To use pictures as a slide show

1. Click to open Screen Saver Settings.
2. Click the Screen saver list, and then click Photos.
3. If you want to specify a location for the pictures you want to use in your screen saver, modify the slide show speed, or configure any other screen saver settings, click Settings. After you make your changes, click Save.
4. Click OK.

User account picture

A user account picture helps identify your account on a computer. The picture is displayed on the Welcome screen and on the Start menu. You can change your user account picture to one of the pictures included with Windows, or you can use your own picture.

Windows Sidebar

Windows Sidebar provides a way to organize the information, games, and tasks that you want to access quickly without cluttering your workspace. It's made up of gadgets, which are customizable mini-programs that can display continuously updated headlines, a picture slide show, contacts, and more, without having to open a new window.

Phone and Modem Options

The following are descriptions of the settings on the Dialing Rules, Modems, and Advanced tabs in Phone and Modem Options.

Click to open Phone and Modem Options.

If you haven't opened Phone and Modem Options before, a dialog box will be displayed, prompting you to type your area code and other access codes.

Dialing Rules tab

The Dialing Rules tab lists all currently defined dialing locations (sets of rules applied to outgoing phone calls from your computer's modem). Use this tab to add, delete, or configure dialing locations. When you specify the destination phone number, the rules associated with the dialing location determine whether the area code must be included, whether a calling card should be used, and so on.

The following table describes the options on the Dialing Rules tab.

Locations: Lists all of the currently defined locations on your computer. The currently selected location appears in bold text, and its rules apply to any phone calls made from your computer. Double-clicking a location opens the Edit dialog box, where you can make changes to the rules associated with that location.

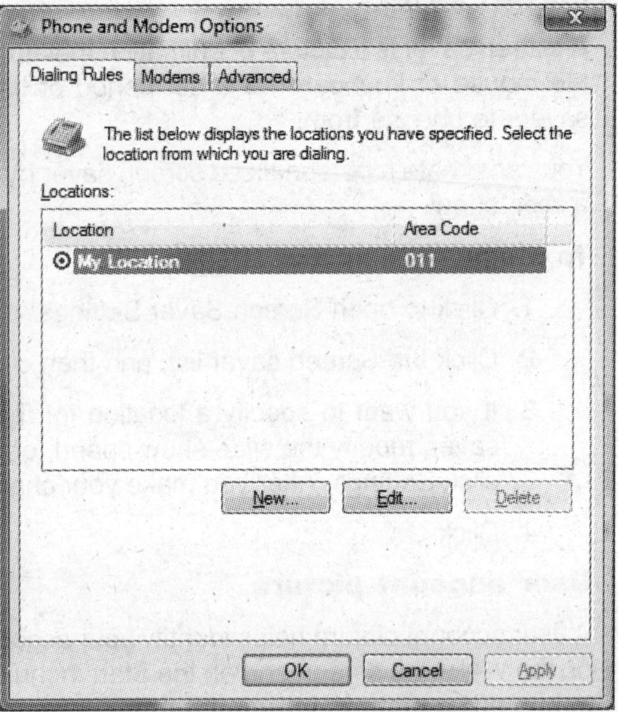

New: Allows you to create a new location and specify the rules associated with that location.

Edit: Allows you to edit the rules for the currently selected location.

Delete: Removes the currently selected location and all rules associated with it. It does not remove any existing calling card definitions.

Modems tab

The Modems tab lists all modems currently installed on your computer. Use this tab to add, remove, and configure modems.

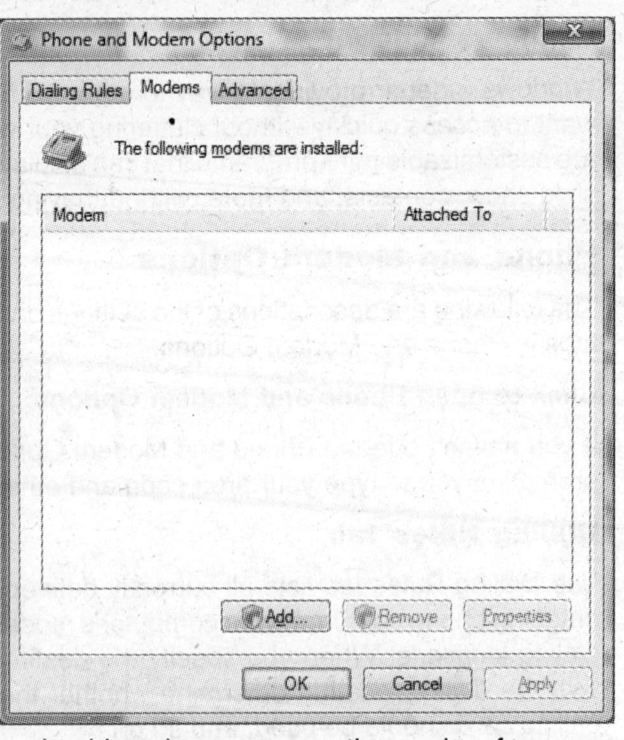

The following table describes the options on the Modems tab.

The following modems are installed: Lists the modems currently installed on your computer, and the communications port your computer uses to communicate with each modem.

Add: Allows you to install a new modem on your computer. If the drivers for your new modem are not already installed on your computer, you will be asked to install the drivers provided by the modem manufacturer.

Remove: Uninstalls the currently selected modem from your computer. You should unplug or remove the modem from your computer after uninstalling it, or it could be detected and reinstalled the next time you start your computer.

Properties: Allows you to view or change the configuration of the currently selected modem. The options available depend on the make and model of the modem.

Advanced tab

The Advanced tab lists the telephony providers (software used to communicate with telephony hardware, such as modems) currently installed on your computer. Use this tab to add, remove, and configure providers.

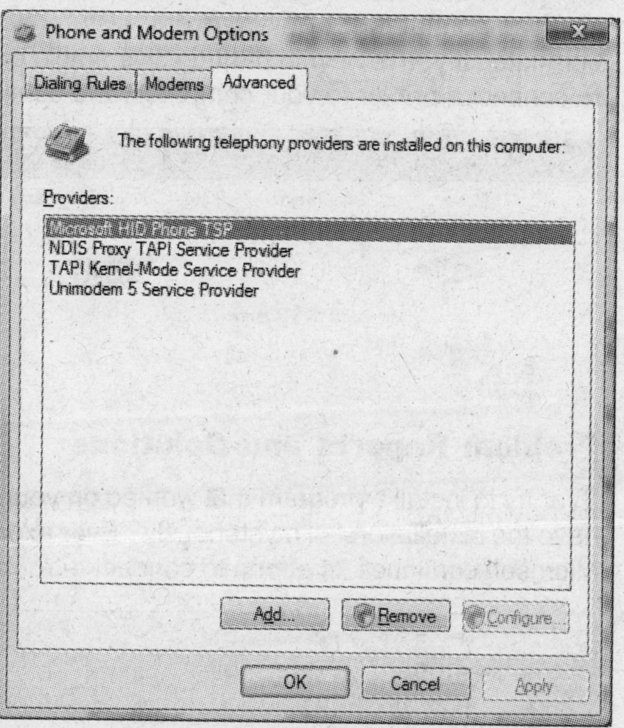

The following table describes the options on the Advanced tab.

Providers: Lists the telephony providers currently installed on your computer.

Add: Allows you to add a Telephony Application Programming Interface (TAPI) service provider to the list and make it available to telephony programs. To do this, you must have the drivers for the TAPI-supported telephony hardware already installed on your computer.

Remove: Removes the selected TAPI service provider from the list. Removing a TAPI service provider makes it unavailable to telephony programs. It does not delete any files from your computer.

Configure: Allows you to view or change the properties of the selected TAPI service provider. If this is unavailable, there are no configurable properties for the service provider.

Power Options

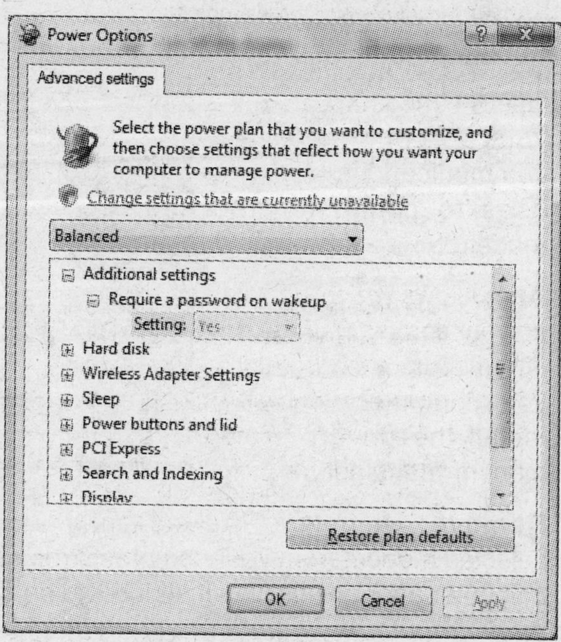

The Power Options program manages the power consumption of your computer. That's a big deal when you are running off a laptop's battery, of course, but it's also important if you'd like to save money (and the environment) by cutting down on the juice consumed by your desktop PC.

In Vista, Microsoft has tried to simplify the business of managing the electricity/speed tradeoff in two ways. First, it has abandoned the old name power scheme and adopted a new one: power plan.

Printers

You can print almost any document, picture, webpage, or file that you can view on your computer. If you're new to printing, this article can help you understand printer types, how to connect a printer to your computer, and common print options.

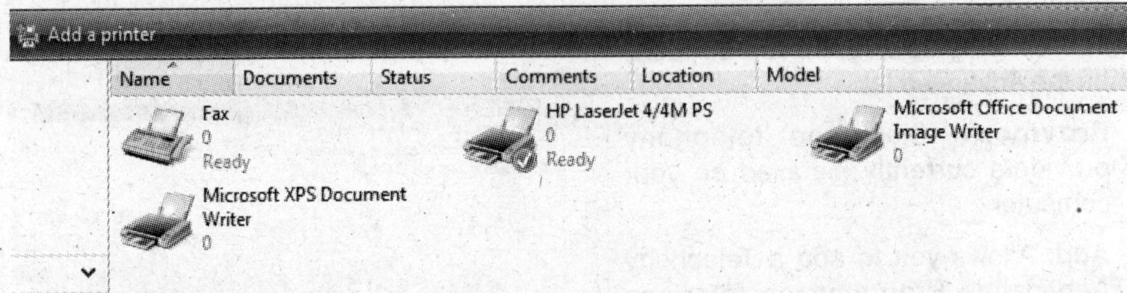

Problem Reports and Solutions

Ever try to install a program that worked on your old computer onto a new computer? Ever have the installation fail mysteriously? Ever experience a hang, freeze, or crash? In Vista, Microsoft continues its efforts to conduct a troubleshooting session on a worldwide scale.

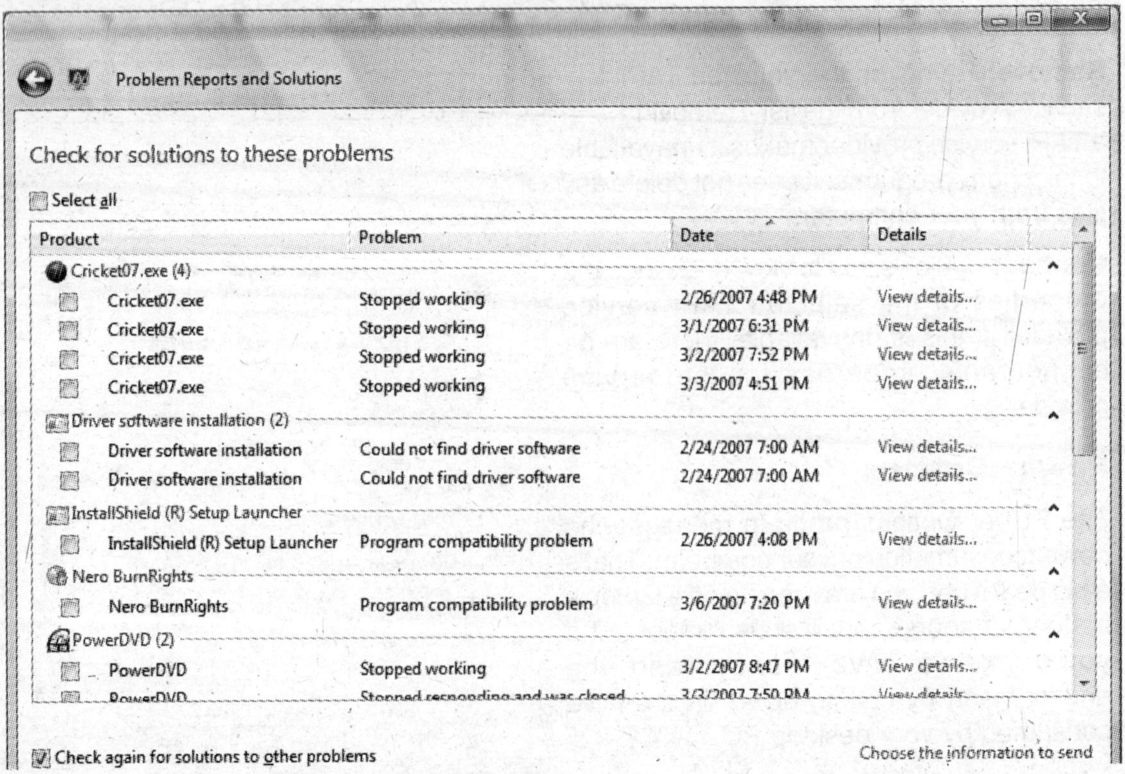

Problem Reports and Solutions

Check for solutions to these problems

Select all

Product	Problem	Date	Details
Cricket07.exe (4)			
Cricket07.exe	Stopped working	2/26/2007 4:48 PM	View details...
Cricket07.exe	Stopped working	3/1/2007 6:31 PM	View details...
Cricket07.exe	Stopped working	3/2/2007 7:52 PM	View details...
Cricket07.exe	Stopped working	3/3/2007 4:51 PM	View details...
Driver software installation (2)			
Driver software installation	Could not find driver software	2/24/2007 7:00 AM	View details...
Driver software installation	Could not find driver software	2/24/2007 7:00 AM	View details...
InstallShield (R) Setup Launcher			
InstallShield (R) Setup Launcher	Program compatibility problem	2/26/2007 4:08 PM	View details...
Nero BurnRights			
Nero BurnRights	Program compatibility problem	3/6/2007 7:20 PM	View details...
PowerDVD (2)			
PowerDVD	Stopped working	3/2/2007 8:47 PM	View details...
PowerDVD	Stopped responding and was closed	3/3/2007 7:50 PM	View details

Check again for solutions to other problems

Choose the information to send

Programs and Features

It is about managing the software you have installed, managing updates, and buying software online. It replaces the old Add/Remove Programs program. The Windows is useful for fixing, which might simply mean reinstalling, changing, and uninstalling existing programs, and is the only place you can go to turn on, or off, Windows features like Fax and Scan, Games, Meeting Space and more.

Regional and Language Options

You can change the format Windows uses to display information (such as dates, times, currency, and measurements) so that it matches the standards or language used in the country or region where you are located. For example, if you work on documents in both French and English, you can change the format to French so that you can display currency in Euros or display dates in the day/month/year format.

If you need to type and edit documents in more than one language, you can add input languages. Many input languages support a variety of keyboard layouts, input method editors (IMEs), and speech and handwriting recognition programs. Deciding which of these options to use is usually a matter of personal preference. Experiment with the options to discover which work best for you. Even if you do most of your work in one language, you might want to try other keyboard layouts. For example, if you need to type accented letters in English, it might be easier to use the United States-International keyboard layout instead of the standard U.S. keyboard layout.

When you add input languages, keyboard layouts, input method editors, or speech or handwriting recognition programs, Windows displays the Language bar on your desktop. The Language bar provides a quick way to change the input language or keyboard layout from your desktop.

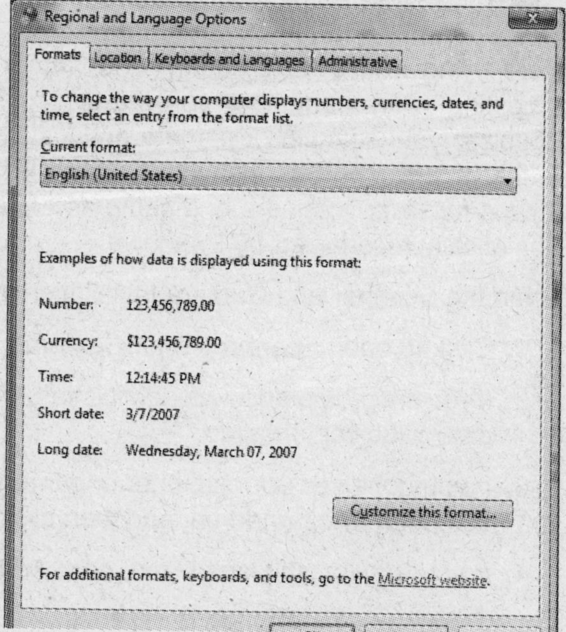

You can also change the display language—the language that the user interface text is displayed in—so that you can view wizards, dialog boxes, menus, and other items in the user interface in a different language. Some display languages are installed by default and others require you to install language files.

Formats tab

If you think 7/4 means July 4 and that 1,000 is the number of heads you have, skip this section. But, in some countries 7/4 means April 7, and 1,000 means one thousand. If your PC isn't showing numbers, times, currency, symbols, or dates in a familiar way, choose your country from the "Current format" button to rearrange the sequence of date elements.

Location tab

This tab, new to Vista, identifies you computer's location. The point is so that when you go online to check local news and weather, you'll get the right news and weather—a handy feature if you're travelling with a laptop.

Keyboards and Languages tabs

The symbols you use when you're typing in English. Microsoft solved this problem by creating different keyboard layouts, one for each language, or more, like Qwerty or Dvorak for English. Each keyboard layout rearranges the letters that appear when you press the keys. For example, in the Swedish layout, pressing the semicolon key produces an Ö—not a simicolon(;).

General tab

In order to even use Windows Vista, you must have an input language. The default is US English. If yours is different, then choose it from the drop-down list. This is the language that Vista will use to communicate with you, and the standard language for your keyboard.

Administrative tab

The "Change system locale" button this tab lets you specify—which language handles error messages and the occasional dialog box. The "Copy to reserved account" button lets the newly configured language settings apply to new user accounts, so anyone who gets a new account on this computer will have your language, format, and keyboard settings conveniently available to them.

Scanners and Cameras

Before trying to use the Scanner and Camera Installation Wizard, you should first try connecting your scanner or camera to your computer and turning it on. If Windows recognizes your scanner or camera and installs the appropriate driver, you don't need to use the wizard. The Scanner and Camera Installation Wizard helps you to install driver software for older scanners and cameras—and some networked scanners—that are not automatically recognized by Windows.

To start the Scanner and Camera Installation Wizard

1. Click to open Scanners and Cameras.
2. If you are prompted for an administrator password or confirmation, type the password or provide confirmation.
3. If you don't see your scanner or camera listed, ensure that it is connected to your computer and turned on, and then click Refresh.
4. If your device still isn't listed, click Add Device to start the Scanner and Camera

Installation Wizard, and then follow the instructions to install the necessary driver software.

- The wizard will ask you to select your scanner or camera from a list. If your scanner or camera isn't listed, you will need to obtain driver software for it, either from the manufacturer's website or from a disc provided by the manufacturer, and then click Have Disk when asked to choose your scanner or camera.

Security Center

Windows Security Center can help enhance your computer's security by checking the status of several security essentials on your computer, including firewall settings, automatic updates, anti-malware software settings, Internet security settings, and User Account Control settings. If Windows detects a problem with any of these security essentials (for example, if your antivirus program is out of date), Security Center displays a notification and places a Security Center icon in the notification area. Click the notification or double-click the Security Center icon to open Security Center and get information about how to fix the problem.

Firewall

A firewall can help prevent hackers or malicious software (such as worms) from gaining access to your computer through a network or the Internet. A firewall can also help stop your computer from sending malicious software to other computers.Windows checks if your computer is protected by a software firewall. If the firewall is off, Security Center will display a notification and put a Security Center icon in the notification area.

To turn on Windows Firewall

1. Click to open Security Center.
2. Click Firewall, and then click Turn on now. If you are prompted for an administrator password or confirmation, type the password or provide confirmation.
3. If you have a firewall other than Windows firewall, check the information that came with the firewall or go to the manufacturer's website to find out how to turn it on.
4. Windows does not detect all firewalls. If you are sure that you have a firewall installed and turned on, you can click Show me my available options to stop receiving notifications from Security Center about your firewall. If you do this, Windows will not monitor your firewall status or alert you if it is off.

Automatic updating

Windows can routinely check for updates for your computer and install them automatically. You can use Security Center to make sure Automatic updating is turned on. If updating is turned off, Security Center will display a notification and put a Security Center icon in the notification area.

To turn on automatic updating

1. Click to open Security Center.
2. Click Automatic updating, and then click Turn on now. If you are prompted for an administrator password or confirmation, type the password or provide confirmation.

Malicious software protection

Malicious software (malware) protection can help protect your computer against viruses, spyware, and other security threats. Security Center checks if your computer is using up-to-date antispyware and antivirus software. If your antivirus or antispyware software is turned off or out of date, Security Center will display a notification and put a Security Center icon in the notification area.

To install or update your anti-malware software

1. Click to open Security Center.
2. Click Malware protection, click the button under Virus protection or Spyware and other malware protection, and then choose the option that you want.

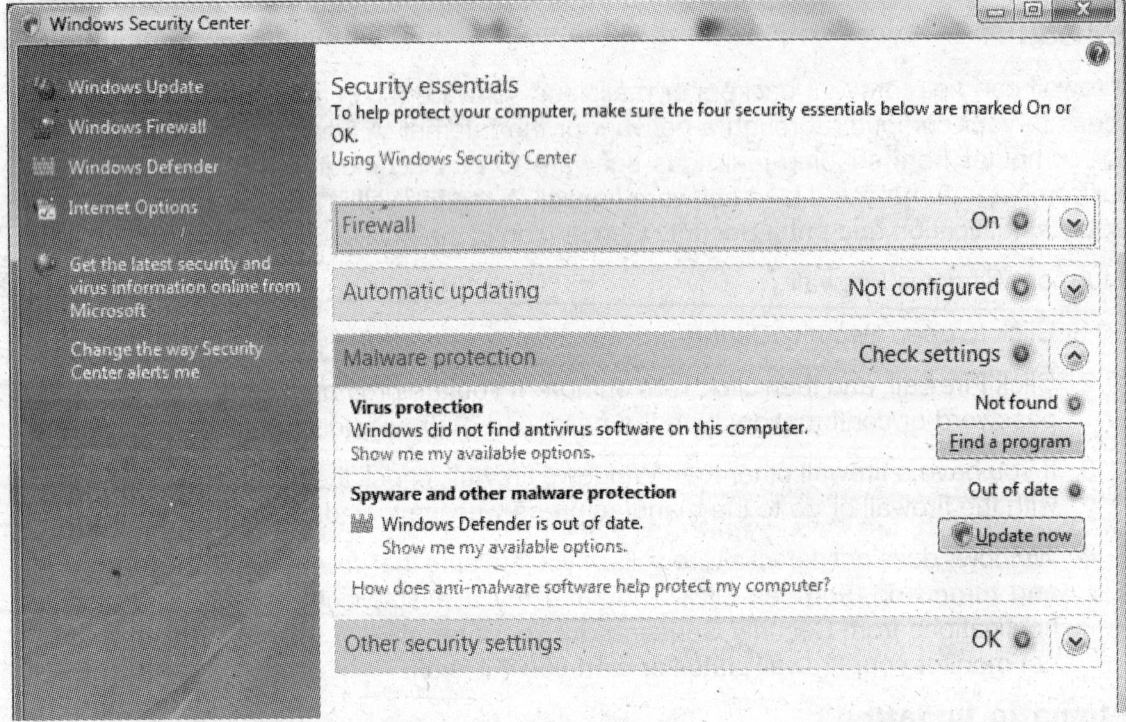

3. Windows does not detect all antivirus and antispyware software. If you are sure that you have anti-malware software installed, it is turned on, and it is up to date, you can click I have an antivirus program that I'll monitor myself or I have an antisypware program that I'll monitor myself to stop receiving notifications from Security Center about your anti-malware software. If you do this, Windows will not monitor your anti-malware software status or alert you if it is off.

Other Security Settings

Windows checks your Internet security settings and User Account Control settings to make sure they are set at the recommended levels. If your Internet or User Account Control settings are changed to a security level that is not recommended, Security Center will display a notification and put a Security Center icon in the notification area.

To restore Internet settings to recommended levels

1. Click to open Security Center.
2. Click Other security settings.
3. Under Internet security settings, click Restore settings.
4. Do one of the following:

- To automatically reset the Internet security settings that are at risk to their default level, click Restore my Internet security settings now.
- To reset the Internet security settings yourself, click I want to restore my Internet security settings myself. Click the security zone you want to change settings for, and then click Custom level.

To restore User Account Control settings to recommended levels

1. Click to open Security Center.
2. Click Other security settings.
3. Under User Account Control, click Turn on now. If you are prompted for an administrator password or confirmation, type the password or provide confirmation

Sound

In Vista, the Sound dialog box has been simplified. It now contains only three tabs that control every aspect of your microphone and speakers: Playback, Record, and Sounds.

Playback and Recording tabs

These tabs simply contain the icon for each attached sound device. To change a device's settings, select it, and then click Configure.

Sounds tab

Windows Vista comes with a new, freshly composed suite of little sound effects—beeps, musical ripples, and chords—that play when you turn on the PC, trigger an error message, empty the Recycle Bin, and so on. And if you like, you can hear them on many other occasions, such as when you open or exit a program, open a menu, restore a window, and so on. The tab lets you specify which sound effect plays for which situation.

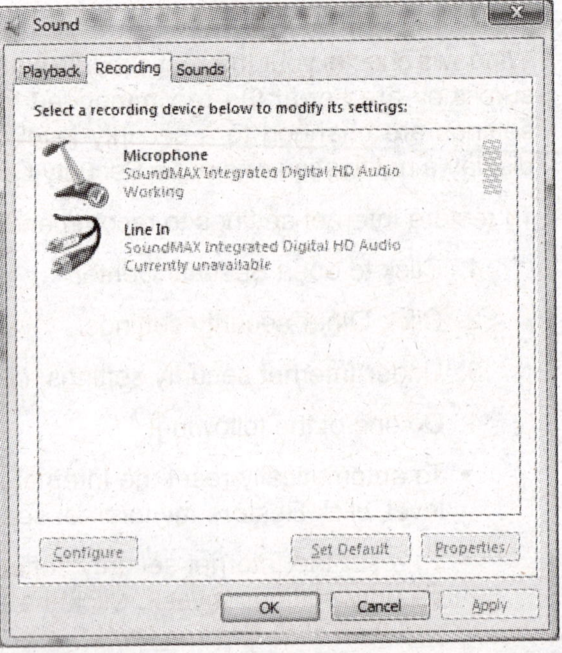

SoundMAX

A sound card is a device installed in your computer that processes information from a computer program, such as a media player, and then sends a signal to your computer's speakers that you can hear. Some motherboards have sound capabilities built into them, but computers often have a dedicated sound card, which usually improves the quality of the sound the computer can produce.

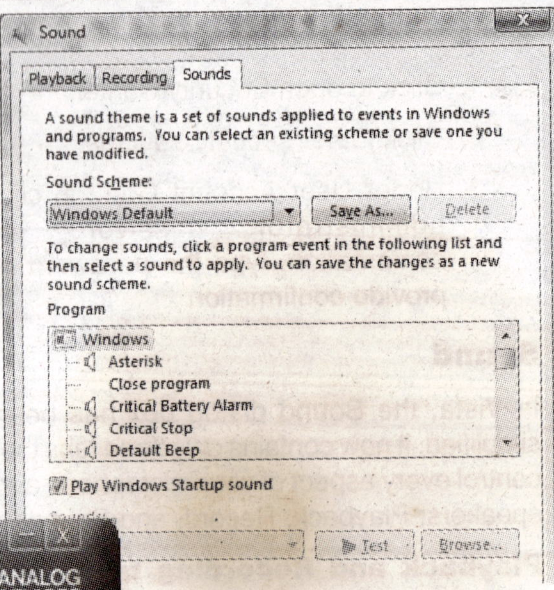

Almost every computer is capable of playing sounds. Check the back or front of your computer for jacks to plug in a microphone, headphones, or external speakers. You can also use Device Manager to check for a sound card.

You must be logged on as an administrator to perform these steps.

Click to open Device Manager. If you are prompted for an administrator password or confirmation, type the password or provide confirmation. Expand the Sound, video, and game controllers section to see the sound card that you have installed. If that section isn't displayed or no sound card is listed, either your computer doesn't have a sound card, or the driver for the sound card hasn't been properly installed.

Speech Recognition

To use Speech Recognition, the first thing you need to do is set it up on your computer. To learn how to do that, see Set up Speech Recognition. When you're ready to use Speech Recognition, you need to speak in simple, short commands. The tables below include some of the more commonly used commands.

1. Click to open Windows Speech Recognition.
2. Speech Recognition is not available in all languages.

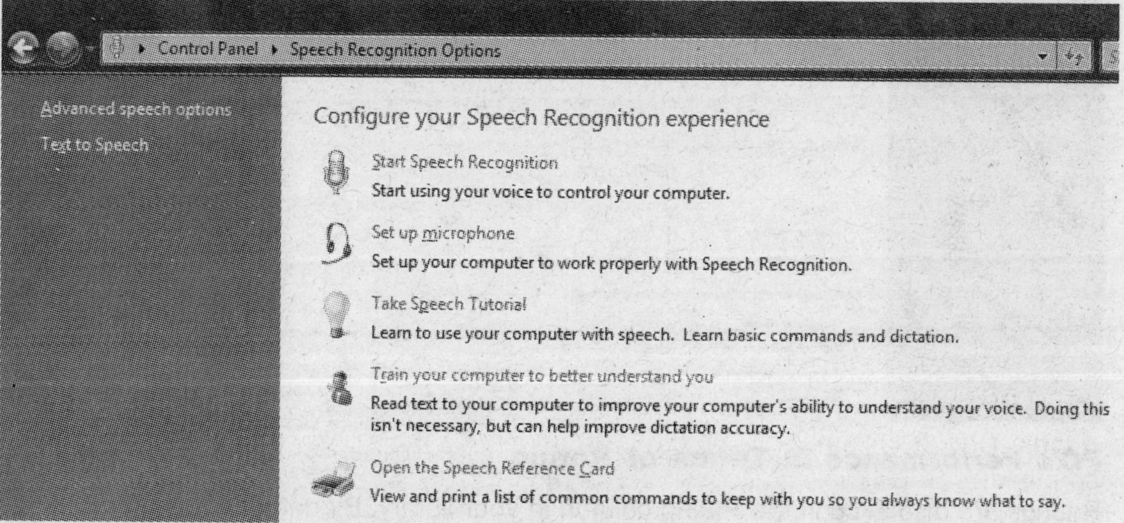

Sync Center

Sync is short for synchronization. In Windows, sync is the process of keeping two or more versions of the same file stored in different locations matched with each other. If you add, change, or delete a file in one location, Windows can add, change, or delete the same file in the other locations that you choose to sync with, whenever you choose to sync.

Sync Center is a feature of Windows that allows you to keep information in sync between your computer and Mobile devices that you plug in to your computer or to which you connect wirelessly (such as portable music players, digital cameras, and mobile phones).

- Files stored in folders on network servers. (These are called offline files because you can access them even when your computer or the server is not connected to the network.)
- Programs that support Sync Center.

System

The system dialog box has the following information.

What edition of Vista is installed on your computer?

As you know, Vista comes in several editions. Not all editions are made equal; if you're failing to find some feature that you could have sworn is supposed to be in Vista, it's good to check here. You might find out that the feature you want is available only on higher-priced versions.

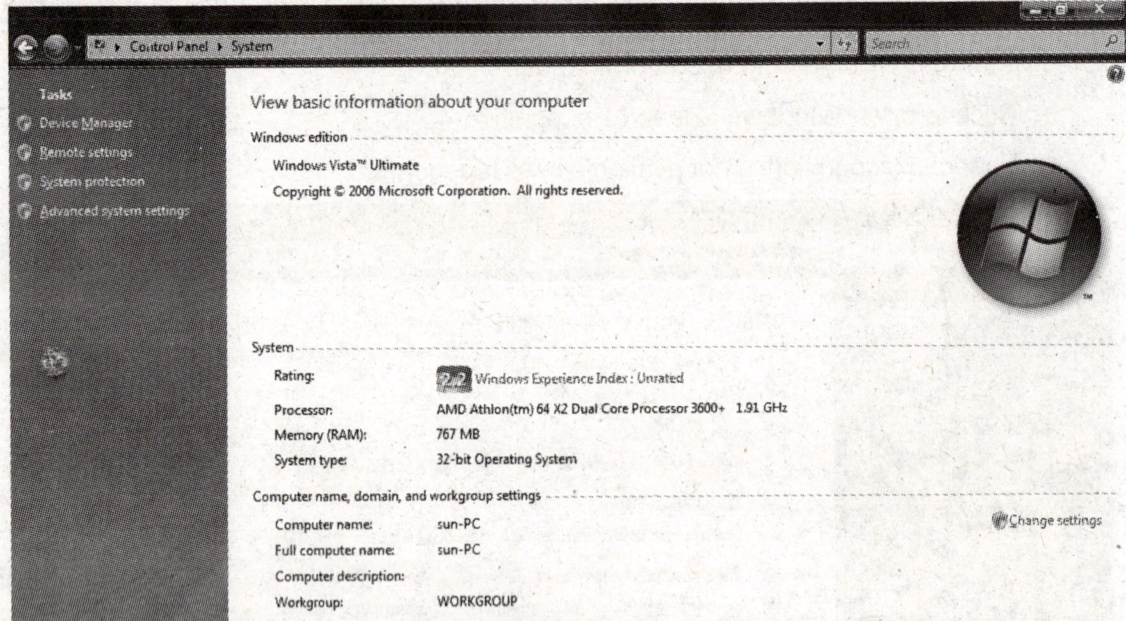

PC's Performance in Terms of Rating

Ratings are displayed in the Rating column in your library. By default, most items in your library are automatically given an auto rating. The auto rating is controlled by non-Microsoft data providers, such as AMG and some online stores. You can override an auto rating by explicitly choosing a new user rating. You can distinguish between the two types of ratings by the appearance of the stars, which are blue for auto ratings and bright yellow for user ratings.

The model name and speed of your PC's processor chip

Such as Pentium 4, 2.6 GHz

How much memory your PC has?

That's a very helpful number to know, particularly if you need to improve your computer's speed.

Your computer's name, domain or workgroup

Remember, your computer name and description are primarily useful on a network, since that's how other people will identify your computer. Unless you tell it otherwise, Vista names your computer after you login name, somtheing like SUN-PC.

Table PC Settings

This applet is all about managing a Table PC, one of those touchscreen laptop things.

Here, you will find settings that focus on tablet display orientation and calibration, handwriting recognition, and configuring pen input.

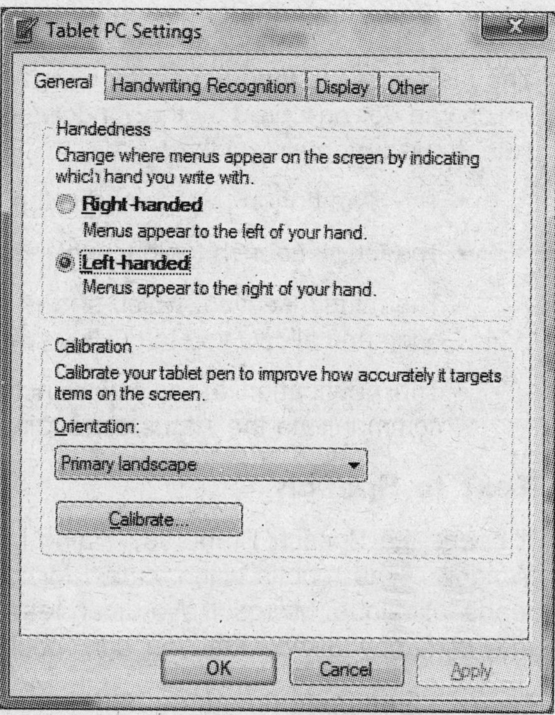

Taskbar and Start Menu

The Start menu is the main gateway to your computer's programs, folders, and settings. It's called a menu because it provides a list of choices, just as a restaurant menu does. And as "Start" implies, it's often the place that you'll go to start or open things.

Use the Start menu to do these common activities:

- Start programs
- Open commonly used folders
- Search for files, folders, and programs
- Adjust computer settings
- Get help with the Windows operating system
- Turn off the computer

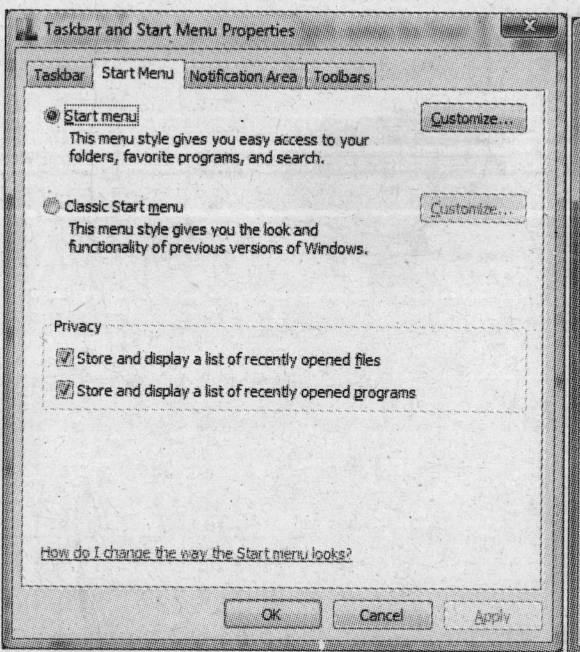

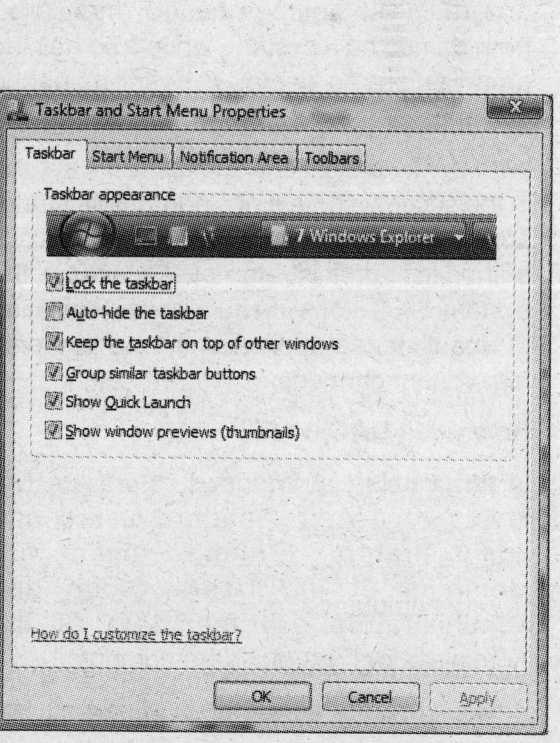

- Log off from Windows or switch to a different user account

The taskbar is the long horizontal bar at the bottom of your screen. Unlike the desktop, which can get obscured by the windows on top of it, the taskbar is visible almost all the time. It has four main sections:

- The Start button , which opens the Start menu.
- The Quick Launch toolbar, which lets you start programs with one click.
- The middle section, which shows you which programs and documents you have open and allows you to quickly switch between them.
- The notification area, which includes a clock and icons (small pictures) that communicate the status of certain programs and computer settings.

Text to Speech

It opens the Speech Properties dialog box. Here is where you configure the voice of Windows—the robotic voice, called Microsoft Anna—that you head any time Windows reads text aloud. Microsoft Word can read text to you, however, and for that reason, you may be happy to know that you can specify Anna's rate of speaking using the dialog box.

User Accounts

User Account Control (UAC) is a new set of infrastructure technologies in this version of Windows that helps prevent malicious programs, sometimes called "malware," from damaging a system, while also helping organizations to deploy a better-managed desktop.

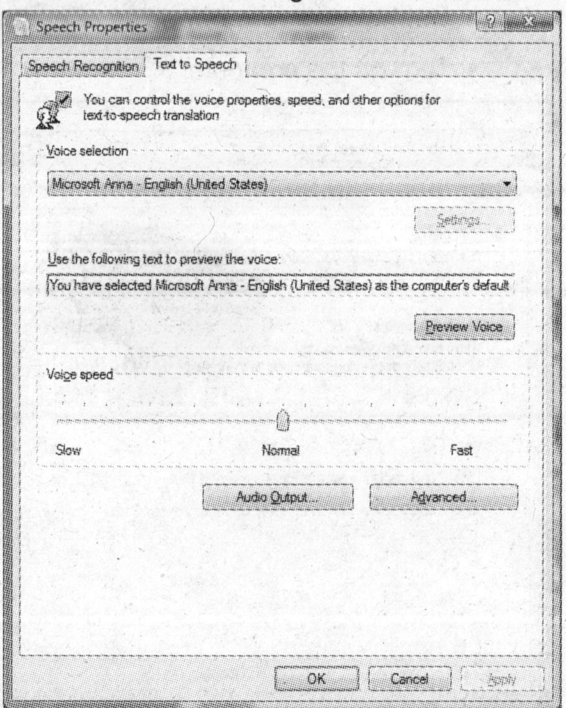

With UAC, applications and tasks always run in the security context of a non-administrator account, unless an administrator specifically authorizes administrator-level access to the system. UAC stops the automatic installation of unauthorized applications, and prevents inadvertent changes to system settings.

How does UAC work?

In this version of Windows, there are two levels of users: standard users and administrators. Standard users are members of the Users group and administrators are members of the Administrators group on the computer.

Unlike previous versions of Windows, both standard users and administrators access resources and run applications in the security context of standard users by default. When any user logs on to a computer, the system creates an access token for the user. This access token contains information about the level of access that the user is granted, including specific security identifiers (SIDs) and Windows privileges. When an administrator logs on, this version of Windows creates two separate access tokens for the user: a standard user access token and an administrator access token. The standard user access token contains the same user-specific information as the administrator access token, but the administrative Windows privileges and SIDs have been removed. The standard user access token is used to start applications that do not perform administrative tasks ("standard user applications").

When the administrator needs to run applications that perform administrative tasks ("administrator applications"), this version of Windows prompts the users to change or "elevate" their security context from a standard user to an administrator. This default administrator user experience is called Admin Approval Mode. In this mode, applications require specific permission to run as an administrator application (an application that has the same access as an administrator).

When an administrator application is starting, by default a User Account Control message appears. If the user is an administrator, the message gives a choice to allow the application to start or to prevent it from starting. If the user is a standard user, the user can enter the user name and password of an account that is a member of the local Administrators group.

Welcom Center

The Welcome Center, a new Vista feature, is the window that welcomes you every single time you log in. This window conveniently displays how to get started with Vista and pay Microsoft for more products and services.

Windows CardSpace

Ever have to fill out a form on the Internet—name, address, email address—only to go to a differnt site that requests exactly the same information. CardSpace is Microsoft's attempt to solve that duplication-of-effort problem. You are supposed to create a profile containing this kind of information, like a digital ID card. You show your card at a site, and the site gest your information off the card, saving you all that retyping.

Windows Defender

It's important to run antispyware software whenever you're using your computer. Spyware and other potentially unwanted software can try to install itself on your computer any time you connect to the Internet. It can also infect your computer when you install some programs using a CD, DVD, or other removable media. Potentially unwanted or malicious software can also be programmed to run at unexpected times, not just when it is installed.

Windows Defender offers three ways to help keep spyware and other potentially unwanted software from infecting your computer:

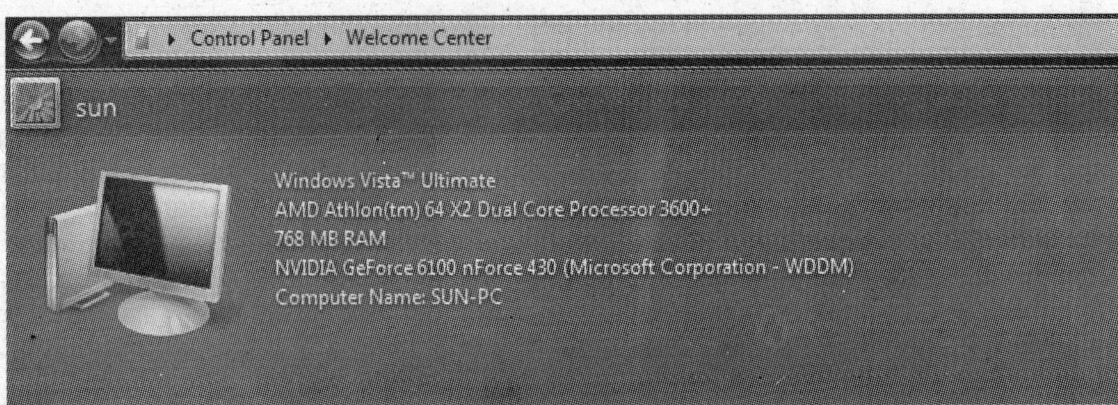

1. Get started with Windows (14)

 View computer details

 Transfer files and settings

 Add new users

 Windows Ultimate Extras

 What's new in Windows Vista

 Personalize Windows

Show all 14 items...

2. Offers from Microsoft (7)

 Go online to learn about Windows Live

 Download Windows Live Toolbar

 Sign up online for Windows Live OneCare

 Download Windows Live Mail desktop

 Download Windows Live Messenger

 Sign up online for technical support

☐ Run at startup (Welcome Center can be found in Control Panel, System and Maintenance)

- Real-time protection.Windows Defender alerts you when spyware or potentially unwanted software attempts to install itself or to run on your computer. It also alerts you when programs attempt to change important Windows settings.
- SpyNet community. The online Microsoft SpyNet community helps you see how other people respond to software that has not yet been classified for risks. Seeing if other members of the community allow software can help you choose whether to allow it on your computer. In turn, if you participate, your choices are added to the community ratings to help other people choose what to do.

- Scanning options. You can use Windows Defender to scan for spyware and other potentially unwanted software that might be installed on your computer, to schedule scans on a regular basis, and to automatically remove any malicious software that is detected during a scan.

When you use Windows Defender, it's important to have up-to-date definitions. Definitions are files that act like an ever-growing encyclopedia of potential software threats. Windows Defender uses definitions to determine if software that it detects is spyware or other potentially unwanted software, and then to alert you to potential risks. To help keep your definitions up to date, Windows Defender works with Windows Update to automatically install new definitions as they are released. You can also set Windows Defender to check online for updated definitions before scanning.

Windows Firewall

A firewall is software or hardware that checks information coming from the Internet or a network, and then either blocks it or allows it to pass through to your computer, depending on your firewall settings.

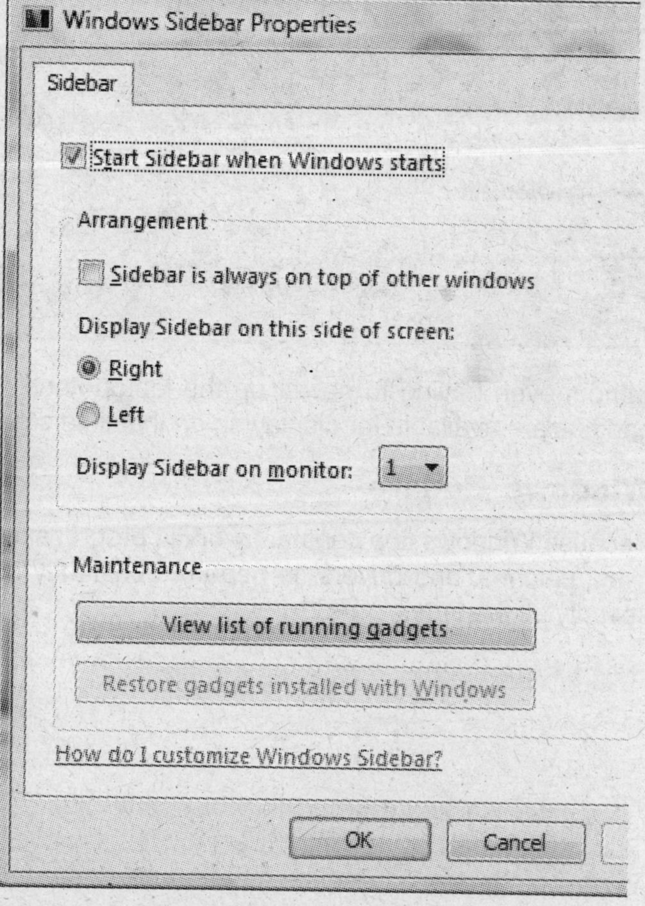

A firewall can help prevent hackers or malicious software (such as worms) from gaining access to your computer through a network or the Internet. A firewall can also help stop your computer from sending malicious software to other computers.

Windows Sidebar Properties

In Vista, there is a set of hybrid entities that Microsoft calls gadgets. They appear, all at once, floating in fornt of your other windows, at the right side of the screen. They are there when you first fire up Vista, or whenever you press Start + Space bar.

Gadgets are shown on the next page.

Windows SlideShow

It is a secondary screen, like a tiny text only display on specially made ShideShow—compatible laptops or desktop keyboards. Its designed to offer quick lookups of your email, calendar, Internet news feeds, and so on—

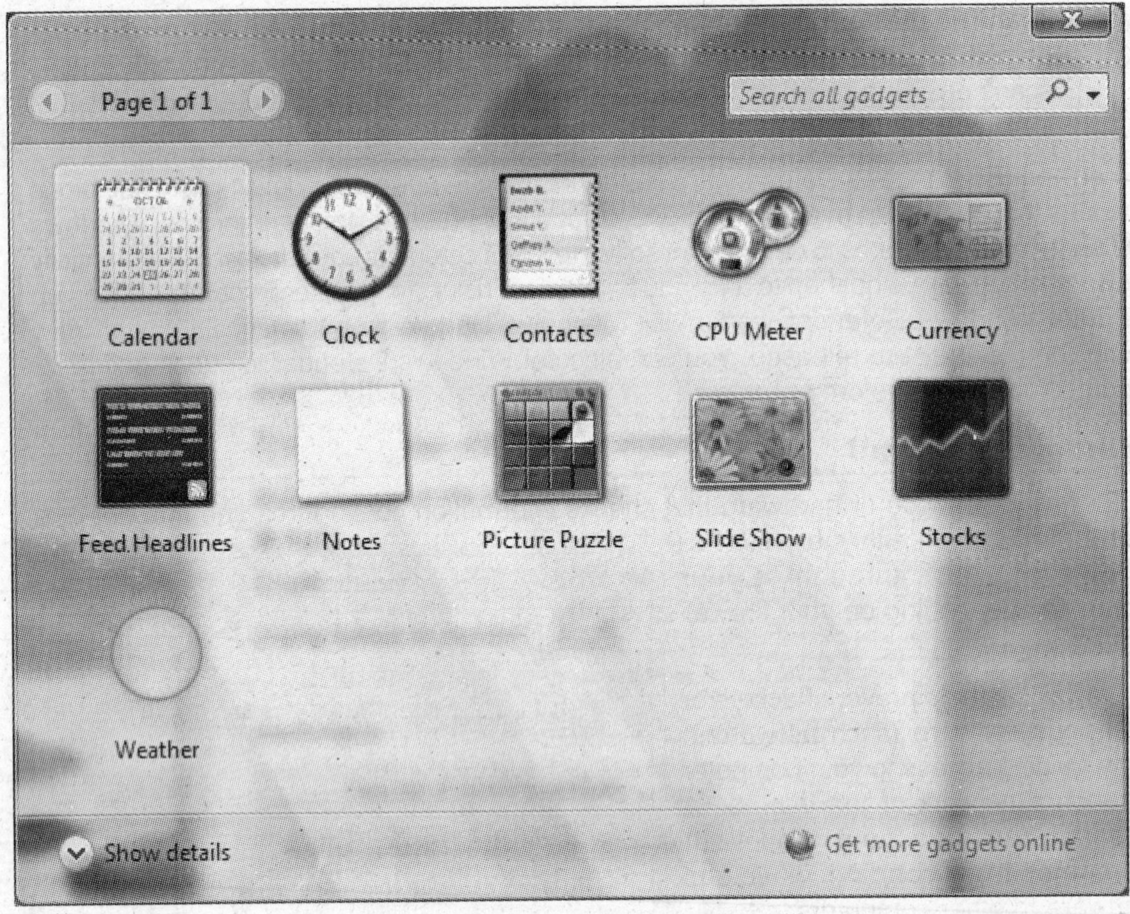

without even having to power up the laptop itself. This applet lets you configure which gadgets are available for displaying on that little screen.

Windows Update

Because Windows is a constant work in progress, Microsoft frequently releases updates, fixes, patches, and drivers, in hope of constantly improving your computer's speed and security all the time.

2 Introduction to Microsoft Word 2007

Introduction to Microsoft Office Word 2007

Since we are already familiar with other versions of Microsoft Word, let us first try to find out what is new in this version of Word.

What's New in Microsoft Office Word 2007

Microsoft Office Word 2007 helps you produce professional-looking documents by providing a comprehensive set of tools for creating and formatting your document in a new interface. Rich review, commenting, and comparison capabilities help you quickly gather and manage feedback from colleagues. Advanced data integration ensures that documents stay connected to important sources of business information.

Create professional-looking documents

Office Word 2007 provides editing and reviewing tools for creating polished documents more easily than ever before.

Spend more time writing, less time formatting

A new, results-oriented interface presents tools to you when you need them, in a clear and organized fashion:

- Save time and get more out of the powerful Word capabilities by selecting from galleries of predefined styles, table formats, list formats, graphical effects, and more.
- Word eliminates the guesswork when you apply formatting to your document. The galleries of formatting choices give you a live visual preview of the formatting in your document before you commit to making a change.

Add preformatted elements with just a few clicks

Office Word 2007 introduces building blocks for adding preformatted content to your documents:

- When you are working on a document from a particular template type, such as a report, you can select from a gallery of preformatted cover pages, pull quotes, and headers and footers to make your document look more polished.
- If you want to customize the preformatted content, or if your organization often

uses the same piece of content, such as legal disclaimer text or customer contact information, you can create your own building blocks that you select from the gallery with a single click.

Communicate more effectively with high-impact graphics

New charting and diagramming features include three-dimensional shapes, transparency, drop shadows, and other effects.

Instantly apply a new look and feel to your documents

When your company updates its look, you can instantly follow suit in your documents. By using Quick Styles and Document Themes, you can quickly change the appearance of text, tables, and graphics throughout your document to match your preferred style or color scheme.

Easily avoid spelling errors

The following are some new features of the spelling checker:

- The spelling checker has been made more consistent across the 2007 Microsoft Office system programs. Examples of this change include:
  - Several spelling checker options are now global. If you change one of these options in one Office program, that option is also changed for all the other Office programs.
  - In addition to sharing the same custom dictionaries, all programs can manage them using the same dialog box.
- The 2007 Microsoft Office system spelling checker includes the post-reform French dictionary. In Microsoft Office 2003, this was an add-in that had to be separately installed.
- An exclusion dictionary is automatically created for a language the first time that language is used. Exclusion dictionaries let you force the spelling checker flag words you want to avoid using. They are handy for avoiding words that are obscene or that don't match your style guide.
- The spelling checker can find and flag some contextual spelling errors. Have you ever typed a mistake similar to the following? I will see you their. In Office Word 2007, you can enable the Use contextual spelling option to get help with finding and fixing this type of mistake. This option is available when checking the spelling of documents in English, German or Spanish.
- You can disable spelling and grammar checking for a document or for all documents you create.

Share documents confidentlys

When you send a draft of a document to your colleagues for their input, Office Word 2007 helps you efficiently collect and manage their revisions and comments. When you are ready to publish the document, Office Word 2007 helps you ensure that any unresolved revisions and comments aren't still lurking in the published document.

Quickly compare two versions of a document

Office Word 2007 makes it easy to find out what changes were made to a document. When you compare and combine documents, you can see both versions of the document — with the deleted, inserted, and moved text clearly marked in a third version of the document.

Find and remove hidden metadata and personal information in documents

Before you share your document with other people, you can use the Document Inspector to check the document for hidden metadata, personal information, or content that may be stored in the document. The Document Inspector can find and remove information like comments, versions, tracked changes, ink annotations, document properties, document management server information, hidden text, custom XML data, and information in headers and footers. The Document Inspector can help you ensure that the documents you share with other people do not contain any hidden personal information or any hidden content that your organization might not want distributed. Additionally, your organization can customize the Document Inspector to add checks for additional types of hidden content.

Add a digital signature or signature line to your documents

You can help provide assurance as to the authenticity, integrity, and origin of your document by adding a digital signature to the document. In Office Word 2007 you can either add an invisible digital signature to a document, or you can insert a Microsoft Office Signature Line to capture a visible representation of a signature along with a digital signature.

The ability to capture digital signatures by using signature lines in Office documents makes it possible for organizations to use paperless signing processes for documents like contracts or other agreements. Unlike signatures on paper, digital signatures provide a record of exactly what was signed and they allow the signature to be verified in the future.

Convert your Word documents to PDF or XPS

Office Word 2007 supports exporting your file to the following formats:

- Portable Document Format (PDF) PDF is a fixed-layout electronic file format that preserves document formatting and enables file sharing. The PDF format ensures that when the file is viewed online or printed, it retains exactly the format that you intended, and that data in the file cannot be easily changed. The PDF format is also useful for documents that will be reproduced by using commercial printing methods.
- XML Paper Specification (XPS) XPS is an electronic file format that preserves document formatting and enables file sharing. The XPS format ensures that when the file is viewed online or printed, it retains exactly the format that you intended, and that data in the file cannot be easily changed.

Instantly detect documents that contain embedded macros

Office Word 2007 uses a separate file format (.docm) for macro-enabled documents, so you can instantly tell whether a file is capable of running any embedded macros.

Prevent changes to a final version of a document

Before you share a final version of a document with other people, you can use the Mark As Final command to make the document read-only and communicate to other people that you are sharing a final version of the document. When a document is marked as final, typing, editing commands, and proofing marks are disabled, and people who view the document cannot inadvertently change the document. The Mark As Final command is not a security feature. Anyone can edit a document that is marked as final by turning off Mark As Final.

Go beyond documents

Now more than ever, when computers and files are interconnected, it pays to store documents in files that are slim, sturdy, and supportive of a wide variety of platforms. To meet this need, the Microsoft Office system achieves a new stage in its evolution of XML support. The new XML-based file format enables Office Word 2007 files to be smaller, more robust, and deeply integrated with information systems and external data sources.

Reduce file sizes and improve corruption recovery

The new Word XML format is a compressed, segmented file format that offers a dramatic reduction in file size and helps ensure that damaged or corrupted files can be easily recovered.

Connect your documents to business information

In your business, you create documents to communicate important business data. You can save time and reduce the risk of error by automating the process of this communication. Create dynamic smart documents that update themselves by using new document controls and data binding to connect to your back-end systems.

Manage document properties in the Document Information Panel

The Document Information Panel makes it easy to view and edit document properties while you work on your Word document. The Document Information Panel displays at the top of your document in Word. You can use the Document Information Panel to view and edit both standard Microsoft Office document properties and properties for files that are saved to a document management server. If you use the Document Information Panel to edit the document properties for a server document, the updated properties will be saved directly to the server.

For example, you may have a server that keeps track of a document's editorial status. When you put the finishing touches on a document, you can open the Document Information Panel to change the document's editorial status from Draft to Final. When you save the document back on the server, the change in editorial status is updated on the server.

If you store document templates in a library on a Microsoft Windows SharePoint Services 3.0 server, the library might include custom properties that store information about the templates. For example, your organization may require you to categorize documents in the library by filling in a Category property. Using the Document Information Panel, you can edit properties like this directly within the Word environment.

Recover from Computer Problems

2007 Microsoft Office system provides improved tools for recovering your work in the event of a problem in Office Word 2007.

Office Diagnostics

Microsoft Office Diagnostics is a series of diagnostic tests that can help you to discover why your computer is crashing. The diagnostic tests can solve some problems directly and may identify ways that you can solve other problems. Microsoft Office Diagnostics replaces the following Microsoft Office 2003 features: Detect and Repair and Microsoft Office Application Recovery.

Program Recovery

Office Word 2007 has improved capabilities to help avoid losing work when the program closes abnormally. Whenever possible, Word tries to recover some aspects of the state of the program after it restarts.

For example, you are working on several files at the same time. Each file is open in a different window with specific data visible in each window. Word crashes. When you restart Word, it opens the files and restores the windows to the way they were before Word crashed.

Opening Screen of Microsoft Word Screen

Gone are the days of Menu, for example, File menu, Edit menu, etc. Now everything is there on the screen. You have to just click it and presto, you have the command available to you. But, first have a look at the opening screen, which is shown next. There are some main Tabs, which are basic substitutions for the menus. They are: Home, Insert, Page Layout, References, Mailings, Review, and View. Let us see what each one of them contains.

Home Panel

It has the various options of changing the style and type of text. Among the various important features are: Clipboard, Font, Paragraph, Styles, and Editing. Let us look at them one by one.

Clipboard

Most important commands here are: Cut, Copy, Paste and Format Painter. The Format Painer is used for copying formattting from one place and applying it to another. Paste includes options like, Paste Special and Paste as Hyperlink.

Paste

Clipboard

Font

Various options of the font dialog box are all here. You can choose Font, Font size, Grow font, Lower font, Clear formatting in the first row.

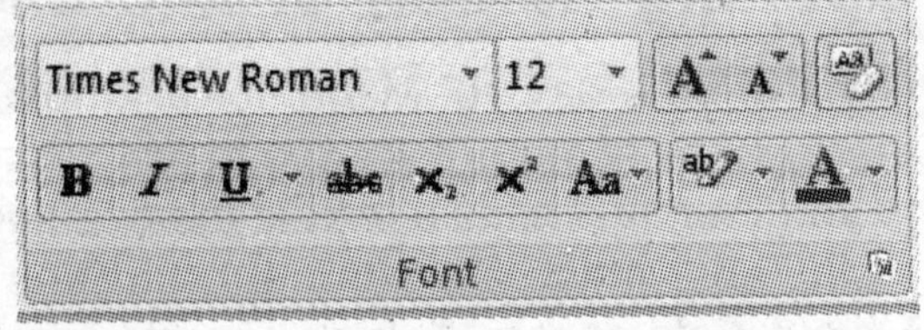

The second row contains options for Bold, Italics, Underline, Strikethrough, Subscript, Superscript, Change case, Text highlighting, and Text colour. The underlining option contains options for different type of lines which can be chosen for underlining and then choosing the colour of the same too. In Change case you have the option of changing the case to Sentence case, lowercase, UPPERCASE, Captalize Each Word and tOGGLE cASE. Text highlighting and colours have various options too.

Paragraph

It has options for paragraph styling. The first row contains options for Bullets, Numbering, Multilevel numbering, Shifting text to left, Shifting text to right, Sort, Show/hide non printing characters. In the second row you have the options of making paragraph, Left aligned, Centrally aligned, Right aligned, Box aligned, Line spacing,

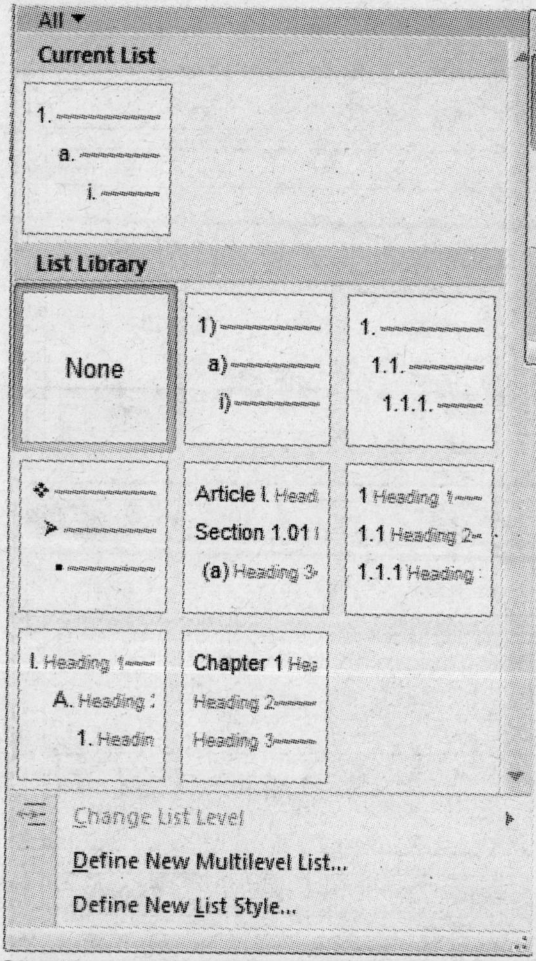

All
Current List
List Library
None
Change List Level
Define New Multilevel List...
Define New List Style...

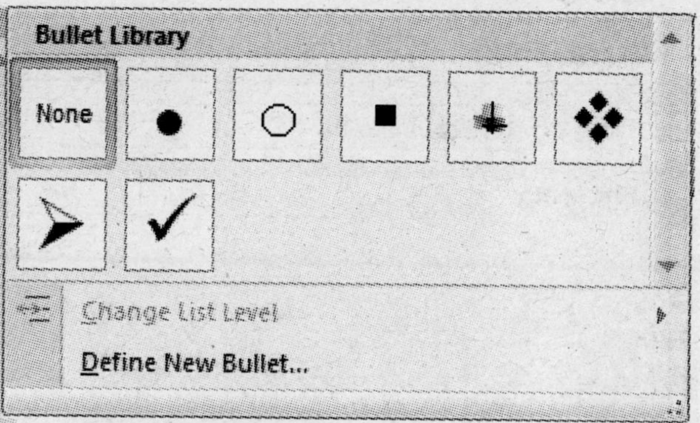

Bullet Library
None
Change List Level
Define New Bullet...

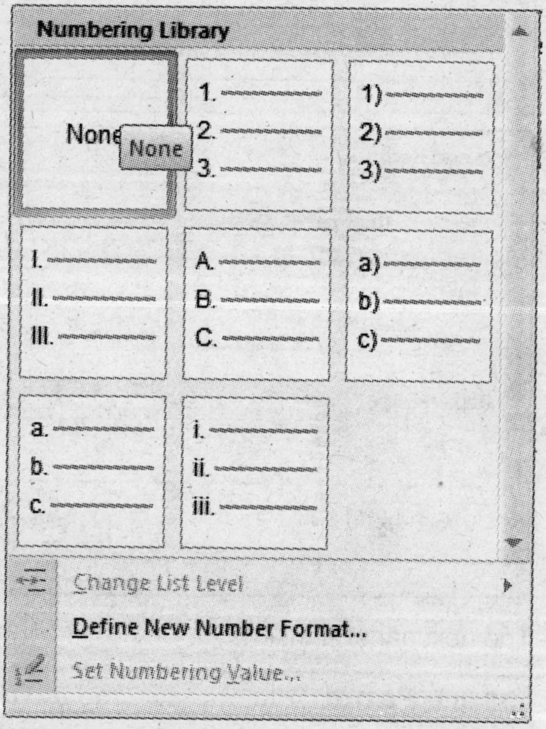

Numbering Library
None
Change List Level
Define New Number Format...
Set Numbering Value...

Shading, and Bottom border. Bullets have different options. Numering can be done in different styles too. So can be done in the case of Multilevel numbering.

Styles

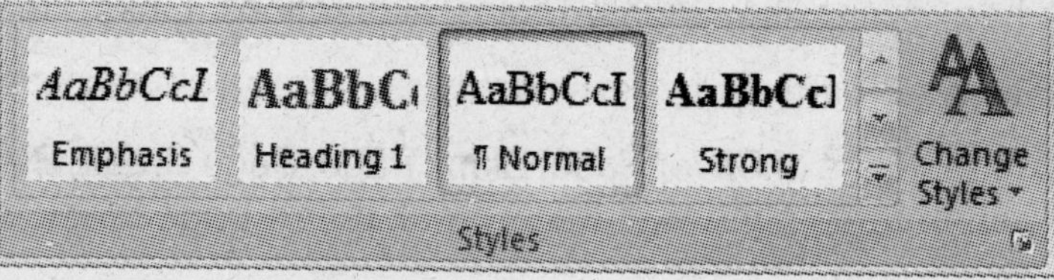

It displays the various styles which you have created. Just click at the one you want to apply to your text and it will be done. You can also Change Styles and create your own style from it.

Editing

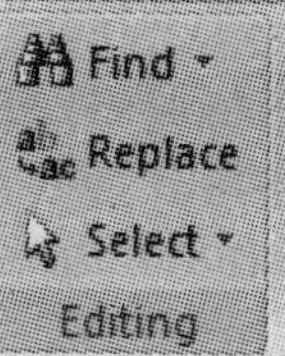

It has various other editing options, like, Find, Replace, and Select. Find allows you to find a particular word in the text. Replace allows you to find the word and replace it with another one. Select allows you to select text, select objects or the text with similar formatting.

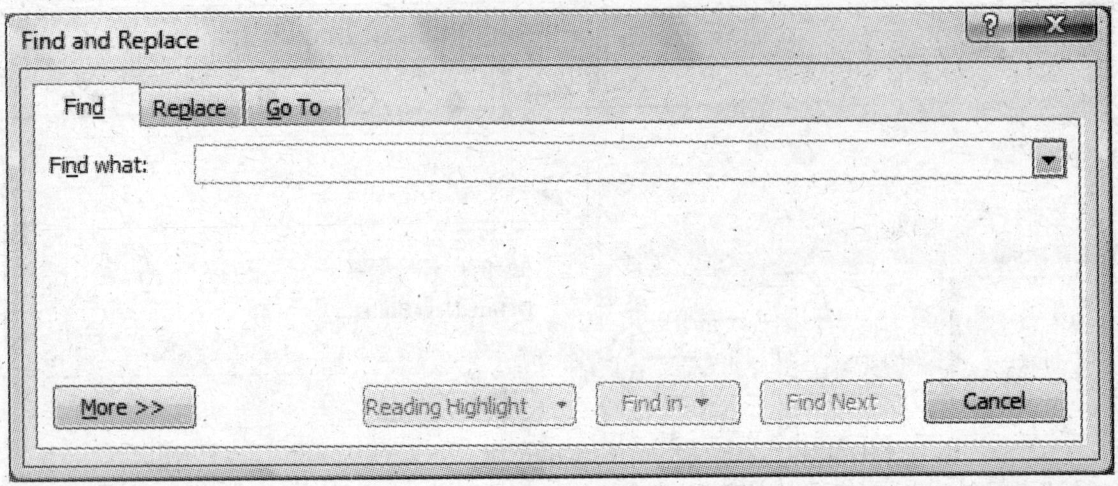

Find and Replace

Find | Replace | Go To

Find what:

More >> | Reading Highlight | Find in | Find Next | Cancel

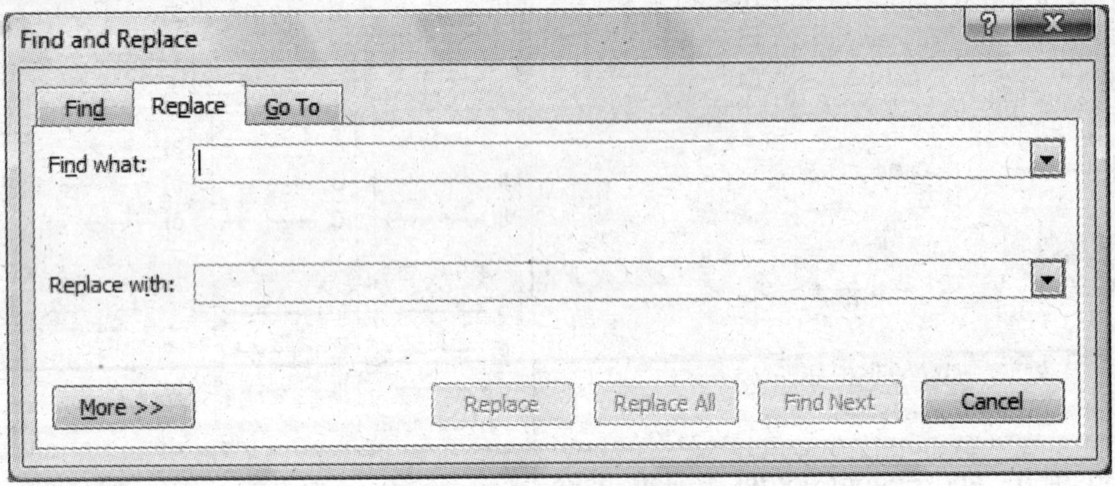

Find and Replace

Find | Replace | Go To

Find what:

Replace with:

More >> | Replace | Replace All | Find Next | Cancel

The next panel is Insert.

Insert Panel

It has options like: Pages, Tables, Illustrations, Links, Header & Footer, Text, and Symbols.

Pages

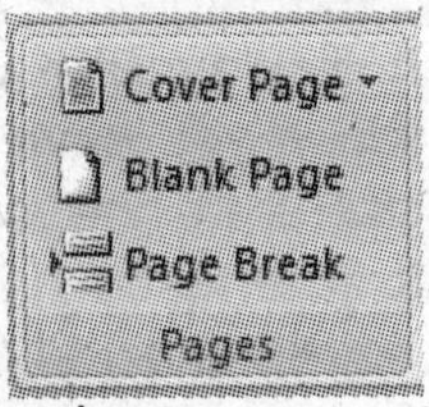

Cover Page
Blank Page
Page Break
Pages

It has options of Cover Page, Blank Page, Page Break. Blank page inserts a blank page in the text. Page break puts a page break in the text.

Tables

Inserts table format in the text. If you click at the arrow, you will see the options shown here, which not only describe the type of table you are choosing but also draws the table in the text simultaneously. You can also insert as a table, an Excel Spreadsheet. There is option of Quick Tables too, which allows you to save a table format, which can be called later for quickly creating a table.

Illustrations

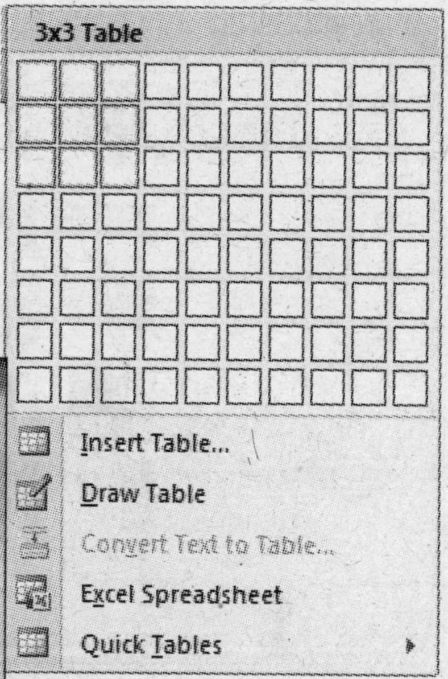

The various type of illustrations which can be inserted into the text of the document are: Picture, Clip Art, Shapes, SmartArt, and Charts. All of these have options, which are shown here.

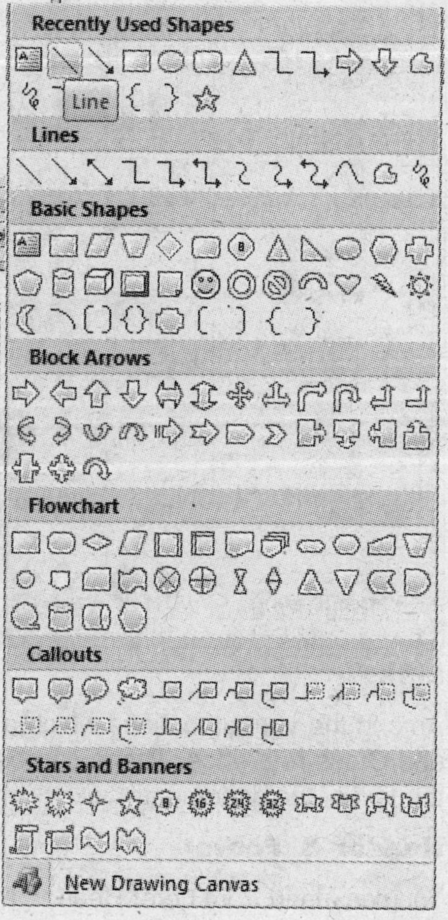

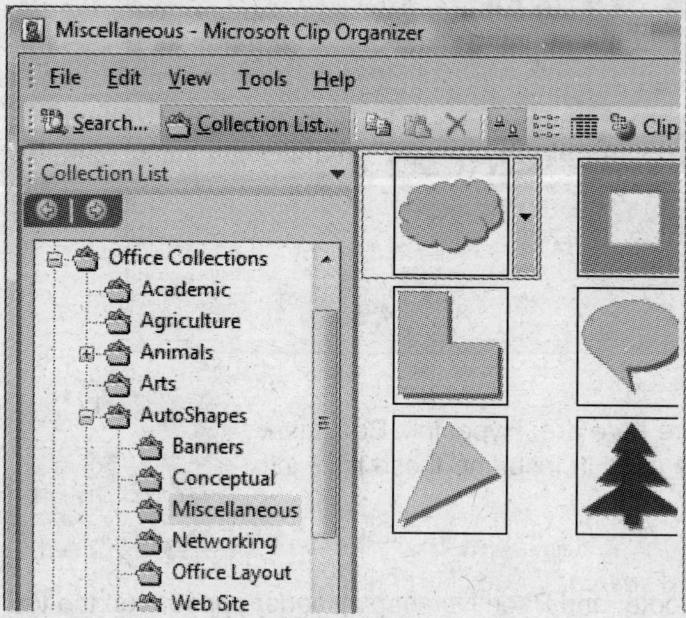

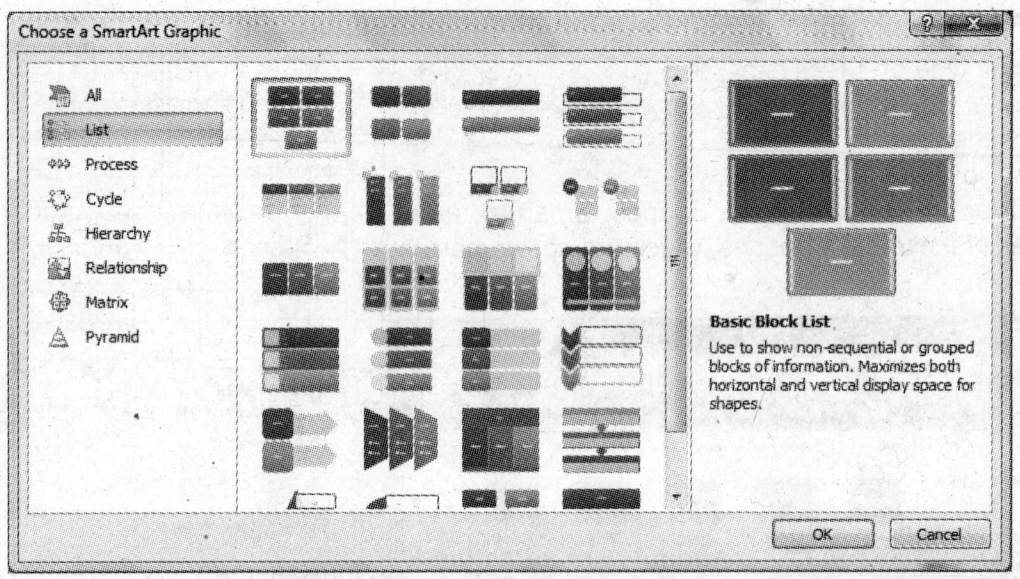

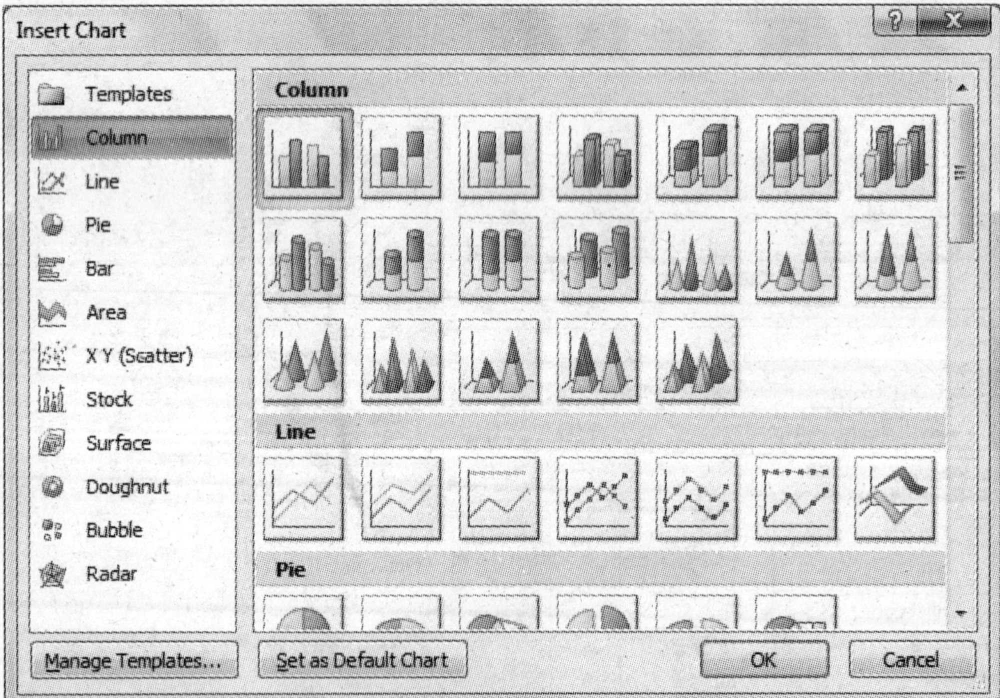

Links

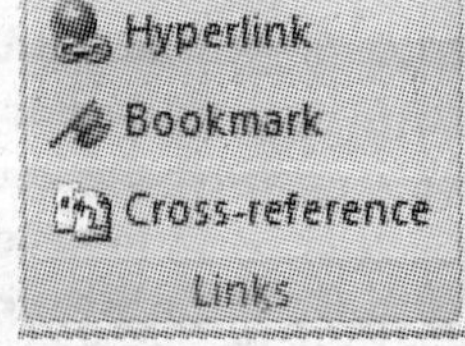

Among the various options which are here are: Hyperlink, Bookmark, and Cross-reference. These can be used in inserting these links into the text of the document.

Header & Footer

You can insert from here, Header, Footer and Page Numbers. Header appears on the top of each printed page. The content of the Footer appears at the bottom of the printed page. Header and Footer both of options of Editing and Removing them. Page number options are Top of Page, Bottom of Page, Page Margins, Current Position, Format Page Numbers and Remove Page Numbers.

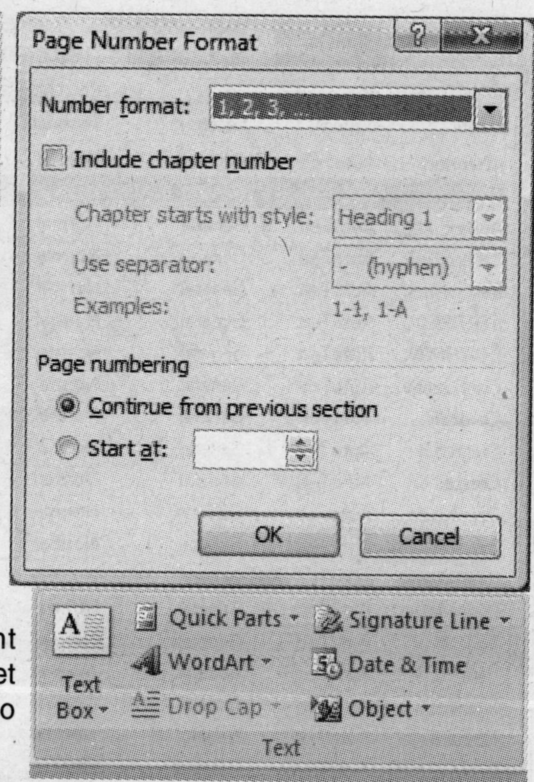

Text

Various options here are: Text Box, Quick Parts, Word Art, Drop Cap, Signature Line, Date and Time, and Object. Text box creates a box which can be filled up with the text and is independent of the document text.

Quick Parts has the options of Document Property, Field, Building Blocks Organizer, Get More on Office Online, and Save Selection to Quick Part Gallery.

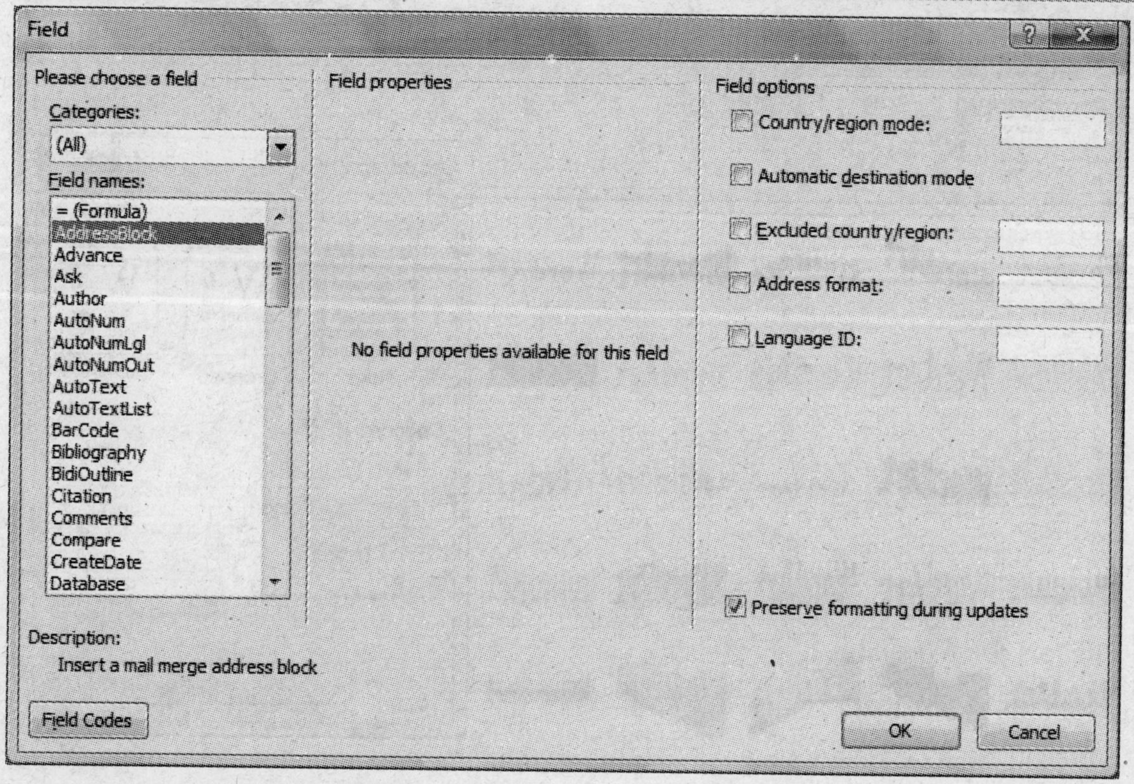

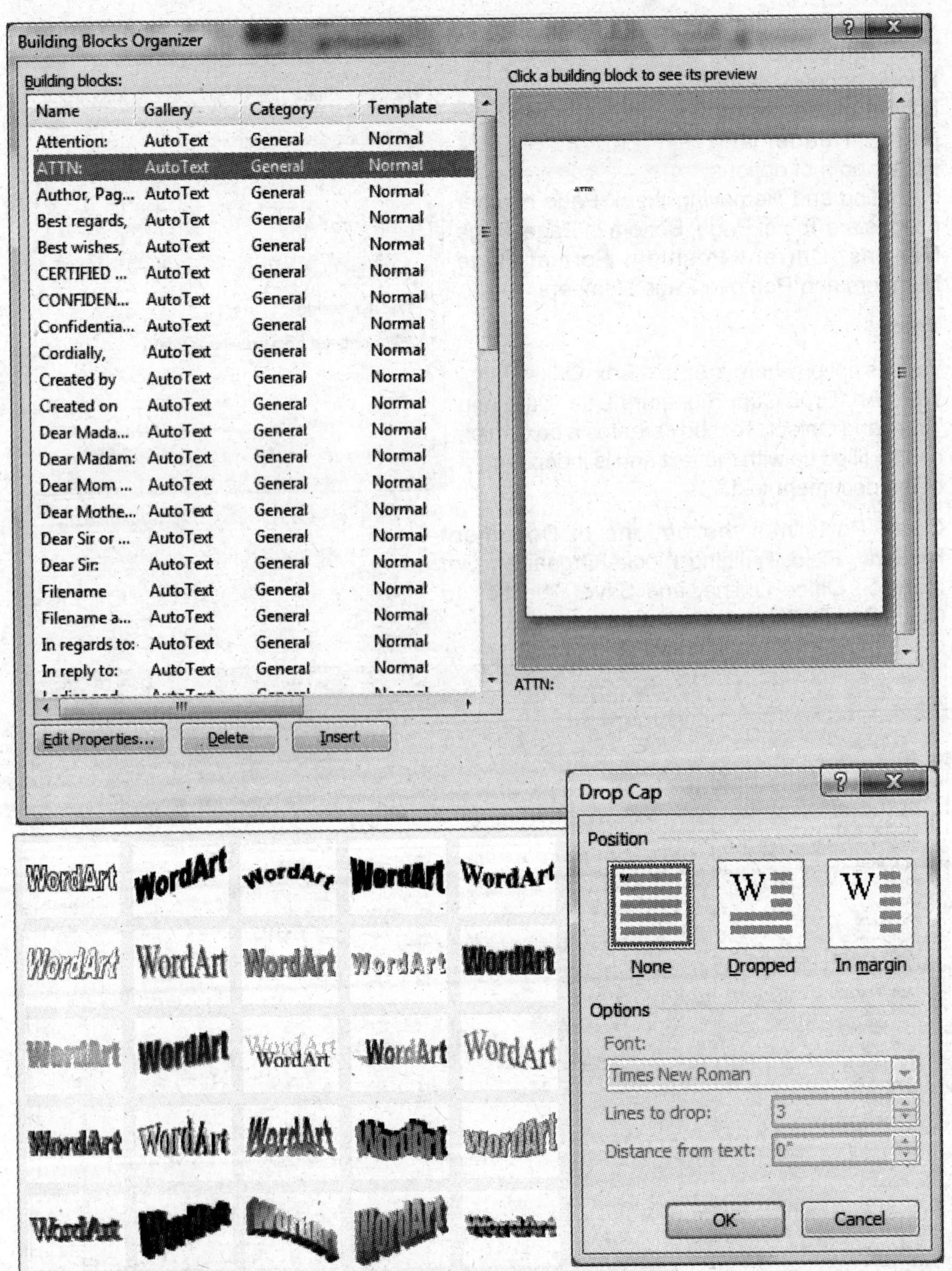
Building Blocks Organizer
Building blocks:
Name
Gallery
Category
Template
Attention: AutoText General Normal
ATTN: AutoText General Normal
Author, Pag... AutoText General Normal
Best regards, AutoText General Normal
Best wishes, AutoText General Normal
CERTIFIED ... AutoText General Normal
CONFIDEN... AutoText General Normal
Confidentia... AutoText General Normal
Cordially, AutoText General Normal
Created by AutoText General Normal
Created on AutoText General Normal
Dear Mada... AutoText General Normal
Dear Madam: AutoText General Normal
Dear Mom ... AutoText General Normal
Dear Mothe... AutoText General Normal
Dear Sir or ... AutoText General Normal
Dear Sir: AutoText General Normal
Filename AutoText General Normal
Filename a... AutoText General Normal
In regards to: AutoText General Normal
In reply to: AutoText General Normal
Click a building block to see its preview
ATTN:
Edit Properties...
Delete
Insert
Drop Cap
Position
None
Dropped
In margin
Options
Font:
Times New Roman
Lines to drop:
3
Distance from text:
0"
OK
Cancel

WordArt is an independent program which allows you to create and insert an independent text.

Drop Cap allows you to put a capital letter in the beginning of the text. It can cover 2-3 lines of the text to highlight the alphabet.

Signature Line allows you to insert a signature line.

Date and Time would insert date and time in the text, in the format selected by you.

Object allows you to insert objects in the text. It also allows you to insert text from another file.

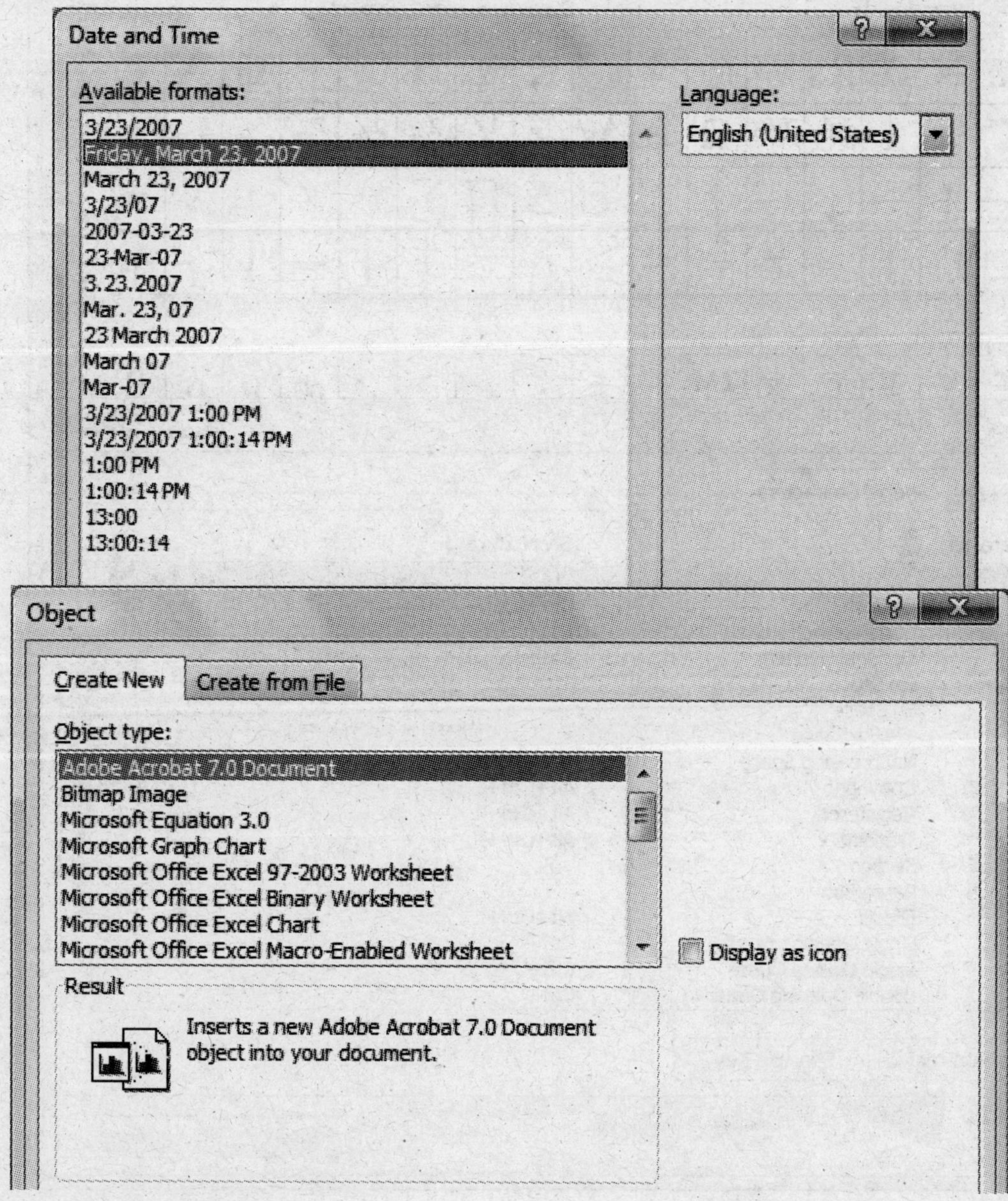

Symbols

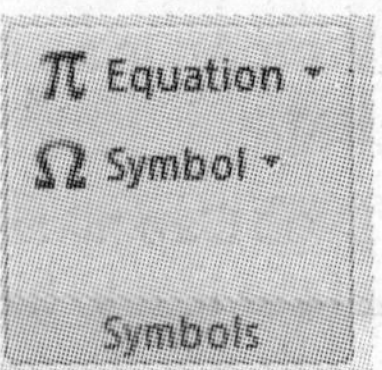

It has two options: Equation and Symbol. Equation allows you to enter equations in the text, after creating it using the various symbols available under it. It is quite a big topic and can be discussed in an advanced book. Symbol button allows you insert a symbol from the list shown here.

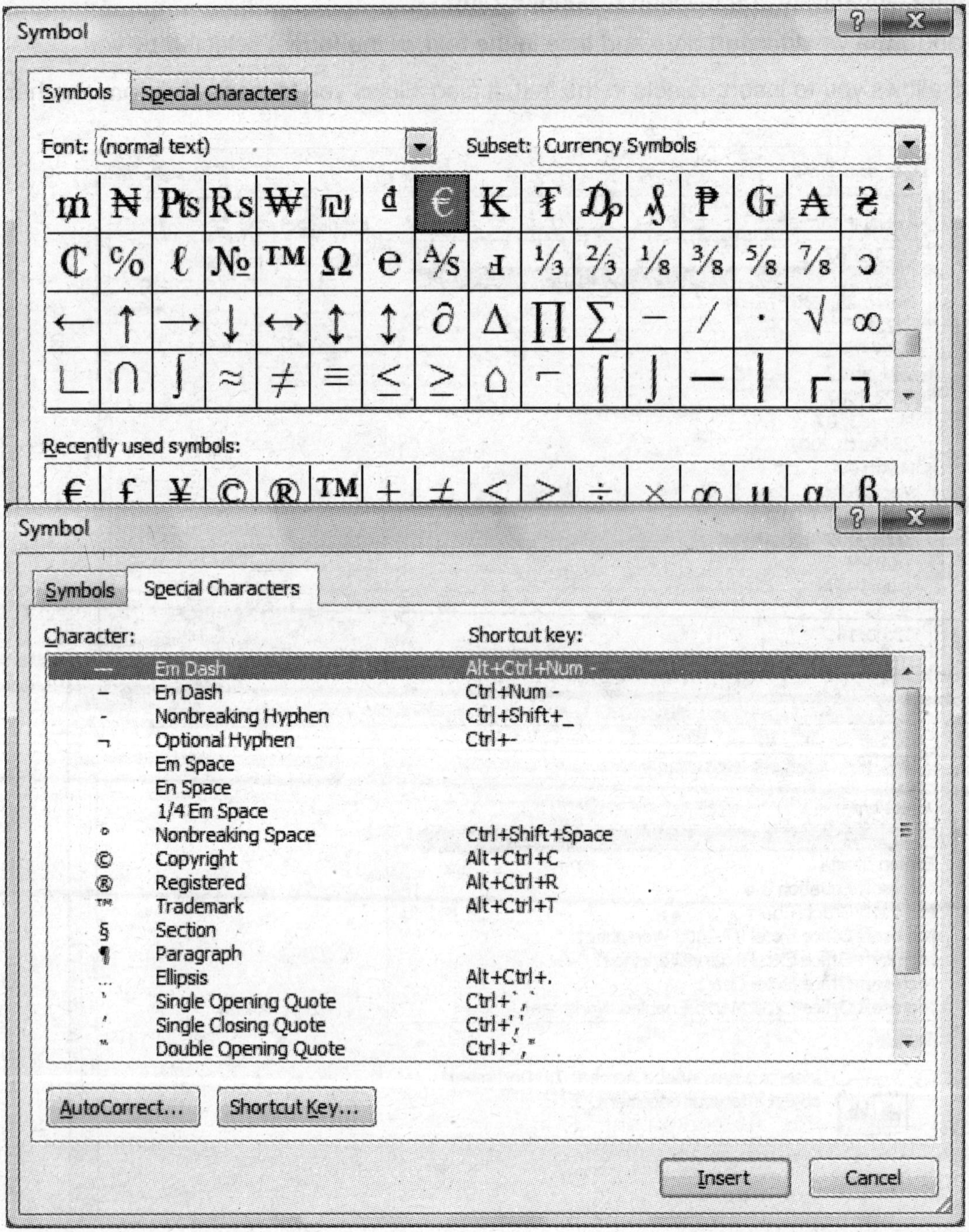

Symbol

Symbols | Special Characters

Font: (normal text) Subset: Currency Symbols

Recently used symbols:

Symbol

Symbols | Special Characters

Character:		Shortcut key:
—	Em Dash	Alt+Ctrl+Num -
–	En Dash	Ctrl+Num -
-	Nonbreaking Hyphen	Ctrl+Shift+_
¬	Optional Hyphen	Ctrl+-
	Em Space	
	En Space	
	1/4 Em Space	
°	Nonbreaking Space	Ctrl+Shift+Space
©	Copyright	Alt+Ctrl+C
®	Registered	Alt+Ctrl+R
™	Trademark	Alt+Ctrl+T
§	Section	
¶	Paragraph	
…	Ellipsis	Alt+Ctrl+.
'	Single Opening Quote	Ctrl+`,`
'	Single Closing Quote	Ctrl+','
"	Double Opening Quote	Ctrl+`,"

AutoCorrect... Shortcut Key...

Insert Cancel

Now we come to Page Layout.

Page Layout Panel

It has the following options: Themes, Page Setup, Page Background, Paragraph, and Arrange.

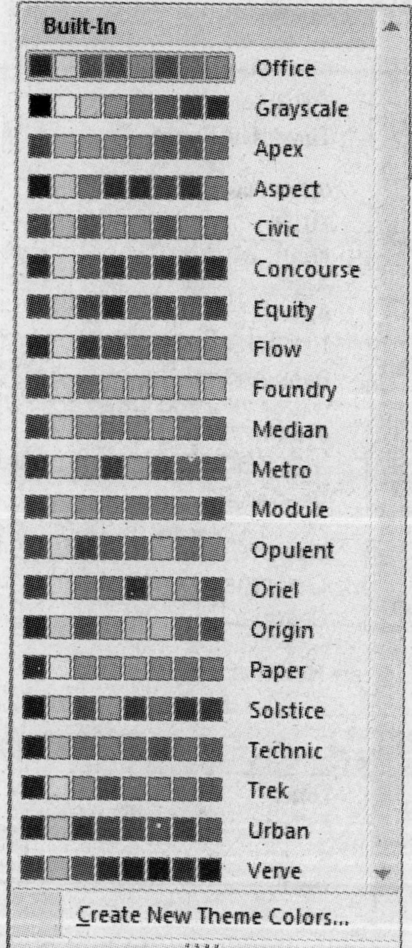

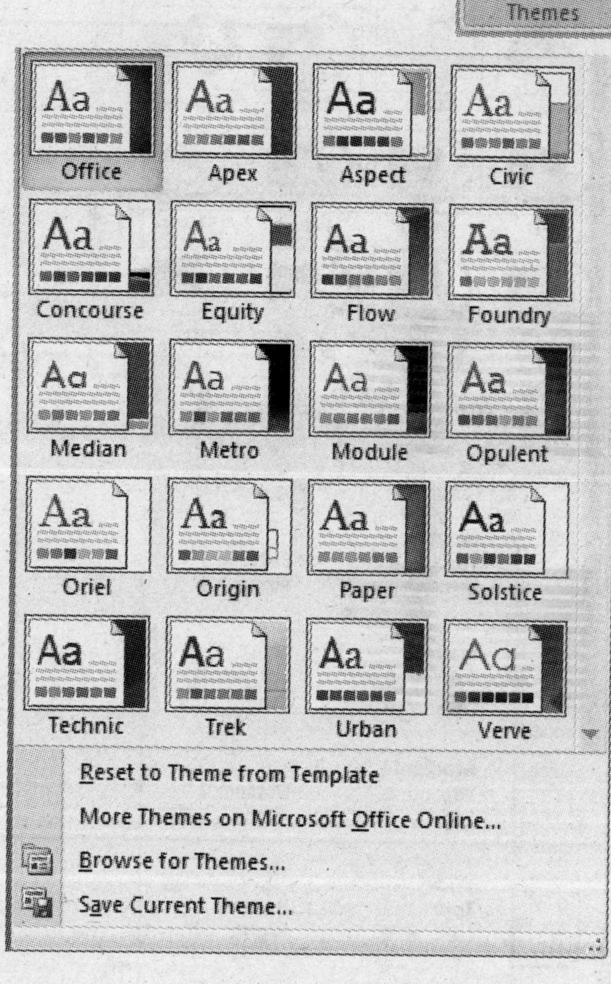

Themes

Among the various option which you can choose here are: Colours, Fonts and Themes. Each one of them have their own set of options, as shown here.

Page Setup

Among the various options available here are: Margins, Orientation, Size, Columns, Breaks, Line Numbers and Hyphenation.

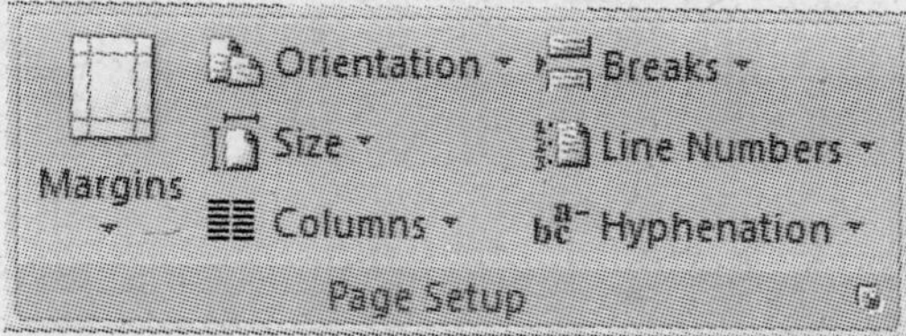

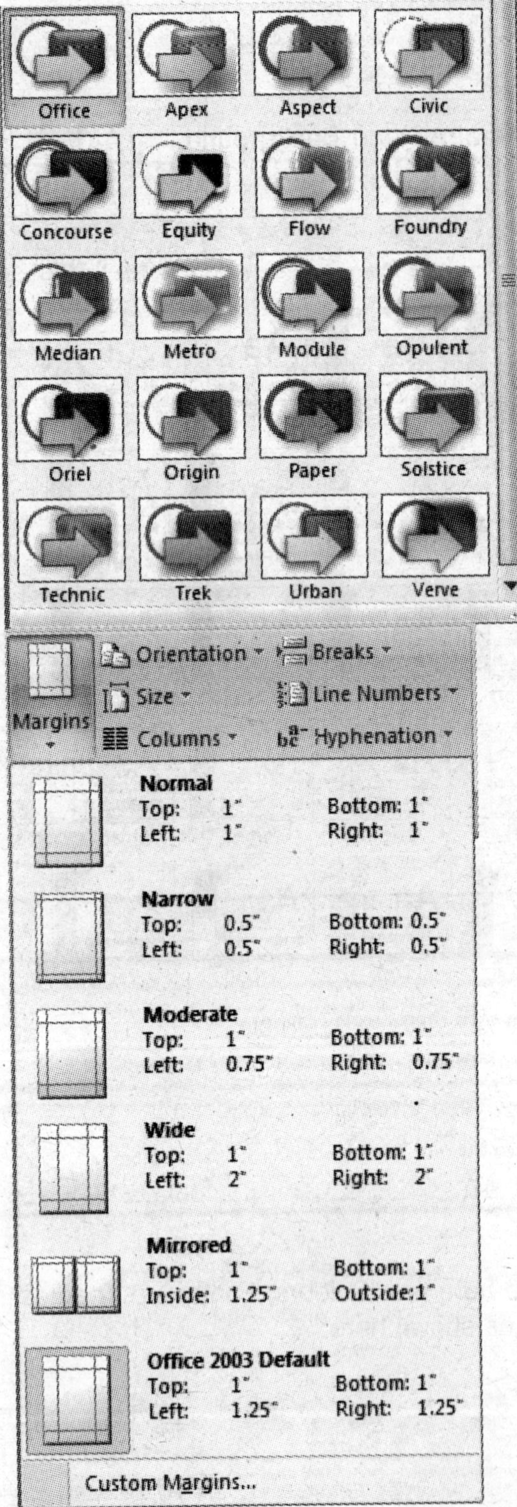

Office
Apex
Aspect
Civic
Concourse
Equity
Flow
Foundry
Median
Metro
Module
Opulent
Oriel
Origin
Paper
Solstice
Technic
Trek
Urban
Verve
Margins
Orientation
Breaks
Size
Line Numbers
Columns
Hyphenation
Normal
Top: 1" Bottom: 1"
Left: 1" Right: 1"
Narrow
Top: 0.5" Bottom: 0.5"
Left: 0.5" Right: 0.5"
Moderate
Top: 1" Bottom: 1"
Left: 0.75" Right: 0.75"
Wide
Top: 1" Bottom: 1"
Left: 2" Right: 2"
Mirrored
Top: 1" Bottom: 1"
Inside: 1.25" Outside:1"
Office 2003 Default
Top: 1" Bottom: 1"
Left: 1.25" Right: 1.25"
Custom Margins...

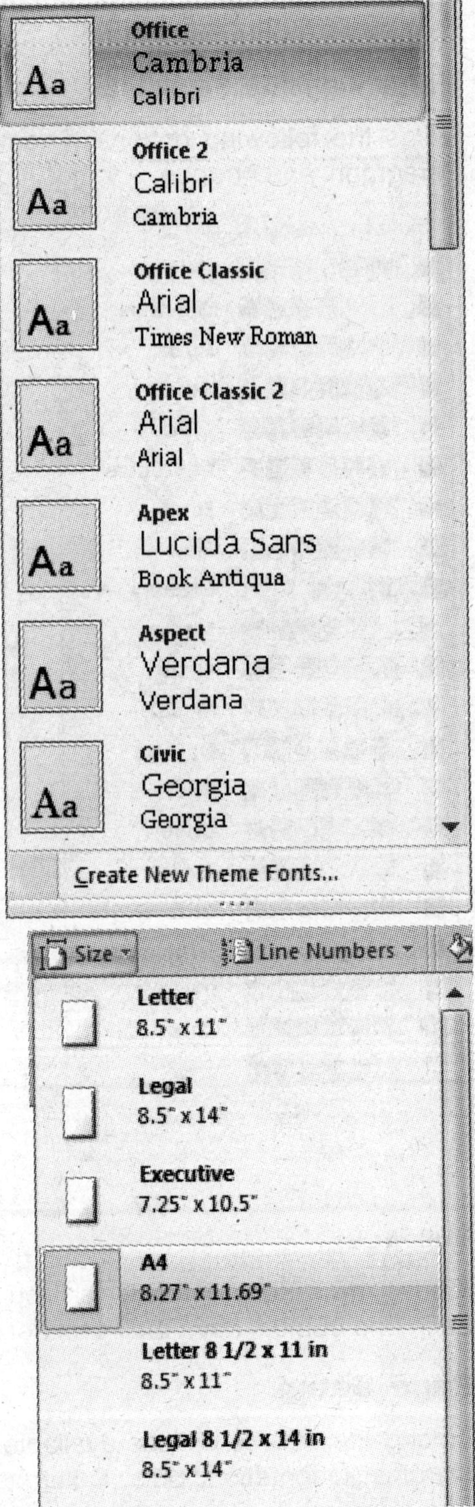

Office
Cambria
Calibri
Office 2
Calibri
Cambria
Office Classic
Arial
Times New Roman
Office Classic 2
Arial
Arial
Apex
Lucida Sans
Book Antiqua
Aspect
Verdana
Verdana
Civic
Georgia
Georgia
Create New Theme Fonts...
Size
Line Numbers
Letter
8.5" x 11"
Legal
8.5" x 14"
Executive
7.25" x 10.5"
A4
8.27" x 11.69"
Letter 8 1/2 x 11 in
8.5" x 11"
Legal 8 1/2 x 14 in
8.5" x 14"

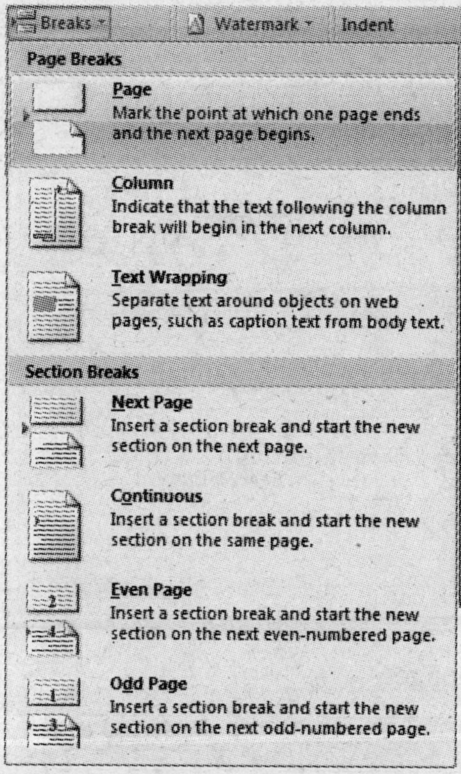

Breaks
Watermark
Indent
Page Breaks
Page
Mark the point at which one page ends and the next page begins.
Column
Indicate that the text following the column break will begin in the next column.
Text Wrapping
Separate text around objects on web pages, such as caption text from body text.
Section Breaks
Next Page
Insert a section break and start the new section on the next page.
Continuous
Insert a section break and start the new section on the same page.
Even Page
Insert a section break and start the new section on the next even-numbered page.
Odd Page
Insert a section break and start the new section on the next odd-numbered page.

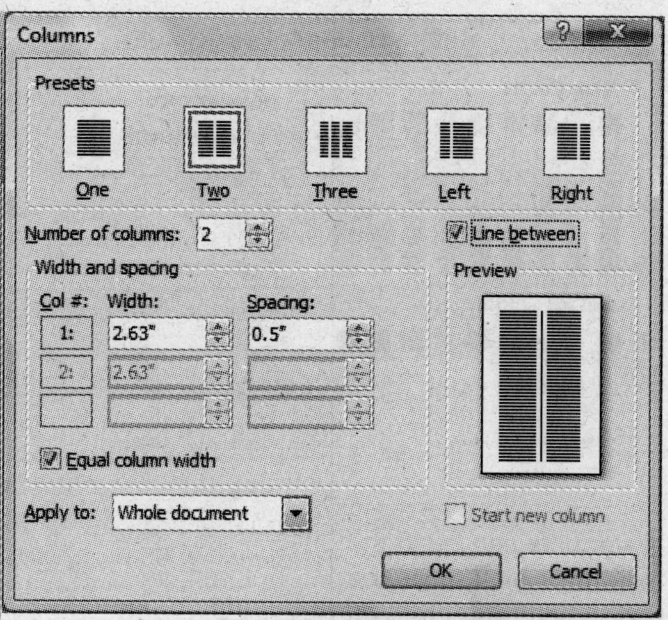

Columns
Presets
One
Two
Three
Left
Right
Number of columns: 2
Line between
Width and spacing
Preview
Col #: Width: Spacing:
1: 2.63" 0.5"
2: 2.63"
Equal column width
Apply to: Whole document
Start new column
OK
Cancel

Margins allows you to set margins of the page, i.e., margins from the left and right of the page.

Orientation has two options: Portrait and Landscape.

Size allows you to choose from the various size of the paper normally used globally.

Columns allow you to set the page into various columns with line in-between or not.

Line Numbers
Add line numbering
Start at: 1
From text: Auto
Count by: 1
Numbering:
Restart each page
Restart each section
Continuous
OK
Cancel

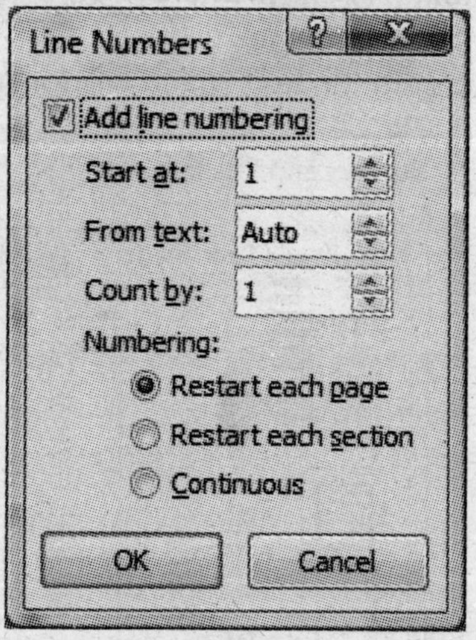

Breaks inserts break into the text in the form of line, page, etc.

Line Numbers are inserted using this option. Various options of the dialog box are shown here.

Watermark
Page Color
Page Borders
Page Background

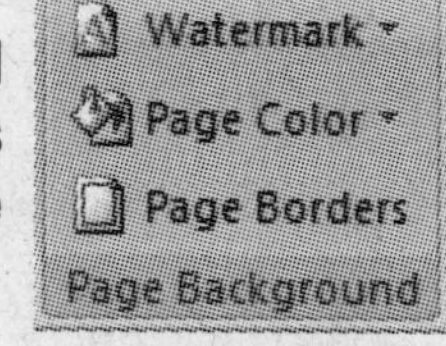

Hyphenation allows to have hyphens in the paragraph or not.

Hyphenation
Automatically hyphenate document
Hyphenate words in CAPS
Hyphenation zone: 0.25"
Limit consecutive hyphens to: No limit
Manual...
OK
Cancel

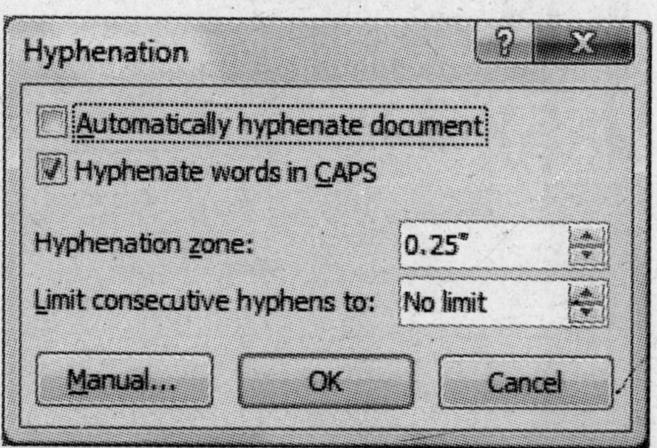

Page Background

As shown here, it has three options in the form of Watermark, Page Color, Page Borders.

Page Color
Left:
Theme Colors
Standard Colors
No Color
More Colors...
Fill Effects...

Printed Watermark
No watermark
Picture watermark
Select Picture...
Scale:
Auto
Washout
Text watermark
Language:
English (United States)
Text:
ASAP
Font:
Times New Roman
Size:
Auto
Color:
Automatic
Semitransparent
Layout:
Diagonal
Horizontal
Apply
OK
Cancel

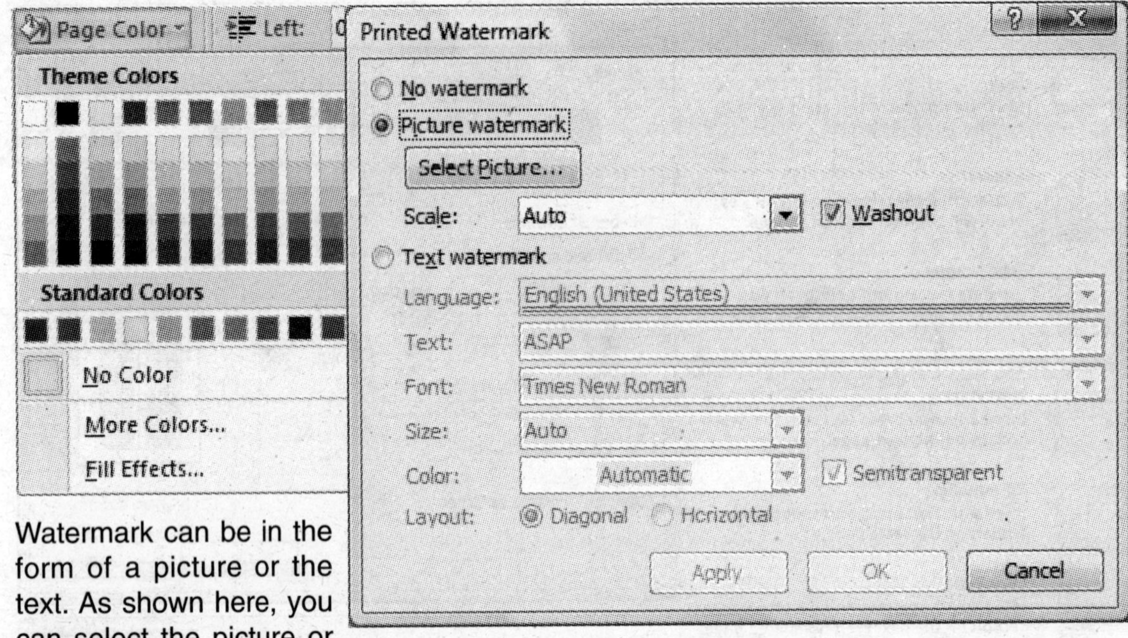

Watermark can be in the form of a picture or the text. As shown here, you can select the picture or create the text which will form the background of the page.

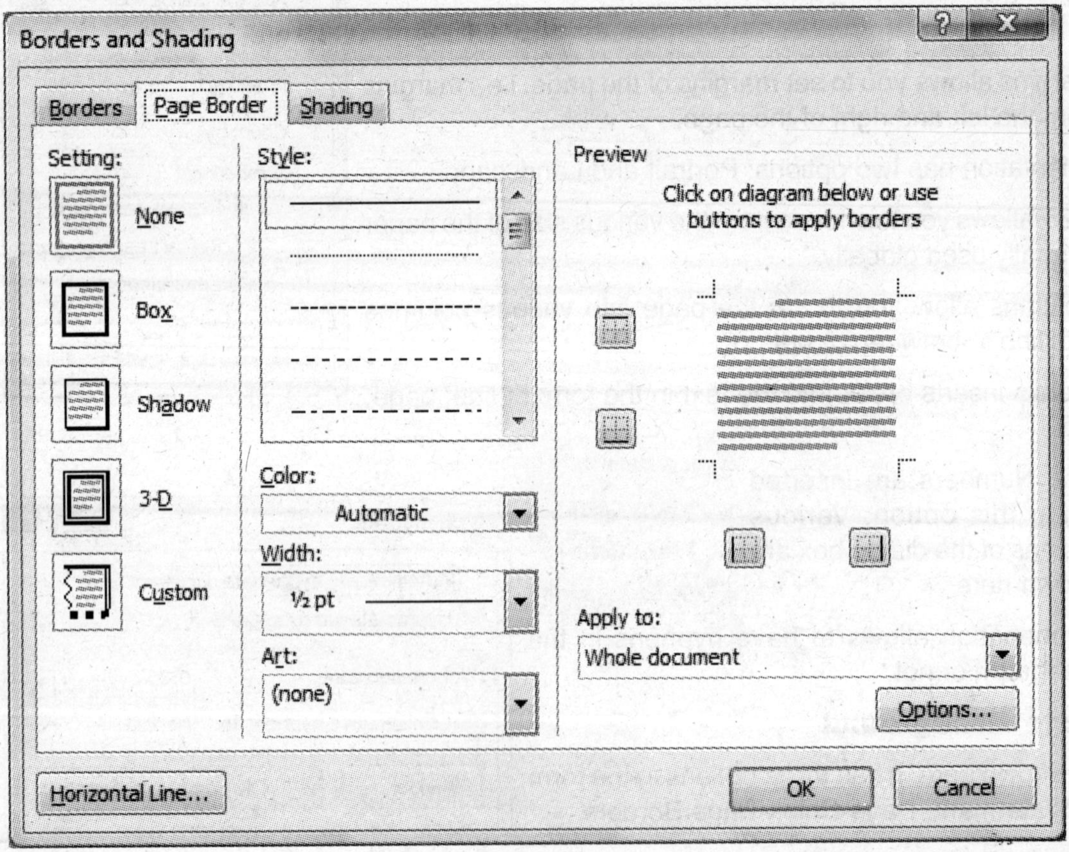

Borders and Shading
Borders
Page Border
Shading
Setting:
None
Box
Shadow
3-D
Custom
Style:
Color:
Automatic
Width:
½ pt
Art:
(none)
Preview
Click on diagram below or use buttons to apply borders
Apply to:
Whole document
Options...
Horizontal Line...
OK
Cancel

Page Color allows you to choose the color of the background.

Page Borders allows you place a border in the background of the page.

Paragraph

It has two main options: Indent and Spacing.

Indent allows you to set the left and right indent.

Spacing allows you to set the Before and After paragraph space.

Arrange

It has the following options: Position, Bring to Front, Send to Back, Text Wrapping, Align, Group and Rotate.

Position allows you to position the picture/object as per the options available.

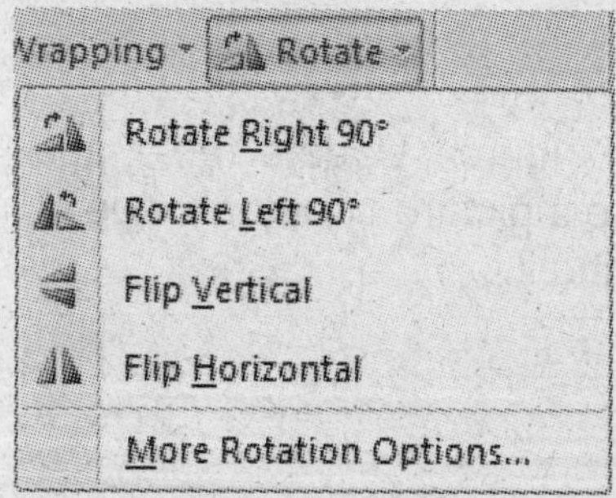

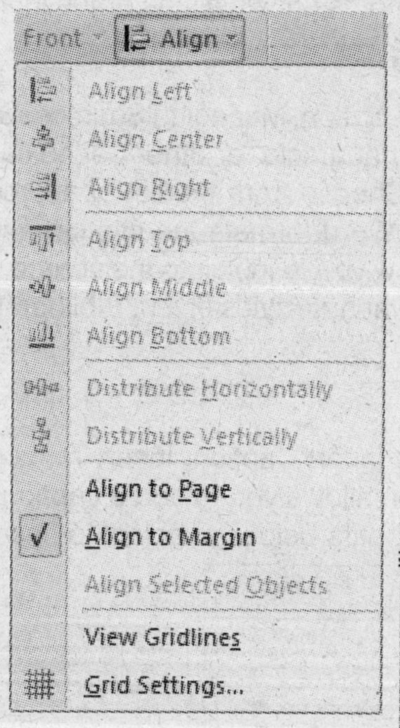

Bring to Front and Send to Back are used when you have to rearrange the picture/object with respect to the text.

Align allows you to align the text, as per the options shown here.

Group allows you to group two or more objects together.

Rotate allows you to rotate the inserted object as per the options shown here.

References Panel

It has the following options: Table of Contents, Footnotes, Citations and Bibliography, Captions, Index, and Table of Authorities.

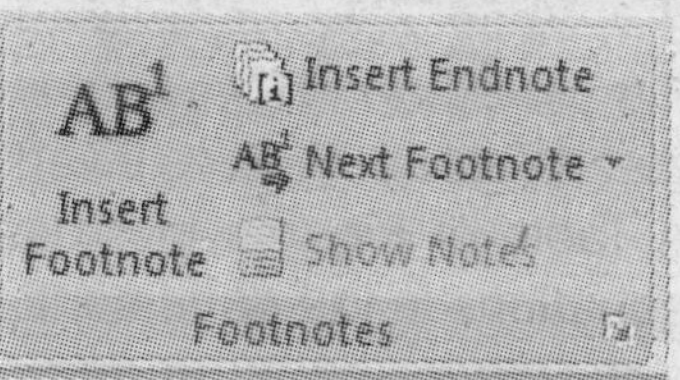

Table of Contents

It has the options: Table of Contents, Add Test and Update Table. Table of Contents allows you create table of contents of the text. Add Text allows you to set levels of the text. Update Table updates an existing table of contents.

Footnotes

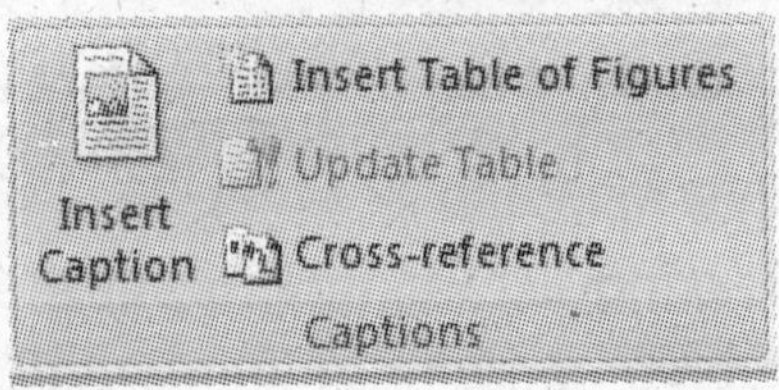

It has the options: Insert Footnote, Insert Endnote, Next Footnote, and Show Notes. Insert Footnote allows you to insert a footnote in the text. Insert Endnote allows you to insert endnote. Next footnote allows to insert the next or prev footnote, endnote. Show notes shows all the notes in the text.

Citations & Bibliography

It has the options of Inserting a Citation, Managing Sources, Style, and Bibliography. Citation allows you to cite a book, journal article, or other periodical as the source for a piece of information in the document. Choose from the list of sources you have created or enter information for a new source. Word formats the citation according to the style you have selected. Manage Sources allow you to look into the source manager and manage it. Style allows you to choose from the various styles given. Bibliography allows you to maintain the various references.

Captions

This has the following options: Insert Caption, Insert Table of Figures, Update Table, and Cross-reference. Insert Caption allows you to add a caption to a picture or other image. A caption is a line of text that appears below an object to describe it.

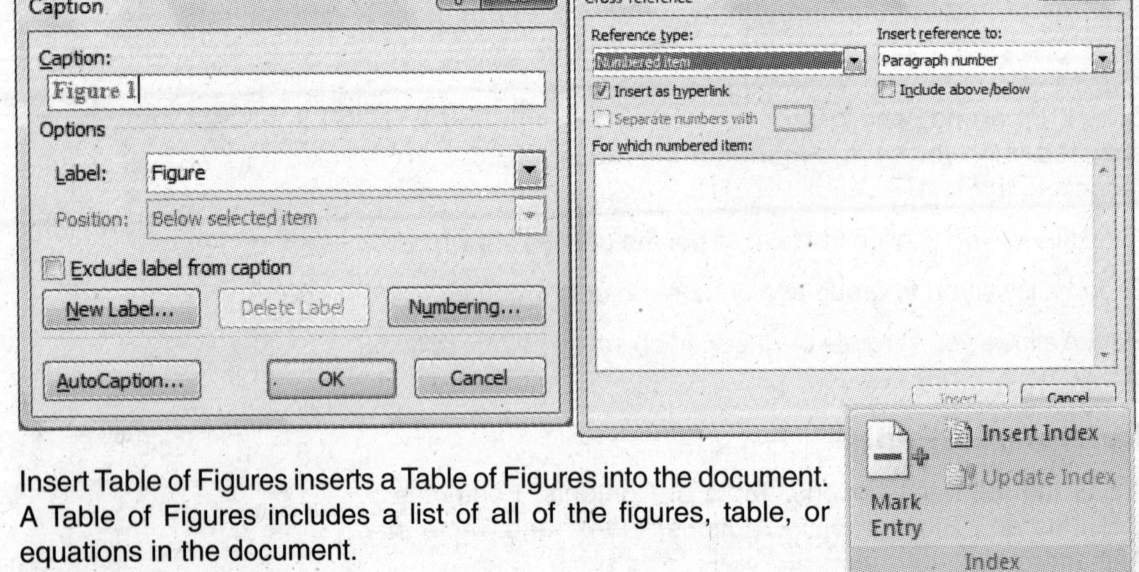

Insert Table of Figures inserts a Table of Figures into the document. A Table of Figures includes a list of all of the figures, table, or equations in the document.

Cross-reference refers to items such as headings, figures, and tables by inserting a cross reference such as, "See Table 6 below" or "Turn to page 8." Cross references are automatically updated if the content is moved to another location. By default, cross references are inserted as hyperlinks.

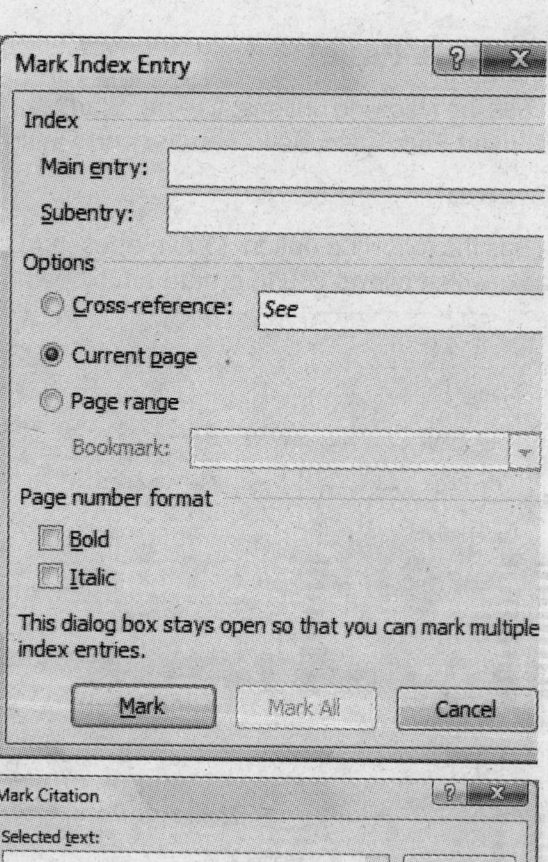

Index

It has the following commands: Mark Entry, Insert Index, and Update Index.

Mark Entry allows you to include the selected text in the index of the document.

Insert Index inserts an index into the document. An index is a list of keywords found in the document along with the page numbers the words appear on.

Table of Authorities

It has the option called Mark Citation, Insert Table of Authorities, and Update Table of Authorities. Mark Citation adds the selected text as an entry in the Table of Authorities.

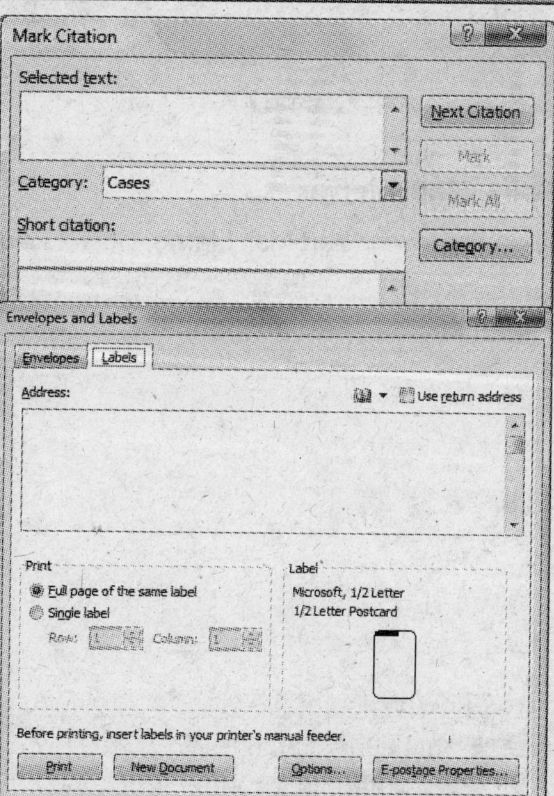

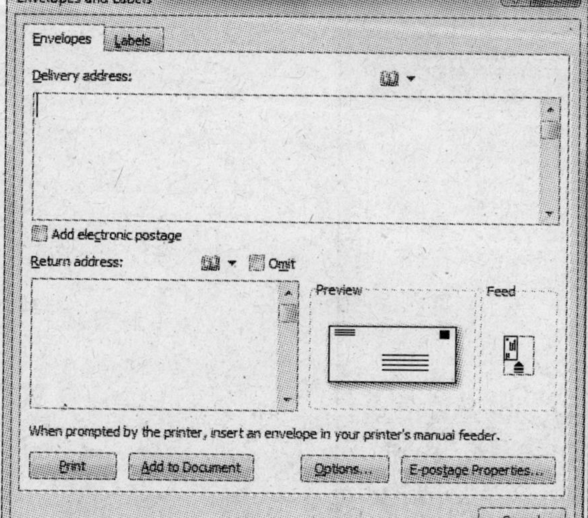

Mailings Panel

It has the following options: Create, Start Mail Merge, Write & Insert Fields, Preview Results, and Finish.

Create

It has the following options: Envelopes, and Labels. Each one of them gives rise to a dialog box, which allows you to create envelopes and labels.

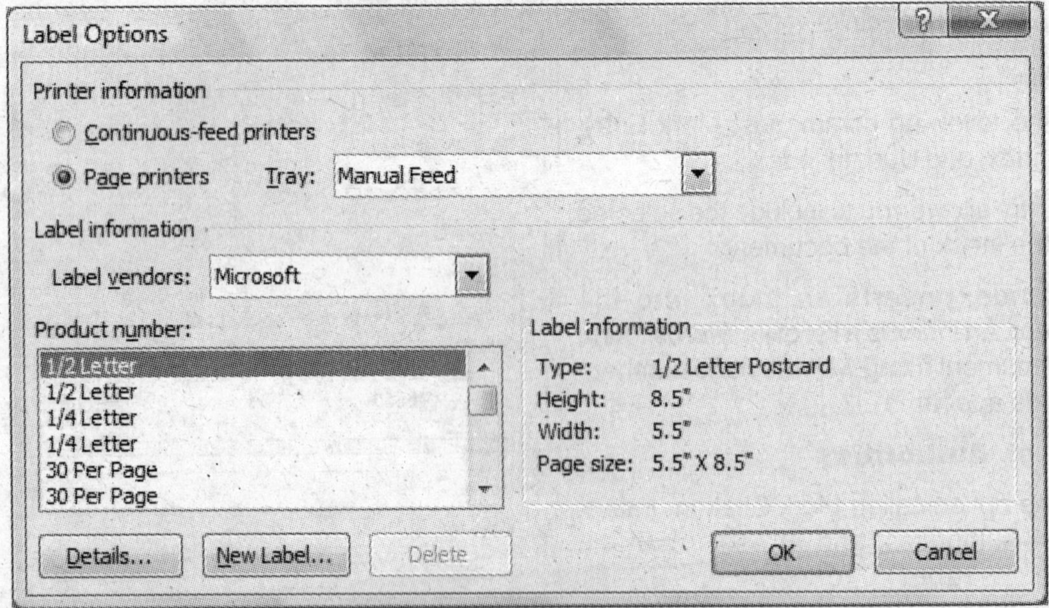

Start Mail Merge

It has options to Start Mail Merge, Select Recipients and Edit Recipients List.

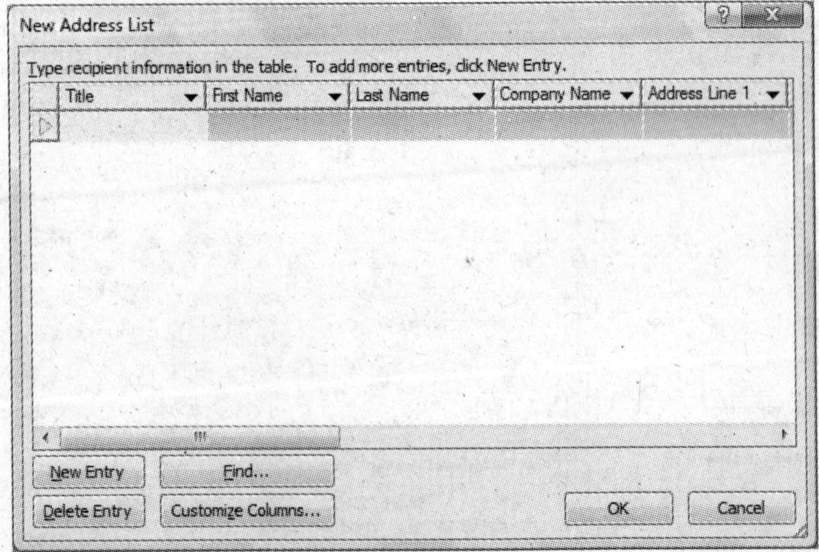

Start Mail Merge allows you to select the options of Letters, E-Mail Messages, Evelopes, Labels, Directory or start the Step by Step Mail Merge Wizard.

Select Recipients allows you to choose the list of people you intend to send the letter to. You can type you own list, use your Outlook contacts, or connect to a database. It also has options to Type New List, Use Existing List or Select from Outlook Contacts.

Write & Insert Fields

It has the options to Highlight Merge Fields, Address Block, Greeting Line, Insert Merge Field, Rules, Match Fields, and Update Labels.

Highlight Merge Fields highlights the fields you have inserted into the document. This makes it easy to see what part of your form letter will be replaced by information from the recipient list you have chosen.

Addresss Block adds an address to your letter. You specify the formatting and location, and Word will replace it with actual addresses from your recipient list when you finish the mail merge.

Greeting Line adds a greeting line such as "Dear<<First Name>>", to your document.

Insert Merge Field adds any field from your recipient list to the document, such as "Last Name," "Home Phone," "Company Name," or any other field.

When you finish the mail merge, Word will replace these fields with the actual information from the recipient list.

Rules specifies rules to be added decision-making ability to the mail merge. For instance, you could use If...Then...Else to check the address of recipient and show a local phone number to recipients near you and an international phone number for recipients outside of your country.

Match Fields allows you to tell Word the meaning of different fields in your recipient list. For example, you can indicate that your custom field "Home" is equivalent to normal built-in field "Home Phone."

Update Labels allow you to create labels, update all the labels in the document to use information from the recipient list. For a mail merge to a printed letter or e-mail, this command is not necessary.

Preview Results

It has the options to Preview Results, Find Recipient, and Auto Check for Errors.

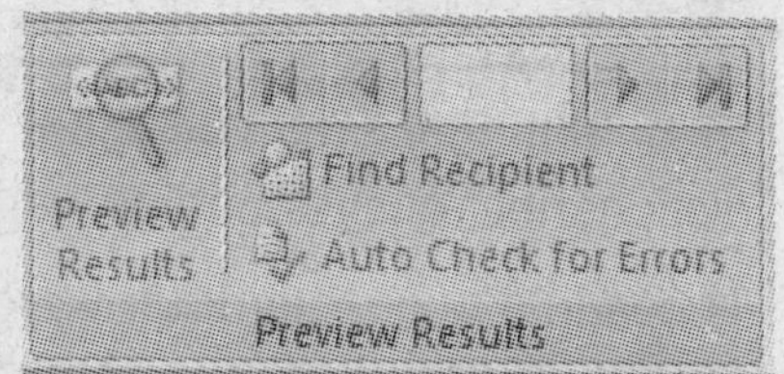

Preview Results replaces the merge fields in your document with acutal data from your recipient list so you can see what it looks like.

Find Recipient finds and previews a specific record in the recipient list by searching for text.

Auto Check for Errors specifies how to handle errors that occur when completing the mail merge. You also have the option of simulating the mail merge to see if any errors would occur.

Finish

It has the options to Finish & Merge. It completes the mail merge. You can create separate documents for each copy of the letter, send them all directly to the printer, or send them via e-mail.

Review Panel

It has the following options: Proofing, Comments, Tracking, Changes, Compare, and Protect.

Proofing

It has the following options: Spelling & Grammer, Research, Thesaurus, Translate, Translation ScreenTip, Set Language, Word Count.

Spelling & Grammar checks the spelling and grammar of text in the document.

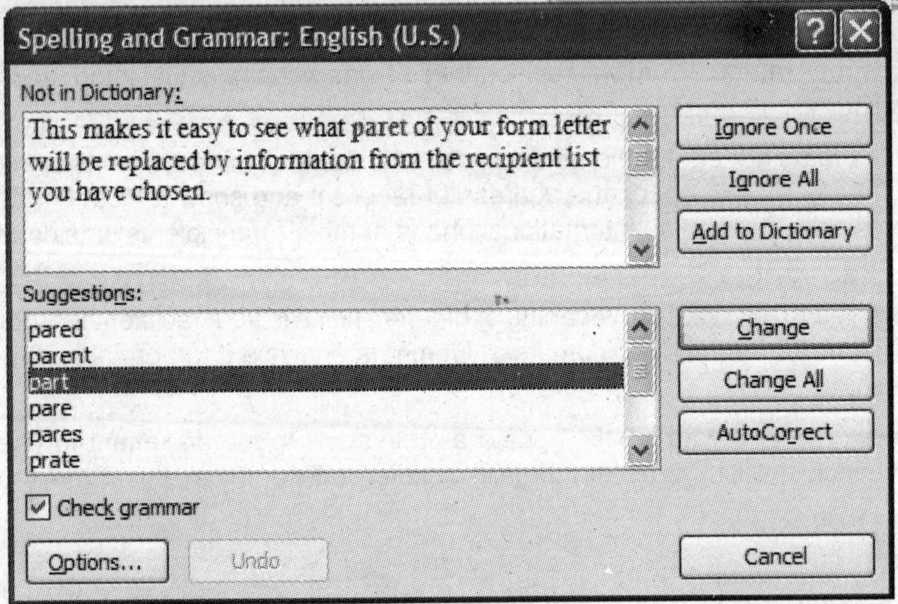

Research opens the Research Task Pane to search through reference materials, such as dictionaries, encyclopedias, and translation services.

Thesaurus suggests other words with a similar meaning to the word you have selected.

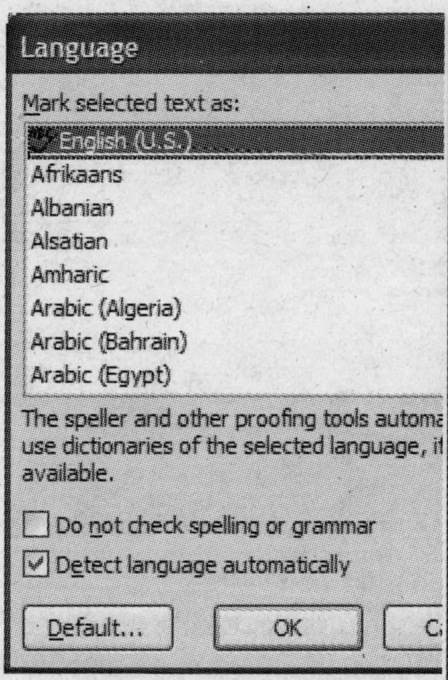

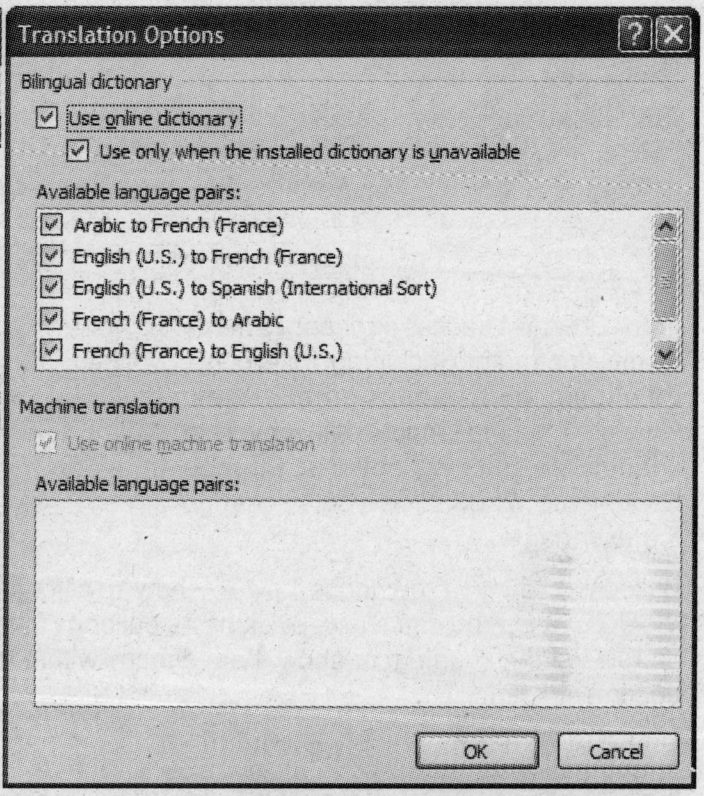

Translates the selected text into a different language.

Translation ScreenTip enables a ScreenTip that translates words you pause your cursor over into another language.

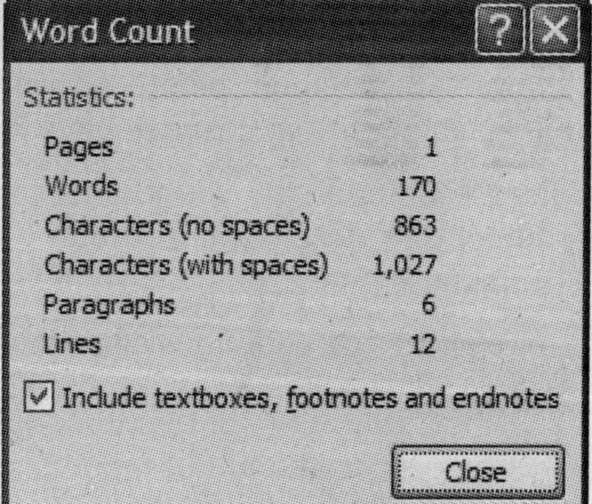

Set Language sets the language used to check the spelling and grammar of the selected text.

Word Count finds out the number of words, characters, paragraphs, and lines in the document. You can also find the word count in the status bar at the bottom of the window.

Comments

This has the following options: New Comment, Delete, Previous, and Next.

New Commnet adds a selection over the selection.

Delete command deletes an existing comment.

Previous locates the previous comment.

Tracking

This has the following options: Track Changes, Balloons, Final Showing Markup, Show Markup, and Reviewing Pane.

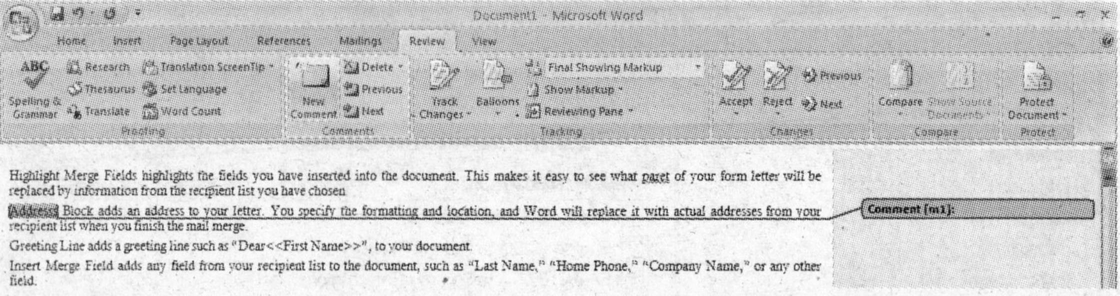

Track Changes trackes all changes made to the document, including insertions, deletions, and formatting changes. Change Tracking Options allows you to change the tracking options. Change User Name would allow you to change the user name.

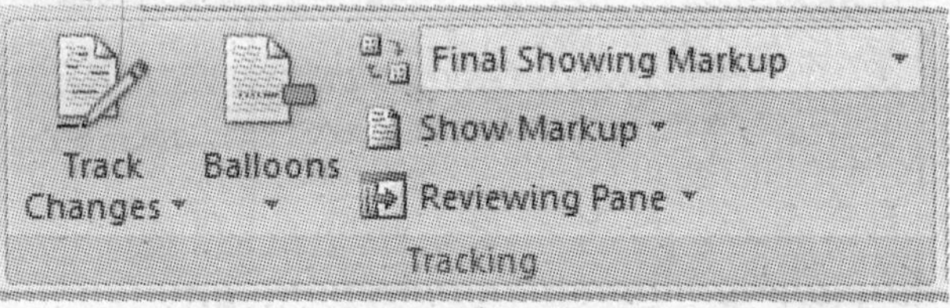

Track Changes
Change Tracking Options...
Change User Name...

Balloons allow you to choose how to show revisions to the document. You can show revisions as balloons in the margins of the coument or show them directly within the document itself.

Show Revisions in Balloons
Show All Revisions Inline
✓ Show Only Comments and Formatting in Balloons

Display for Review allows you to choose how to view the proposed changes to the document. Final shows the document with all proposed changes included; Original shows the document before any changes were made. The markup shows what changes have been proposed.

Final Showing Markup
Final
Original Showing Markup
Original

Show Markup allows you to choose what kind of markup to show in the document. You can hide or show comments, insertions and deletions, formatting changes, and other kinds of markup.

Reviewing Pane shows revisions in a separate window.

Changes

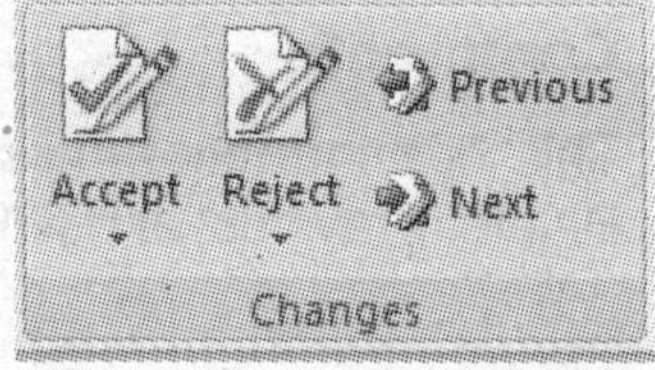

This has the following options: Accept, Reject, Previous, and Next.

Accept and Move to Next allows you to access other options such as accepting all changes in the document.

Reject and Move to Next allows you to access other options such as rejecting all changes in the document.

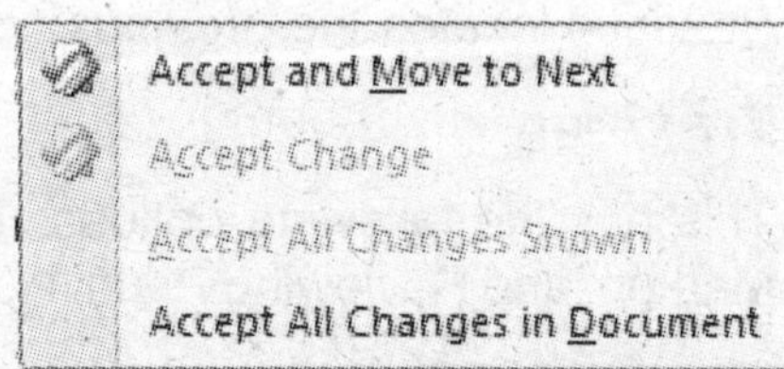

Previous Change allows you to navigate to the previous revision in the document so that you can accept or reject it.

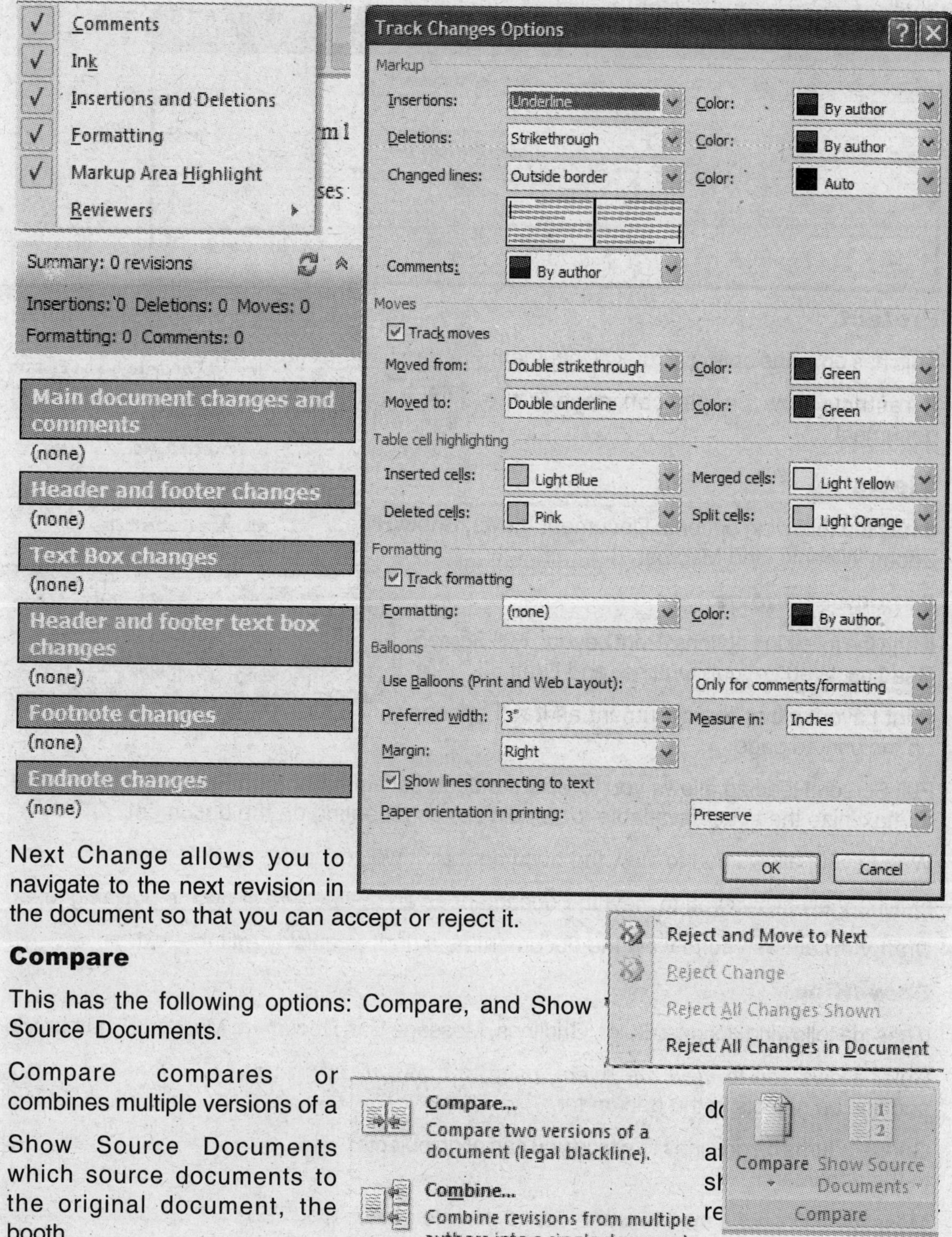

Next Change allows you to navigate to the next revision in the document so that you can accept or reject it.

Compare

This has the following options: Compare, and Show Source Documents.

Compare compares or combines multiple versions of a dc

Show Source Documents al which source documents to sh the original document, the re booth.

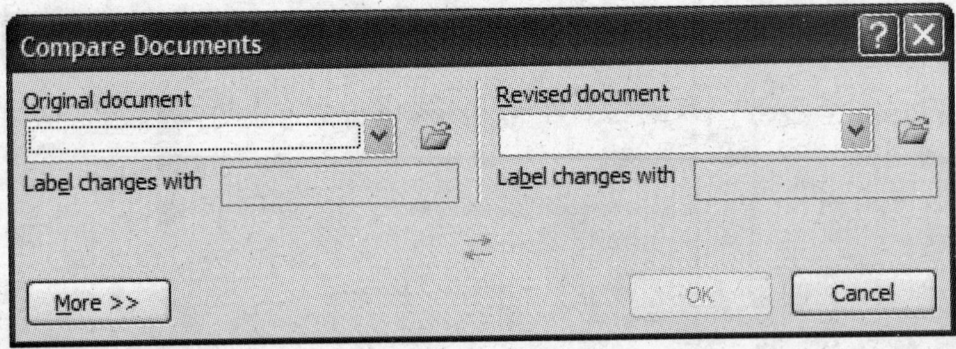

Protect

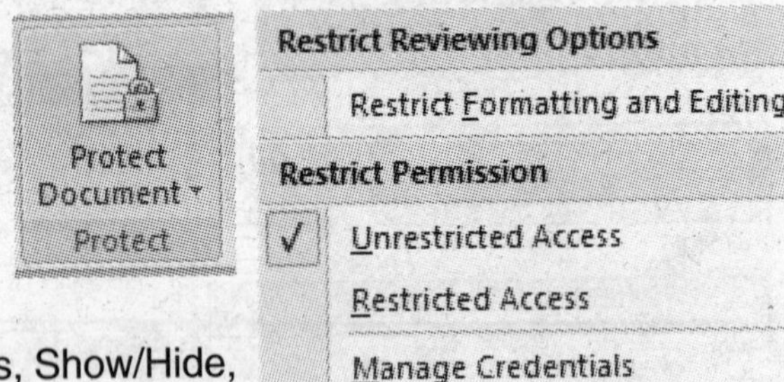

This has only one option: Protect Document.

It restricts how people can access the document.

Views

It has the following options: Document Views, Show/Hide, Zoom, Window, and Macros.

Document Views

It has the following options: Print Layout, Full Screen Reading, Web Layout, Outline, and Draft.

Print Layout views the document as it will appear on the printed page.

Full Screen Reading allows you to view the document in full screen Reading View in order to maximize the space available for reading or commenting on the document.

Web Layout allows you to view the document as it would look as a Web page.

Outline View allows you to view the document as an outline and show the outlining tools.

Draft View allows you to view the document as a draft to quickly edit the text.

Show/Hide

It has the following options: Ruler, Gridlines, Message Bar, Document Map, and Thumbnails.

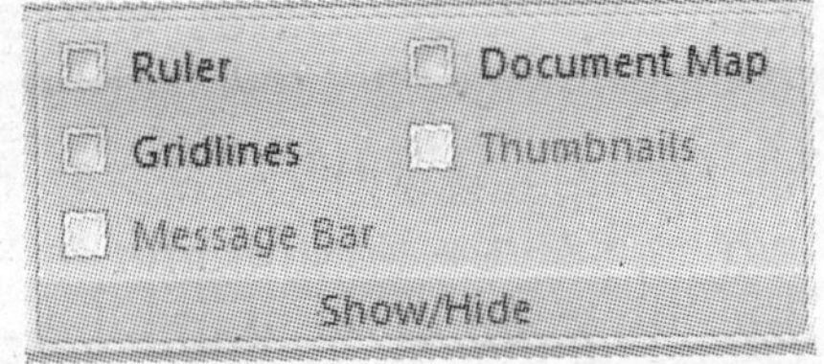

Ruler allows you to view the rulers, used to measure and line up objects in the document.

Gridlines turns on gridlines to which you can align objects in the document.

Message Bar opens the Message Bar to complete any required actions on the document.

Document Map opens the Document Map, which allows you to navigate through a structural view of the document.

Thumbnails opens the Thumbnails pane, which you can use to navigate a long document through small pictures of each page.

Zoom

It has the following options: Zoom, 100%, One Page, Two Pages, and Page Width.

Zoom opens the Zoom dialog box to specify the zoom level of the document. In most cases, you can alos use the zoom controls in the status bar at the bottom of the window to quickly zoom the document.

100% zooms the document to 100% of the normal size.

One Page zooms the document so that an entire page fits in the window.

Two Pages zooms the document so that two pages fit in the window.

Page Width zooms the document so that the width of the page matches the width of the window.

Window

It has the following options: New Window, Arrange All, Split, View Side by Side, Synchronous Scrolling, Reset Window Position, and Switch Windows.

New Window allows you to open a new window containing a view of the current document.

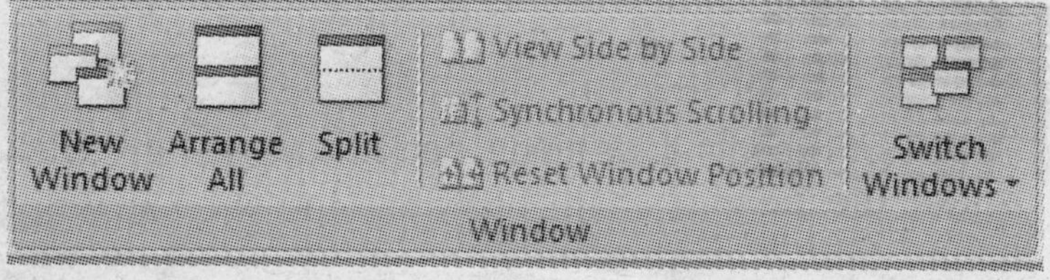

Arrange All tiles all open program windows side-by-side on the screen.

Split Window splits the current window into two parts so that you can view different sections of the document at the same time.

View Side by Side allows you to view two documents side-by-side so that you can compare their contents. Synchronous Scrolling synchronizes the scrolling of two documents so that they scroll together. To enable this feature, turn View Side by Side.

Reset Window Position resets the window position of the documents being compared side-by-side so that they share the screen equally. To enable this feature, turn on View Side by Side.

Switch Windows allows you to switch to a different currently open window.

Macros

It has only one option, i.e., Macros.

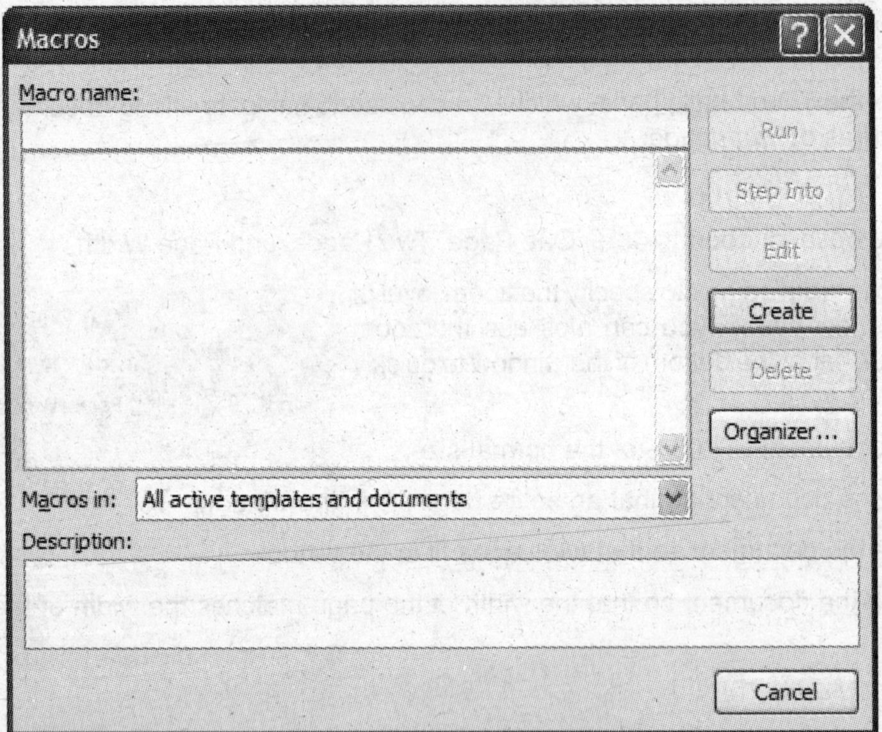

Macros command allows you to view macros. Click here to record a macro or to access other macro options.

Office Button

Besides, the commands mentioned till now, we have a set of commands, under the so called Office Button. These are the commands which were there in File menu of the earlier version. Well, most of them. I will not go through them since they have been there since the earliest version of Word.

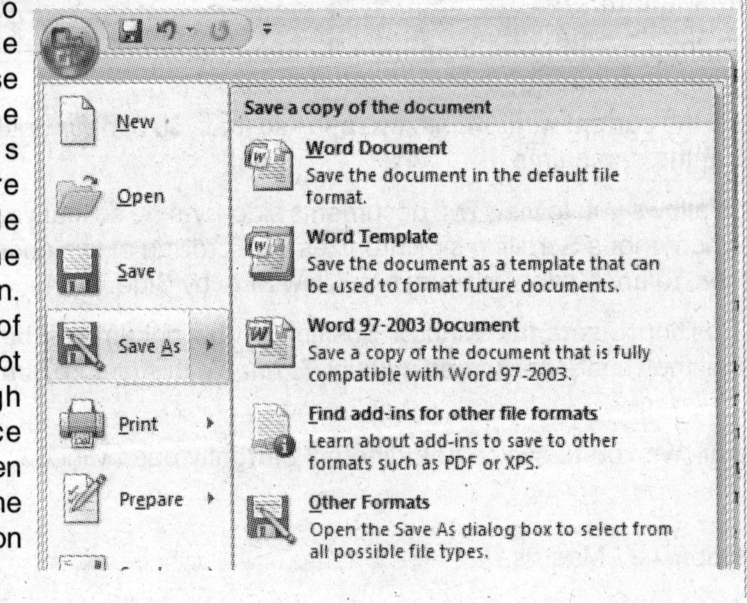

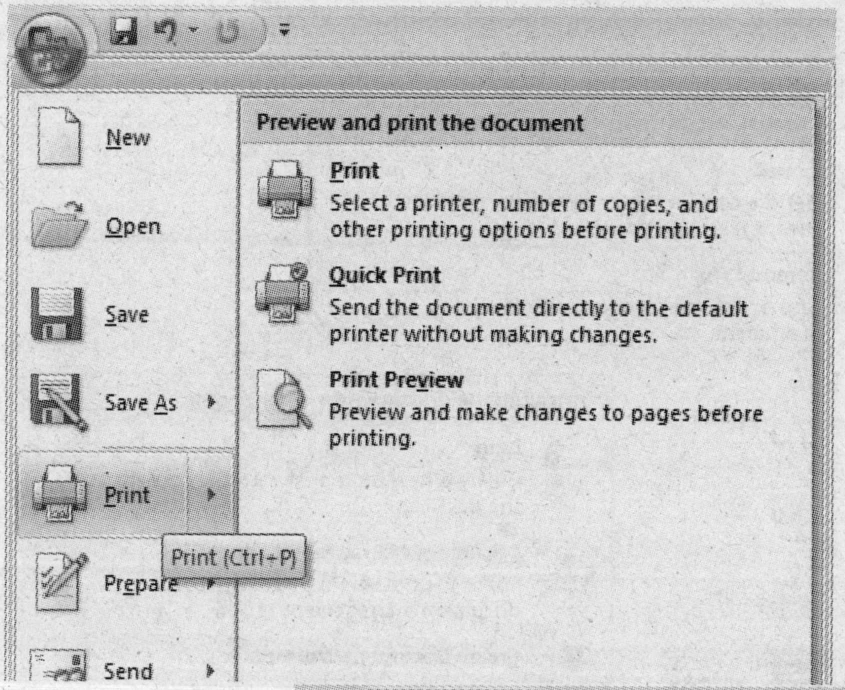
New
Open
Save
Save As
Print
Prepare
Send
Print (Ctrl+P)
Preview and print the document
Print
Select a printer, number of copies, and other printing options before printing.
Quick Print
Send the document directly to the default printer without making changes.
Print Preview
Preview and make changes to pages before printing.

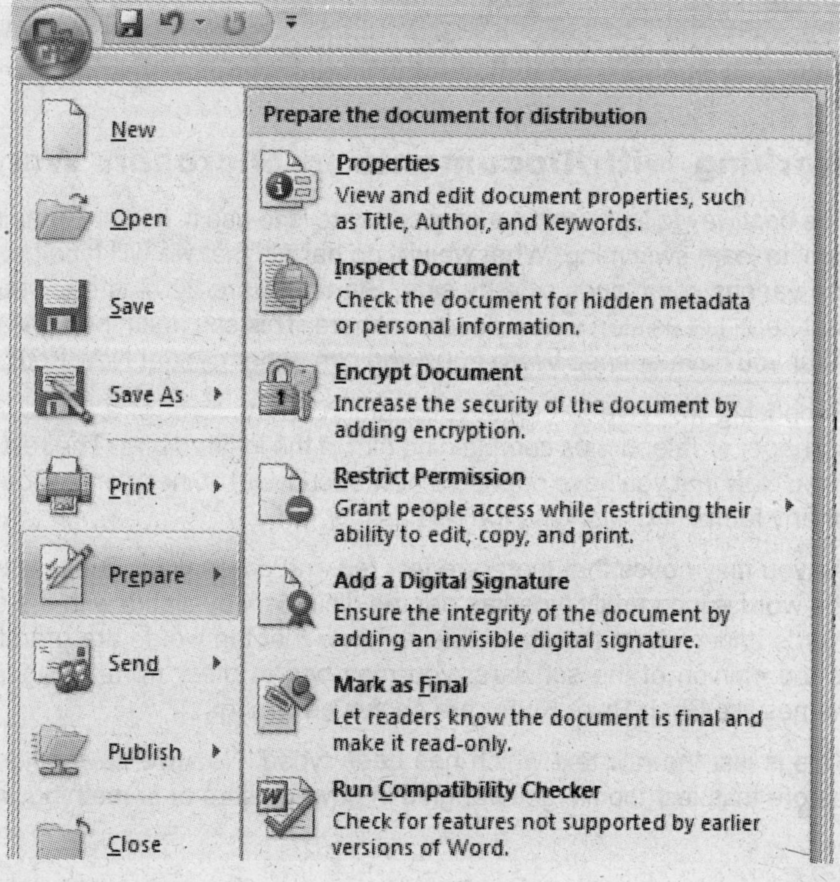
New
Open
Save
Save As
Print
Prepare
Send
Publish
Close
Prepare the document for distribution
Properties
View and edit document properties, such as Title, Author, and Keywords.
Inspect Document
Check the document for hidden metadata or personal information.
Encrypt Document
Increase the security of the document by adding encryption.
Restrict Permission
Grant people access while restricting their ability to edit, copy, and print.
Add a Digital Signature
Ensure the integrity of the document by adding an invisible digital signature.
Mark as Final
Let readers know the document is final and make it read-only.
Run Compatibility Checker
Check for features not supported by earlier versions of Word.

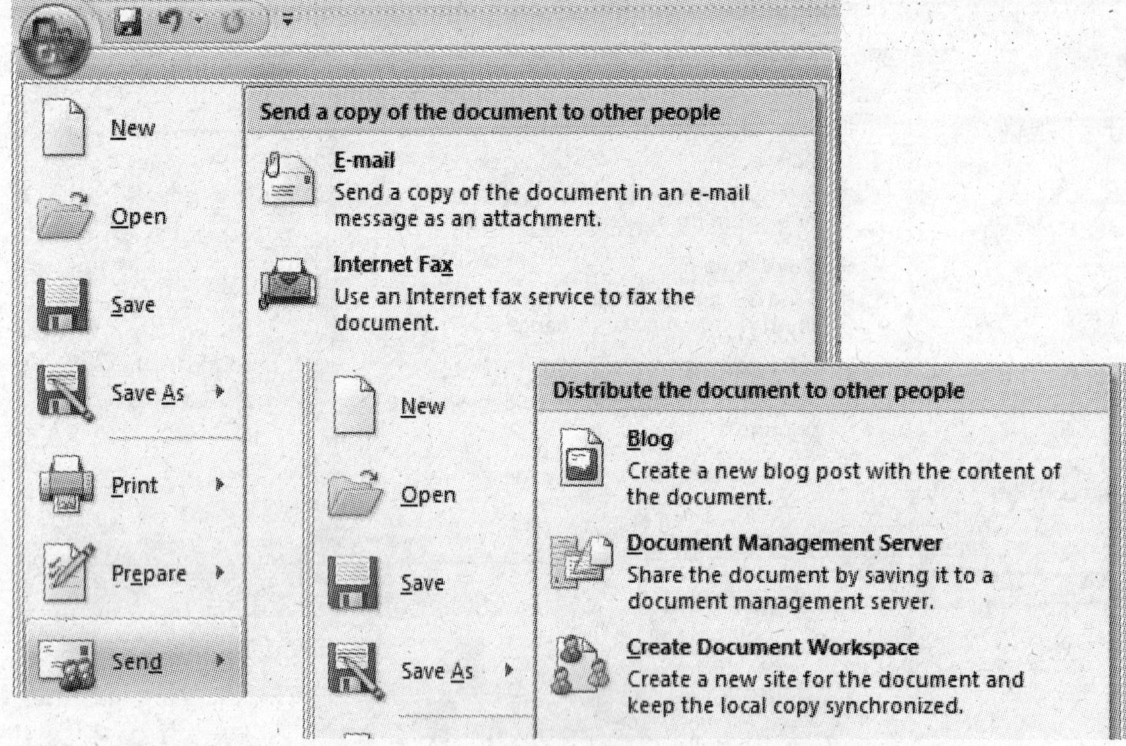

Working with Documents in Microsoft Word 2007

The best way to learn about a new software is to use it. It is like jumping into the swimming pool to learn swimming. What we will do here is that we will type our document and learn the various commands side by side. Starting Word 2007 is easy so I am not discussing that here. Let us start a new document here. This can again be done from the Start button. After you have opened Word 2007 you can either click at New from the Office button.

Supposing we have to create a document in the form of a letter written to the General Manager of Telephones complaining him of the inflated bills. The text of the letter is shown next. Now that you have opened a new document, do not worry about any typing mistakes or any formatting, just type the text as it is.

As you may notice that there are few red and green wavy lines. The red lines, show that the word is incorrectly typed as per the dictionary available with the system and the word/ words under whom the green line is, show that the words are grammatically wrong. This is the opinion of the software, you may beg to differ from it. Since most of the proper names like Shah Rukh Khan, are shown as wrong.

This is just the raw text which has been typed. Now we have to do the formatting. But, before that, lest the file gets tangled in power failure or something, we must save the file.

11th January, 2007

To,

The General Manager

Mahanagar Telephones Nigam Limited

Khurshid Lal Bhawan

New Delhi - 110 001

Ref: Telephone No. 4611098

Sir,

I am in receipt of bill for the above telephone number dated 11.12.2006 for an amount of Rs. 4,678.90. This bill is to be paid by 21.1.2000. While going through the bill, I notice that I have been charged at two accounts for the calls which have not been made by me. These enteries are:

Called Id	***Duration***	***Amount***
0017249873769	120	1,008.00
0013245934234	60	675.90

As you can notice that both these entries pertain to **International calls** and since my phone does not have this facility, these calls could not have been made from my phone.

I hope that you would look into and send me the revised bill, so that I can make the payment in time.

Hoping for an early action,

Thanking you,

Yours faithfully,

Shah Rukh Khan

3695 Ballimaran, Delhi - 110 006

* This letter has few errors, which will be corrected in Word 2007

Saving the file

It is the process by which you give the name to the file and save under that name. Since our letter pertains to the inflated bill, we will call our file as Bill. For saving, just select the Save option under Office button. You will get the following dialog box. Just type the name Bill in the space provided for typing the filename and click Save. Your file will be saved under this name and automatically the title bar will show the name of the file on the top of the Word 2007 screen.

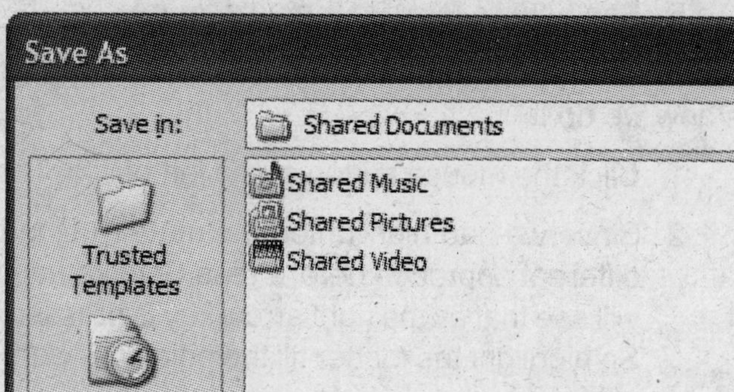

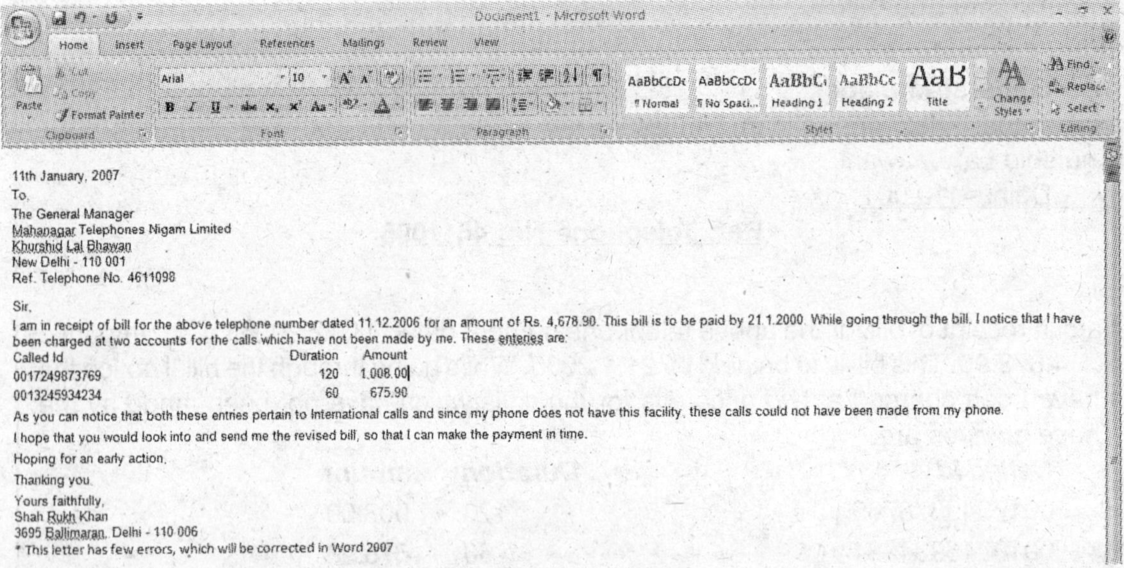

11th January, 2007
To,
The General Manager
Mahanagar Telephones Nigam Limited
Khurshid Lal Bhawan
New Delhi - 110 001
Ref. Telephone No. 4611098

Sir,
I am in receipt of bill for the above telephone number dated 11.12.2006 for an amount of Rs. 4,678.90. This bill is to be paid by 21.1.2000. While going through the bill, I notice that I have been charged at two accounts for the calls which have not been made by me. These enteries are:

Called Id	Duration	Amount
0017249873769	120	1,008.00
0013245934234	60	675.90

As you can notice that both these entries pertain to International calls and since my phone does not have this facility, these calls could not have been made from my phone.

I hope that you would look into and send me the revised bill, so that I can make the payment in time.

Hoping for an early action,

Thanking you.

Yours faithfully,
Shah Rukh Khan
3695 Ballimaran, Delhi - 110 006
* This letter has few errors, which will be corrected in Word 2007

Now we come to other fomatting tools.

Formatting the text

Let us now start our formatting from the top. The first line containing address has nothing to be done.

The second line containing To, has to be *italized*.

For this do the following:

1. Click the mouse button at the left of T of To.
2. Now drag the mouse, still having it pressed to the right so that the next character o also gets highlighted. At this stage both T and o are highlighted.
3. Now leave the mouse with To highlighted.
4. With the mouse, click at I in the formatting toolbar to make To as *To*.
5. See how To looks in the next figure.

Now we come to the line having The General Manager. This line has to be made bold. This is how we do it.

1. Click the mouse button at the left of T of The General Manager.
2. Since we had highlighted the matter using mouse in the case of To, we will use a different approach here. Press Shift key and start pressing right arrow key ⇨. You will see that as the right arrow key is pressed the matter on the right gets highlighted. So highlight the matter till the point you want it to highlight. In this case highlight till r of Manager.

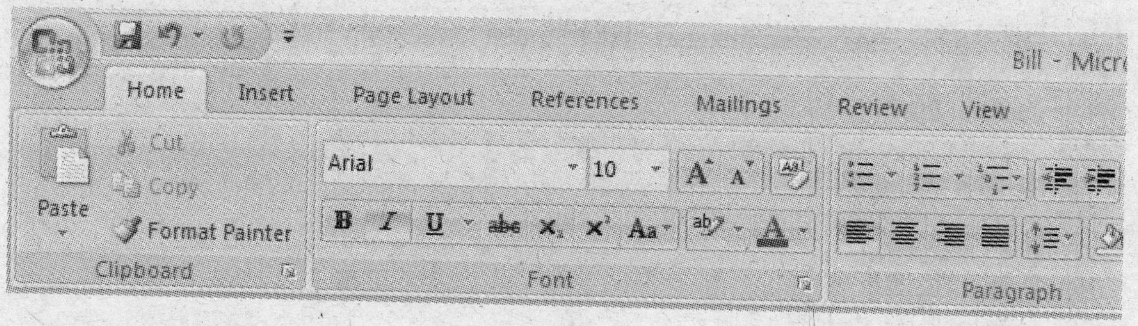

3. Now leave the shift key.
4. With the mouse, click at B in the formatting toolbar to make the highlighted text as **Bold**.
5. In the figure below, see how the text looks now.

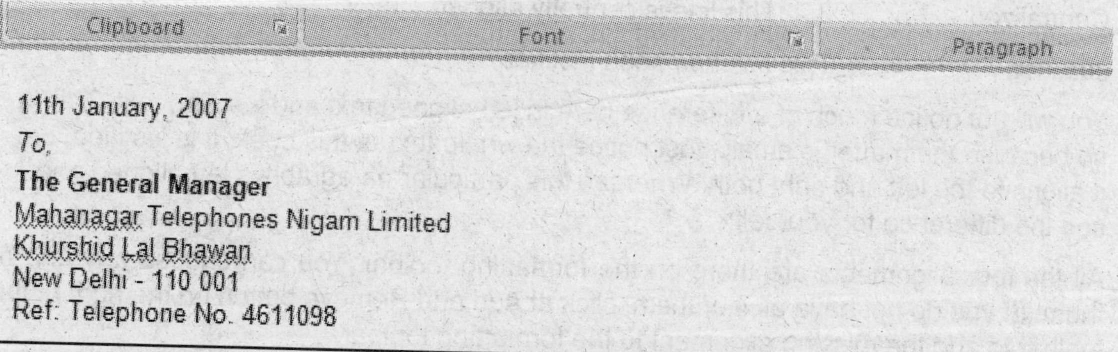

Next in the line is the address, whose last line New Delhi - 110 001 has to be underlined. Word 2007 allows you the option of underlining the word with one or more lines. This option is available under Font. But for the time being, we will stick to single underline.

For this do the following:

1. Click the mouse button at the left of N of New Delhi - 110 001.
2. Using any of the two methods described above, highlight the text to be underlined.
3. With the mouse, click at U in the formatting toolbar to make the highlighted text **Underlined**.
4. You can see the text underlined next.

Coming down now you see the line containing the telephone number. This line has to be underlined and centralized. I am not describing here the method to underline this line since

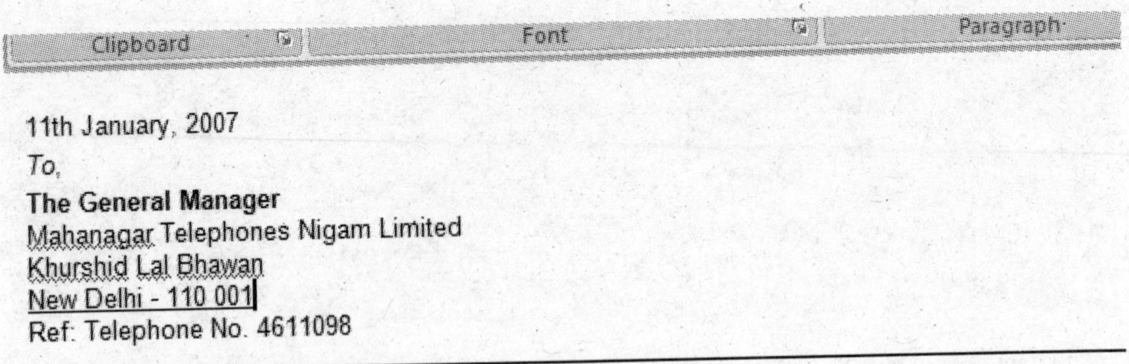

Clipboard | Font | Paragraph

11th January, 2007

To,

The General Manager

Mahanagar Telephones Nigam Limited

Khurshid Lal Bhawan

New Delhi - 110 001

Ref: Telephone No. 4611098

---

it is similar to the one followed by you in the above case. I am sure you can do it yourself. Let us now concentrate on alignment. Let us see how it is done in Word 2007.

Alignment of Text

Word 2007 gives you the option of placing the text in four different alignments. These are:

Left aligned   This line is left aligned.

Right aligned   This line is right aligned.

Centralized   This line is centrally aligned.

Justified   This line has been justified.

You will not notice much of a difference here in left aligned text and justified text. This is so because the matter is small. Just notice the whole text of this book, it is justified, i.e., it aligns to the left and right both. Whereas this particular paragraph is left aligned and see the difference for yourself.

All the four alignments are there on the formatting toolbar. You can choose any one of them. (If you do not have all 4 of them, click at Add and Remove button on the right of the toolbar to add the missing alignment to the formatting toolbar.

Coming back to our text. We have to centrally align the line containing the telephone number.

For that do the following:

1. Click the mouse button at the left of R of Reference: Telephone No. 4611098.
2. Click at the icon which shows the centralized alignment.
3. Notice here that you do not have to highlight the text for alignment. This is so since the whole matter of the paragraph has to be aligned to the same alignment. It is not possible to align one word to one alignment and another word to another alignment.
4. You can see the text underlined and centralized aligned in the figure next.

Now that the next lines have nothing much to be done, expect that International calls and Shah Rukh Khan have to be made bold. This I presume you will be able to do without any difficulty.

11th January, 2007

To,

The General Manager
Mahanagar Telephones Nigam Limited
Khurshid Lal Bhawan
New Delhi - 110 001

Ref: Telephone No. 4611098

Sir,

I am in receipt of bill for the above telephone number dated 11.12.2006 for an amount of Rs. 4,678.90. This bill is to be paid by 21.

It is time to save the document again so as to make sure that the changes made by you are stored in the hard disk.

Next, let us try to put some fancy things on the text. First among them is Font.

Applying fonts

It is upto you to select the same font for the whole text or have different fonts for different paragraphs.

Let us see how it is done.

1. Click at any place in the text with the mouse.
2. Click at Select All in the Edit menu or simply press Ctrl and then A. This will highlight the whole text in the document.
3. Now you can select the font of your liking in the whole text. You can also change the size of the font too.
4. Select Arial for font and size 12 for the whole text in the Formatting toolbar.
5. This will make the whole text 12 points and will have Arial as the font.
6. The previous changes made by you in terms of **Bold**, *Italics* will remain intact and will not be disturbed by doing this.
7. Now if you want you can change the font of particular items like address, etc., to make it more decorative.

Now that our letter is ready, we can just print it, but before that we must check the spelling in the document so as no typological errors remain in the document.

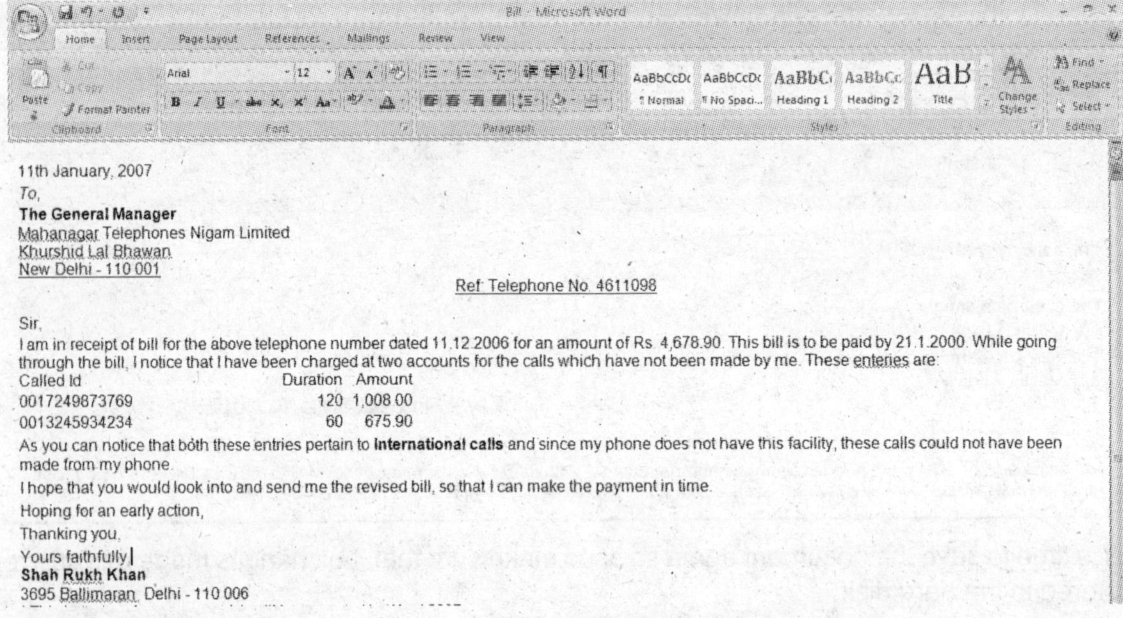

11th January, 2007

To,

The General Manager

Mahanagar Telephones Nigam Limited

Khurshid Lal Bhawan

New Delhi - 110 001

Ref: Telephone No. 4611098

Sir,

I am in receipt of bill for the above telephone number dated 11.12.2006 for an amount of Rs. 4,678.90. This bill is to be paid by 21.1.2000. While going through the bill, I notice that I have been charged at two accounts for the calls which have not been made by me. These enteries are:

Called Id	Duration	Amount
0017249873769	120	1,008.00
0013245934234	60	675.90

As you can notice that both these entries pertain to **International calls** and since my phone does not have this facility, these calls could not have been made from my phone.

I hope that you would look into and send me the revised bill, so that I can make the payment in time.

Hoping for an early action,

Thanking you,

Yours faithfully,

Shah Rukh Khan

3695 Ballimaran, Delhi - 110 006

Spell Checking

As was mentioned in the options, Word 2007 points out the spelling errors by underling the word/words with red wavy line. Since our document is just one page long. It is not difficult to pin point the errors.

There are two methods of correcting these errors. One method is to correct these errors one by one, picking them up. Secondly, you spell check the whole document. Let us do both on our document.

Looking from top to bottom of the text in the document file Bill, you will see few of the words underlined by wavy red line. Few of them are the proper words and thus cannot be corrected.

Words like Mahanagar is basically a *Hindi* word, so it cannot be in the dictionary of Word 2007 and that is why it has been shown as an error. Similar is the case with enteries which is wrong and needs to be corrected. For this follow the following procedure:

1. Click with the mouse at any place within the word to be corrected, in this case enteries.
2. Now right click the mouse button.
3. A pop-menu will pop-up as shown next.
4. Among the various options are:

   Alternative words: Word 2007 displays few words which are similar to the word in question with a hope that these may had been word in your mind while typing this word wrongly. You can choose any one of them, which you feel is the right word by just clicking and selecting that and leaving the mouse. The word will stand corrected with the new word and will replace the wrong word.

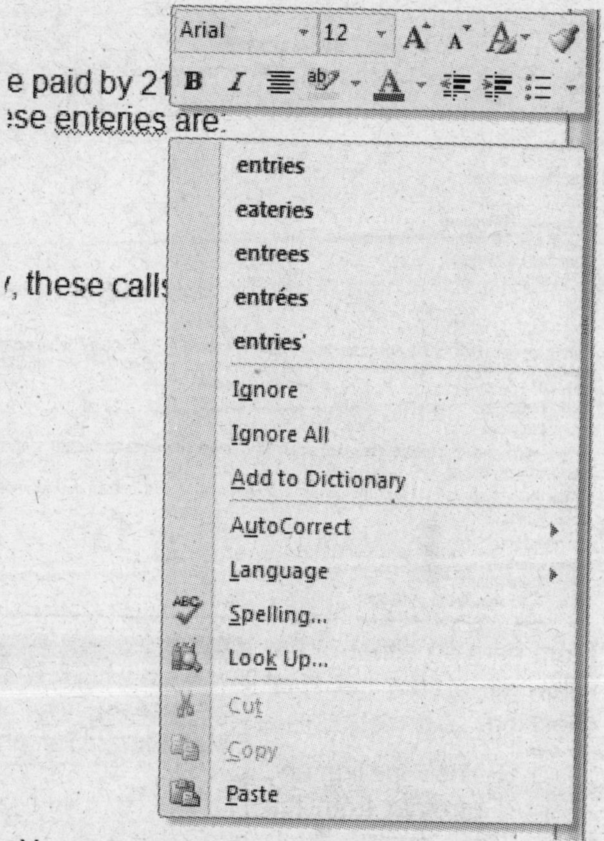

Ignore: It is like over ruling the dictionary and saying that whatever you have typed is right and would like the dictionary to ignore this not only at this place but also at all other places within the document.

Ignore All: This will allow you to ignore this error thoughout the document.

Add to Dictionary: You feel that this word is right and would like this word to be added to the dictionary so that it is not shown as an error in the future.

AutoCorrect: You will learn about AutoCorrect later. But, only thing to understand here is that it is a list of mostly misplaced word which can be corrected without referring to the dictionary. For example, you may have the bad habit of typing *the* as *teh*. You can add this to AutoCorrect to correct *teh* to *the* always without even telling you.

Language: You feel that this particular word which has been pointed as wrong by the current dictionary would be available in other language dictionary. So mention here the name of the other dictionary where this word could be found. If you do not have a second dictionary loaded, just ignore this.

Spelling: By clicking at this, you can start the spell checking of the whole document from this point onward.

Look Up: It looks for an alternative word in the Thesaurus.

Cut, Copy and Paste: These can be used for transferring the word to some other place in the document by cutting or copying it at this place and pasting it there.

5. In our case we will accept entries as the correct substitute for the wrong word enteries.

Since there is no other word which is to be corrected here. The corrected text would now look like the one shown next. Now we come to the second way of spell checking which is checking the whole document. In this case place the cursor at the beginning of the text in the document. In our case we will place the cursor at the left of 1 of 11th January.

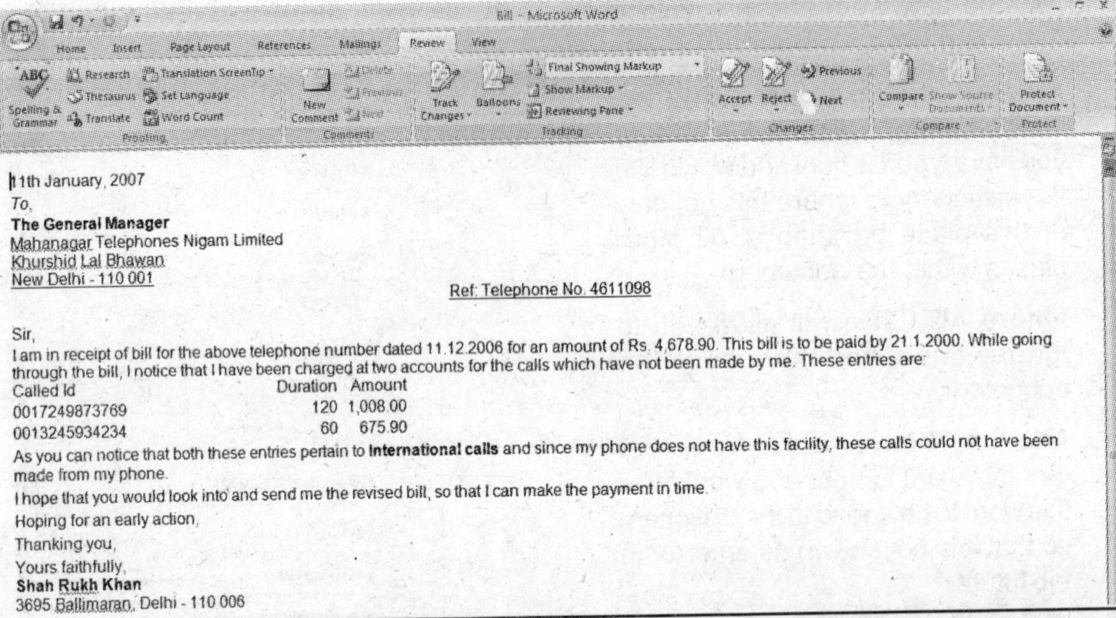

11th January, 2007

To,

The General Manager
Mahanagar Telephones Nigam Limited
Khurshid Lal Bhawan
New Delhi - 110 001

Ref: Telephone No. 4611098

Sir,

I am in receipt of bill for the above telephone number dated 11.12.2006 for an amount of Rs. 4,678.90. This bill is to be paid by 21.1.2000. While going through the bill, I notice that I have been charged at two accounts for the calls which have not been made by me. These entries are:

Called Id	Duration	Amount
0017249873769	120	1,008.00
0013245934234	60	675.90

As you can notice that both these entries pertain to **International calls** and since my phone does not have this facility, these calls could not have been made from my phone.

I hope that you would look into and send me the revised bill, so that I can make the payment in time.

Hoping for an early action,

Thanking you,

Yours faithfully,

Shah Rukh Khan
3695 Ballimaran, Delhi - 110 006

From here do either of the following to start the spell checking.

1. Select Spelling and Grammar from the Tools menu.

   Or

2. Press F7

   Or

3. Click at Spell Grammar in Proofing panel of Review.

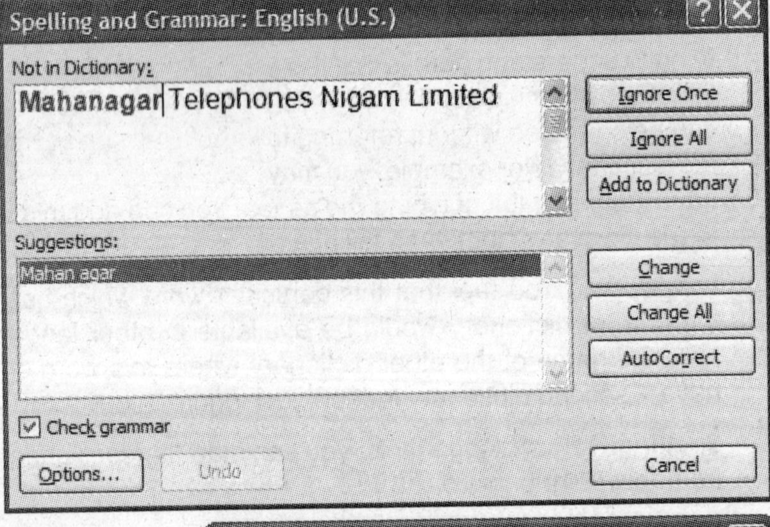

This will initiate the spell checking process and will start the spell checking of the document with each word of the document being searched with the similar word with the words available in the dictionary. If not found it will point out.

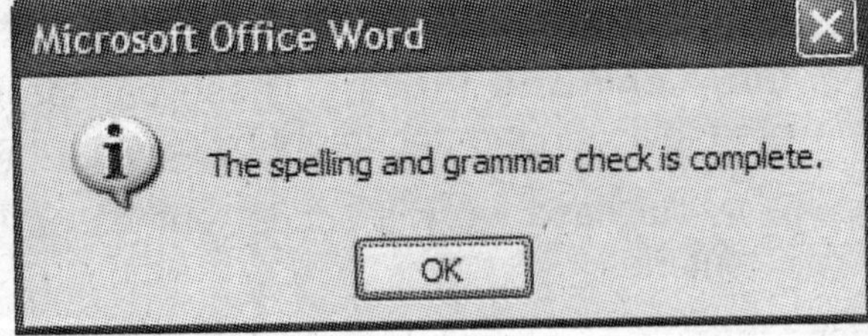

In our case it will select *Mahanagar* of **Mahanagar Telephones Nigam Limited**. As was mentioned before it is a proper *Hindi* word, so it cannot be corrected. Ignore it to proceed further. Other words in the document are also correct. So keep clicking Ignore for all of them till you reach the end of the document and it stops checking the spelling of the document.

After this there is no other word to correct and the spell checking ends with a dialog box, saying that the spelling checking is complete.

Remember, you can spell check a portion of the text or a word by just highlighting it and then clicking at Spell Checking Icon.

Then there is another option called Thesaurus.

Consulting Thesaurus

Thesaurus is there to help you find Synonym, words with similar meanings and Antonym, words with opposite meanings. Using the thesaurus not only helps your vocabulary, but gives you alternatives to using the same word over and over again throughout your text.

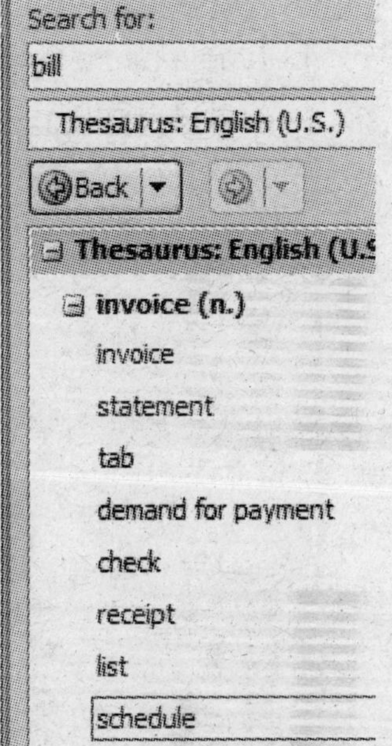

Let us try to use this option in our text. We would like to see the alternatives to the word Bill. For this we do the following:

1. Select the word bill in the second line of the paragraph.
2. Now select Thesaurus from the Proofing panel.
3. You will get the dialog box as shown here.
4. The options given here are Invoice as the main. But there are others too like statement, check, etc.
5. You have the option to select a new word Invoice or other or let the bill remain as it is.

Assign Character Styles

Styles are sets of formatting attributes that you can apply to text in your document. Typically styles are applied to whole paragraphs and allow you to use preset formatting for headings, captions, numbered paragraphs, and so forth. However, Character styles are useful when you find yourself using the Format Painter over and over again to apply character formatting.

Character styles add to the current formatting of text. For example, if the text is 12 point Arial italics and your character style applies **bold** and **strikethrough**, the text to which you apply the character style will be 12 point **Arial bold**, *italic*, and ~~strikethrough~~.

Assign a Character Style

1. To apply a style to existing text, select the text to which you want to assign the style. If you want to apply a style as your are entering new text, place your insertion point where you want the newly styled text to appear.
2. Choose a style from the Style panel on the Home menu. When you click the Style box, you see each style name displayed in the style's font. An underlined "a" indicates a character style.

3. Click the name of the style you want to use to apply the style to the selected text.

When you want to remove the character style from selected text, apply the character style Default Paragraph Font. The text reverts to the formatting defined in the paragraph style assigned to the paragraph in which the selected text is located.

Create a Character Style

1. Open the Home menu and choose Styles. Click at the bottom right hand corner.
2. Choose New Style icon at the left hand bottom.
3. This will give you a dialog box, as shown next.
4. Type a name for the new style in the Name box.
5. Choose Paragraph from the Style Type box.

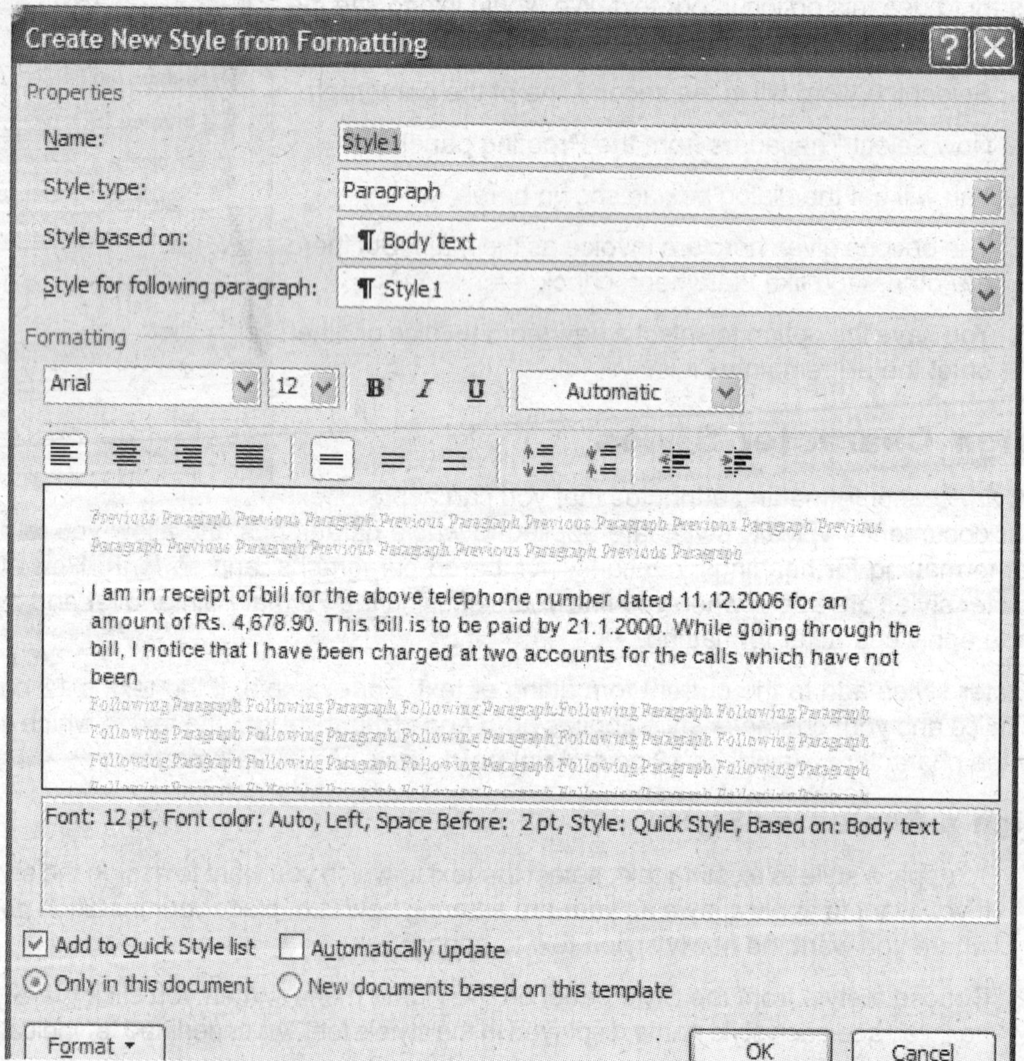

6. Choose Format then Font to set the style's attributes from the Font dialog box. Choose Ok.
7. To add a border or shading to the new character font, choose Format and then Border to open the Borders and Shading dialog box. Make your selections and then choose OK.
8. Choose Ok to close the New Style dialog box.
9. Choose Apply to apply the new style to current text. Choose Close to save the new style definition without assigning it to any text.

Creating a character style is easiest when you select text first, apply the font attributes you want in the new style, and then follow steps 1-5 above. You won't have to select any formatting, so skip to steps 7-8 to finish creating the style.

Borders and Shading

Word 2007 allows you to highlight headlines, captions, and other text of importance by applying a border or shading to that text. You can apply it to a piece of text or to the full text.

Apply Borders and Shading

1. Select the text on which you want to apply Borders or Shading. Basically the rules to follow this are:

- If no text is selected, the paragraph where the cursor is, will be taken as the starting point.
- If you select text within a single paragraph, but the paragraph mark itself is not included in the selection, the results affect only the selected text.
- If you select text included in more than one paragraph (so that at lease one paragraph mark is included in the selection), the results affect all the paragraphs in which any of the selected text resides.

2. Open the Page Layout menu, and select Page Border.
3. Click Borders to work with options available under it.

- Under Setting, click one of the preset border options.
- Select None to remove all borders from the selected paragraph(s), Box to insert a box border around the selected paragraph(s), and Shadow to insert a box border around the selected paragraph(s) and apply preset shadow formatting to the border.
- Select 3-D to insert a box border around the selection and apply preset 3D border formatting. Choose Custom to create a border using the options you click in the Preview window. When you choose any of these settings, the current selections in Style, Colour, and Width apply to the borders.

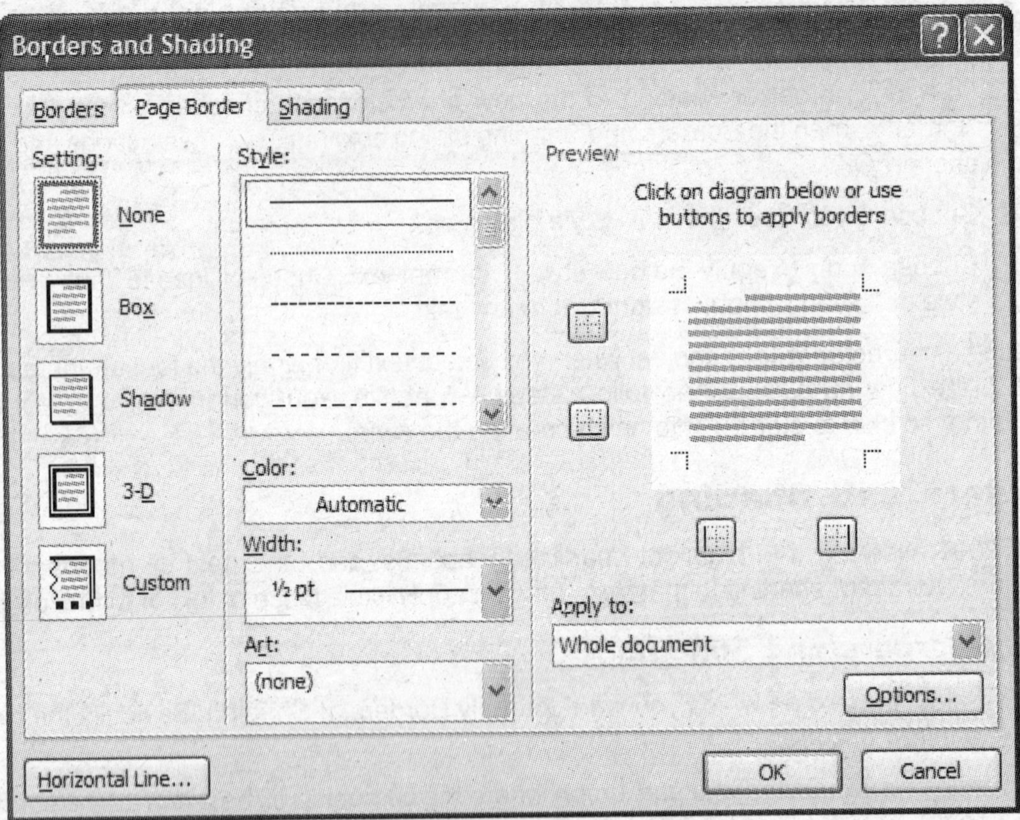

- From the Style list, select the type of line you want to use for the border, including *dotted*, *dashed*, and *wavy lines*.
- Click the Color drop-down list to select a colour to apply to the border.
- From the Width drop-down list, choose the thickness of the border line from ¼ point to 6 points.
- In the Preview box, click the individual border lines or use the border line buttons to apply or remove borders or change the attributes of a particular border (select the attributes first and then add the border).
- From the Apply To drop-down list, select whether to apply the border to just the selected text or to the whole paragraph(s).

4. Select Shading to choose shading options.

- Under Fill, select the colour or shade of gray with which you want to fill the selection. Click More Colors to see a larger selection of colours.
- From the Patterns Style drop-down list, choose a shading percentage for the colour you selected under Fill or a pattern of lines such as Lt Horizontal or Dk Trellis.
- If you selected a pattern of lines, select the Color of the lines from the drop-down list. The Fill colour then becomes the background colour for the pattern.

- From the Apply To drop-down list select whether to apply the shading options to just the selected text or to the whole paragraph(s).

5. Click Ok.

You can use all these options of Borders and Shading from the Tables and Border toolbar, which can be called from toolbar options.

This will allow you to select shading colours, border line styles, border line colours, and border line widths, etc.

Following are the button on the toolbar that apply to borders and shading.

Button	***Description***
Line Style	Sets the style of the border lines (dotted, dashed, wavy, double, and so on)
Line Weight	Sets the thickness of the border lines
Border Color	Sets the colour of the border lines
Borders	Specifies where the border appears (top, bottom, left, right, or box)
Shading Color	Sets the colour of the background shading for the paragraph (you cannot specify the percentage)

Since our letter is a formal one, we would not like to use any of these decorations. They have been told here so that they can be used at a later stage in another document.

Now that our letter is final. What we would do now is that we will close the file and then reopen and finally print. This is deliberately done so as to learn the concept of closing and opening of the file. If you want you can print the file as it is.

Closing of the File

As you would have noticed that there is no Close command in File menu. All you have to do is close the file using the ☒ button on the extreme right top of the word document. But don't forget to save the file before closing else the software will ask you to do so.

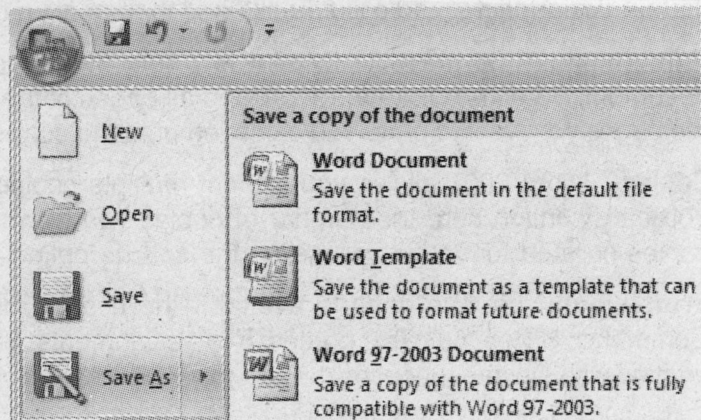

Save as option

Unlike the earlier options of Save As, this time in Word 2007 has different options for Save As. These can be seen here in the dialog box. The options are: Word

Document, Word Template, Word 97-2003 Document, Find add-ins for other file formats, and Other Formats. These are self explanatory.

Printing Your Document

As mentioned earlier, no document preparation process is complete without printing it. For this we have the Print option under the File menu.

Once clicked it gives rise to a dialog box as shown here. The various options, which can differ depending upon the printer, which you are working on, of the dialog box are as follows:

Printer: Select the printer to which you want to send the printing. From the drop-down list, you can select one of the many printers which you may have installed under Windows.

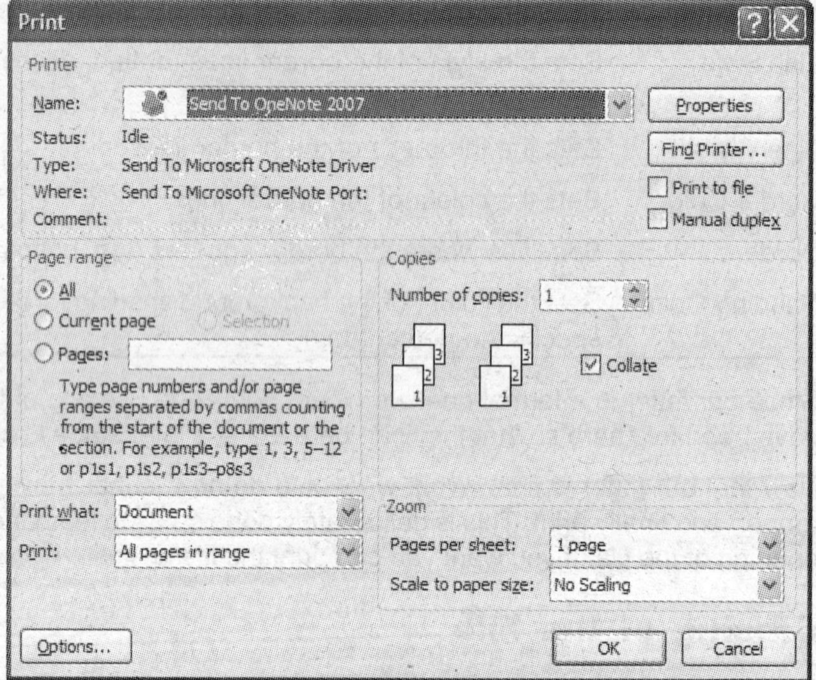

Properties: Clicking at it would lead to a dialog box having the properties of the selected printer. If some adjustments are to be made in the properties of the selected printer, they can be done here.

Print to file: Sometimes it is possible that you may like to print the document to the printer which is not installed in your computer. In this case you will select this option and create a print file for that particular printer and copy the file and then print on that printer where it is installed.

Print range: You may like to print few selective pages instead of printing the whole document. So either click **All**, for printing all pages of the document or **Pages**, for defining the pages you want to print. You can even print the current page, i.e., page on the screen.

Copies: Word 2007 allows you to print multiple copies of the pages in the document. You can mention here the number of copies you want. What's more you can have the copies collated for you, if you select the **collate** option.

Print what: Various options available here are Document, Document properties, Comments, Styles, AutoText entries, Key assignments. But, most of the time you would be printing with Document option.

Print: You have the option of printing all pages or all **odd pages** or all **even pages**.

Zoom: Pages per sheet allows you to print 1 to 16 pages of the document on one sheet. Scaling allows you to scale your document to the various sizes of the paper.

Options: This will lead to the print options, already described under **Options** and select the option of your choice.

Once you are sure that you have selected all the options required by you, just click Ok to for document to start printing. However, do not forget to have the Printer ON before giving the final print command.

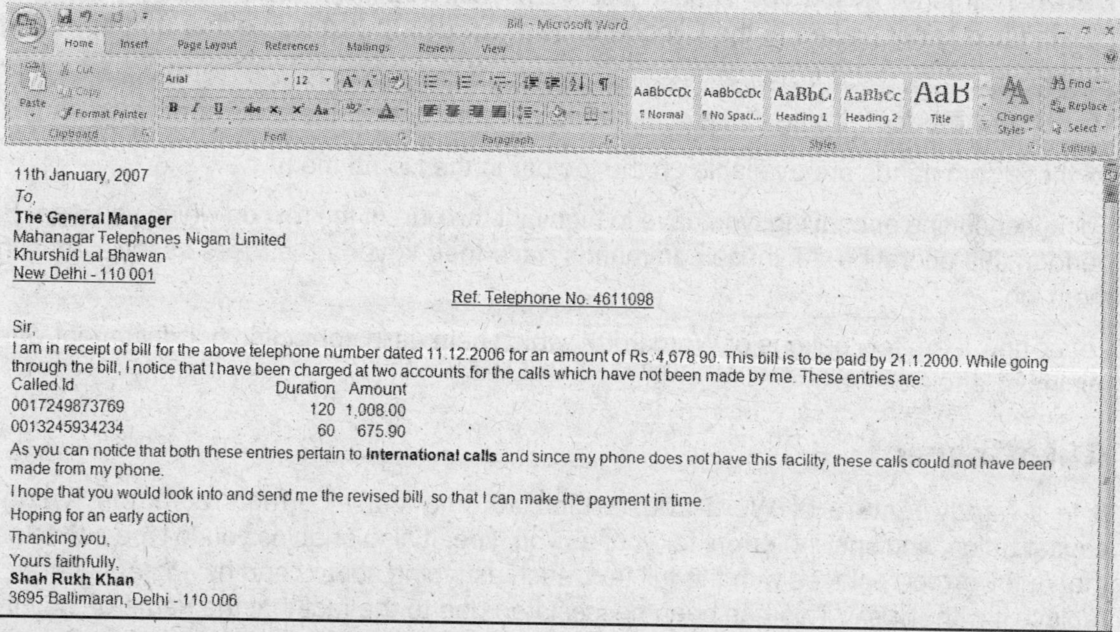

11th January, 2007

To,

The General Manager

Mahanagar Telephones Nigam Limited

Khurshid Lal Bhawan

New Delhi - 110 001

Ref. Telephone No. 4611098

Sir,

I am in receipt of bill for the above telephone number dated 11.12.2006 for an amount of Rs. 4,678 90. This bill is to be paid by 21.1.2000. While going through the bill, I notice that I have been charged at two accounts for the calls which have not been made by me. These entries are:

Called Id	Duration	Amount
0017249873769	120	1,008.00
0013245934234	60	675.90

As you can notice that both these entries pertain to **International calls** and since my phone does not have this facility, these calls could not have been made from my phone.

I hope that you would look into and send me the revised bill, so that I can make the payment in time.

Hoping for an early action,

Thanking you,

Yours faithfully,

Shah Rukh Khan

3695 Ballimaran, Delhi - 110 006

Editing the Document

Now that you have printed the document, you may want to either correct few words which you have realized that they do not look good in the letter. Even otherwise you may want to enhance the overall look of the letter. Besides this you would also learn how to do the tailor's job, i.e., Cut, Copy and Paste. There are other options too which may not be used in this letter but are quite useful overall for editing. Let us start with the proofing tools.

Editing Tools

Many editing functions are performed on selected text, such as cut, copy, move, and delete. There are various tools provided by Word to help you edit text:

Cut, Copy: Cutting and copying items places them on the Clipboard and you can paste these items anywhere in the document, wherever required. These items can be text, graphics, tables and any other object which is there in the word document. Cut and Copy can be performed using mouse and key strokes.

Paste: It is the command used to paste whatever is available on the Clipboard to paste it in the document. This is also done by the use of mouse and key strokes.

Move: It is an action associated with the mouse. However, if you cut and paste from one place to another, it can also be called move.

Insert Mode: It is the feature that adjusts spacing when you add new text to the document.

Overtype Mode: This option replaces the existing text with your new text.

Delete: It is an action you should reserve for text you want to permanently remove. Deleted text is not placed in the Clipboard. You can delete text with either mouse or key strokes.

Undo and Redo: Using these commands you can reverse the tasks performed earlier.

All these commands are available on the toolbar in the Home menu.

For either cutting or copying, you have to highlight the part of the text on which you want to perform this operation. All these commands have their keyboard strokes associated with them too.

Let us now learn few options of Word 2007 which help us in correcting our document with minimum efforts.

AutoCorrect

It is a handy feature of Word 2007 which automatically corrects common typing, capitalization, and spelling errors for you, as you type. It also enables you to type shortcuts that AutoCorrect replaces with the full text, such as typing BOMBAY and having AutoCorrect replace it with MUMBAI. This has been neccesiated due to the fact that the name of the city has been changed as thus. Although Word 2007 has a number of default AutoCorrect entries, you can add your own common misspellings and shortcuts.

It only checks whole words, so if you type TEH, Word won't replace it with THE until your press the spacebar, period, or some other key that indicates that the word is complete. It is also useful tool for applying formatting options. In a business letter, for example, you might want your company name to always appear in a certain font and size, regardless of the font you are using for the letter. By creating an AutoCorrect entry of your company name with formatting options, you eliminate the need to format while you type, or to run search and replace when you are finished with the letter.

Add AutoCorrect Entries Without Formatting

1. From the Office button, select Word Options, and then AutoCorrect options.
2. Click Replace Text as You Type to place a check mark there, if it isn't already checked.

3. In the replace box, enter the text you want AutoCorrect to automatically replace for you, such as your initials or a word you commonly misspell.
4. Click Plain Text if it is not selected to inserted text without formatting options.
5. Choose Add. If the text in the Replace box is already listed, choose Replace to replace the existing replacement text with the text you entered in the With box.
6. Click Ok.

Text your new AutoCorrect entry by typing the word in a document and pressing the Spacebar.

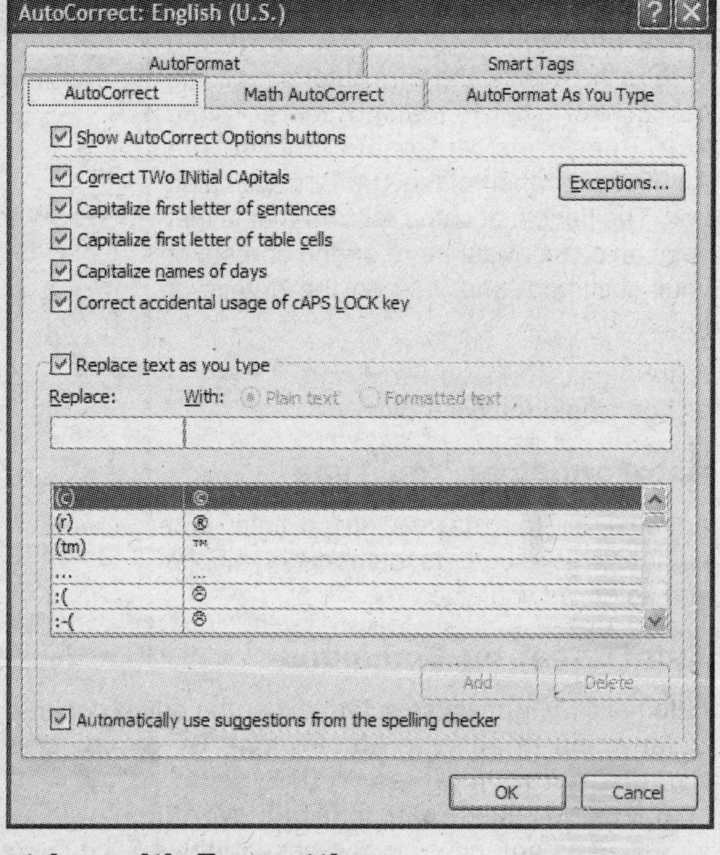

Add New AutoCorrect Entries with Formatting

1. Type the text in your document and format it.
2. Select the text. To store paragraph formatting with your entry, include the paragraph mark at the end of the text, in your selection.
3. From the Office button, select Word Options and AutoCorrect AutoCorrect. The AutoCorrect dialog box appears.
4. In the Replace text box, type a name for the AutoCorrect entry (an abbreviation, or the entire word or phrase).
5. Click Formatted Text.
6. To save the entry and close the dialog box, click Add.

Here you have an option for Math AutoCorrect tool, which allows you to create mathematical characters, by just writing the english word for it.

AutoFormat

Word 2007 has automated a lot of small, tedious chores that we had to do manually in older word processing programs. Many of these are formatting chores, and Word collects them under the term AutoFormat. You can control what formatting chores Word 2007 performs automatically in the AutoFormat panels of the AutoCorrect dialog box. The benefit of using AutoFormat is that you can concentrate more on the content of your document and less on the details of formatting.

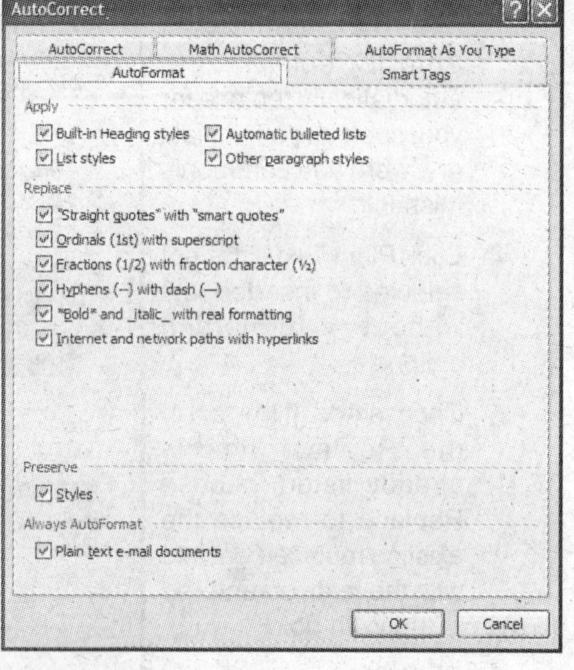

AutoFormat works on two different ways—as you type or on command.

AutoFormat as You Type

Automatically formats headings, bulleted and numbered lists, borders, numbers, symbols, and so on, as you type.

AutoFormat on Command

Automatically formats selected text or the entire document in one pass. You don't have to do anything to activate AutoFormat. By default, AutoFormat as You Type is enabled—you just enter text and Word formats it as you go. You can change the default to AutoFormat on Command, which allows you to manually run AutoFormat. This is similar to the way in which you can spell check a document—as you type, or manually, using the menu commands or toolbar icons.

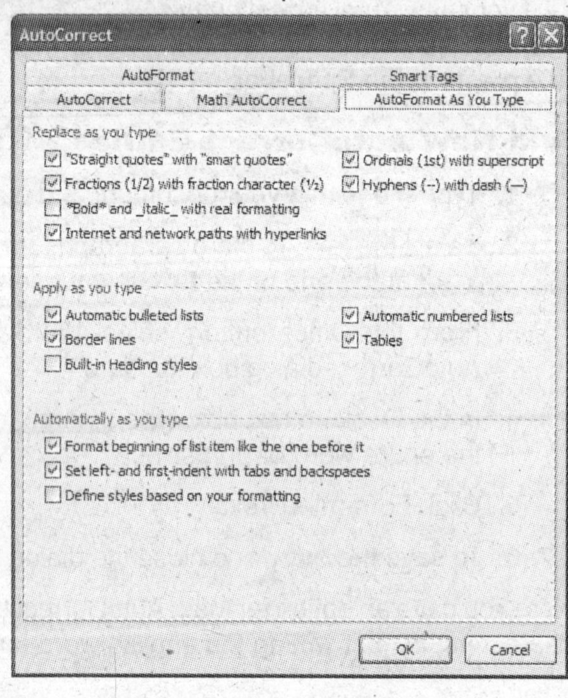

AutoFormatting Text

1. To AutoFormat a block of text, select it. To AutoFormat the entire document, make sure that no text is selected.
2. From the Office button, select Word Options followed by Proofing options. From here click at AutoCorrect options to get the dialog box.
3. Click AutoFormat.

4. Click AutoFormat and Review Each Change if you want the opportunity to accept or reject each change proposed by Word.
5. Choose the type of document you have created in the drop-down list labelled Please Select a Document Type to Help Improve the Formatting Process. This helps Word to AutoFormat the document properly.
6. If you want to limit the types of formatting Word does, choose the Options button to display the AutoFormat panel of the AutoCorrect dialog box. Make your selections and then click Ok to return to the AutoFormat dialog box.
7. Click Ok to begin the AutoFormat process.

If you choose AutoFormat Now, Word 2007 formats the document, and that's that. If you choose AutoFormat and Review Each Change, Word 2007 formats the document and then presents a new AutoFormat dialog box. This version of the document looks very different from the first version.

Find and Replace

Supposing you had prepared a thesis on the working of middle level managers in the city of Bombay. Naturally the word Bombay must have come in it quite a number of times. Then you hear that the Government of that State has decided to change the name of city from **Bombay** to **Mumbai**. What will you do? Will you be able to locate each occurrence of Bombay and physically change it to Mumbai? No! For this Word 2007 has an excellent option called Find and Replace. Once you give this command, Word 2007 will automatically search for Bombay and replace it with Mumbai.

You can use Find and Replace to do the following:

Text strings: Either strings of text embedded in words, or discrete words or whole phrases.

Text strings with formatting: Strings of text that are formatted a particular way, such as Bold.

Formatting: Font formatting options, such as underlining and bold, that are not necessarily associated with words or text.

Styles: Find all instances of a named style or replace one named style with another.

Special characters: Tab markers, forced line breaks, non-breaking spaces, non-breaking hyphens, whitespace, and so on.

This command is actually divided into 2 parts, Find and Replace. Let us see how the find command works first.

Find

This command will find for you the exact text which is mentioned in its box and will stop for further action. Normally the finding of the text starts from the position where the cursor is. If you have selected some text, the finding will be restricted to that block of text only. So if you have to select the entire text, then it is advised to put the cursor at the beginning of the text in the document.

To start the Find command, click at Find in the Home menu.

Find and Replace dialog box, as shown here will appear.

This is how you will use the Find command.

1. Type the text that you are seeking in the Find What? text box. This word or phrase is also referred to as the search string.

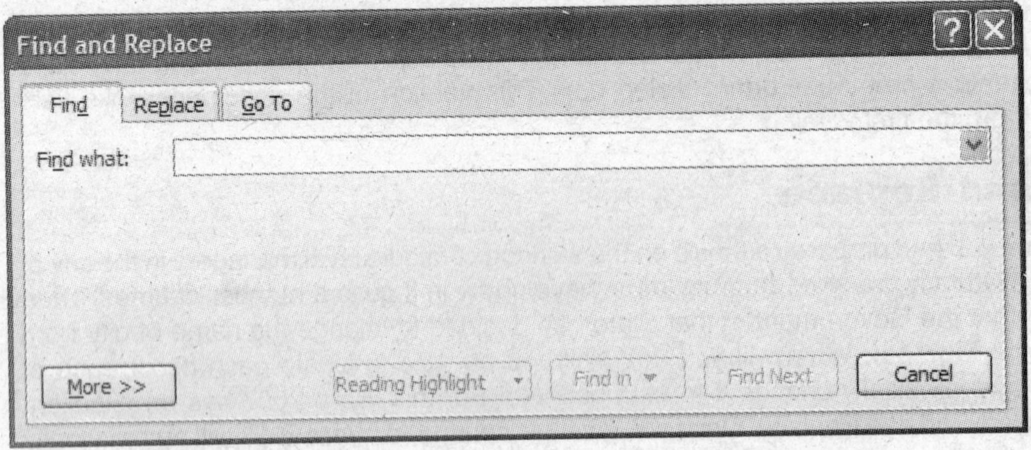

2. Choose the More button (if necessary) to specify search options.
3. Choose Find Next. Find looks through the document for text that matches your search strings. When it finds matching text, Word highlights the text in the document and stops. The Find and Replace dialog box remains on screen.
4. Choose Find Next if you want to continue the search for another instance of the search string. Click Cancel or press Esc to close the dialog box and return to the document. The text in the document is still highlighted.

When Word finishes the entire document, or if it could not find the search string in the document, a dialog box displays a message to that effect. Choose Ok to continue working in the document.

Replace Text

Next step after finding the required text is to replace it with some other text. For this we would call the command called Replace. To get the replace command click at Replace in the Home menu.

Now on the Find and Replace dialog box click at the Replace panel and do the following:

1. Type the text you want to replace in the Find What text box (in this case, *Bombay*).

You can leave this field blank if you have to search for a formatting only. However, you have to search for something.

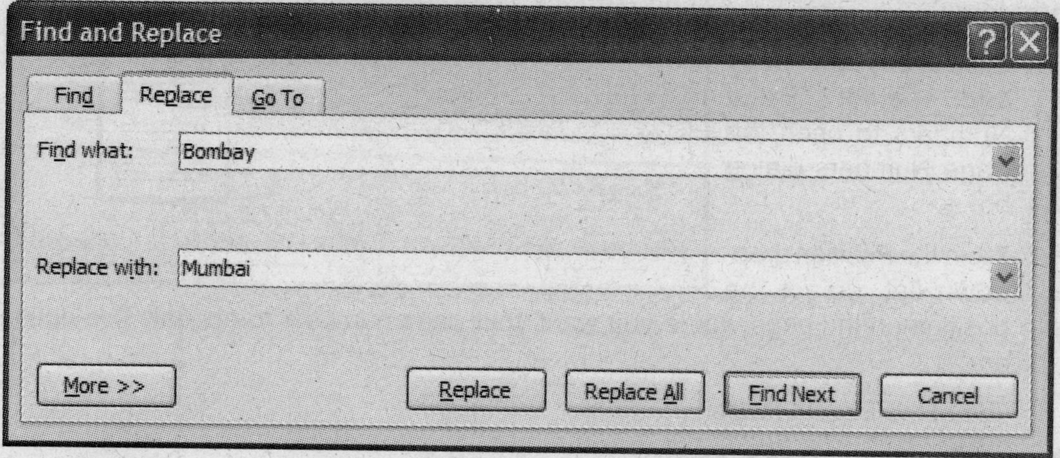

2. Type the text you want to replace it with in the Replace With text box (in this case, *Mumbai*). If you search for text and leave this field blank, you are in effect telling Word to delete all instances of the search strings, because they would be replaced by a blank.
3. Choose the More button (if necessary) to specify search options.
4. Choose Find Next to locate and highlight the first occurence of text that matches your search string.
5. Then do one of the following:

- Choose Replace to replace the text matching the search string with the replacement text and then locate the next occurrence of the search string in your document.
- Choose Find Next to leave the text matching the search string unchanged and to locate the next occurence of the search string.
- Choose Replace All to replace text in the entire document that matches the search string with the replacement text.

6. Choose Cancel. Alternatively, press Esc to close the Find and Replace dialog box and return to the your document.

When Word has finished searching through the document and has replaced all occurrences of the search text or can't find any further occurrences, a message box appears. Click Ok to return to your document.

Page Numbering

Printed documents longer than one page should have page numbers. You can set up page numbering in two ways. Either insert a page number code while editing headers and footers, or insert page numbers from the Insert menu. Both methods insert a page number code in you documents' header or footer, but there are two differences.

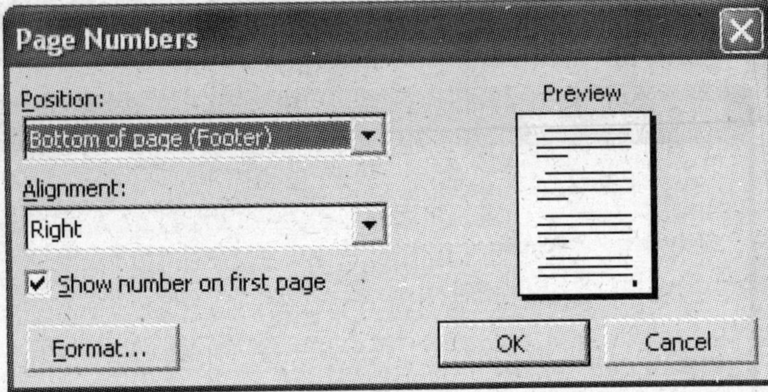

1. Click the Insert menu and select Page Numbers to open the Page Numbers dialog box.
2. From the Position drop-down list, select the position on the page where you want your page numbers to appear. The options are:

   Top of the Page (Header)

   Bottom of the Page (Footer)
3. From the alignment drop-down list, select Left, Center, or Right to specify the horizontal position of the page number in relation to the right or left margins.
4. If you want the page number to appear on the first page, Show number on first page to place check mark there. Deselecting this option creates a separate header or footer for the first page.
5. Click Ok.

When you insert a page number, Word automatically switches you to Print Layout view so you can scroll to the portion of the page where the page number appears to check its appearance.

Header and Footer

As you must be knowing that Header appears on the top of the page and Footer appears on the bottom of the page. Word 2007 allows you to put both of them on the document pages. Once clicked they give you the options to choose from.

Headers and footers can vary within a document. Choices include:

1. The same header and footer on every page.
2. A different header and footer for the first page only
3. Different headers and footers for odd numbered pages than those on even numbered pages.
4. Different headers and footers for each section of the document.

Footnotes and Endnotes

These are used in the documents to provide references to the source documents for the document text, to provide more detailed explanations and definitions that might otherwise distract the reader if left in the main body of the document.

The two parts to each footnote or endnote are the reference mark—a number, character, or combination of characters appearing in the body of the document—and the note text. You may automatically number the marks or create your own custom marks. If you use the automatic numbering, Word renumbers the note reference marks if you add, delete, or move notes. The note can be of any length and format, and you can format the line that separates the notes from the body of the document.

To view the note text, rest the mouse pointer on the note reference mark. The note text appears in a pop-up box above the mark. Double-click the note reference mark to display the note text in a note pane at the bottom of the screen. If you are using Print Layout view, footnotes display at the bottom of the page, endnotes at the end of the document.

Add a Footnote or Endnote

1. Place curosr where you want the note reference mark to appear.
2. Choose the Reference menu and select Insert Footnote. The Footnote dialog box appears.
3. Select Footnote or Endnote.
4. Under Numbering, select AutoNumber or Custom Mark. If you choose Custom Mark, insert the symbol or symbols for the reference mark or choose Symbol to open the Symbol dialog box. Choose a font, click the symbol you want to use, and then click Ok.
5. Choose Ok to close the Footnote and Endnote dialog box.
6. Type the note text in the footnote pane. Apply formatting as desired or, better yet, reformat the Footnote text style (which automatically appears in the Style list when you insert your first footnote).
7. Choose Close to close the footnote pane or click in the document to continue typing.

Splitting Panes

You can split a document window into two panes. Then, you can display different portions of the same document at the same time. This lets you compare two portions of a single document. It also makes it easier for you to move or copy text from one portion of a document to another. When you make a change to the document from either pane, the change is applied to the same document. As a result, the change can be found in both panes.

Splitting Document into Two Panes

1. Choose the New window command from the View menu, drag the separator bar to where you want to split the window, and click the left mouse button.

2. Use Remove Split to remove the split.

Tiling of the Documents

With tiling you can display two or more different documents at the same time. This makes it easy for you to compare two or more documents, or to move and copy text from one document to another. However, this works best when only two documents are open. Otherwise, the windows get too small for effective use. To return the display so only one window shows, just maximize the window that you want dispalyed.

To Tile Open Document Window

1. Choose the Arrange All command from the View menu.
2. The Arrange All command sizes the open documents windows so they are all the same height and so they are as wide as possible within Word's application window.
3. You can use standard Windows techniques to move, size and maximize the document windows and to switch between them.

Using MailMerge in Word 2007

MailMerge is one of the very important application of any word processing software. It has been given an important panel in the Word 2007. Word has indeed made it very easy to operate. In MailMerge you have the variable data coming from a data source which can be either a database file, spreadsheet, or even a text file with fields marked in it. Then you have the document file whose text remains the same for all the subsequent merged files changing only the data which has been received from the source. So in fact you create multiple documents having the same text but having different fields depending upon the source.

Well, one can think of various usages of the MailMerge. The most important being sending the same letter to various parties. Sending the same invitation to various guests. Sending payment reminders to various creditors. Calling all the directors to the same board meeting. In all these cases, the text would remain more or less the same but the name and address of the receiver would change. You can even change the salutation too, for example, Dear Mr. so and so, picking the name from the data source.

MailMerge in Word is done in steps. Creating document (text), data source and then merging them before printing. Let us see how it is done. For your information, here I am creating a appreciation letter for the various members of the victories Indian Cricket Team. So, lets start.

1. Start Word 2007.
2. On the Panels menu, select Mailings.
3. From here on the Start Mail Merge, click at Step by Step Mail Merge Wizard.
4. As shown here, the first step is to select the document type.

5. Select Letters as shown here.
6. Click at Next to start document.
7. The second step as mentioned is to select the document.
8. You have the option of using the current document, starting from an existing document or from a template.
9. Step 3 asks you to type your letter.
10. We have written a letter to various people inviting them to the marriage.
11. As shown next the letter for the same has been type.
12. Now comes the part of selecting the recipients of the letter.
13. In the top portion of the Wizard, choose the Type a new list option and click at Create.

Mail Merge

Select document type

What type of document are you working on?

Letters
E-mail messages
Envelopes
Labels
Directory

Letters

Send letters to a group of people. You can personalize the letter that each person receives.

Click Next to continue.

Step 1 of 6

Next: Starting document

14. You would be given a blank dialog box to create a New Address Book. Here various options of filling the name, address, company's name, etc are given. Type the ones you want to use and ignore others. When you have types one, click at New Entry to go for the next entry.
15. Once you have typed all the entries, click at Ok. You would be asked to save the address list with a name.
16. Once again the same list would be shown to you for making the last minute correction, addition, deletion, etc. You can even change the sequence by sorting it.
17. In the next step, you would insert the field name at the place where it would be displayed. For this choose the option of Insert Merge Field, and then the field name, where it would be replaced with the actual data.

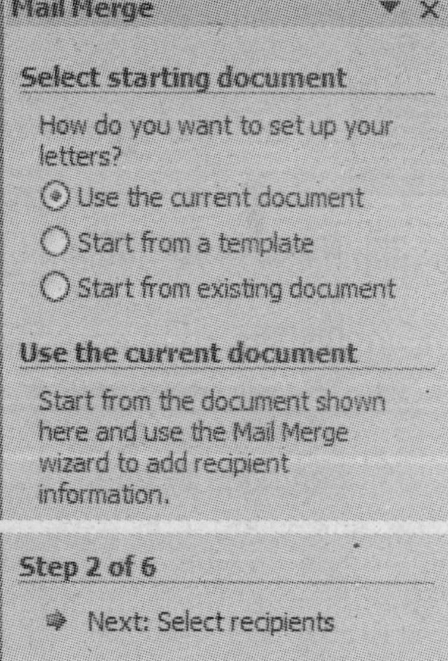

18. You will notice that the fields are shown within << and >>.
19. Next step would show you the preview of the letter by inserting the actual data from first entry into the letter.

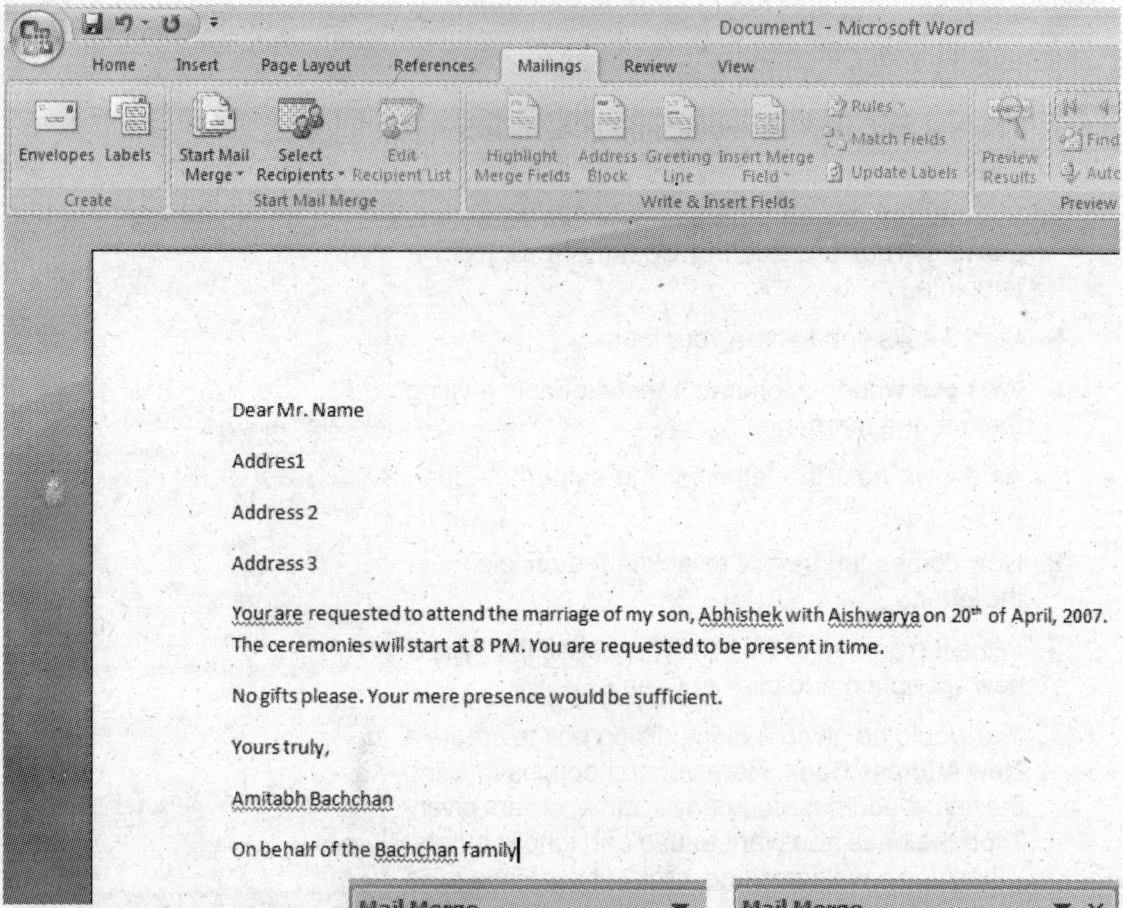

Document1 - Microsoft Word

Home | Insert | Page Layout | References | Mailings | Review | View

Envelopes Labels (Create) | Start Mail Merge, Select Recipients, Edit Recipient List (Start Mail Merge) | Highlight Merge Fields, Address Block, Greeting Line, Insert Merge Field, Rules, Match Fields, Update Labels (Write & Insert Fields) | Preview Results, Find, Auto (Preview)

Dear Mr. Name

Addres1

Address 2

Address 3

Your are requested to attend the marriage of my son, Abhishek with Aishwarya on 20th of April, 2007. The ceremonies will start at 8 PM. You are requested to be present in time.

No gifts please. Your mere presence would be sufficient.

Yours truly,

Amitabh Bachchan

On behalf of the Bachchan family

20. Next step is to complete the merge.
21. This will create a file of all letters to be sent, one by one.

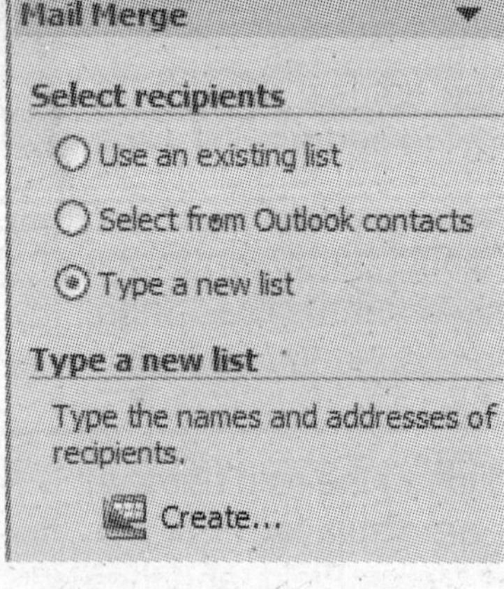

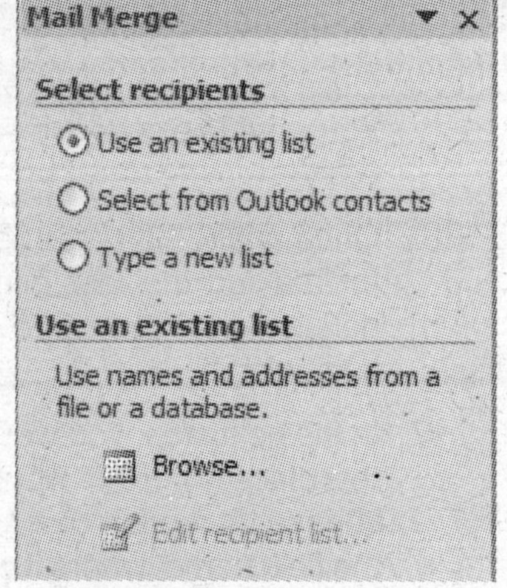

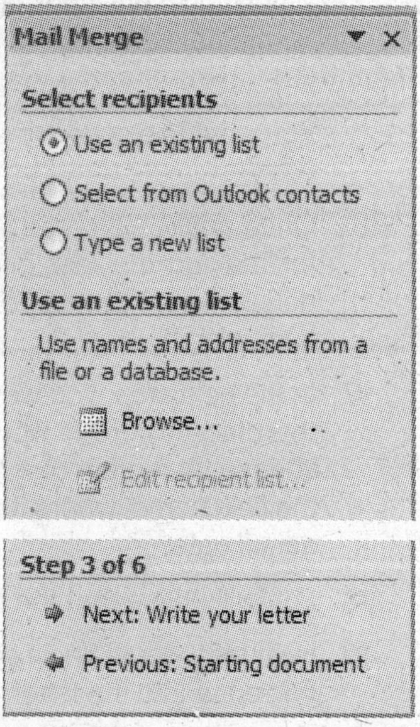

New Address List
Type recipient information in the table. To add more entries, click New Entry.
Title
First Name
Last Name
Company Name
Address Line 1
Mr
Sanjay
Dutt
Mumbai
Mrs
Sonia
Gandhi
Delhi
Mr
Karan
Johar
Mumbai
Mr
Rituparno
Ghosh
Kolkatta
Mr
Shah Rukh Khan
Mumbai
New Entry
Find...
Delete Entry
Customize Columns...
OK
Cancel

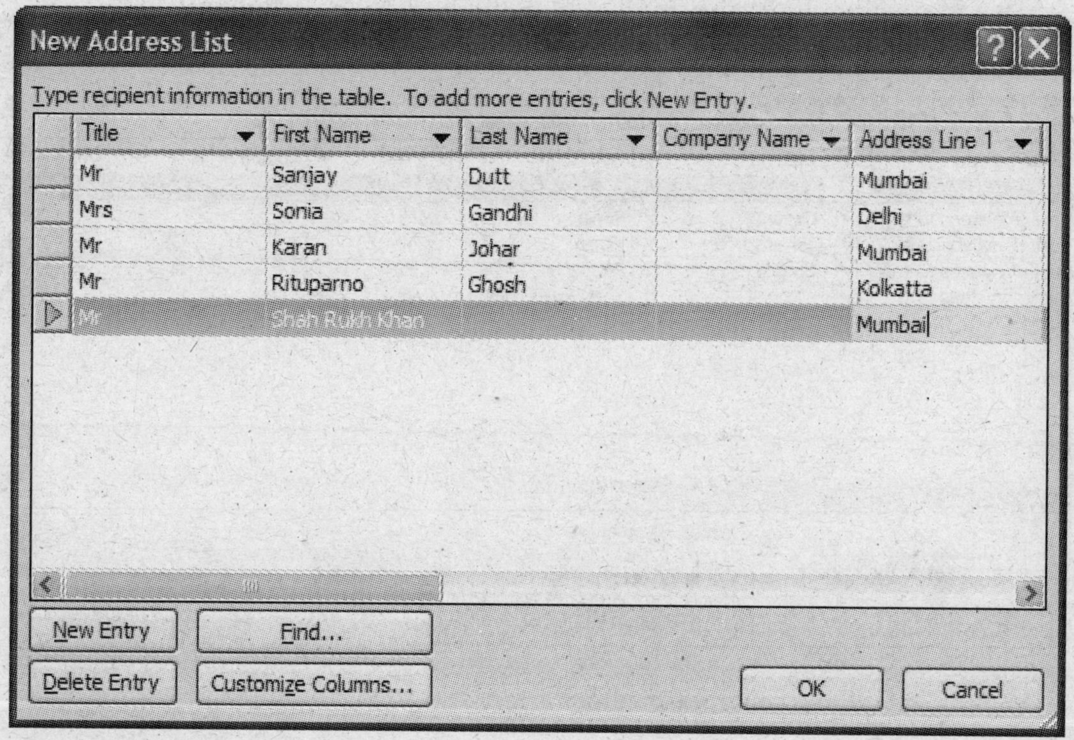

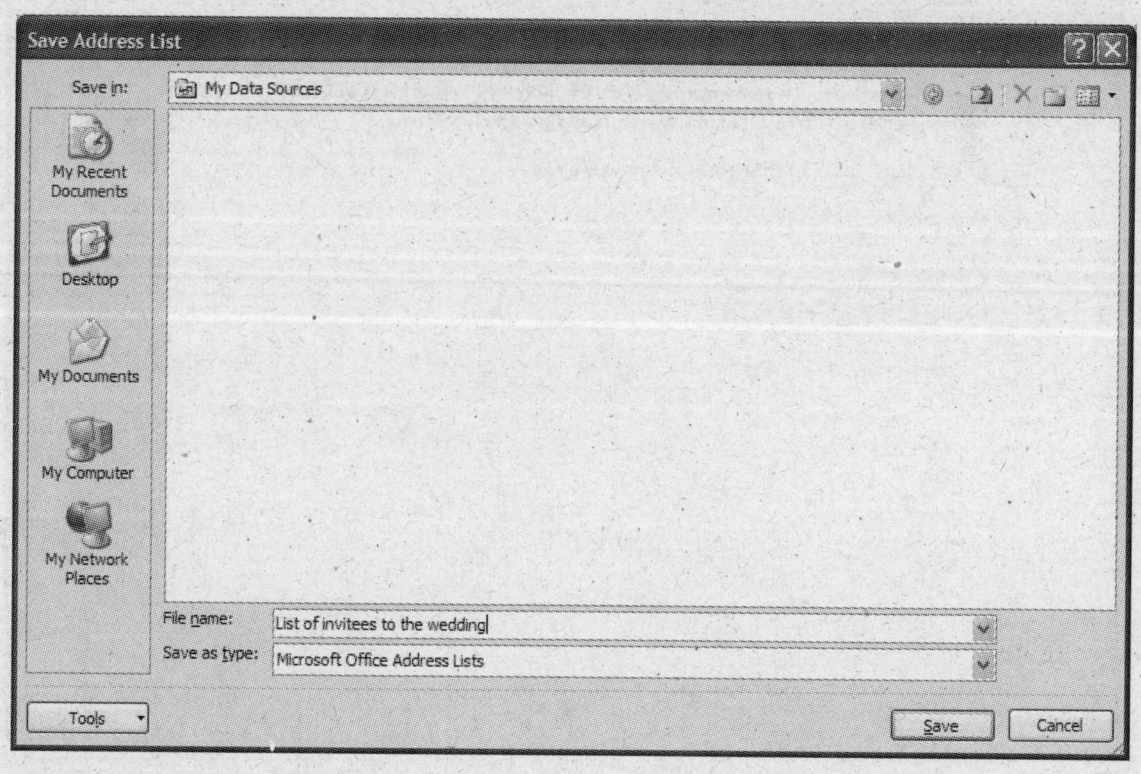

Save Address List
Save in:
My Data Sources
My Recent Documents
Desktop
My Documents
My Computer
My Network Places
File name:
List of invitees to the wedding
Save as type:
Microsoft Office Address Lists
Tools
Save
Cancel

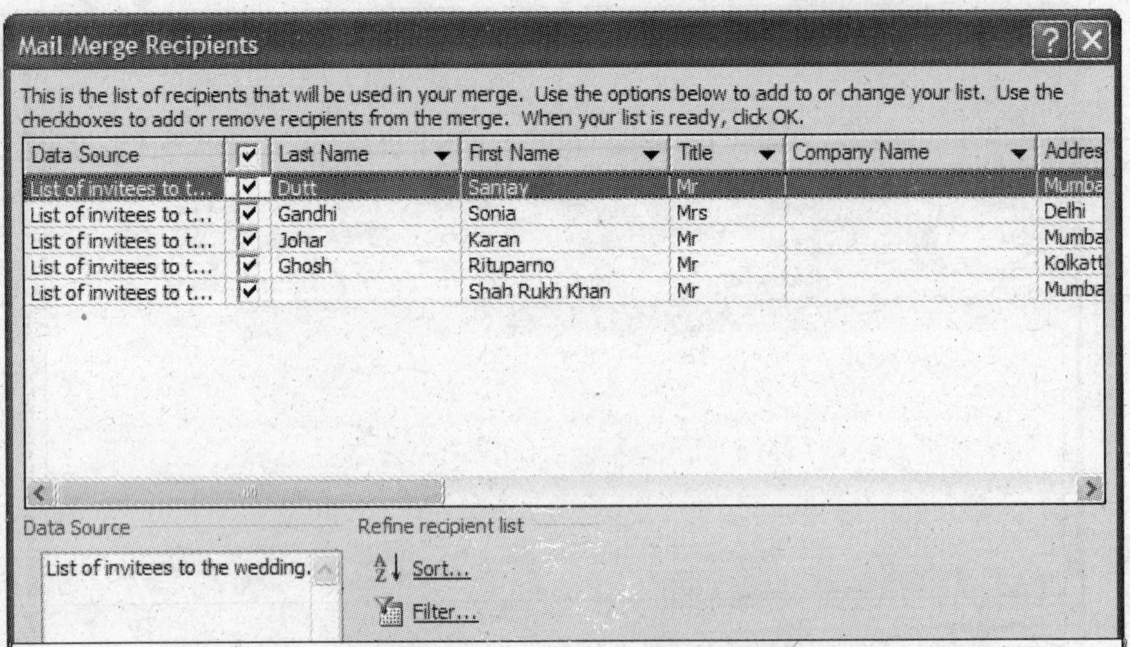

Mail Merge Recipients

This is the list of recipients that will be used in your merge. Use the options below to add to or change your list. Use the checkboxes to add or remove recipients from the merge. When your list is ready, click OK.

Data Source	☑	Last Name	First Name	Title	Company Name	Addres
List of invitees to t...	☑	Dutt	Sanjay	Mr		Mumba
List of invitees to t...	☑	Gandhi	Sonia	Mrs		Delhi
List of invitees to t...	☑	Johar	Karan	Mr		Mumba
List of invitees to t...	☑	Ghosh	Rituparno	Mr		Kolkatt
List of invitees to t...	☑		Shah Rukh Khan	Mr		Mumba

Data Source

List of invitees to the wedding.

Refine recipient list

Sort...

Filter...

Dear Mr. «First_Name» «Last_Name»

«Address_Line_1»

Your are requested to attend the marriage of my son, Abhishek with Aishwarya on 20th of April, 2007. The ceremonies will start at 8 PM. You are requested to be present in time.

No gifts please. Your mere presence would be sufficient.

Yours truly,

Amitabh Bachchan

On behalf of the Bachchan family

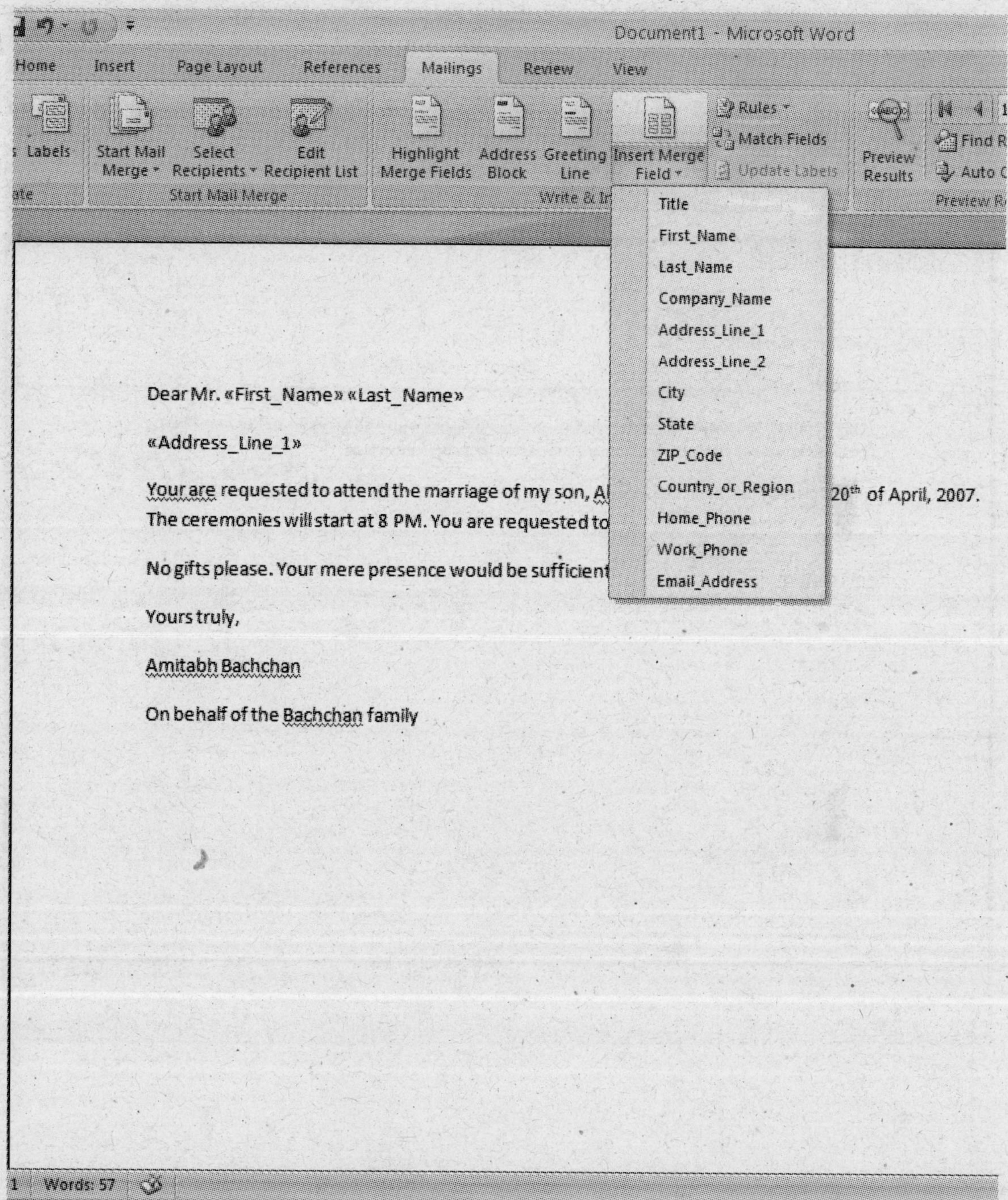

Document1 - Microsoft Word
Home
Insert
Page Layout
References
Mailings
Review
View
Labels
Start Mail Merge
Select Recipients
Edit Recipient List
Start Mail Merge
Highlight Merge Fields
Address Block
Greeting Line
Insert Merge Field
Rules
Match Fields
Update Labels
Preview Results
Title
First_Name
Last_Name
Company_Name
Address_Line_1
Address_Line_2
City
State
ZIP_Code
Country_or_Region
Home_Phone
Work_Phone
Email_Address
Dear Mr. «First_Name» «Last_Name»
«Address_Line_1»
Your are requested to attend the marriage of my son, Al 20th of April, 2007.
The ceremonies will start at 8 PM. You are requested to
No gifts please. Your mere presence would be sufficient
Yours truly,
Amitabh Bachchan
On behalf of the Bachchan family
Words: 57

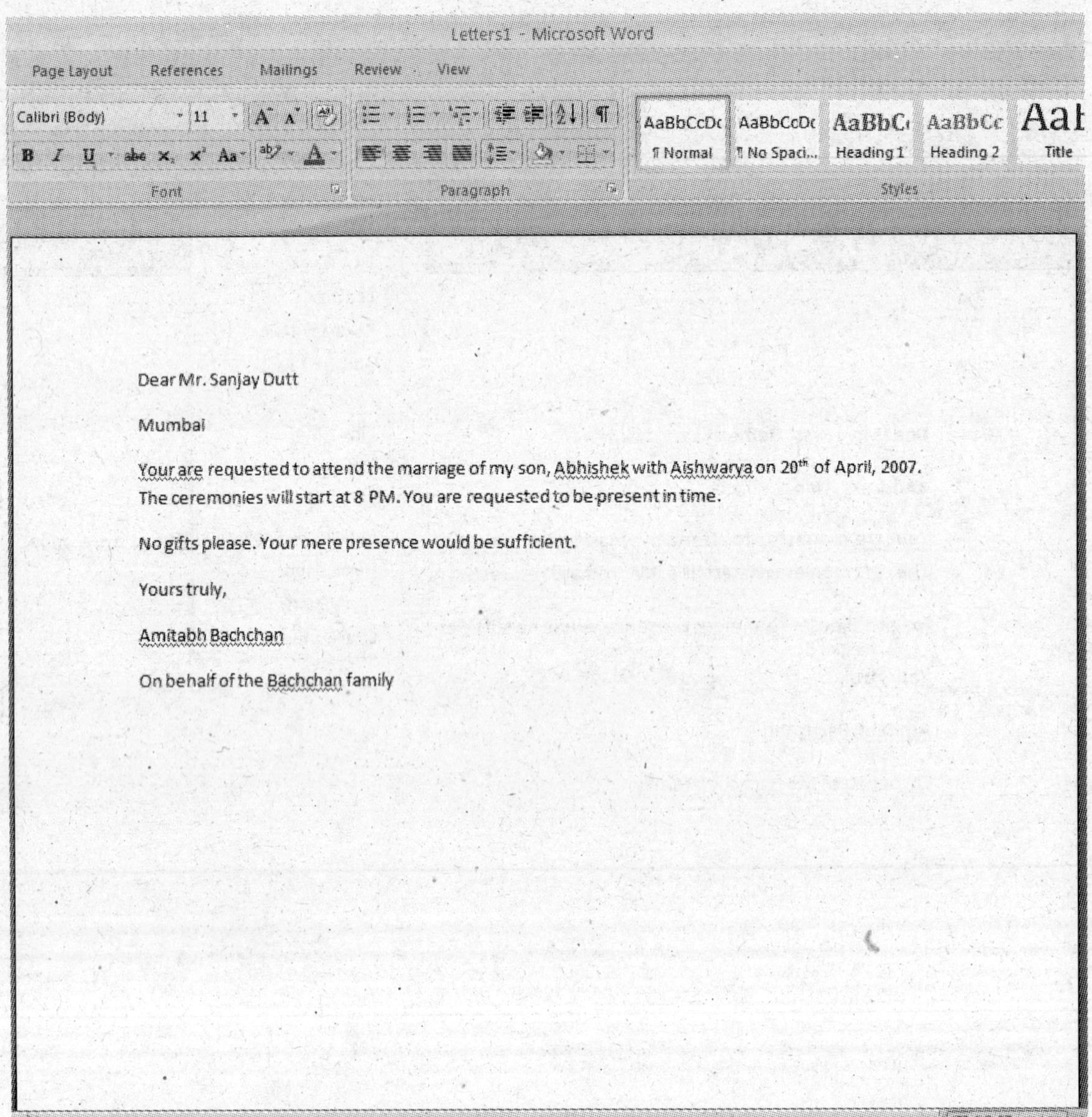
Letters1 - Microsoft Word

Page Layout References Mailings Review View

Calibri (Body) 11

AaBbCcDc ¶ Normal | AaBbCcDc ¶ No Spaci... | AaBbC Heading 1 | AaBbCc Heading 2 | AaB Title

Font | Paragraph | Styles

Dear Mr. Sanjay Dutt

Mumbai

Your are requested to attend the marriage of my son, Abhishek with Aishwarya on 20th of April, 2007. The ceremonies will start at 8 PM. You are requested to be present in time.

No gifts please. Your mere presence would be sufficient.

Yours truly,

Amitabh Bachchan

On behalf of the Bachchan family

3 Introduction to Microsoft Excel 2007

Understanding Spreadsheets

Before we go into understanding the various commands of Excel, let us first understand the working of a spreadsheet. A spreadsheet as the name suggests is a sheet which is spread in such a way that it divides itself into the various horizontal rows and vertical columns. Rows are numbered from 1 onwards and Columns are numbered from A onwards. Graphically they can be represented as:

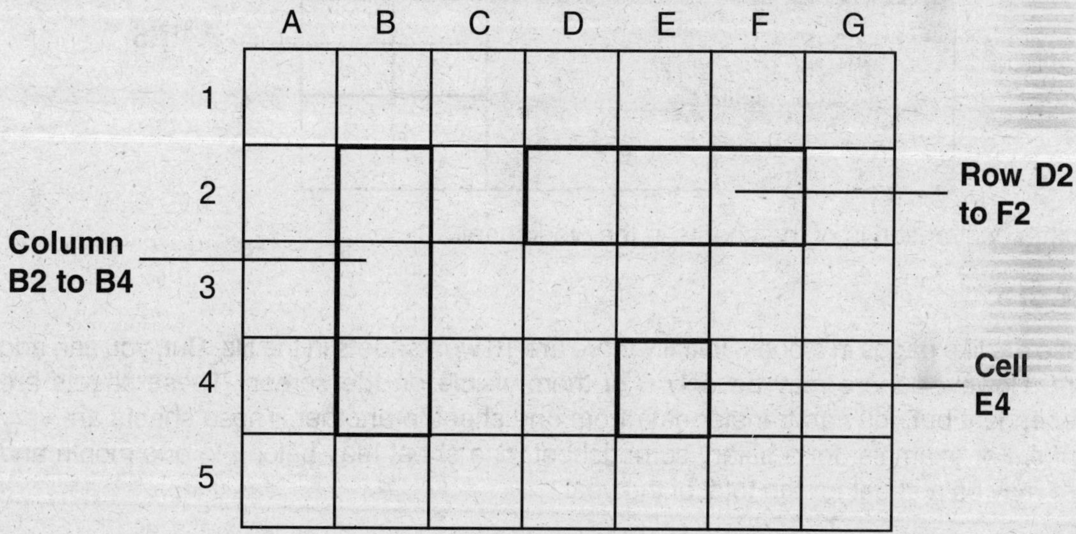

When we take this to the computer and see it electronically using our software Excel, this becomes Electronic Spreadsheet, also called Worksheet. The main features of the worksheets are:

Rows These are the horizontal cells which can contain any information.

Columns These are vertical cells which can also contain information.

Cell It is the interaction of a row with a column. Each cell is identified with its position.

Naming Conventions

It is not that I have named rows from 1 onwards and columns A onwards on my own but they are so numbered by the software itself. These are the standard way of expressing these columns and rows.

If we have to name a large number of cell or columns, for that too we have the convention which asks us to call them with starting cell address and last cell address with colon in between. For example, see the following addressed cells, shown below.

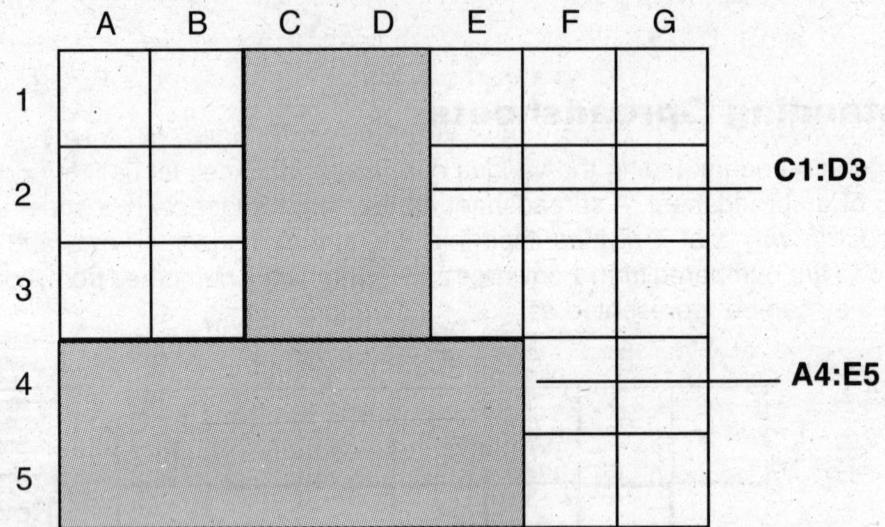

Another convention is of the sheets in the worksheet.

Sheets

These are like pages in a book. Initially there are 16 worksheets in the file. But, you can add more. However, there may be only 6 of them visible on the screen. These sheets are independent but you can transfer data from one sheet to another. These sheets are very helpful. For example, for a salary spreadsheet, one sheet may belong to one month and there may be a sheet for the total of the year.

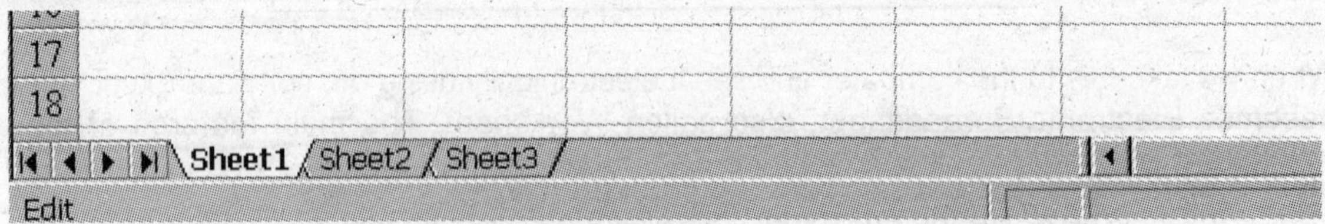

To understand the software better, let us create a worksheet in Excel 2007 and apply the various options/commands on it to see the working of the software. This will give you an idea about creating a workshett and applying the commands.

Creating a Worksheet in Excel 2007

We have learnt quite a number of commands and naturally would like to use them in a worksheet. So let us create a worksheet and use these commands side-by-side to see how they work out. Supposing we have the financial highlights of a company as given below:

Year	Total Income (A)	Interest Paid (B)	Profit (C)	Tax (D)	Profit After Tax (E)
1999	4,500	To be	To be	To be	To be
2000	5,500	Calculated	Calculated	Calculated	Calculated
2001	7,000	as 15%	as Income	as 12% of	as Profit
2002	8,000	of the	minus	the Profit	minus Tax
2003	9,000	Total	Interest		(C) - (D)
2004	12,000	Income	(A) - (B)		
2005	15,000				
2006	20,000				

As you can see that there are quite a number of fields which have to be calculated. This will act as a good exercise for you to do. Let us start from the very beginning, i.e., start the software Microsoft Excel 2003. You will end up with a blank worksheet, ready for you to take action, with the first cell **A1**, totally at your command to do something, as shown in the figure below.

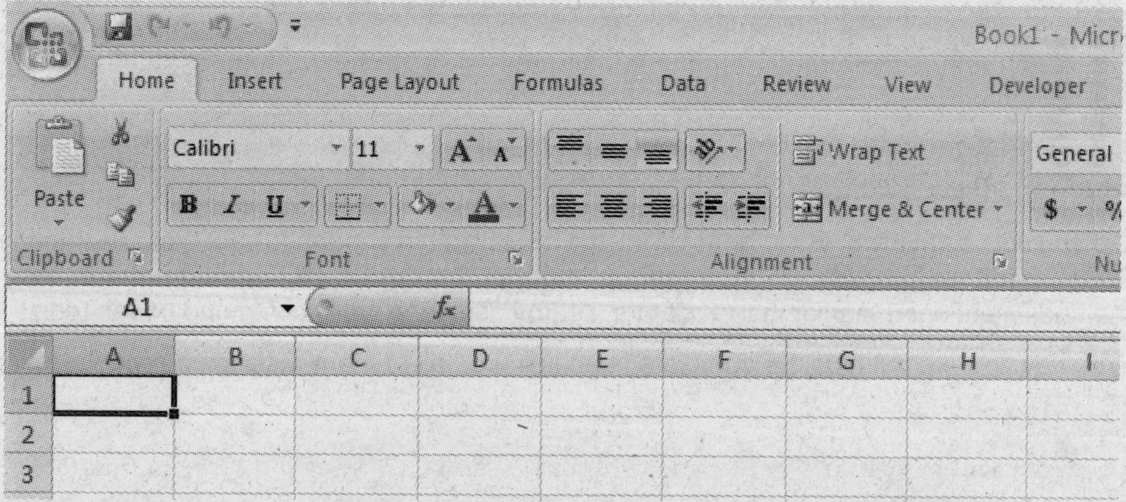

So what we have to do here. We have to type "Year". So just type the word Year and press **Enter**. You will see the word being shown in the formula bar too. This will also take you to the cell **A2**. But, for typing the next heading, you have to go to the cell **B1**. So use the arrow keys right and up to reach **B1**.

Next we have to type "Total Income". (Please note that for the sake of convenience I had shown this heading in 2 lines, but, if permitted we will type it in one line. Also (A), (B), etc., in the table are just symbolic and are not to be typed).

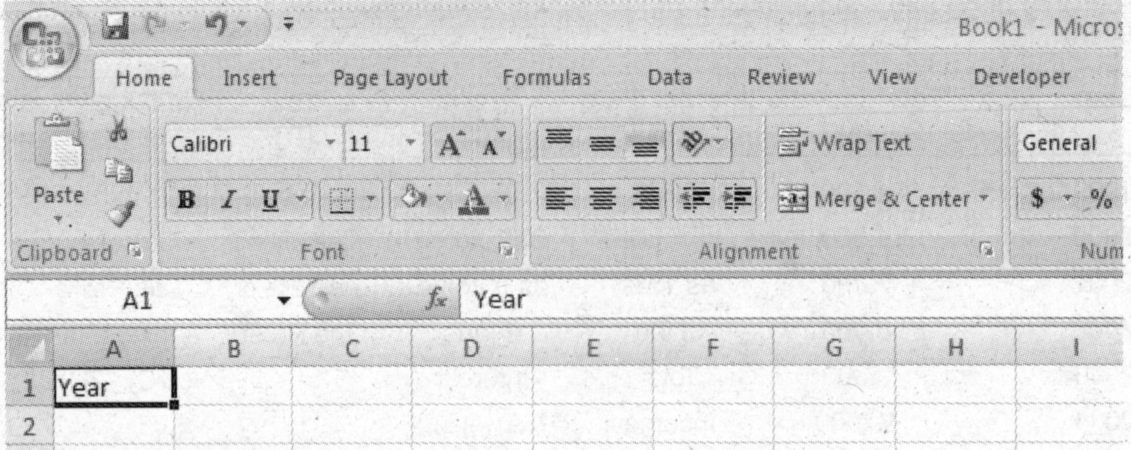

So for type the next heading, "Total Income" in the cell **B1**, as shown next.

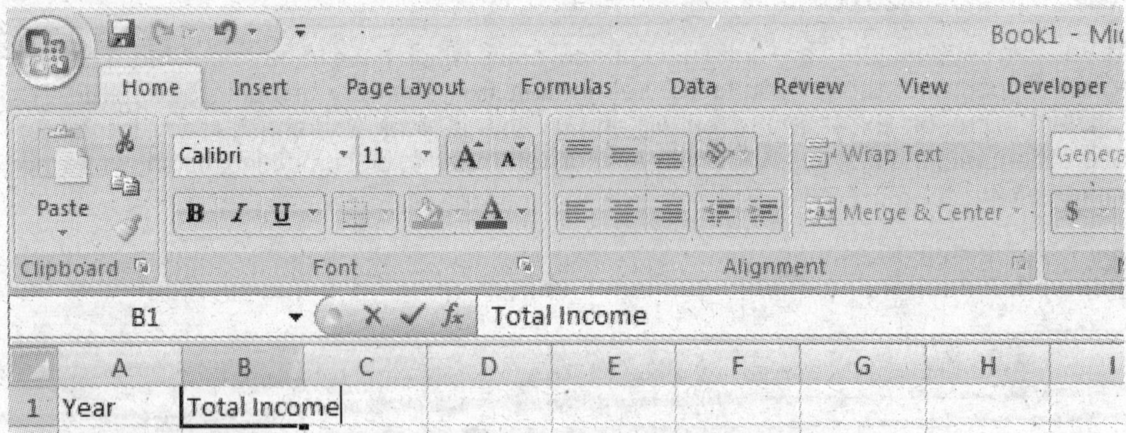

Did you notice anything wrong here? Well, the cell is not big enough to carry your heading. So what will we do? We will increase the width of the column **B**, by using one of the methods mentioned earlier in the chapter, i.e., by using the Cells command under Tools.

This way now we will type the complete headings, i.e., all of them, as shown next.

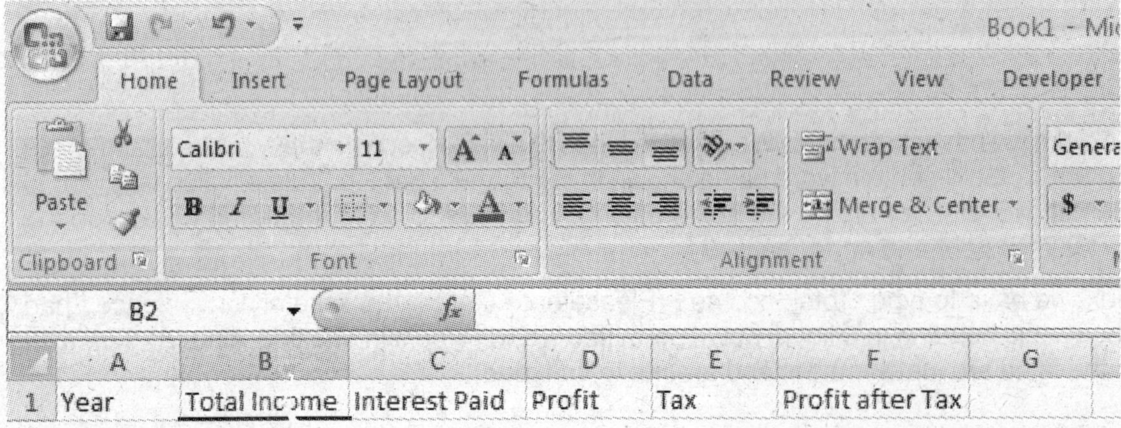

But, since these are headings, and are to be highlighted. We will make them **Bold** and put them in the centre of the cells. This way they will look good.

Highlight all the cells by just clicking at cell **A1** and then while pressing **Shift** key click mouse in the cell **F1**, the whole row gets highlighted.

Now click at B in the formatting bar to make the whole text as Bold.

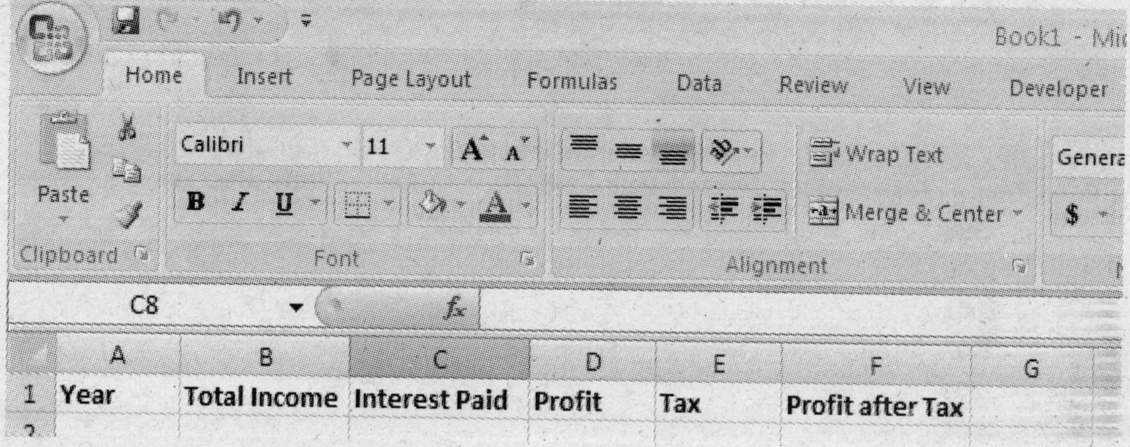

With the text in the cells remaining highlighted, click at [icon] in the alignment panel of Home menu. This will make the text in the cells centralized in all the cells. This is shown in the figure shown next.

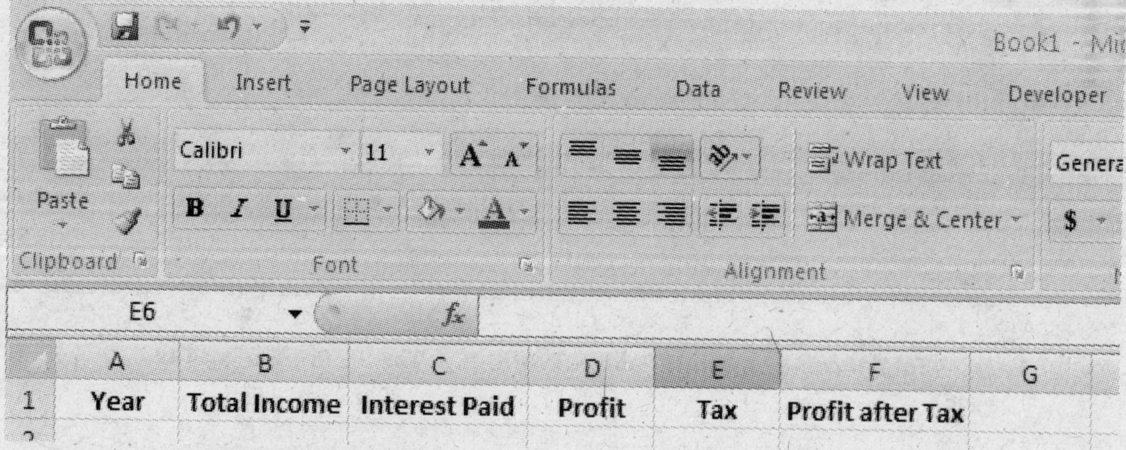

So now we have the headings ready. It was not very difficult, was it? Now all we have is the numeric data. Let us type them too. First of all we will type the various years.

By using the arrow keys, reach the cell **A2**. This is here that we have to type the first year, i.e., **1992**. Type it and press **Enter** to see the data getting aligned to the right. Remember, Excel aligns the numeric data to the right as a default. By pressing **Enter** you must have reached **A3** and this is where you wanted to be for typing the next year, i.e., **1993**.

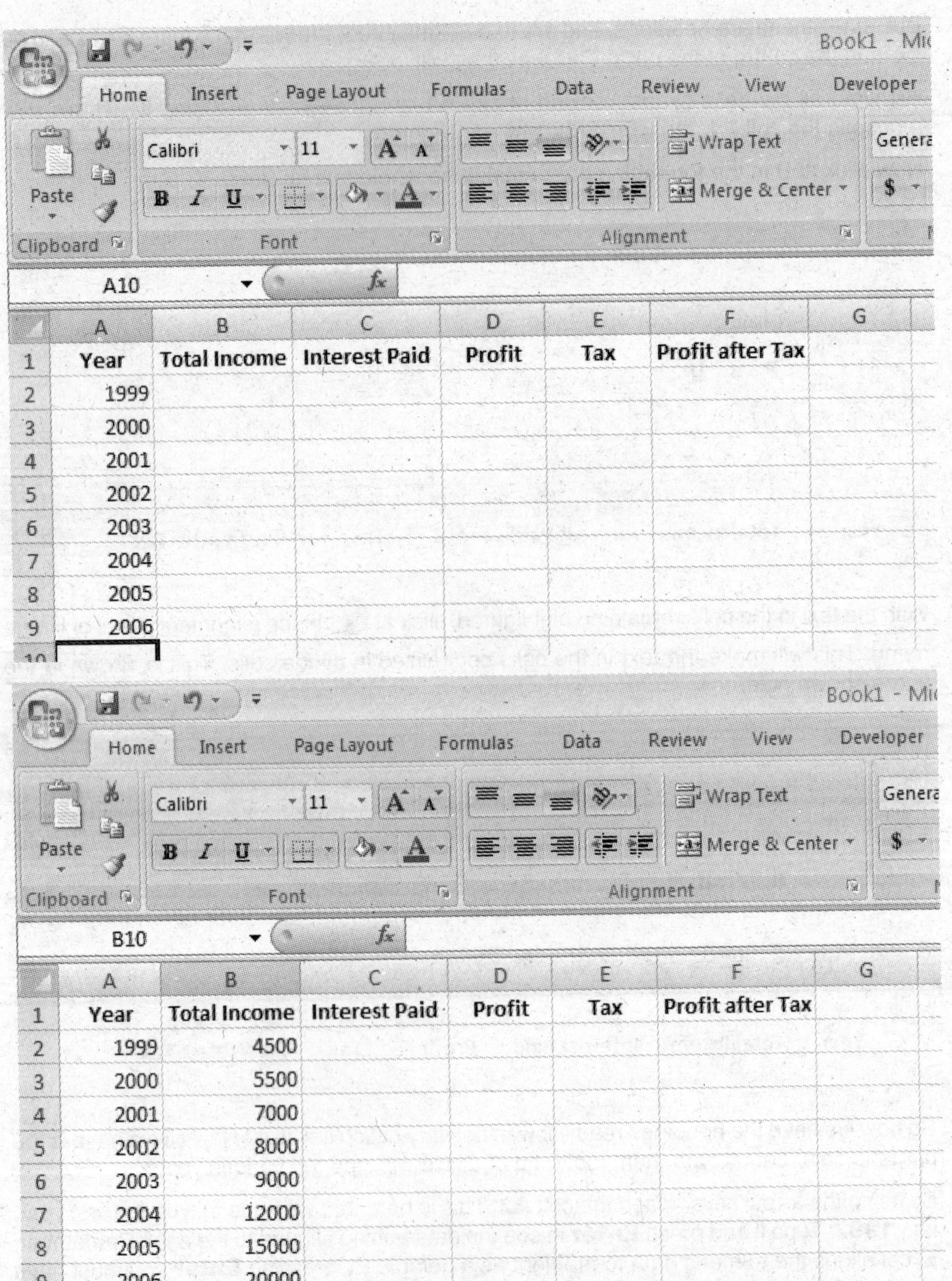
Book1 - Mi
Home
Insert
Page Layout
Formulas
Data
Review
View
Developer
Paste
Clipboard
Calibri
11
Font
Wrap Text
Merge & Center
Alignment
Genera
A10
Year
Total Income
Interest Paid
Profit
Tax
Profit after Tax
1999
2000
2001
2002
2003
2004
2005
2006
Book1 - Mi
Home
Insert
Page Layout
Formulas
Data
Review
View
Developer
Paste
Clipboard
Calibri
11
Font
Wrap Text
Merge & Center
Alignment
Genera
B10
Year
Total Income
Interest Paid
Profit
Tax
Profit after Tax
1999 4500
2000 5500
2001 7000
2002 8000
2003 9000
2004 12000
2005 15000
2006 20000

So now type one year and press **Enter** to reach the next cell for typing the next year, till you reach the last year, i.e., **1999**. At this stage your worksheet will look like the one shown on the next page. Next step is also easy. You have to just type the numbers in the cells **B2** to **B9**. All these figures are available with you. Just type one figure and press **Enter** to reach the next cell and so on till you reach the last cell in the column. After doing this your worksheet will look like the one shown next.

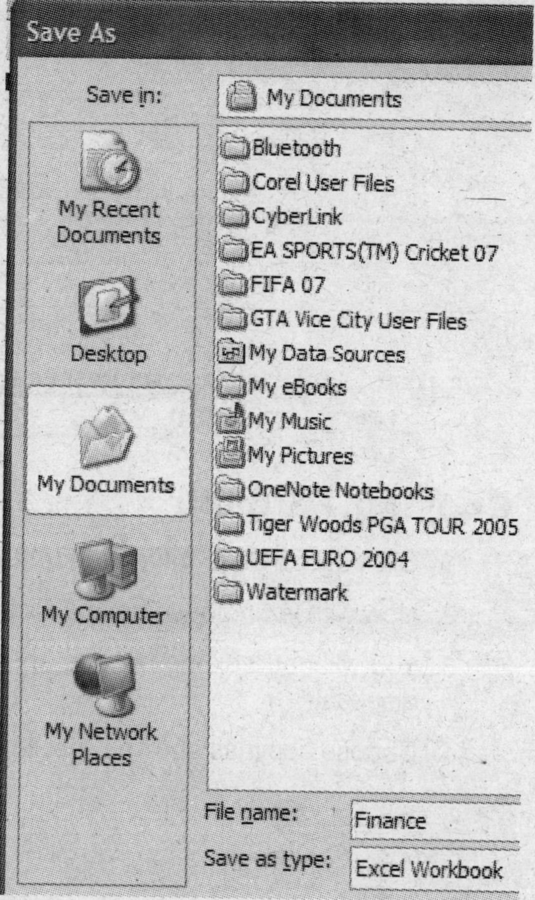

It would not be a bad idea to save this worksheet at this stage. For god forbid, if something happens, like power cut or so. So just press **Ctrl+S** to give the save command, as you would give in any other software. Now all you have to do it to give it a name and decide where you want to save this worksheet. Let us give the name **Finance** to it.

Now we come to the interesting part of this worksheet. So far we have typed whatever was available. Now we have to generate the figures. The column **C** is of Interest Paid which is to be calculated by using the formula.

$$\text{Interest Paid} = \frac{\text{Total Income} \times 15}{100}$$

Transformed to the computer language it will become:

Interest Paid = (Total Income x 15)/100

If we put this in Cell **C2**, it will become:

C2 = SUM(B2*15/100)

Try putting this in the cell **C2** and see the result. It will be as shown below. It has given a figure of 675. Calculate the amount manually to see whether the result is Ok or not. It is correct, isn't it? Now we have to apply this formula to all the cells from **C3** to **C9**. Do you have to put the formula for each cell or there is a method in Excel which allows you to copy the formula in each of the cell.

Well, fortunately there is. So this is how you will do it.

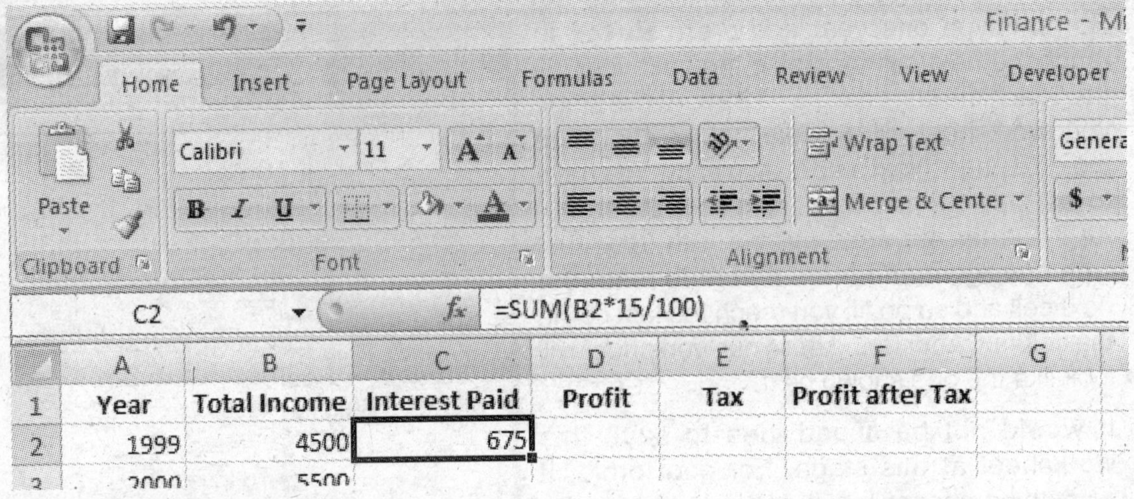

Copying Formula

1. Click at cell C2 to have the formula displayed in the formula bar.
2. Now with your mouse having clicked at cell C2, press the right button of the mouse.
3. You will get a dialog box, as shown below, which has various commands at your disposal.
4. Choose copy, as shown here, to copy the formula.

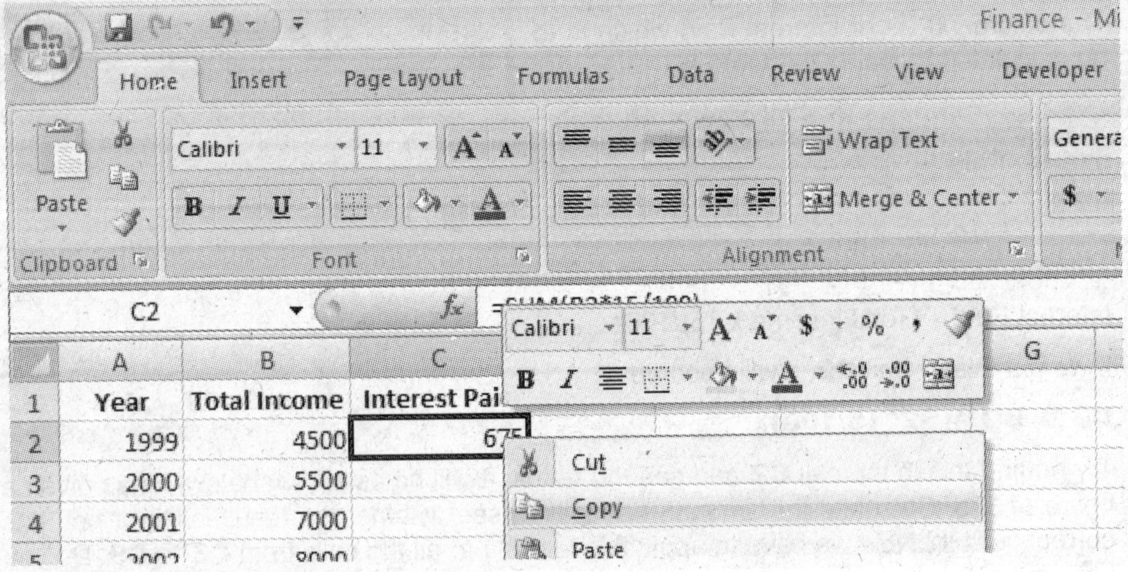

5. Next step now is to paste the formula in their respective cells.
6. Now click at cell C3 with the mouse (left button).
7. Click the right button again to get the dialog box.

8. This time click at Paste instead, as shown next.

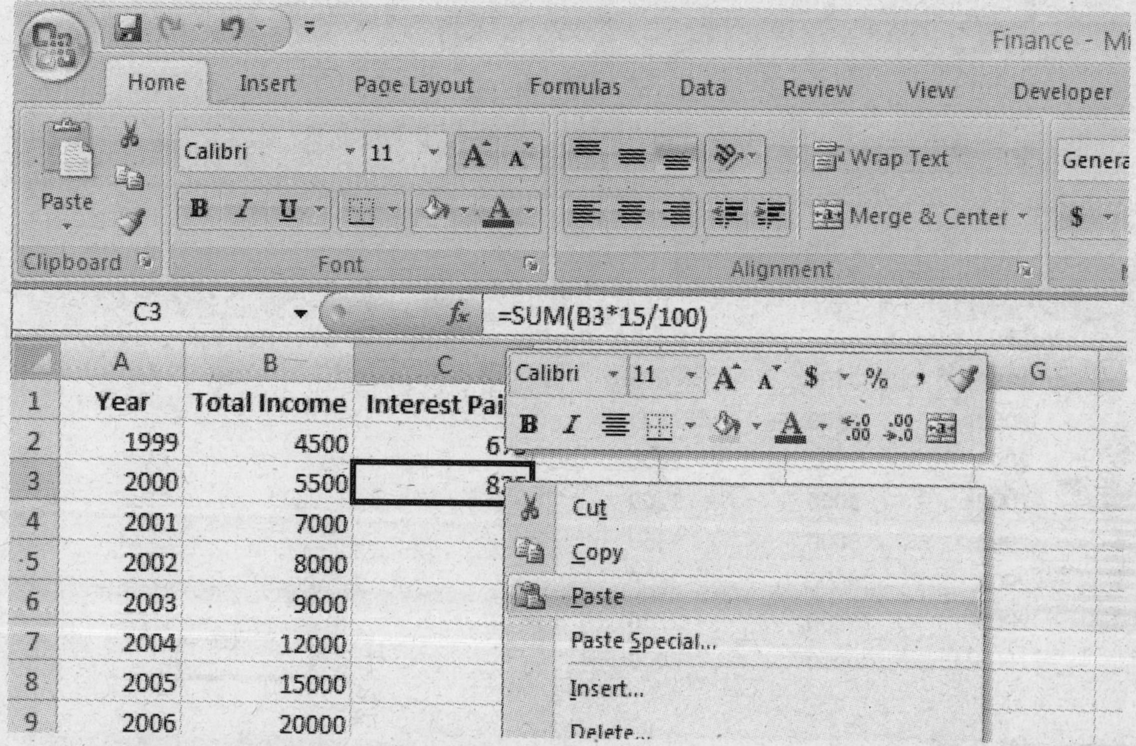

9. Immediately you will get the figure in cell C3.

   This calculation has been based on B3 (see the formula bar) and not B2 which had been copied in our formula. Is it not great? Excel has changed the cell address for you. This is called relative addressing and is a very useful feature of Excel.

10. Similar pasting in the cells from C4 to C9 can also be done.

11. Once done your worksheet should look like the one shown next.

Remember

1. You can take out the dotted lines blinking around the cell C2 by pressing the Esc key.

One look at the worksheet and you will notice that something is wrong. Some figures have no decimals and some have one. This does not look good. So what will you do? You will make them uniform. This is how:

1. Highlight all the cells from C2 to C9.
2. From the Home menu, click at General in Number panel.
3. Choose the category of Number to make all the cell data into 2 digits of numbers.
4. All your cells now have 2 places of decimals, as shown below.

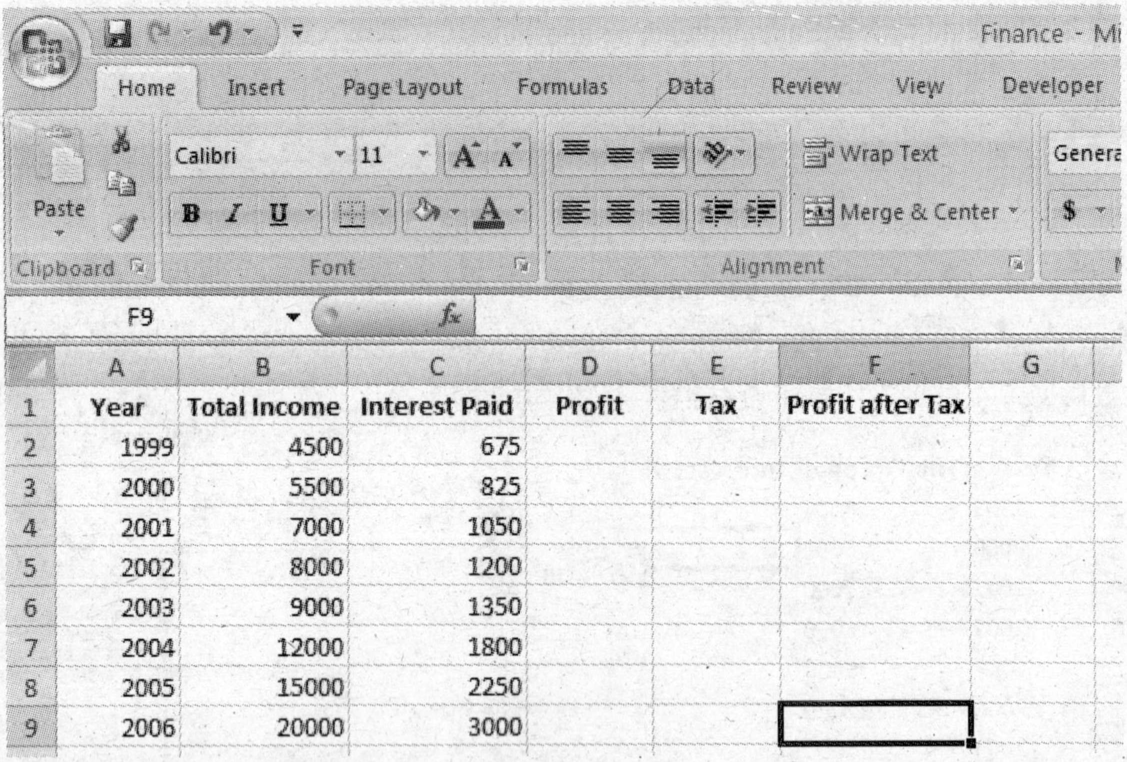

Finance - Mi

Home | Insert | Page Layout | Formulas | Data | Review | View | Developer

F9 | f_x

	A	B	C	D	E	F	G
1	Year	Total Income	Interest Paid	Profit	Tax	Profit after Tax	
2	1999	4500	675				
3	2000	5500	825				
4	2001	7000	1050				
5	2002	8000	1200				
6	2003	9000	1350				
7	2004	12000	1800				
8	2005	15000	2250				
9	2006	20000	3000				

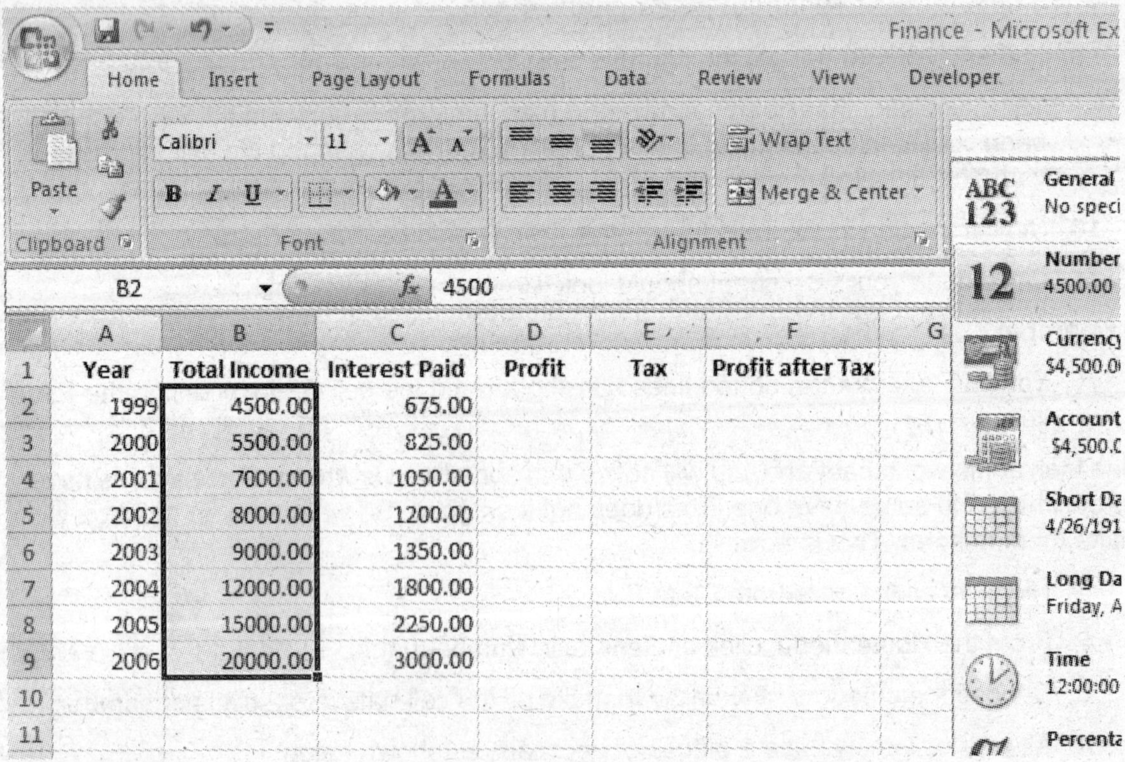

Finance - Microsoft Ex

Home | Insert | Page Layout | Formulas | Data | Review | View | Developer

B2 | f_x | 4500

	A	B	C	D	E	F	G
1	Year	Total Income	Interest Paid	Profit	Tax	Profit after Tax	
2	1999	4500.00	675.00				
3	2000	5500.00	825.00				
4	2001	7000.00	1050.00				
5	2002	8000.00	1200.00				
6	2003	9000.00	1350.00				
7	2004	12000.00	1800.00				
8	2005	15000.00	2250.00				
9	2006	20000.00	3000.00				
10							
11							

General — No speci
Number — 4500.00
Currency — $4,500.0
Account — $4,500.0
Short Da — 4/26/191
Long Da — Friday, A
Time — 12:00:00
Percenta

Now that we have all the figures of Column **C** ready, we can proceed ahead to the next column, i.e., **D**. This column has "Profit", which is nothing but the difference of "Income" and "Interest". So let us calculate that.

Click at cell **D2** and put the formula

=SUM(B2 – C2)

This will give you the figure for **D2**. Calculate it manually to make sure that the formula is right.

Now, as we had done in the earlier case of Interest Paid, we will copy the formula and paste it in other cell, as shown below. One by one you would be able to calculate all the figures of Profit and would be able to fill up the whole column **D**. After you have done so, your worksheet would look like the one shown below. These figures have been corrected to 2 places of decimals as was done in the earlier case.

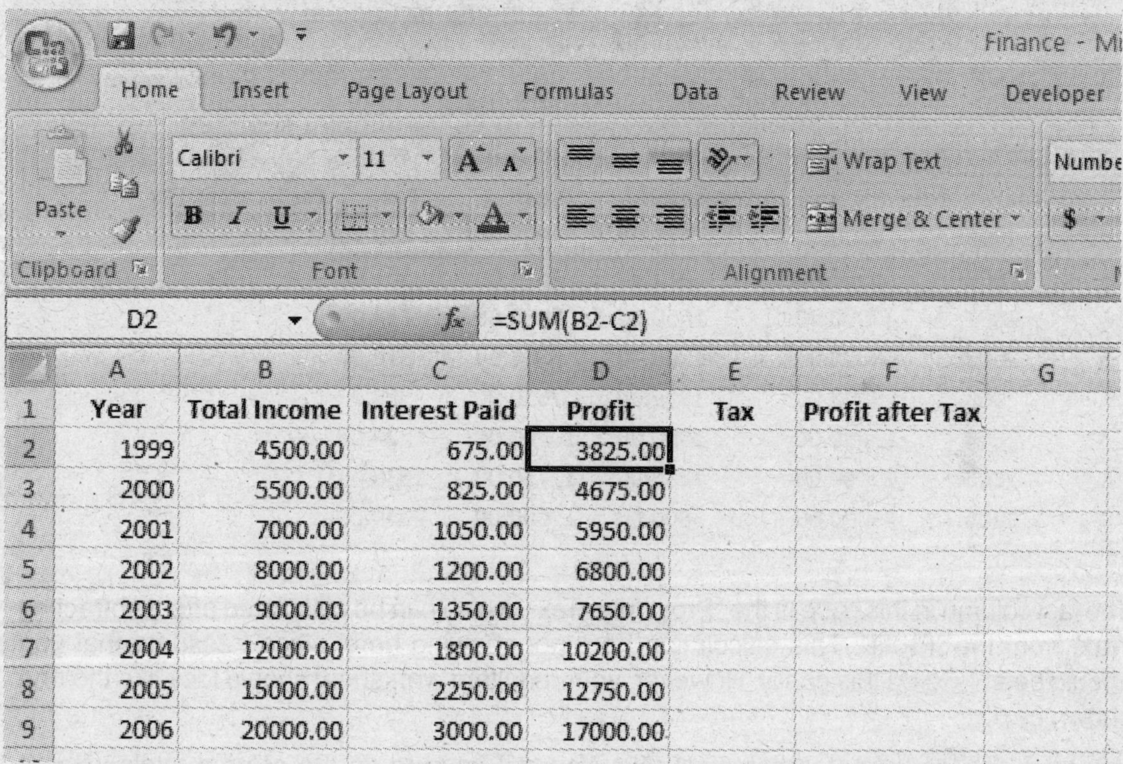

	A	B	C	D	E	F	G
1	Year	Total Income	Interest Paid	Profit	Tax	Profit after Tax	
2	1999	4500.00	675.00	3825.00			
3	2000	5500.00	825.00	4675.00			
4	2001	7000.00	1050.00	5950.00			
5	2002	8000.00	1200.00	6800.00			
6	2003	9000.00	1350.00	7650.00			
7	2004	12000.00	1800.00	10200.00			
8	2005	15000.00	2250.00	12750.00			
9	2006	20000.00	3000.00	17000.00			

Next in line is the column called Tax. This is as said earlier, 12% of the Profit. So this can be calculated as below:

$$\text{Tax} = \frac{\text{Profit} \times 12}{100}$$

Transformed to the computer language it will become:

Tax= (Profit x 12)/100

If we put this in Cell **E2**, it will become:

E2 = SUM(D2*12/100)

Let us apply this formula in **E2** and see what happens. It gives you the result as 459. Copying this formula to the other cells, i.e., from **E3** to **E9**, you can fill up the whole column and make the worksheet look like the one shown next.

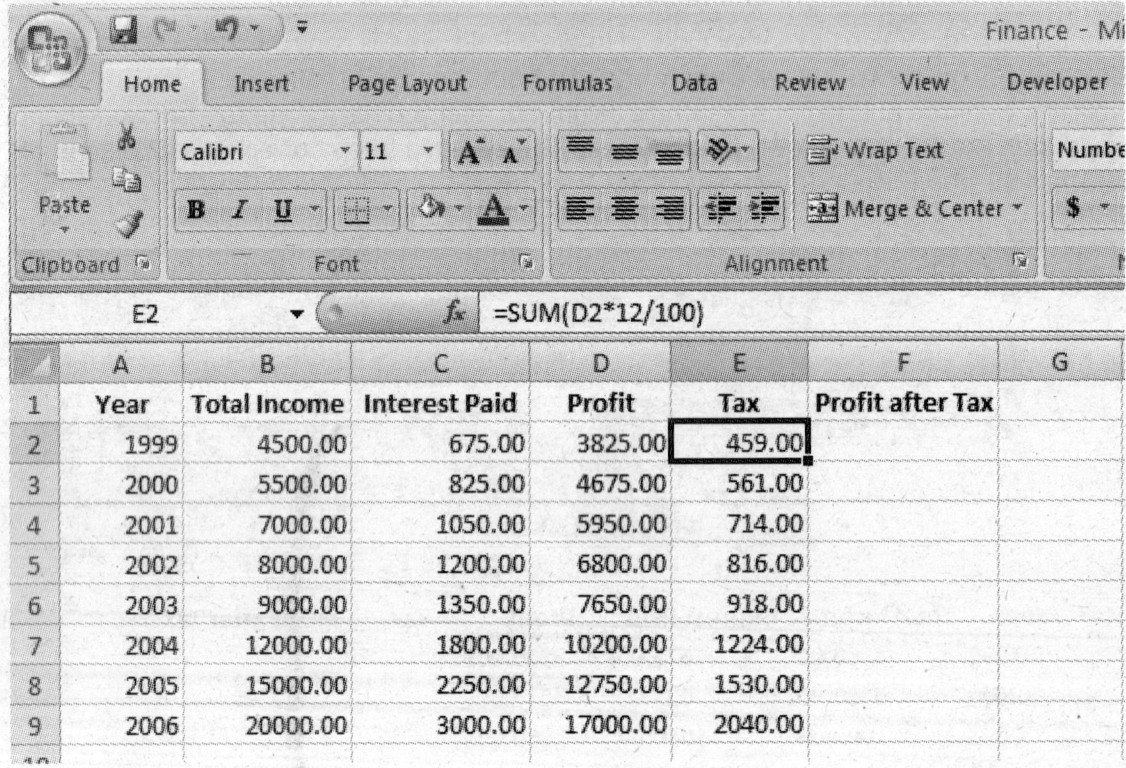

	A	B	C	D	E	F	G
1	Year	Total Income	Interest Paid	Profit	Tax	Profit after Tax	
2	1999	4500.00	675.00	3825.00	459.00		
3	2000	5500.00	825.00	4675.00	561.00		
4	2001	7000.00	1050.00	5950.00	714.00		
5	2002	8000.00	1200.00	6800.00	816.00		
6	2003	9000.00	1350.00	7650.00	918.00		
7	2004	12000.00	1800.00	10200.00	1224.00		
8	2005	15000.00	2250.00	12750.00	1530.00		
9	2006	20000.00	3000.00	17000.00	2040.00		

The last column in this case is the "Profit After Tax", which can be calculated after subtracting "Tax" from the "Profit". This calculation I am not showing here, since I assume that you should be able to do this easily. However, your resultant worksheet should look like the one shown next.

You think the worksheet is complete. No. You still have to do the column totals without which the whole worksheet looks incomplete.

For this follow the following steps.

1. Click at cell B10 to get the total of figures from B2 to B9.
2. Now click at Σ symbol in the Home menu.
3. It will search for the numeric cells above and put the formula for the same and highlight the cells it has selected.

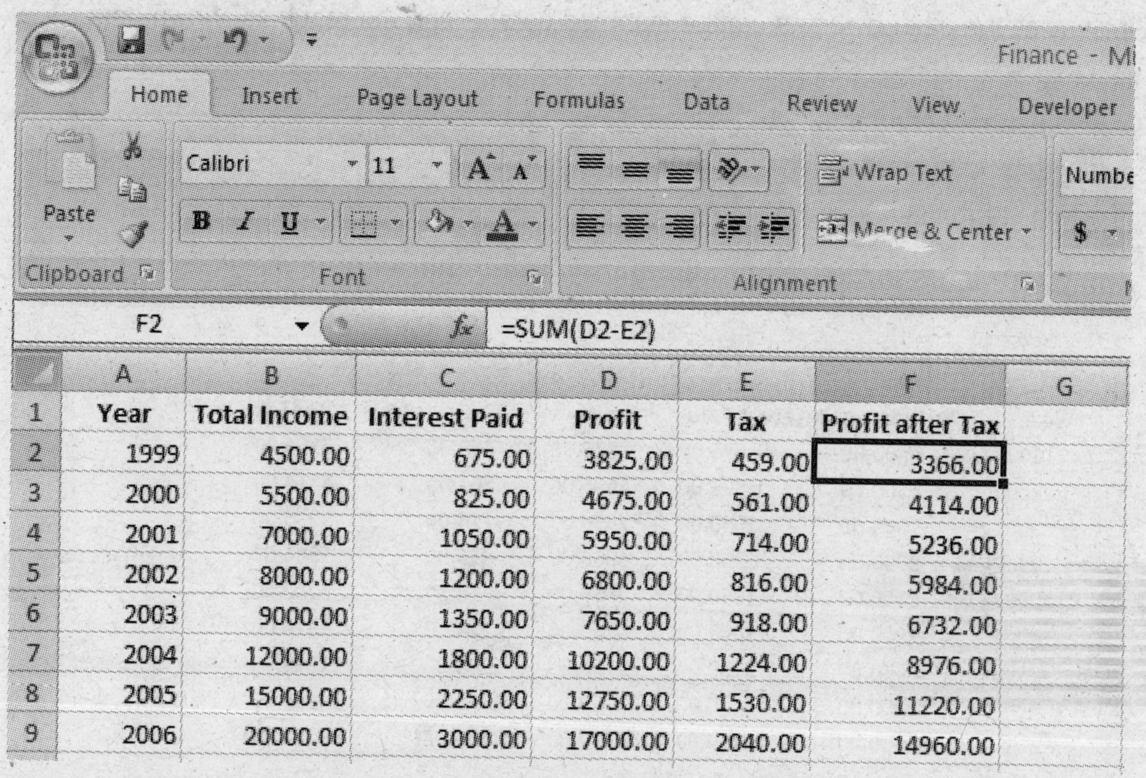

F2 | =SUM(D2-E2)

	A	B	C	D	E	F
1	Year	Total Income	Interest Paid	Profit	Tax	Profit after Tax
2	1999	4500.00	675.00	3825.00	459.00	3366.00
3	2000	5500.00	825.00	4675.00	561.00	4114.00
4	2001	7000.00	1050.00	5950.00	714.00	5236.00
5	2002	8000.00	1200.00	6800.00	816.00	5984.00
6	2003	9000.00	1350.00	7650.00	918.00	6732.00
7	2004	12000.00	1800.00	10200.00	1224.00	8976.00
8	2005	15000.00	2250.00	12750.00	1530.00	11220.00
9	2006	20000.00	3000.00	17000.00	2040.00	14960.00

4. It will wait for your Ok in the form of Enter to put the result.
5. Press Enter to get the total in the cell B10, as shown below.

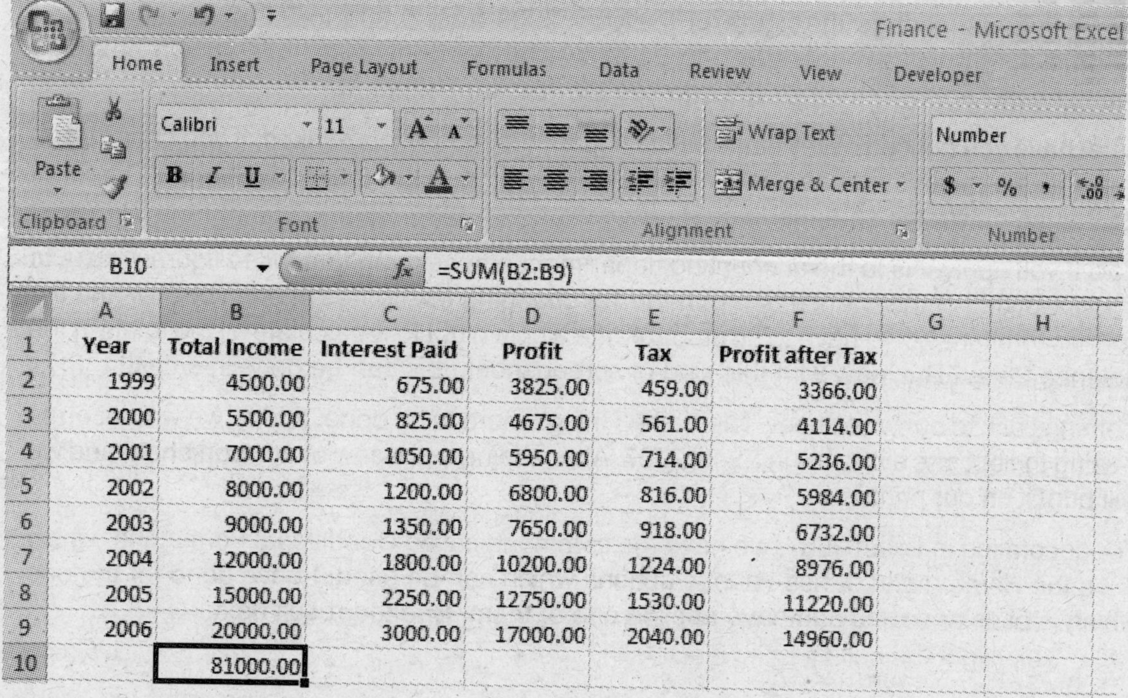

B10 | =SUM(B2:B9)

	A	B	C	D	E	F
1	Year	Total Income	Interest Paid	Profit	Tax	Profit after Tax
2	1999	4500.00	675.00	3825.00	459.00	3366.00
3	2000	5500.00	825.00	4675.00	561.00	4114.00
4	2001	7000.00	1050.00	5950.00	714.00	5236.00
5	2002	8000.00	1200.00	6800.00	816.00	5984.00
6	2003	9000.00	1350.00	7650.00	918.00	6732.00
7	2004	12000.00	1800.00	10200.00	1224.00	8976.00
8	2005	15000.00	2250.00	12750.00	1530.00	11220.00
9	2006	20000.00	3000.00	17000.00	2040.00	14960.00
10		81000.00				

Similarly all the other columns can be summed up showing the result as shown next.

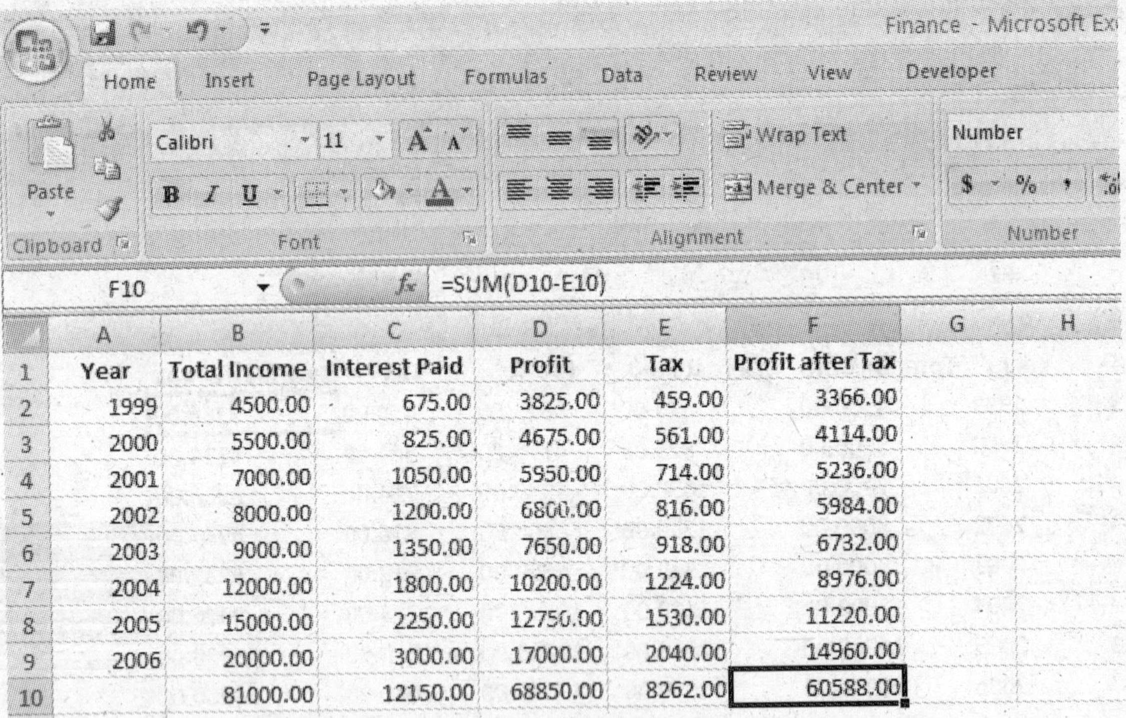

	A	B	C	D	E	F	G	H
1	Year	Total Income	Interest Paid	Profit	Tax	Profit after Tax		
2	1999	4500.00	675.00	3825.00	459.00	3366.00		
3	2000	5500.00	825.00	4675.00	561.00	4114.00		
4	2001	7000.00	1050.00	5950.00	714.00	5236.00		
5	2002	8000.00	1200.00	6800.00	816.00	5984.00		
6	2003	9000.00	1350.00	7650.00	918.00	6732.00		
7	2004	12000.00	1800.00	10200.00	1224.00	8976.00		
8	2005	15000.00	2250.00	12750.00	1530.00	11220.00		
9	2006	20000.00	3000.00	17000.00	2040.00	14960.00		
10		81000.00	12150.00	68850.00	8262.00	60588.00		

Now you can say that your worksheet is complete. But, supposing we want to make any change. This is done delibrately to show you the main advantage of Excel software.

Supposing, we change the figure of the year 2003 from 9,000 to 9,200, which we can assume that it was wrongly given to us or was a typing mistake. It is shown next. Try changing this figure in the cell **B6** and see the resultant effect.

What have you noticed? Well since all the figures are mostly inter-linked, if you change one figure all the relative figures change automatically. This is the main advantage of Excel or for that an electronic spreadsheet.

Now if you apply this to the accounting department and assume that these figures relate to actual working of the finance department. Try changing the figures of one voucher and the poor accountant would have to sit probably the whole night to recalculate all the totals in the Balance Sheet. But, now with this kind of spreadsheet, this can be done in a flash.

Coming back to our worksheet. There are 3 things more to be done. Firstly, we will decorate it using the options available in Excel 2007. After seeing a preview of our worksheet and we will print it on our printer.

For decorating in Excel 2007, we have the command called Conditional Formatting, which is on the Home menu. It has various options which can be used. I have gone for the one which is of color scales and have applied one of them. See the result next.

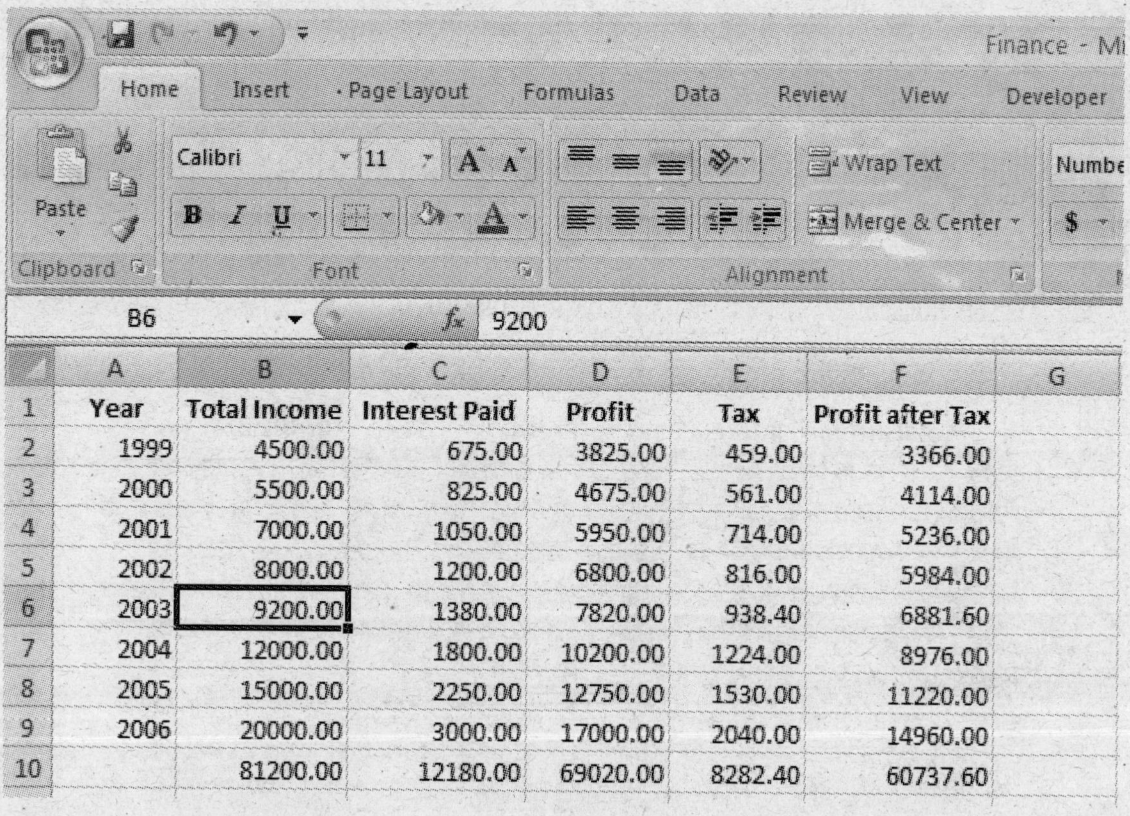

Finance - Mi

Home | Insert | Page Layout | Formulas | Data | Review | View | Developer

Paste | Clipboard | Calibri | 11 | Font | Wrap Text | Merge & Center | Alignment | Number

B6 | f_x 9200

	A	B	C	D	E	F	G
1	Year	Total Income	Interest Paid	Profit	Tax	Profit after Tax	
2	1999	4500.00	675.00	3825.00	459.00	3366.00	
3	2000	5500.00	825.00	4675.00	561.00	4114.00	
4	2001	7000.00	1050.00	5950.00	714.00	5236.00	
5	2002	8000.00	1200.00	6800.00	816.00	5984.00	
6	2003	9200.00	1380.00	7820.00	938.40	6881.60	
7	2004	12000.00	1800.00	10200.00	1224.00	8976.00	
8	2005	15000.00	2250.00	12750.00	1530.00	11220.00	
9	2006	20000.00	3000.00	17000.00	2040.00	14960.00	
10		81200.00	12180.00	69020.00	8282.40	60737.60	

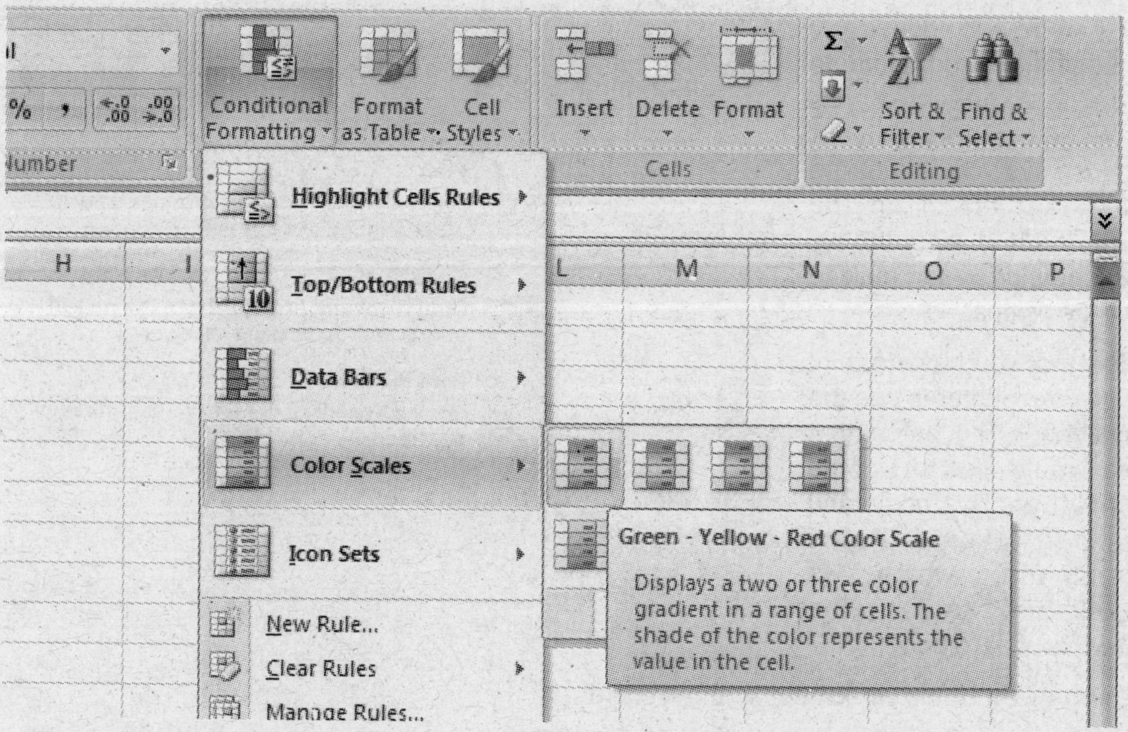

Conditional Formatting | Format as Table | Cell Styles | Insert | Delete | Format | Cells | Sort & Filter | Find & Select | Editing

Highlight Cells Rules

Top/Bottom Rules

Data Bars

Color Scales

Icon Sets

New Rule...

Clear Rules

Manage Rules...

Green - Yellow - Red Color Scale

Displays a two or three color gradient in a range of cells. The shade of the color represents the value in the cell.

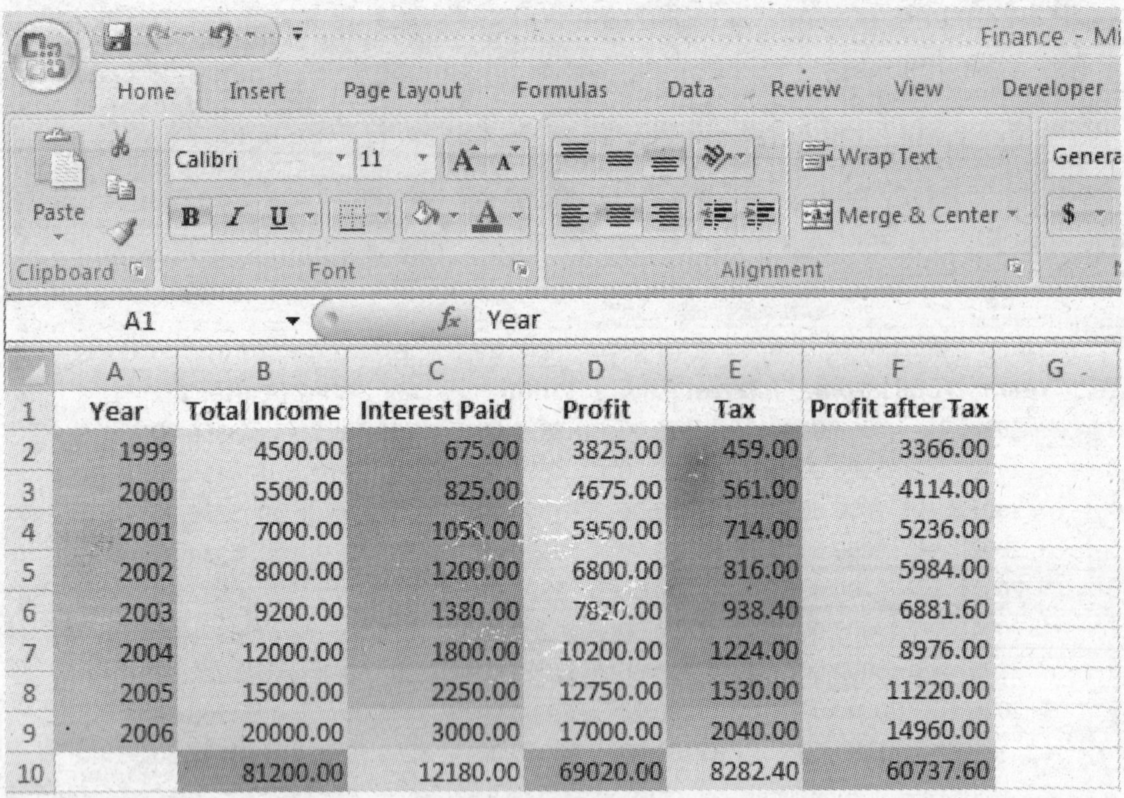

	A	B	C	D	E	F	G
1	Year	Total Income	Interest Paid	Profit	Tax	Profit after Tax	
2	1999	4500.00	675.00	3825.00	459.00	3366.00	
3	2000	5500.00	825.00	4675.00	561.00	4114.00	
4	2001	7000.00	1050.00	5950.00	714.00	5236.00	
5	2002	8000.00	1200.00	6800.00	816.00	5984.00	
6	2003	9200.00	1380.00	7820.00	938.40	6881.60	
7	2004	12000.00	1800.00	10200.00	1224.00	8976.00	
8	2005	15000.00	2250.00	12750.00	1530.00	11220.00	
9	2006	20000.00	3000.00	17000.00	2040.00	14960.00	
10		81200.00	12180.00	69020.00	8282.40	60737.60	

You are free to choose any one of them and decorate your worksheet as you wish. As you move your mouse over the options the resultant effect on the worksheet is also shown, which helps you in making the decisions.

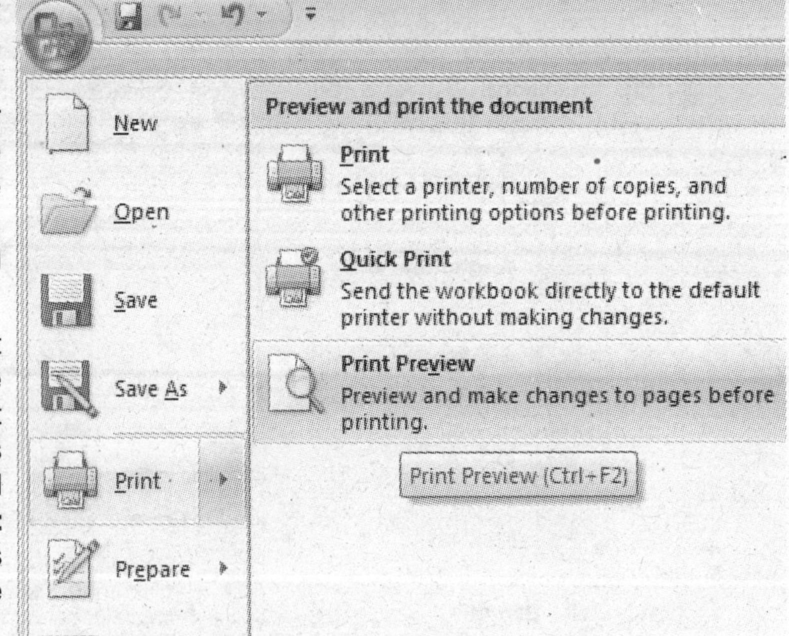

Now that you have to print it on your printer to see the final result. But, before that we would like to see its **Preview**. This command is part of the **Print** command which is available under the **Options button**.

The preview of the worksheet is shown next.

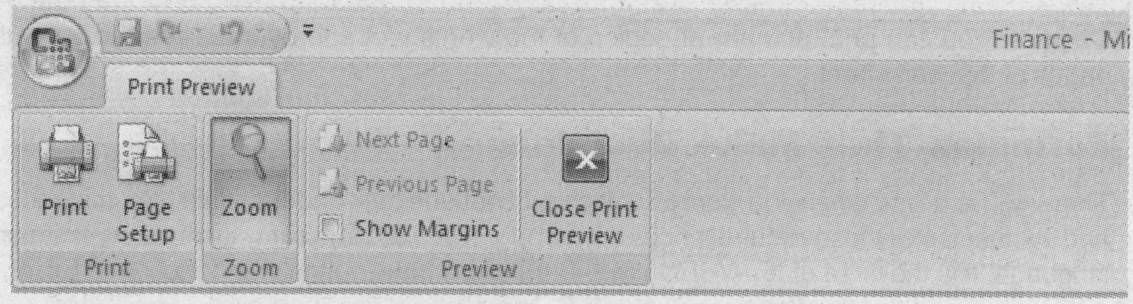

Year	Total Income	Interest Paid	Profit	Tax	Profit after Tax
1999	4500.00	675.00	3825.00	459.00	3366.00
2000	5500.00	825.00	4675.00	561.00	4114.00
2001	7000.00	1050.00	5950.00	714.00	5236.00
2002	8000.00	1200.00	6800.00	816.00	5984.00
2003	9200.00	1380.00	7820.00	938.40	6881.60
2004	12000.00	1800.00	10200.00	1224.00	8976.00
2005	15000.00	2250.00	12750.00	1530.00	11220.00
2006	20000.00	3000.00	17000.00	2040.00	14960.00
	81200.00	12180.00	69020.00	8282.40	60737.60

There are various other options in the print dialog box, shown above, alongwith the print preview of the worksheet.

Printer: You have to specify the various options of your printer. It is usually the printer installed in your Windows.

Print range: You specify whether you want to print the whole file or few selected pages.

Print what: You can choose to print a selected portion of the worksheet, or a full worksheet or even few selected worksheet.

Preview: As said earlier, this gives you the preview of the worksheet which you can see before printing.

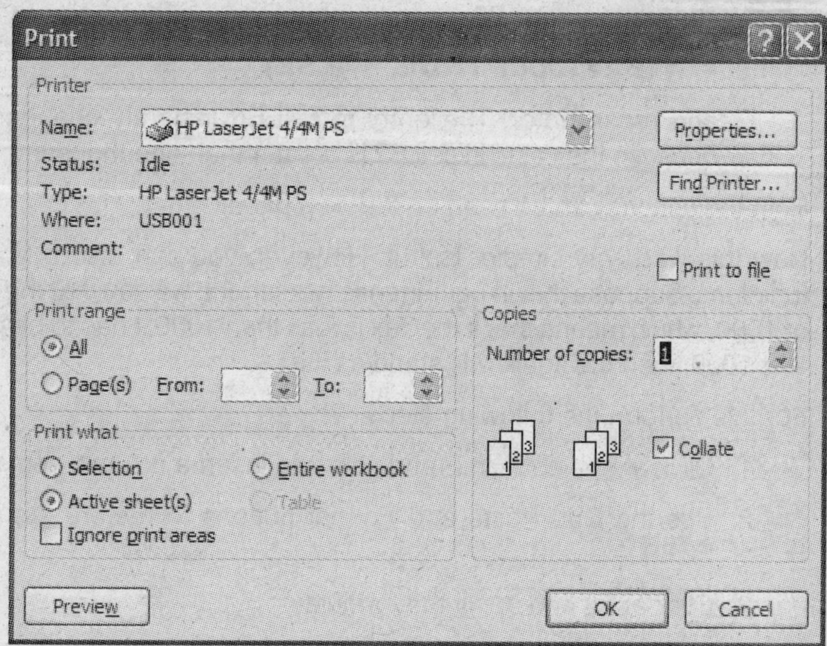

Copies: You can print number of copies of the worksheet and even collate the various pages of the worksheet.

Formulas That Make Decisions

There will be a time when you want Excel to carry out one task under certain circumstances and another task if those circumstances don't apply. If you are familiar with any programming language, it is the case of IF, WHEN or IF, THEN. You have a similar IF function in Excel.

How the IF function works

In its simplest form, the IF function tests the value of a cell and does one thing if the test is positive (**TRUE**) and another if the test is negative (**FALSE**). It requires three arguments: the test data, the action to perform if the test is TRUE and the action to perform if the test is FALSE. You supply the arguments one after the other within the function's parentheses, separating them with commas (no spaces are to be given). The text which you want to appear as it is, i.e., TRUE or FALSE should be given under quotes, reference of cells like **C5**, etc., should be as it is.

Apply this formula in cell **B6** and see the result:

1. Select cell B6, type the following in place of formula and press Enter:

   = IF(B2=0, TRUE, FALSE)

   Excel checks whether the value in cell B2 is zero (the test), and because it isn't zero, it ignores TRUE (the action to perform if the test is TRUE) and displays FALSE (the action to perform if the test is FALSE) in cell B6.

2. Double-click cell B6, change formula to

   = IF(B2>1000, TRUE, FALSE)

   and press Enter. The entry in cell B6 instantly changes from FALSE to TRUE because the value in cell B2 is greater than one thousand; that is, the test is TRUE.

Both the options can be seen on the next page.

Now this was very simple. Isn't it. However, you can also build tests that involve other functions. Suppose that in our Finance worksheet, we say that the Tax has to be a minimum of 1000, which means that if the Tax is less than 1000 it has to be put as 1000 and if it more that 1000, then the figure will stand as it is.

For this perform the following steps.

1. Click at any entry in E and select to insert a column from Insert Menu.
2. Use the Cut, Paste and Format buttons to restore the entries now in E2:E9 to F2:F9.
3. Click at F2 and apply the formula

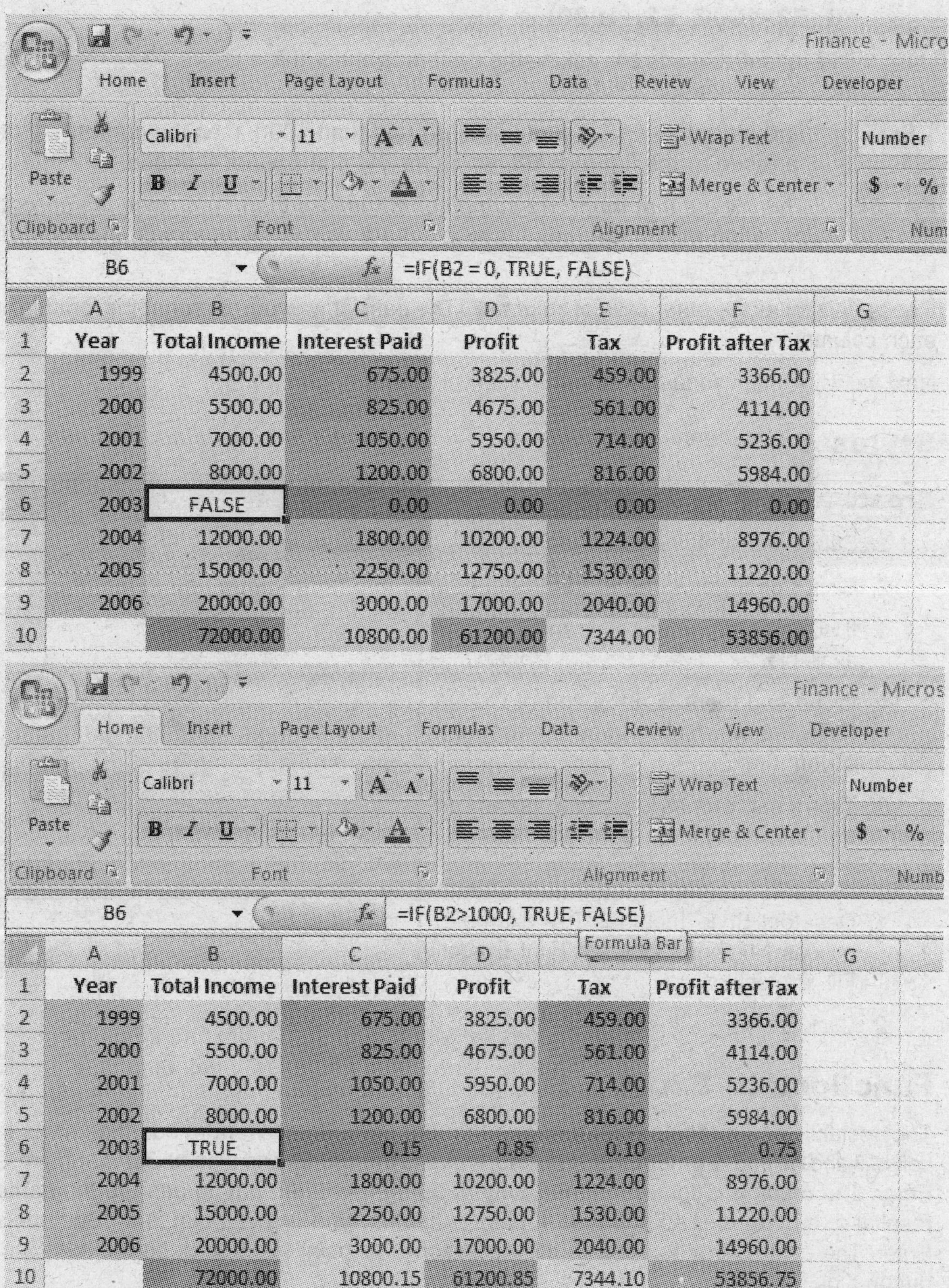

	A	B	C	D	E	F
1	Year	Total Income	Interest Paid	Profit	Tax	Profit after Tax
2	1999	4500.00	675.00	3825.00	459.00	3366.00
3	2000	5500.00	825.00	4675.00	561.00	4114.00
4	2001	7000.00	1050.00	5950.00	714.00	5236.00
5	2002	8000.00	1200.00	6800.00	816.00	5984.00
6	2003	FALSE	0.00	0.00	0.00	0.00
7	2004	12000.00	1800.00	10200.00	1224.00	8976.00
8	2005	15000.00	2250.00	12750.00	1530.00	11220.00
9	2006	20000.00	3000.00	17000.00	2040.00	14960.00
10		72000.00	10800.00	61200.00	7344.00	53856.00

	A	B	C	D	E	F
1	Year	Total Income	Interest Paid	Profit	Tax	Profit after Tax
2	1999	4500.00	675.00	3825.00	459.00	3366.00
3	2000	5500.00	825.00	4675.00	561.00	4114.00
4	2001	7000.00	1050.00	5950.00	714.00	5236.00
5	2002	8000.00	1200.00	6800.00	816.00	5984.00
6	2003	TRUE	0.15	0.85	0.10	0.75
7	2004	12000.00	1800.00	10200.00	1224.00	8976.00
8	2005	15000.00	2250.00	12750.00	1530.00	11220.00
9	2006	20000.00	3000.00	17000.00	2040.00	14960.00
10		72000.00	10800.15	61200.85	7344.10	53856.75

=IF(E2>1000, E2, 1000)

This means that you are asking the system to check if it is above 1000, One of the two possibilities will arise:

TRUE This means that the figure in cell is more than 1000, then the column will be replaced by the figure in **E2**, which means that it is not changed.

FALSE This means that the figure in the cell **E2** is less than 1000, then the second condition will be met, i.e., figure in cell **F2** will be replaced with the figure of 1000.

Repeat this for all the other cells of column **F**. The easiest way out to repeat the formula in each column.

Next we work with various commands of Excel 2007.

Styles

Create a Style by Example

1. Select cell containing desired formats
2. Click Cell Styles in the Home Panel.
3. It will show the various style sheet options available.
4. In the end there is an option of Create New Style which allows you to create one of your own.
3. Type a name for style in Style Name: The style's formats in Style includes box.

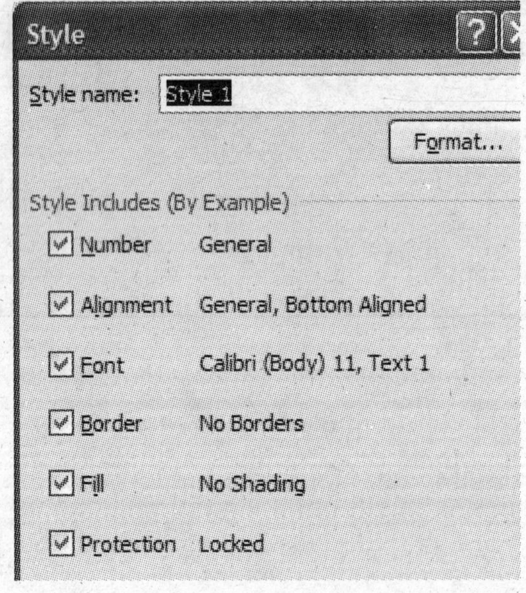

Exclude formats of selected cell from style:

1. Deselect Style Includes (by example) options: Number, Alignment, Font, Border, Fill, Protection
2. Click Ok.

Functions in Excel

They establish relationships between two or more cells. If you want to add the values in cells A3 and A4 and put the result in cell A5, move to the cell A5 and type =A3+A4 and press Enter. The result is displayed immediately in cell A5. Another way to achieve the same result is to move to cell A5 and type +, point to cell A3, type +, then point to A4, and press Enter. The easiest way to achieve this operation is to point to A5, pick up the AutoSum button Σ on the toolbar.

The following symbols have their specific meaning in the formulae which are used in Excel.

Symbol	Description	Symbol	Description
:	Reference operator	,	Argument operator
–	Negation	%	Percentage sign
^	Exponent	*	Multiplication
/	Division	+	Addition
–	Subtraction	&	Text concatenation
>	Greater than	<	Less than
>=	Greater than or equal to	<=	Less than or equal to
<>	Not equal to		

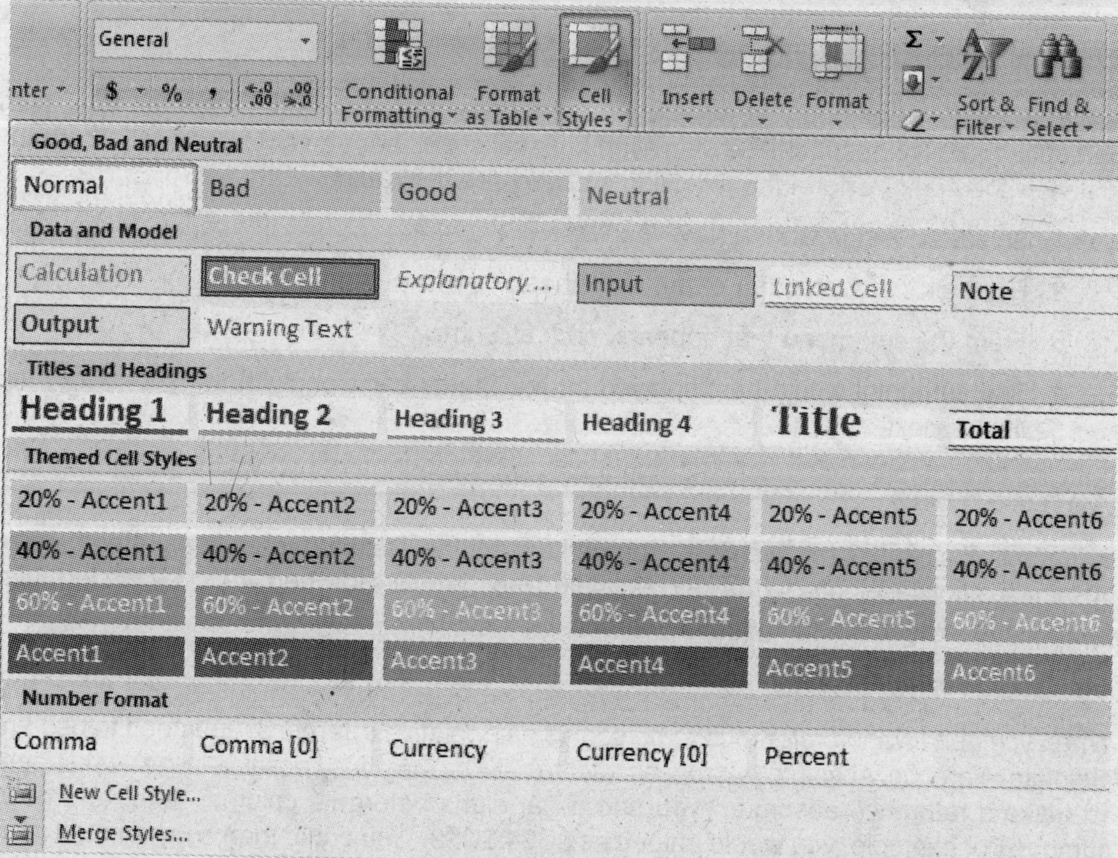

While working with the formulae you would come across the various errors too, which could happen due to wrong use of formula or wrong typing. The following are the common type of errors.

Error Type	Description
# # # #	the column is not wide enough to display the number so either widen the column, or reduce the font size or change the numeric format.
# DIV/0!	Dividing by zero is invalid
# N/A	Data is not available. It happens usually when you refer to a function or value where data is not available
# NAME?	The formula references a name that is unknown to Excel
# NUM !	The formula is using an invalid number
# REF !	A cell reference is not available may be because you deleted that cell or moved another cell onto it.
# VALUE !	The formula contains an invalid operator or argument, for example, adding a text value to a numeric value

Using Autocalculate

It is very useful when you just want to total a number of columns but have the total in a particular field. The result will be displayed in Excel status bar and not in any cell. You can just view the sum. Perform the following steps to see the result.

1. Select the range whose total you want.
2. Right click at Status bar of the worksheet.
3. From the sub menu that appears, click at Sum.
4. The sum total would be displayed on the Status bar alongwith the sub menu, as shown next.

References

By default, Excel uses relative references in its formulae. Relative references refer to cells by their position in relation to the cell containing the formula. So when you copy the formula in cell F5 to cell F6, Excel changes the reference from E5 to E6.

Absolute references

When you don't want a reference to be copied as a relative reference, you need to use an absolute reference. Absolute references refer to cells by their fixed position in the worksheet. To make a reference absolute, you add dollar signs before its column letter and now number. For example, you would enter it as $C$4:$C$9. You could then copy formula that contained this reference anywhere on the worksheet and it would always refer to the range C4:C9.

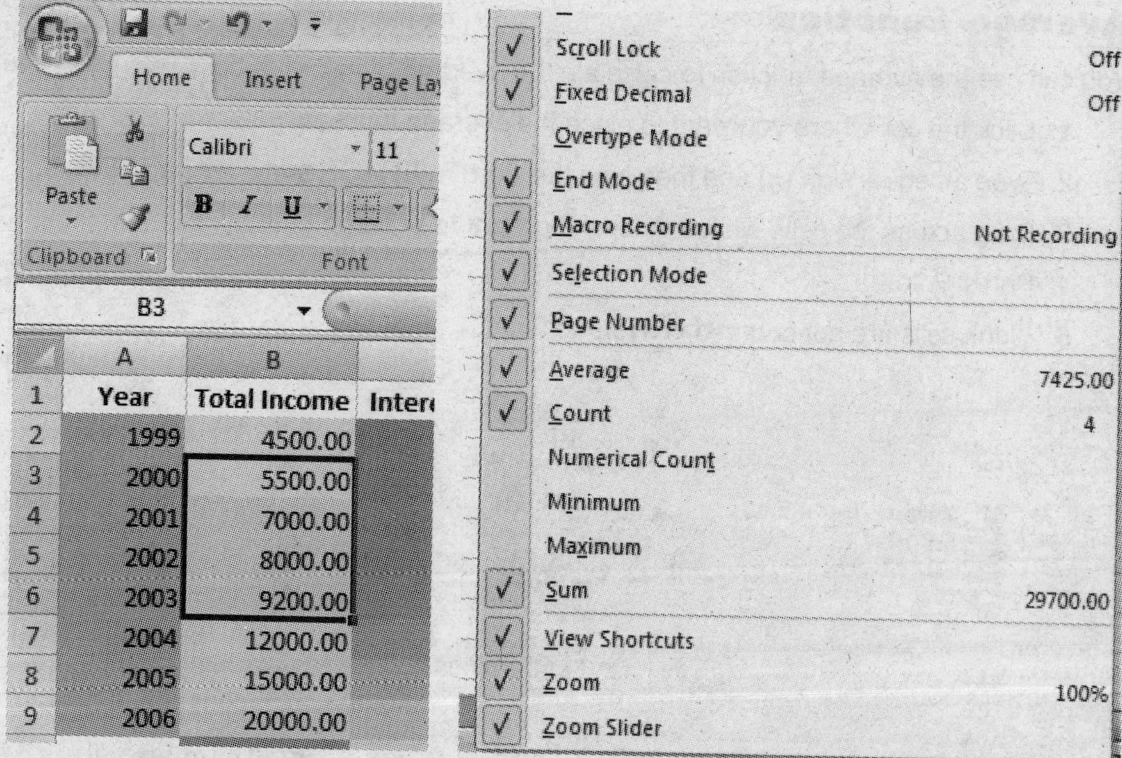

Mixed references

References can also be partially relative and partially absolute. For example, $C3 has an absolute column reference and a relative row reference and C$3 has a relative column reference and an absolute row reference.

Sum Function

The Sum function is perhaps the most commonly used of the Excel functions that carry out mathematical, statistical, financial, date, time, and other calculations.

1. Click the destination cell for the formula.
2. Type an equal sign to start the formula and then type the word SUM and a left parenthesis.
3. Drag down the column of numbers to sum.
4. Press Enter.

Points to Remember

1. You do not need to type the close (right) parenthesis before you press Enter—Excel will do it for you.
2. Use this technique instead of AutoSum to sum ranges of cells that contain blanks.

Average Function

You can use the Average function to calculate the average of values in cells.

1. Click the cell where you want to place the average function.
2. Type an equal sign (=) and then type the word AVERAGE and a left parenthesis.
3. Drag across the cells whose values you want to average.
4. Press Enter.
5. Blank cells are not counted in average.

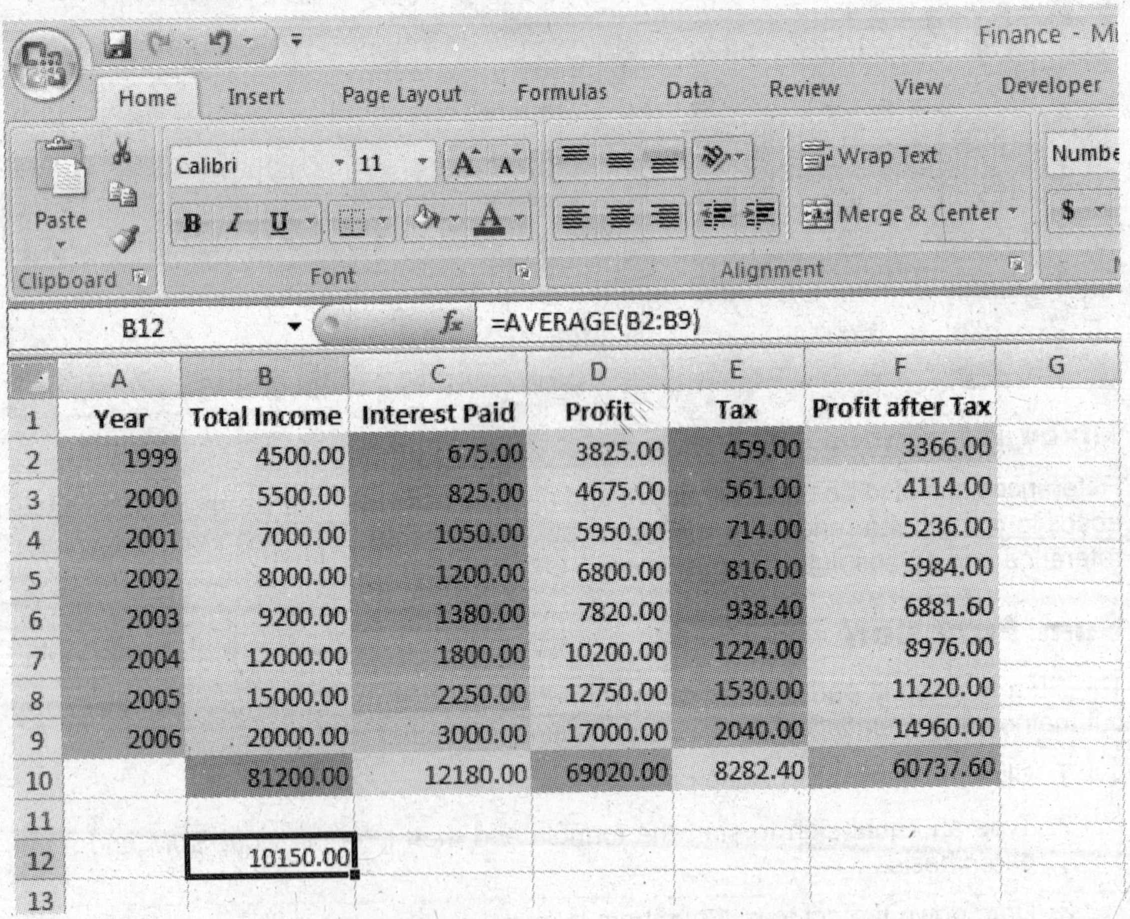

Finance - Mi

Home | Insert | Page Layout | Formulas | Data | Review | View | Developer

Paste | Calibri | 11 | Wrap Text | Merge & Center | Numbe | $

Clipboard | Font | Alignment

B12 | =AVERAGE(B2:B9)

	A	B	C	D	E	F	G
1	Year	Total Income	Interest Paid	Profit	Tax	Profit after Tax	
2	1999	4500.00	675.00	3825.00	459.00	3366.00	
3	2000	5500.00	825.00	4675.00	561.00	4114.00	
4	2001	7000.00	1050.00	5950.00	714.00	5236.00	
5	2002	8000.00	1200.00	6800.00	816.00	5984.00	
6	2003	9200.00	1380.00	7820.00	938.40	6881.60	
7	2004	12000.00	1800.00	10200.00	1224.00	8976.00	
8	2005	15000.00	2250.00	12750.00	1530.00	11220.00	
9	2006	20000.00	3000.00	17000.00	2040.00	14960.00	
10		81200.00	12180.00	69020.00	8282.40	60737.60	
11							
12		10150.00					
13							

Creating Charts in Excel

In the earlier chapter we had created a worksheet and decorated it. There is another method of presenting this worksheet and that is by converting it into graphics and specially in the form of **Charts** in Excel.

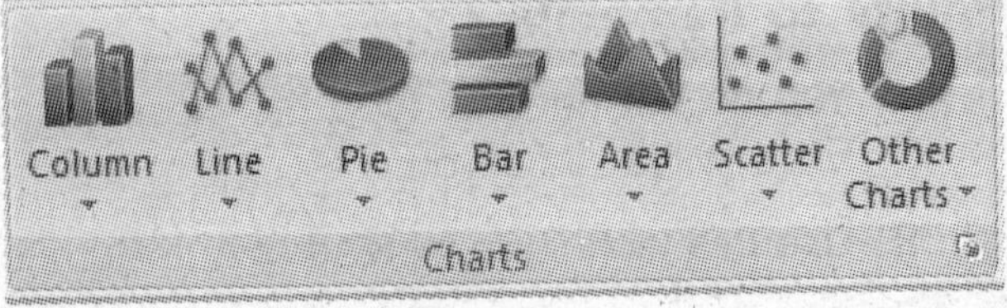

Let us use the same worksheet to make charts of the same. Different type of charts which can be created using Excel 2007 are shown here. Each one of them has various options underneath which can be chosen. For example, the 3-D column chart of the worksheet created earlier would be as shown below.

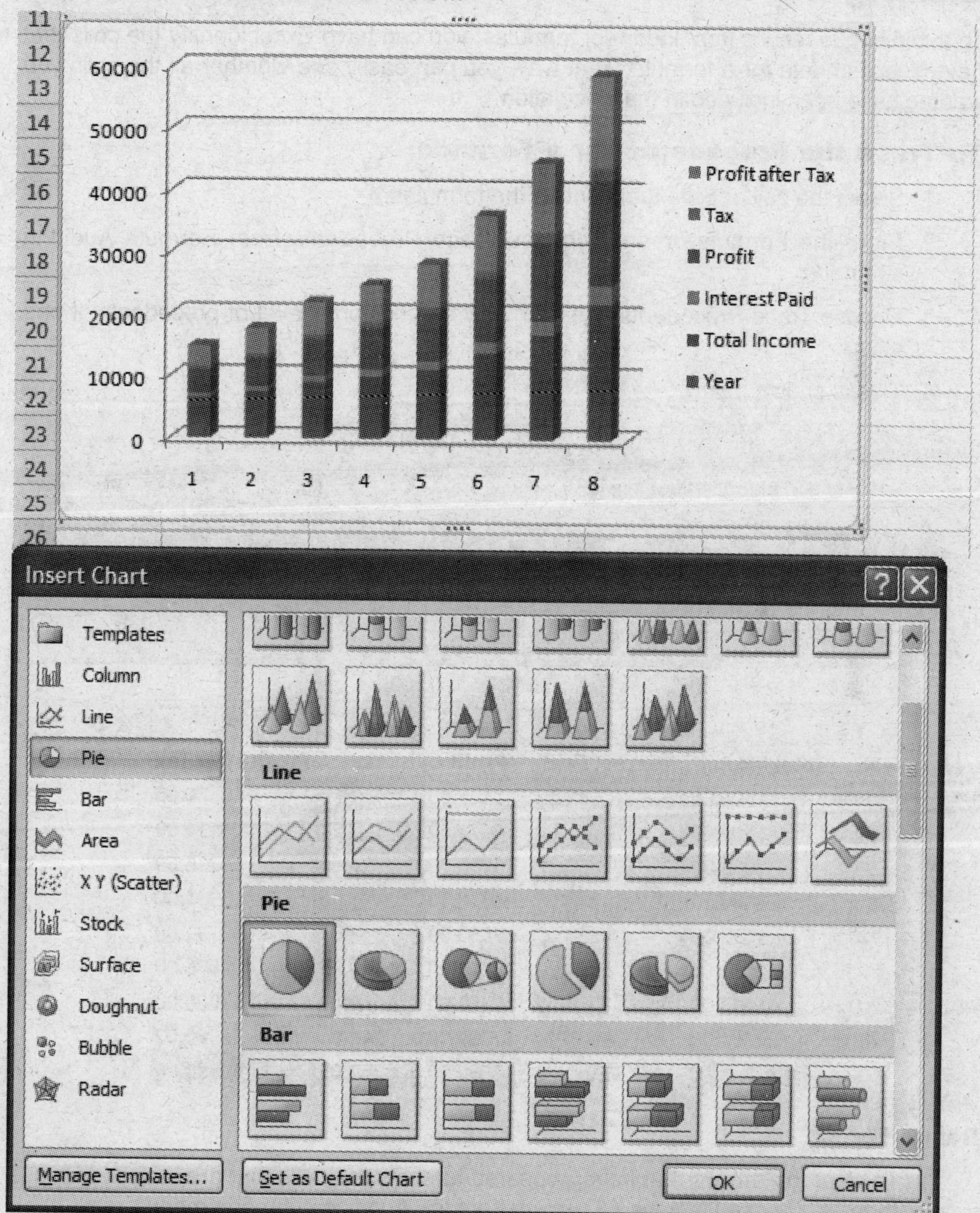

Similary you can create other type of charts. All these charts with their options can also be seen under All Chart Types under Other Charts.

Auditing a Workbook

To avoid bogus results from incorrect formulas, you can have Excel identify the cells that have supplied data for a formula. That way, you can easily see whether all the cells you wanted have been included in the calculation.

To Trace the Precedents for a Formula:

1. Select the cell or cells that contain the formulas.
2. From the Formulas menu, choose Trace Precedents from Formula Auditing submenu.
3. Choose Trace Precedents again to view an additional level of precedents, if one exists.
4. This is shown below.

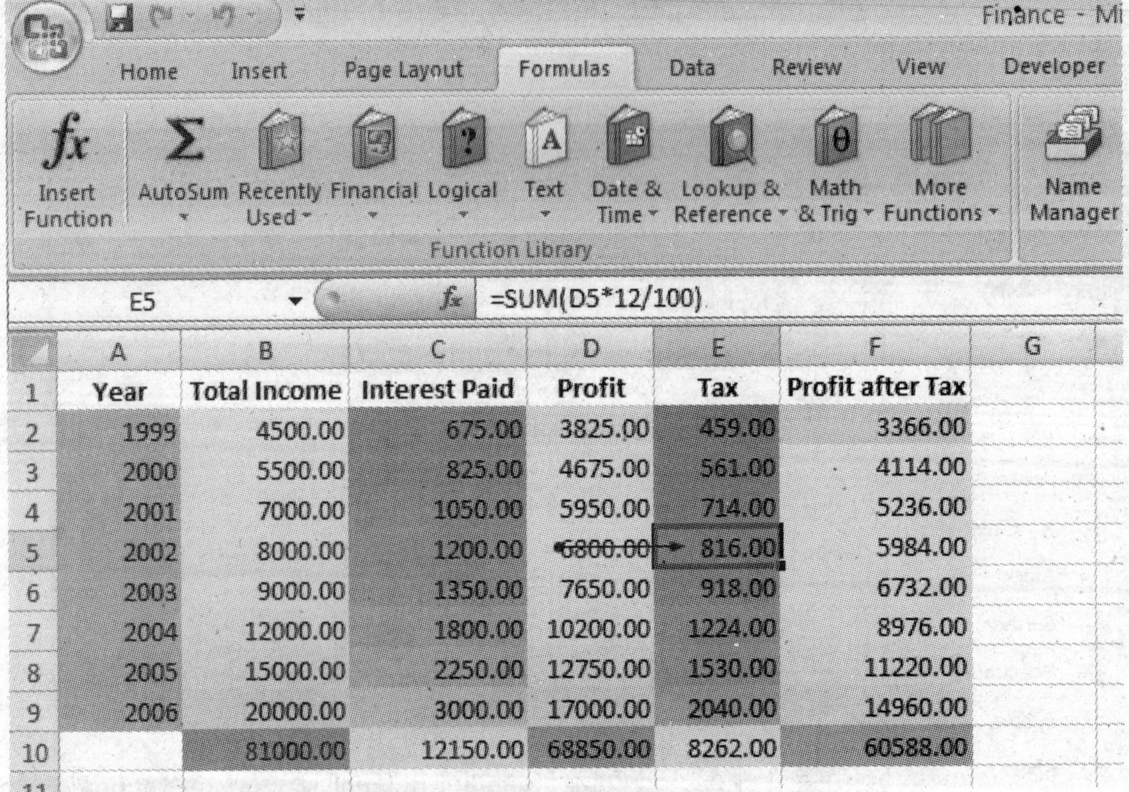

	A	B	C	D	E	F	G
1	Year	Total Income	Interest Paid	Profit	Tax	Profit after Tax	
2	1999	4500.00	675.00	3825.00	459.00	3366.00	
3	2000	5500.00	825.00	4675.00	561.00	4114.00	
4	2001	7000.00	1050.00	5950.00	714.00	5236.00	
5	2002	8000.00	1200.00	6800.00	816.00	5984.00	
6	2003	9000.00	1350.00	7650.00	918.00	6732.00	
7	2004	12000.00	1800.00	10200.00	1224.00	8976.00	
8	2005	15000.00	2250.00	12750.00	1530.00	11220.00	
9	2006	20000.00	3000.00	17000.00	2040.00	14960.00	
10		81000.00	12150.00	68850.00	8262.00	60588.00	

Remember

1. To clear the arrows that have appeared to show the cells that are included in the formula, choose Remove All Arrows from the Auditing submenu menu.

2. The Auditing toolbar contains Trace Precedents and Remove All Arrows buttons. To view the Auditing toolbar, choose Show Auditing Toolbar from the Auditing submenu.

Comments Inserting

A comment is an annotation that you attach to a cell to provide information about the cell's contents. This capability enables several people to review the same worksheet and attach their comments.

To insert a comment:

1. Select the cell to which you want to attach a comment.
2. From the Review menu, choose New Comment from Comments panel.
3. In the yellow text box that opens and displays the text for the comment.
4. Click in another cell to close the text box.

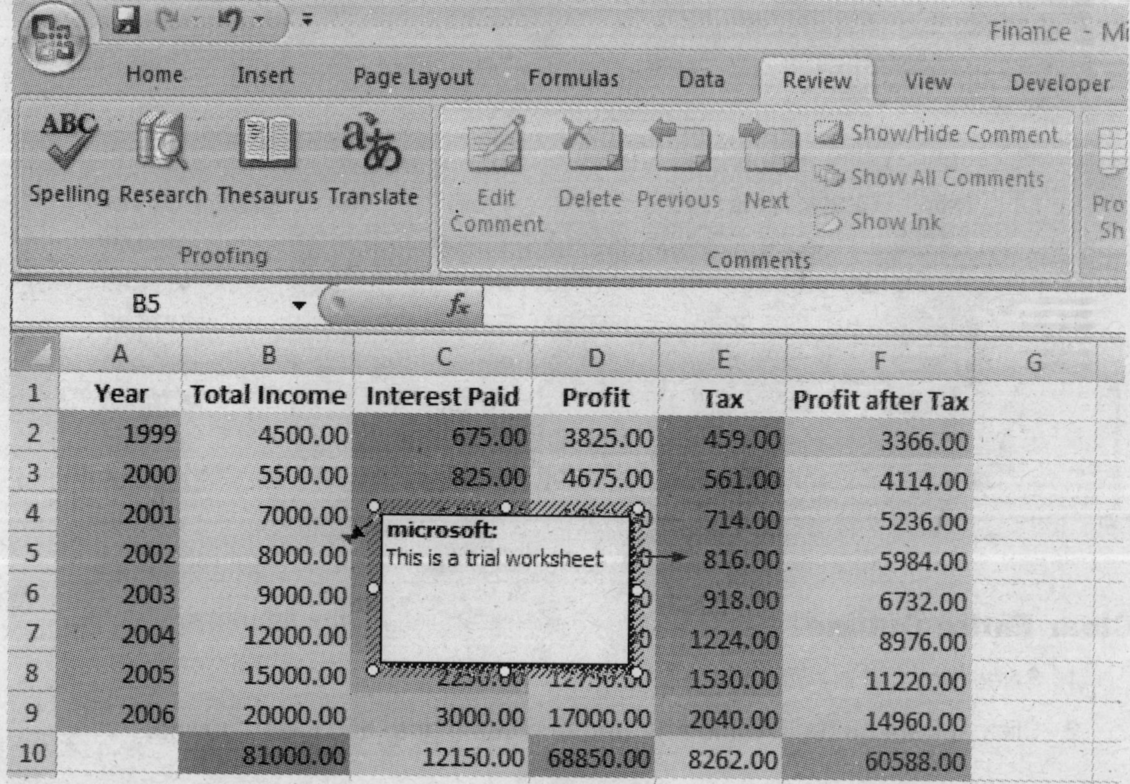

	A	B	C	D	E	F	G
1	Year	Total Income	Interest Paid	Profit	Tax	Profit after Tax	
2	1999	4500.00	675.00	3825.00	459.00	3366.00	
3	2000	5500.00	825.00	4675.00	561.00	4114.00	
4	2001	7000.00			714.00	5236.00	
5	2002	8000.00			816.00	5984.00	
6	2003	9000.00			918.00	6732.00	
7	2004	12000.00			1224.00	8976.00	
8	2005	15000.00	2250.00	12750.00	1530.00	11220.00	
9	2006	20000.00	3000.00	17000.00	2040.00	14960.00	
10		81000.00	12150.00	68850.00	8262.00	60588.00	

Remember

1. A comment is indicated by a comment marker (a small red triangle) at the upper right corner of the cell. To view the comment, pass the cursor over the cell.
2. To remove a comment, right-click in the cell, and choose Delete Comment from the shortcut menu.

Outlines

Outline a Worksheet Automatically

1. Select a single cell to outline or the entire worksheet
2. Select a range of cells to outline
3. Click Data menu, Group and Outline command, and click at Group.

An outline created with outline symbols to the left of the row heading and/or above column headings.

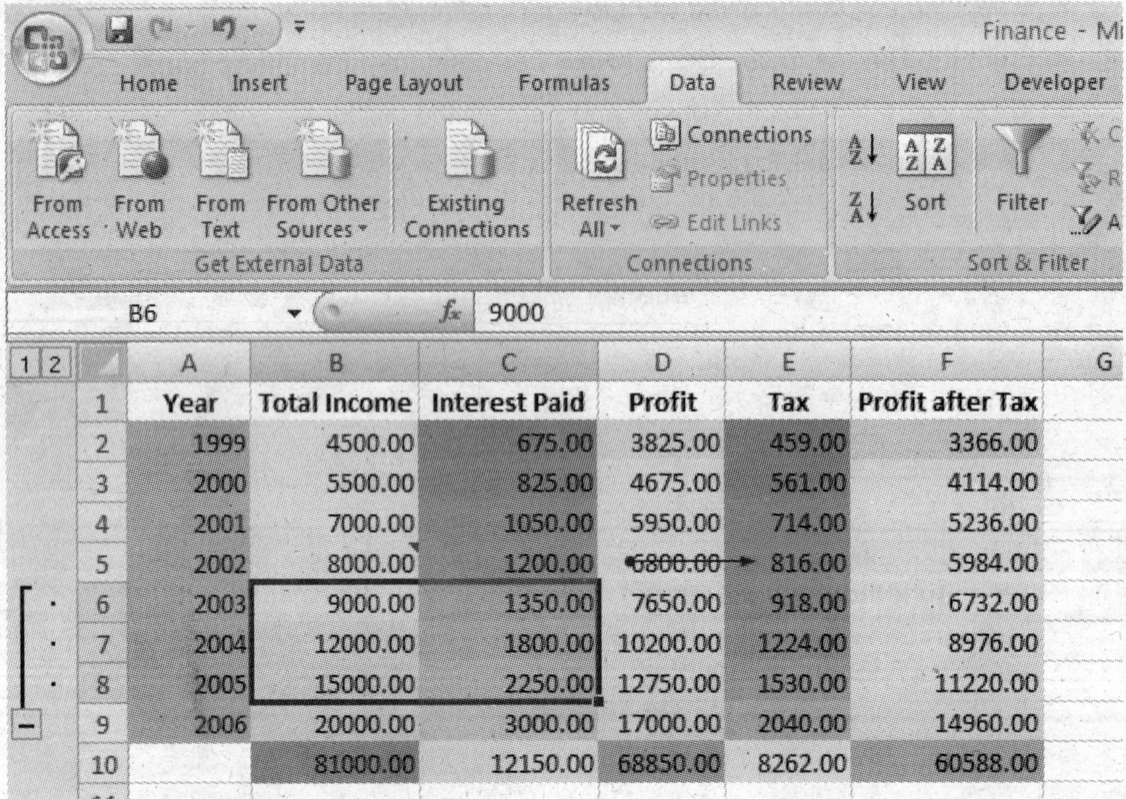

Clear Entire Outline

1. Select any cell in outline
2. Click at Data menu, Outline and Ungroup command, and Clear Outline.

Worksheet Fitting on a Page

If your worksheet is too large to print on one page even after you change the orientation and margins, you might consider using the Fit to option.

This option shrinks the worksheet to make it fit on the specified number of pages. You can specify the document's width and height.

Follow these steps to scale a worksheet to fit on a page:

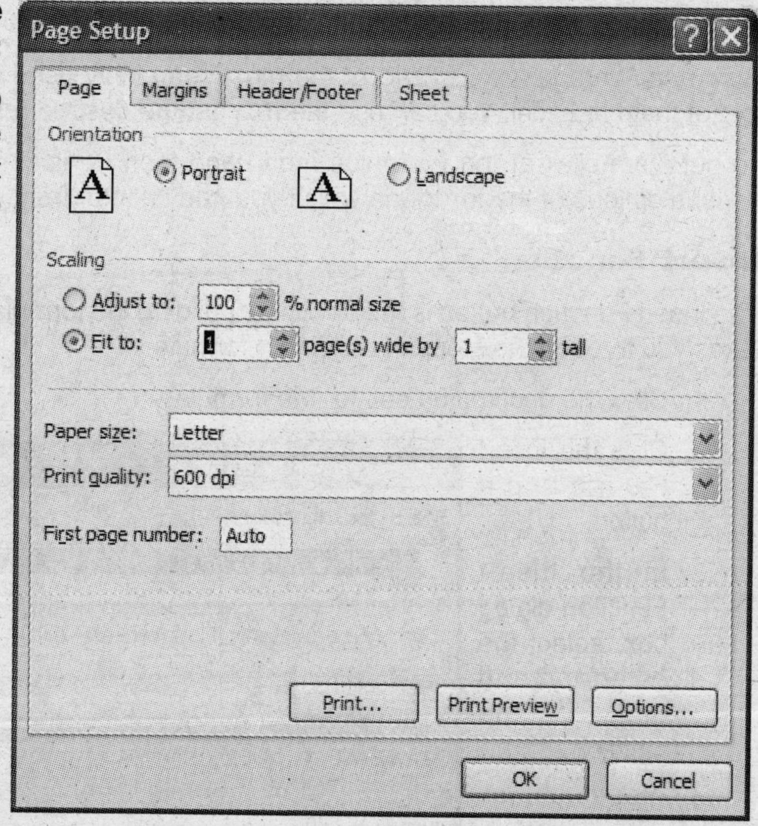

1. Open the Page Setup menu and choose Page Setup and Print Area. The Page Setup dialog box appears.
2. Click the Page tab to display the Page options.
3. In the Fit to XX page wide by XX tall text boxes, enter the number of pages in which you want Excel to fit your data.
4. Click Ok to close the Page Setup dialog box and return to your worksheet. Or click the Print button in the Page Setup dialog box to display the Print dialog box, and then click Ok to print your worksheet.

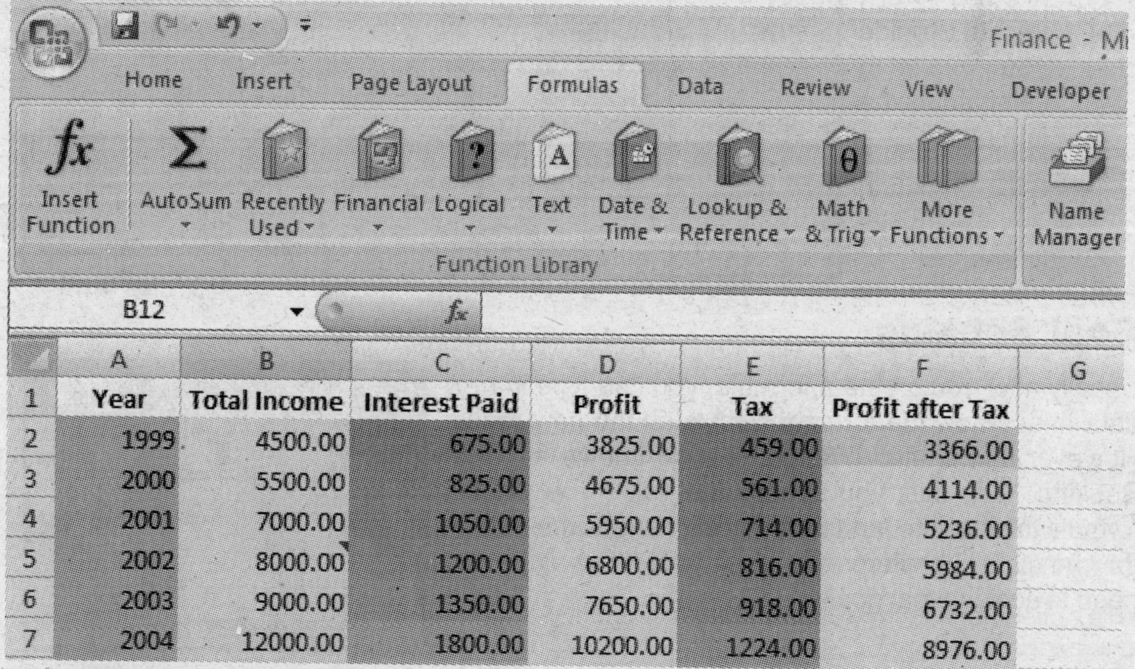

	A	B	C	D	E	F	G
1	Year	Total Income	Interest Paid	Profit	Tax	Profit after Tax	
2	1999	4500.00	675.00	3825.00	459.00	3366.00	
3	2000	5500.00	825.00	4675.00	561.00	4114.00	
4	2001	7000.00	1050.00	5950.00	714.00	5236.00	
5	2002	8000.00	1200.00	6800.00	816.00	5984.00	
6	2003	9000.00	1350.00	7650.00	918.00	6732.00	
7	2004	12000.00	1800.00	10200.00	1224.00	8976.00	

Function Wizard

Sum and Average are just two of the most commonly used functions whereas there are lots of them in Excel. You can use them to get the desired results in a flash.

To get them click at the Formulas menu and then Function Library. Here you have the various options of the functions which you can choose from.

Insert Function

The Insert Function button is the option for building the formula. The Insert Function wizard takes you through the steps of building a formula.

1. Click the destination cell for the formula.
2. Click the Insert Function button.
3. In the Insert Function dialog box, select the category and then the function.
4. Click Ok.
5. Use the Insert Function Wizard to guide you in completing the formula.
6. Click Ok when you have finished.

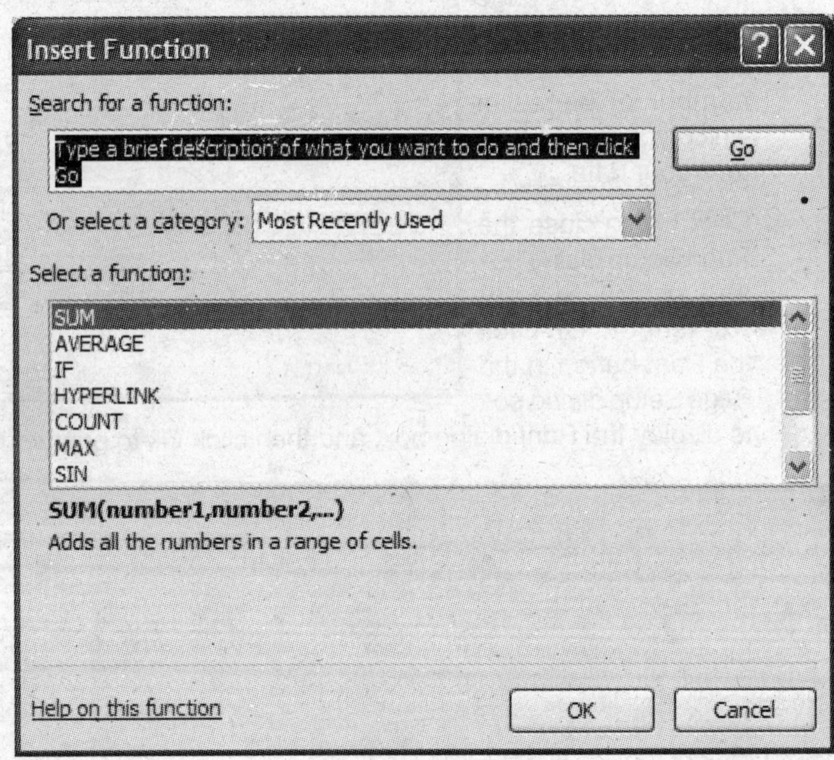

Goal Seeking

Usually after you create a formula, you can type in new data to see how the formula calculates the new result. However, Excel also offers a feature known as Goal Seeking. With this, you specify the value you want a formula to calculate, and then Excel changes the data in thr formula's cell references to tell you what values you need to achieve that goal.

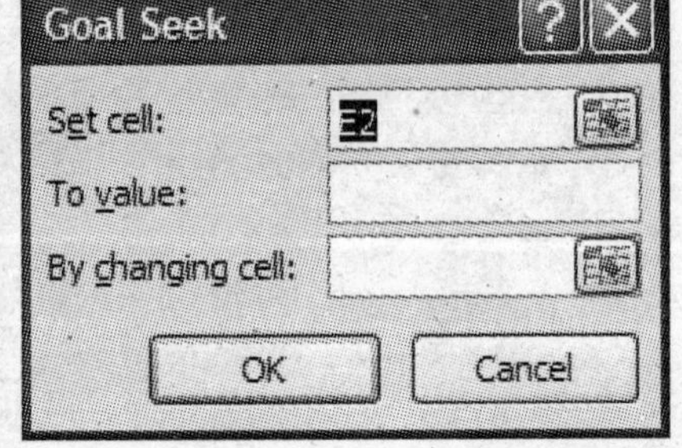

To use Goal Seeking, follow these steps.

1. Click a the cell that contains a formula.
2. Click the Data tab.
3. Click the What-If Analysis Icon in the Data Tools group.
4. Click Goal Seek.
5. Click in the To Value text box and type a number that you want to appear in the formula stored in the cell that you clicked in Step 1.
6. Click in the By Changing Cell text box and click one cell that contains data used by the formula you choose in Step 1.
7. Click Ok.
8. Click Ok (to keep the changes) or click Cancel (to display the origianl vlaue your spreadsheet had before you choose the Goal Seek command)

Scenarios Manager

Human mind is made of What-if situations. The same what-if can be applied to your worksheet to see if the results of the selection displays the good or bad results.

Each time you change the data, the previous solution is lost. To address this limitation, the Scenario Manager helps you keep track of multiple what-if models. Using the Scenarios manager, you can create new forecasting scenarios, view existing scenario, run scenario management commands and display consolidated scenario reports. Let us start with creating a worksheet and then apply the scenario to it.

On the next page a worksheet is shown which has been taken as an example for creating a scenario. Here the figures are very simple and calculated. If you want you can use the constant figures too. Next we perform the following steps to create and view the scenario.

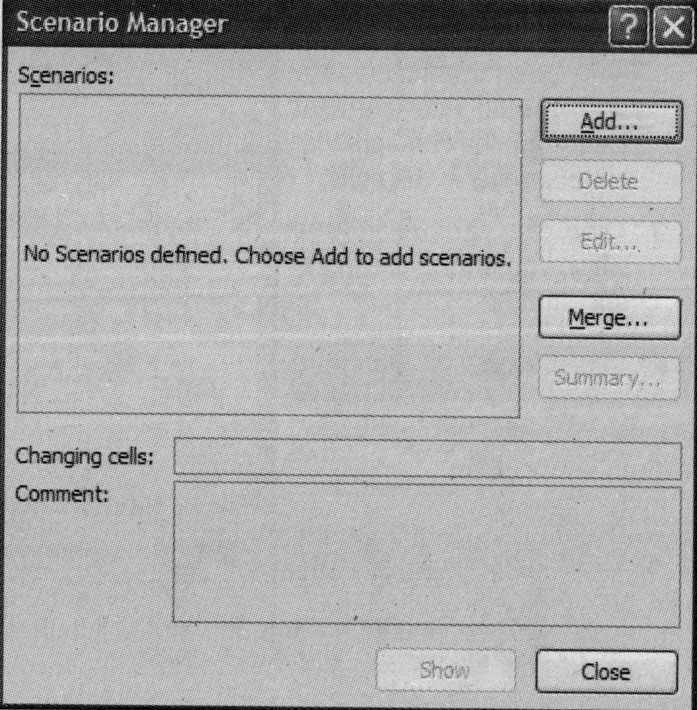

1. Click at Data menu, Data Tools tab and What-If Analysis and then Scenarios manager.

2. A Scenario manager dialog box would appear on the screen, as shown here.
3. As the dialog box says, click at Add to add a scenario.
4. This gives rise to another dialog box, which is called Add scenario.
5. In this dialog box, you have to firstly name the screnario.
6. I have named it as Good.

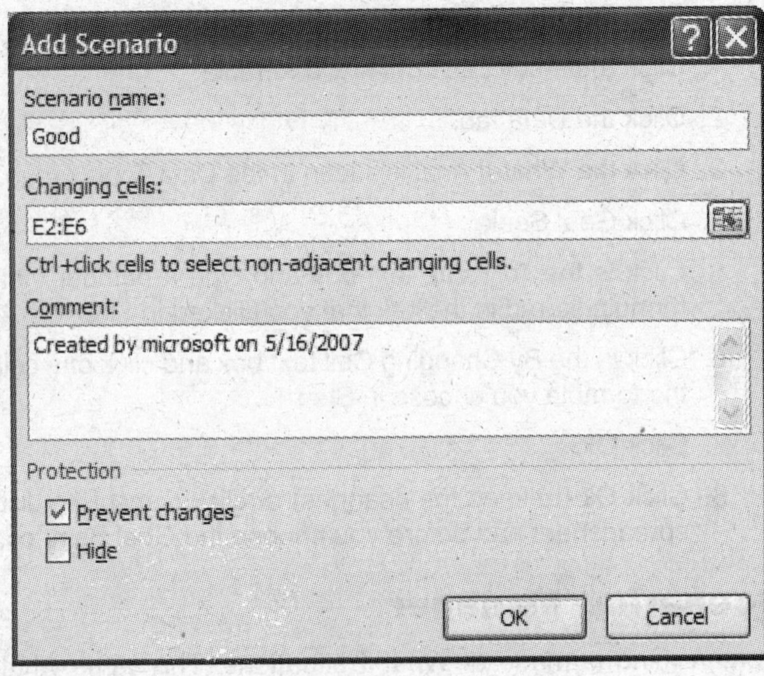

7. You can type the cell names or choose them by clicking at those cells. I have chosen cells from E2 to E4.
8. Click OK to add your scenario to the Scenario Manager. You'll see the Scenario Values dialog box, which asks you for your model's variables. The default values are the numbers that were already in the cells.
9. Type the various values which you want to see in the scenario.

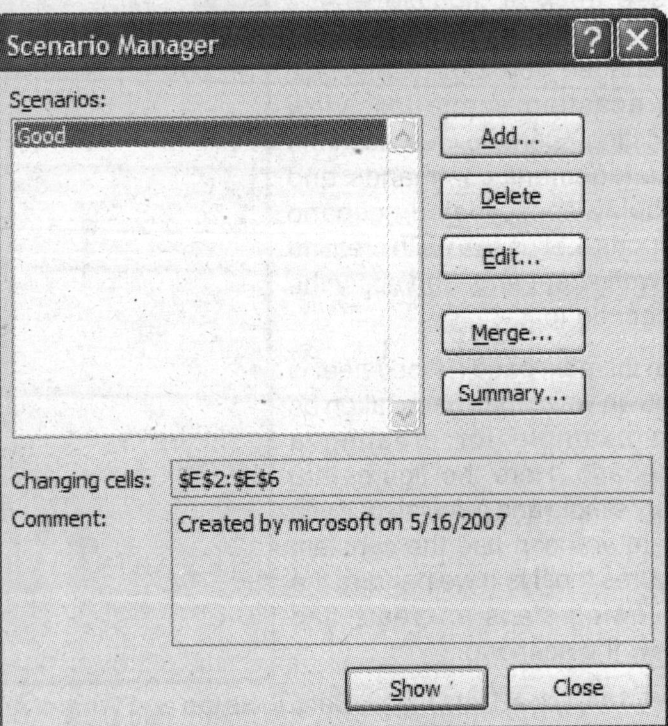

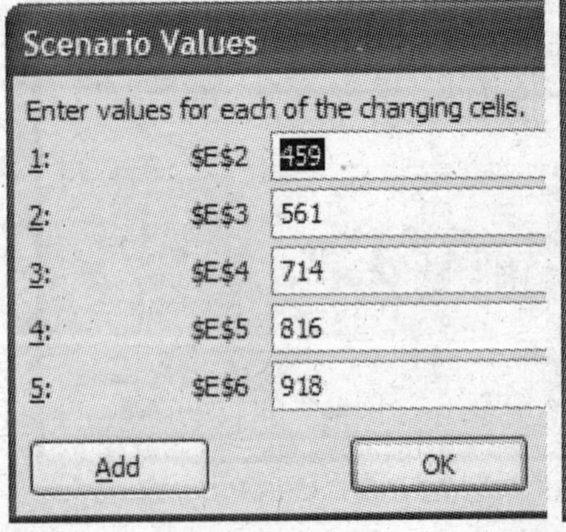

10. Click Add to create a second scenario. If you do not want another set, just click at Ok.
11. This will return you to the scenario manager with your scenario added to it.
12. As mentioned you can add another scenario to it.
13. Now we will see how this scenario works. For this click at Show.

Scenario Summary

Report type

Scenario summary

Scenario PivotTable report

Result cells:

=$E$9

OK Cancel

14. Excel substitutes the values in the scenario for the variables in your worksheet and displays the results in your worksheet, as shown on the next page.
15. Next step is of having the Scenario Reports.
16. For this you choose the button called Summary from the Scenario Manager dialog box.

Scenario Summary		
	Current Values:	Good
Changing Cells:		
$E$4	8,000	8,000
$E$5	10,000	10,000
$E$6	9,000	9,000
$E$7	29,000	29,000
Result Cells:		
$E$9		

17. For this you will have to click at a cell where the summary would be placed.
18. You also have to define whether you want the summary or the PivtoTable report. Click any one of the two.
19. I have taken here Scenario summary and have given E9 as the cell for showing the results.
20. The net results will be shown here.

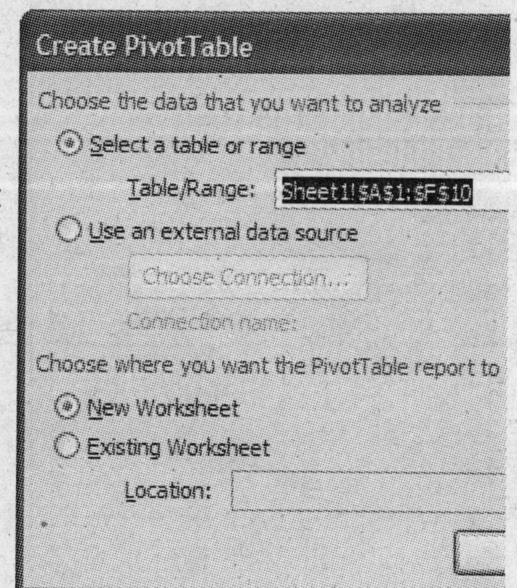

Creating a Pivot Table Report

PivotTable reports can help you look at data in different ways. Once the reports are created, you can swap rows with columns for different views.

1. Click in the selected data area.
2. From the Insert menu, choose PivotTable in the Tables group.
3. Select the cells that contain the data yu want to use in your pivot table. This is optional.
4. Select one of the following radio buttons:

- New Worksheet: Puts the pivot table on a new worksheet.

- Existing Worksheet: Puts the pivot table on an existing worksheet.

5. Click Ok, Excel displays a Pivot Table Fiel List pane.
6. Mark one or more check boxes inside the PivotTable Field List pane.

Rearranging labels in a pivot table

A pivot table organizesdata according to your spreadsheet's columns headings, which appear in a pivot table as row labels. To rearrange column headings in a pivot table, follow these steps:

1. Click the pivot table you want to rearrange.
2. Click the downward-pointing arrow of a lable that appears under the Row Labels group.

   Select one of the following:

   Move Up: Moves the lable one level closer to the beginning.

   Move Down: Moves the lable one level down to the end.

   Move to Beginning: Makes the label the dominant criteria for sorting data.

   Move to End: Makes the label the last criteria for sorting data.

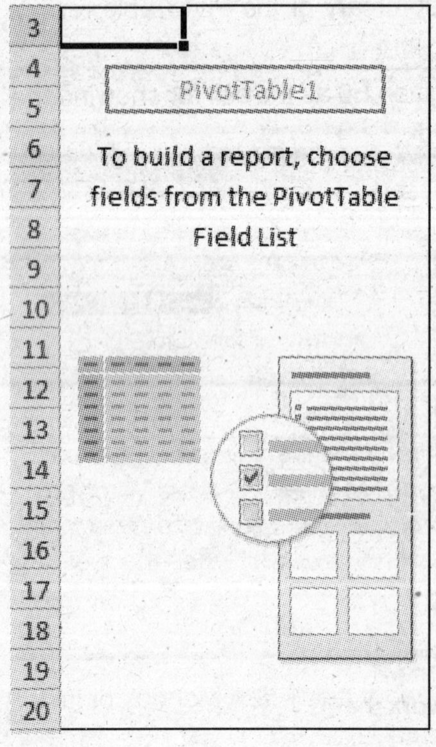

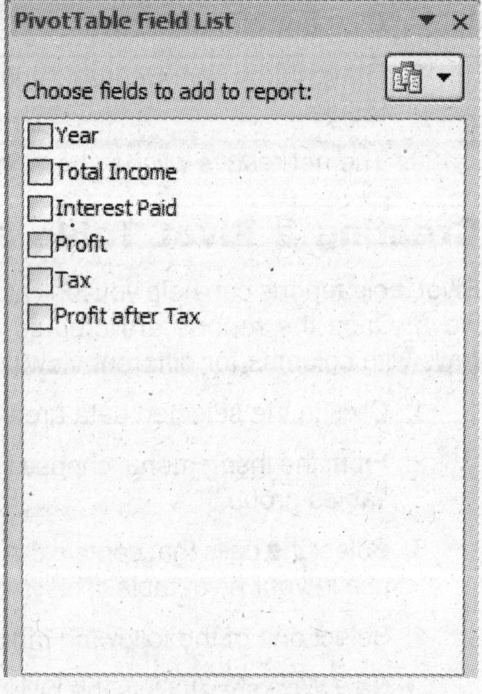

3		Values	
4	Row Labels	Sum of Profit	Sum of Profit after Tax
5	1999	3825	3366
6	2000	4675	4114
7	2001	5950	5236
8	2002	6800	5984
9	2003	7650	6732
10	2004	10200	8976
11	2005	12750	11220
12	2006	17000	14960
13	(blank)	68850	60588
14	**Grand Total**	**137700**	**121176**
15			
16			
17			
18			
19			
20			
21			

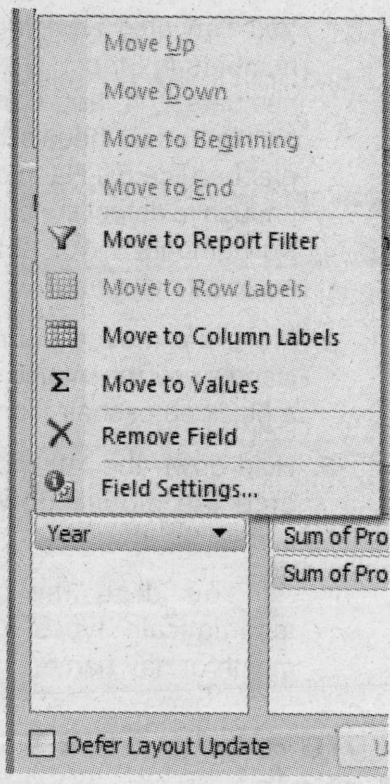

Modifying a Pivot Table

Row labels let you organize data according to different criteria, such as sales per region and then by product. For greater flexibility, you can also turn a row label into a column heading.

To turn row labels into column headings in a pivot table (or vice versa), follow these steps:

1. Click the pivot table you want to modify.
2. Click a heading.
3. Choose Move to Column Labels (or Row Labels).

Typing with AutoFill

If you need to type the names of successive months or days in a row or column (such as January, February, February, March and so on). Excel offers a shortcut to save you from typing all the day or month names yourself. With this shortcut, you just type one month or day and them drag the mouse to highlight all the adjacent cell. Then Excel types the rest of the month or day names in those cells automatically.

To use this shortcut, follow these steps:

1. Click a cell and type a month (like January or just Jan) or a day (like Monday or just Mon).

You can also type in a sequence of numbers in Step 1. So if you typed the numbers 2, 4, and 6 in adjacent cells, highlighted all these adjacent cells, and grabbed the Fill Handle, Excel is smart enough to detect the pattern and display the numbers 8, 10, 12 in the next three adjacent cells.

2. Move the mouse pointer over the Fill Handle until the mouse pointer turns into a black corosshair icon.
3. Hold down the left mouse button and drag the mouse down a column or across the row.

   As you drag the mouse, Excel automatically types in the remaining month or day names.

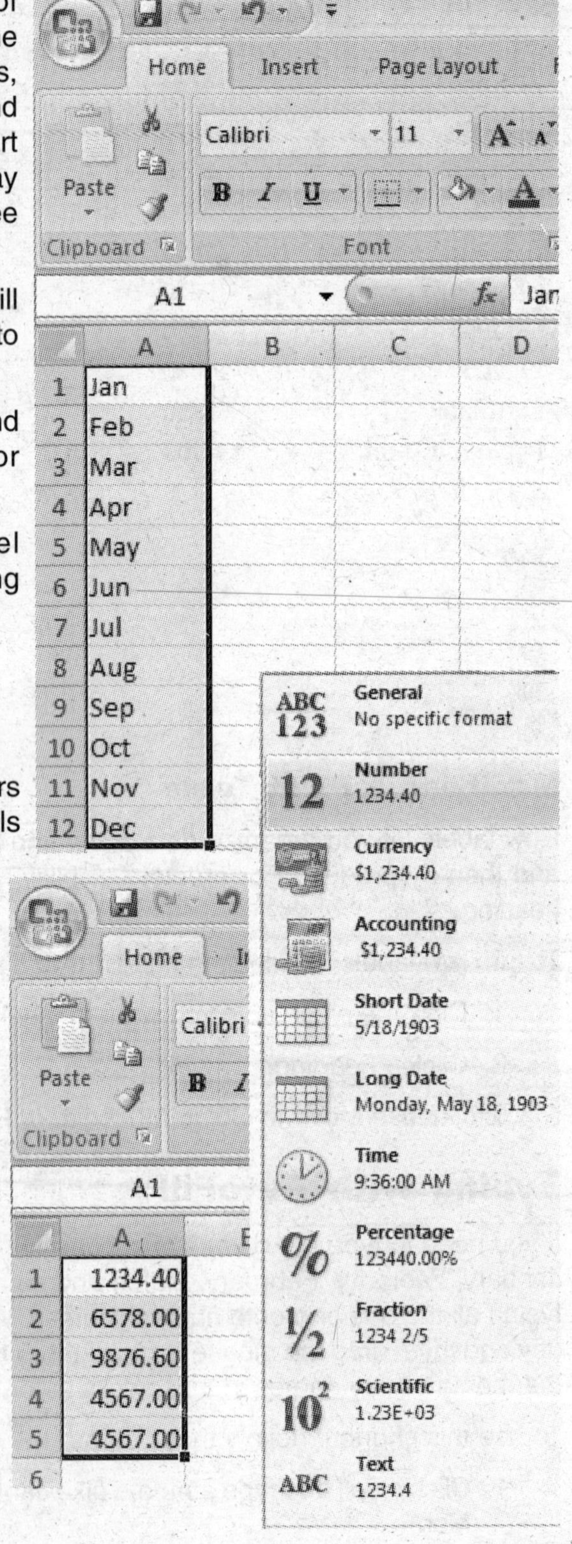

Formatting Numbers and Labels

When you first create a spreadsheet, numbers and labels appear as plain text. Plain labels might look boring, but plain numbers, such as 8495 or 0.29, can be difficult to read and understand it the numbers are supposed to represent currency amounts ($8,495) or percentage (29%). To make labels visually intersesting and numbers appear more description of what they actually represent, you need to format your data after you type it into a spreadsheet.

Formatting Numbers

To format the appearance of numbers, follow these steps:

1. Select one or more cells using the mouse or keyboard.
2. Click the Home tab.
3. Click the Number Format list box in the Number group.

Changing the size of Rows and Columns

If you need to resize a row or columns to a precise value, it's easier to type a specific value into the Row Height or Column Width dialog box instead. To type a value into a Row Height or Column Width dialog box, follow hes steps:

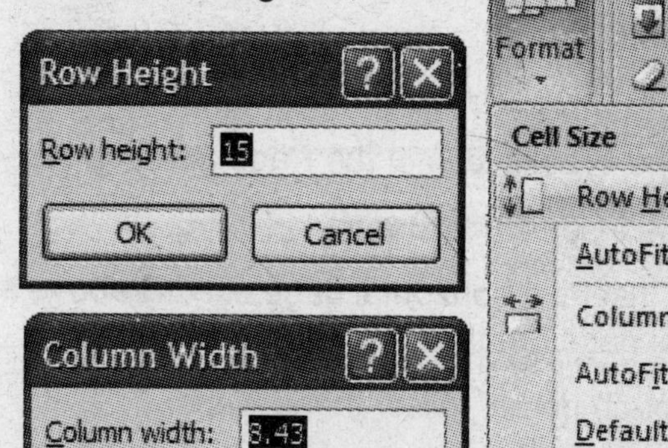

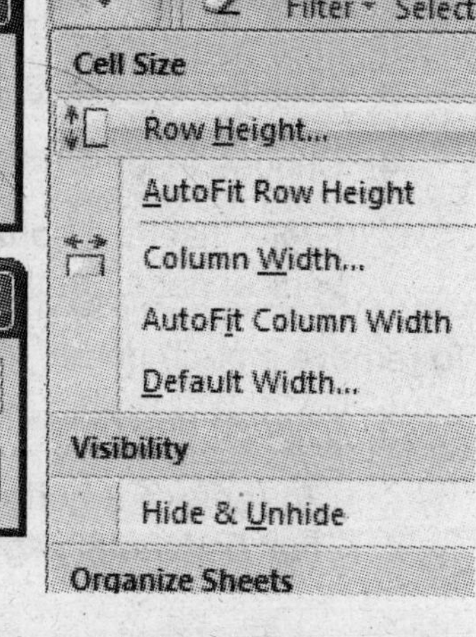

1. Click the Home tab.
2. Click the row or column heading that you want to resize. Excel highlights your entire row or column.
3. Click the Format icon that appears in the Cells group. A pull-down menu appears.
4. Click Height, if you select a row, or Width, if you selected a column.

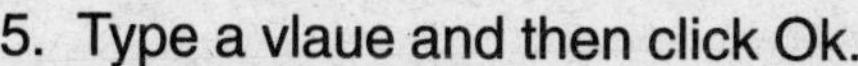

5. Type a vlaue and then click Ok.

Adding and Deleting Rows and Columns

After you type in labels, numbers, and formulas, you may suddenly realize that you need to add or delete extra rows and columns.

To add a row or column, follow these steps:

1. Click at Home Tab.
2. Click the row or column heading where you want to add another row or column.
3. Click the Insert icon in the Cells group.

   Inserting a row adds a new row above the selected row. Inserting a column adds a new column to the left of the selected column.

To delete a row or column, follow these steps:

1. Click at Home tab.
2. Click the row or column heading that you want to delete.
3. Click the Delete icon in the Cells group.

   Deleting a row or colun deletes any data stored in that row or column.

Inserting (and Removing) Page Breaks

One problem with large spreadsheets is that when you print them out, parts may get cut off when printed on separate pages. To correct this problem, you can tell Excel exactly where page breaks should occur.

To insert page breaks, follow these steps:

1. Move the cursor in the cell to define where the vertical and horizontal page breaks will appear.
2. Click the Page Layout tab.
3. Click the Breaks icon in the Page Setup group.
4. Choose Insert Page Break.

   Excfel inserts a horizontal page directly above the cell you selected in Step 1 and a vertical page break to the left of that cell, too.

To remove a page break, follow these steps:

1. Choose one of the following:
   - To remove a horizontal page break: Click in any cell that appears directly below that horizontal page break.

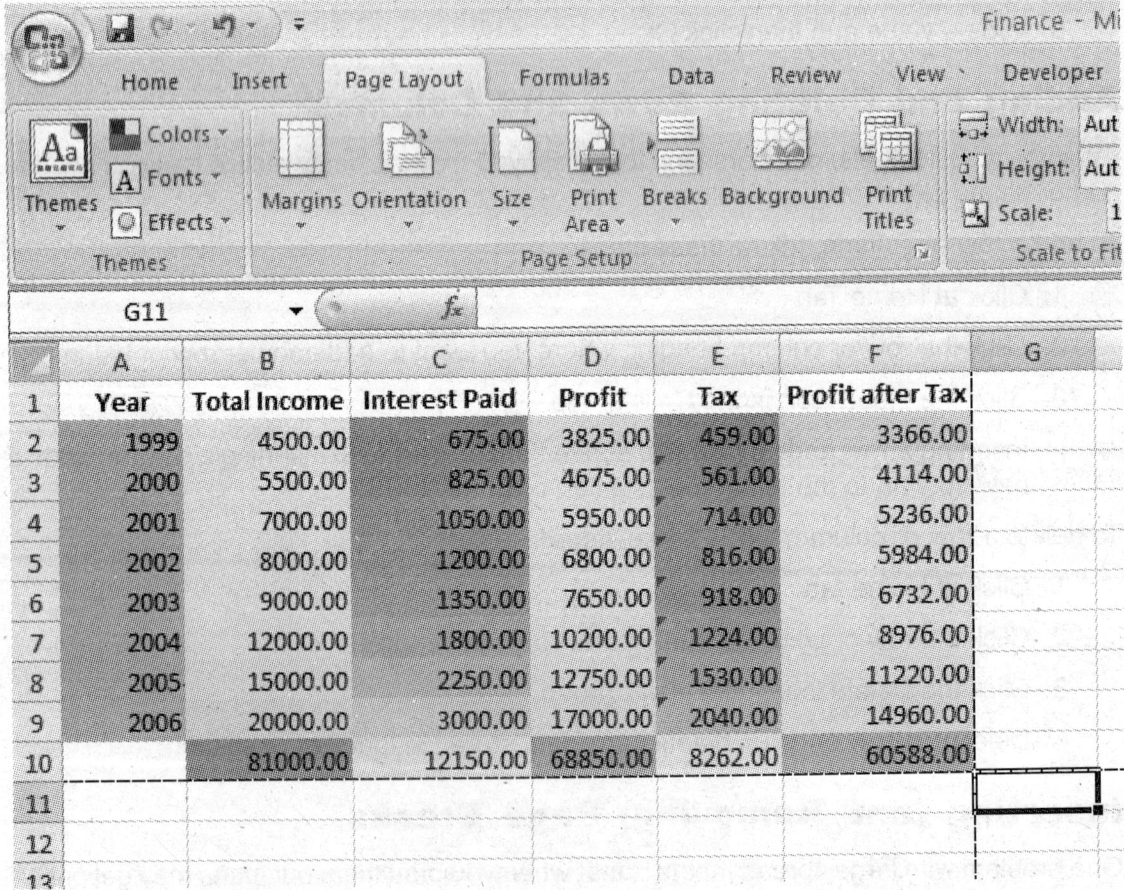

	A	B	C	D	E	F	G
1	Year	Total Income	Interest Paid	Profit	Tax	Profit after Tax	
2	1999	4500.00	675.00	3825.00	459.00	3366.00	
3	2000	5500.00	825.00	4675.00	561.00	4114.00	
4	2001	7000.00	1050.00	5950.00	714.00	5236.00	
5	2002	8000.00	1200.00	6800.00	816.00	5984.00	
6	2003	9000.00	1350.00	7650.00	918.00	6732.00	
7	2004	12000.00	1800.00	10200.00	1224.00	8976.00	
8	2005	15000.00	2250.00	12750.00	1530.00	11220.00	
9	2006	20000.00	3000.00	17000.00	2040.00	14960.00	
10		81000.00	12150.00	68850.00	8262.00	60588.00	
11							
12							
13							

- To remove a vertical page break: Click in any cell that appears directly to the right of the vertical page break and directly underneath the horizontal page break.
- To remove both a vertical and horizontal page break: Click in the cell that appears to the right of the vertical page break and directly underneath the horizontal page break.

2. Click the Page Layout tab.
3. Click the Breaks icon in the Page Setup group.
4. Choose Remove Page Break. Excel removes your chosen page break.

Applying Themes

You can quickly and easily format an entire document to give it a professional and modern look by applying a document theme. A document theme is a set of formatting choices that include a set of theme colors, a set of theme fonts (including heading and body text fonts), and a set of theme effects (including lines and fill effects).

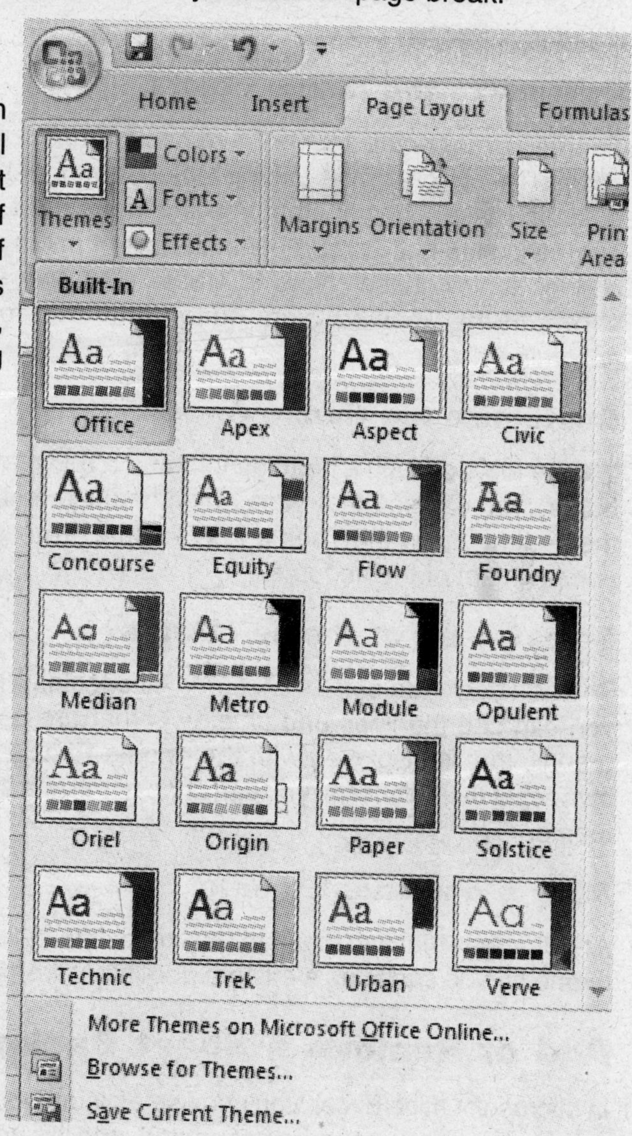

Apply a Document Theme

You can change the document theme that is applied by default in Office programs, such as Word, Excel, and PowerPoint, by selecting another predefined document theme or a custom document theme. Document themes that you apply immediately affect the styles that you can use in your document.

Do one of the following:

- On the Page Layout tab, in the Themes group, click Themes.
- To apply a predefined document theme, click the document theme that you want to use under Built-In.
- To apply a custom document theme, click the document theme that you want to use under Custom.

- Custom is available only if you created one or more custom document themes.
- If a document theme that you want to use is not listed, click Browse for Themes to find it on your computer or a network location.

Customize a Document Theme

To customize a document theme, you start by changing the colors, the fonts, or the line and fill effects that are used. Changes that you make to one or more of these theme components immediately affect the styles that you have applied in the active document. If you want to apply these changes to new documents, you can save them as a custom document theme.

Customize the theme colors

Theme colors contain four text and background colors, six accent colors, and two hyperlink colors. The colors in the Theme Colors button represent the current text and background colors. The set of colors that you see next to the Theme Colors name after you click the Theme Colors button represent the accent and hyperlink colors for that theme. When you change any of these colors to create your own set of theme colors, the colors that are shown in the Theme Colors button and next to the Theme Colors name will change accordingly.

Customize the theme fonts

Theme fonts contain a heading font and a body text font. When you click the Theme Fonts button, you can see the name of the heading font and body text font that is used for each theme font below the Theme Fonts name. You can change both of these fonts to create your own set of theme fonts.

Select a set of theme effects

Theme effects are sets of lines and fill effects. When you click the Theme Effects button , you can see the lines and fill effects that are used for each set of theme effects in the graphic that is displayed with the Theme Effects name. Although you cannot create your own set of theme effects, you can choose the one that you want to use in your own document theme.

Save a document theme

Any changes that you make to the colors, the fonts, or the line and fill effects of a document theme can be saved as a custom document theme that you can apply to other documents.

Add or Remove a Sheet Background

In Microsoft Office Excel, you can use a picture as a sheet background for display purposes only. A sheet background is not printed, and it is not retained in an individual worksheet or in an item that you save as a Web page. Because a sheet background is not printed, it cannot be used as a watermark. You can, however, mimic a watermark by inserting a graphic in a header or footer.

Add a sheet background

1. Click the worksheet that you want to display with a sheet background. Make sure that only one worksheet is selected.
2. On the Page Layout tab, in the Page Setup group, click Background.
3. Select the picture that you want to use for the sheet background, and then click Insert.
4. The selected picture is repeated to fill the sheet.

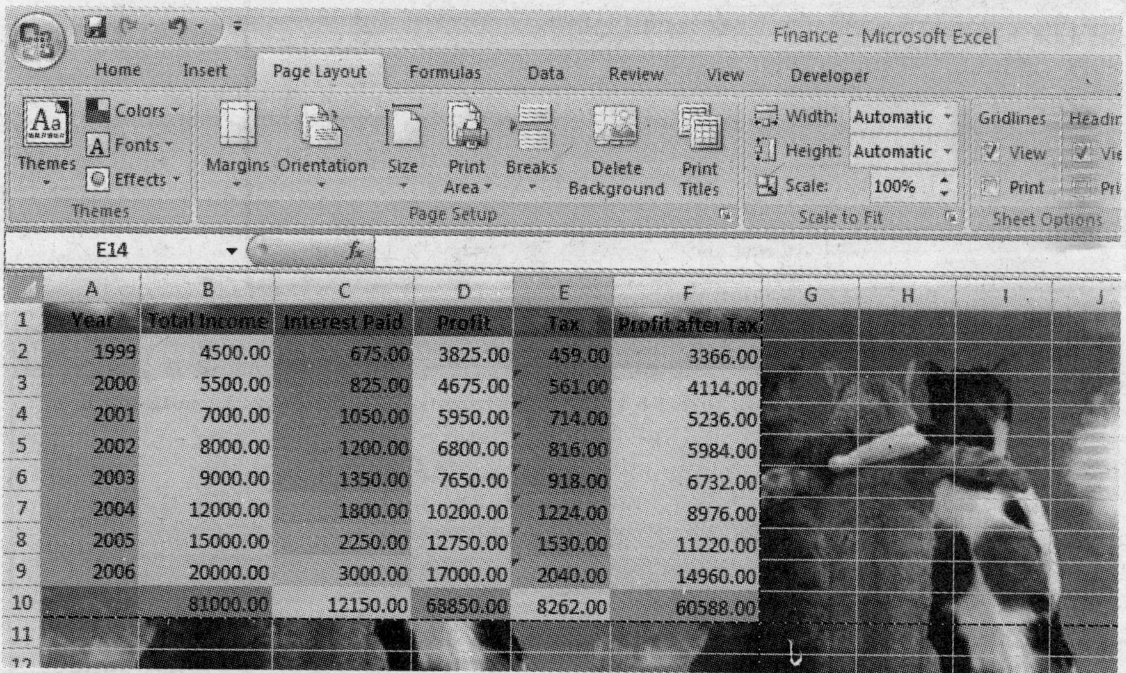

	A	B	C	D	E	F
1	Year	Total Income	Interest Paid	Profit	Tax	Profit after Tax
2	1999	4500.00	675.00	3825.00	459.00	3366.00
3	2000	5500.00	825.00	4675.00	561.00	4114.00
4	2001	7000.00	1050.00	5950.00	714.00	5236.00
5	2002	8000.00	1200.00	6800.00	816.00	5984.00
6	2003	9000.00	1350.00	7650.00	918.00	6732.00
7	2004	12000.00	1800.00	10200.00	1224.00	8976.00
8	2005	15000.00	2250.00	12750.00	1530.00	11220.00
9	2006	20000.00	3000.00	17000.00	2040.00	14960.00
10		81000.00	12150.00	68850.00	8262.00	60588.00

Remove a sheet background

1. Click the worksheet that is displayed with a sheet background. Make sure that only one worksheet is selected.
2. On the Page Layout tab, in the Page Setup group, click Background.

Convert Text to Columns

You can convert text to columns in Excel by using the Wizard called Convet Text to Columns. For this select the text which you want to convert and select the wizard from Data menu and Text to Columns from Data Tools tab. Rest is easy. Just follow the three steps shown here.

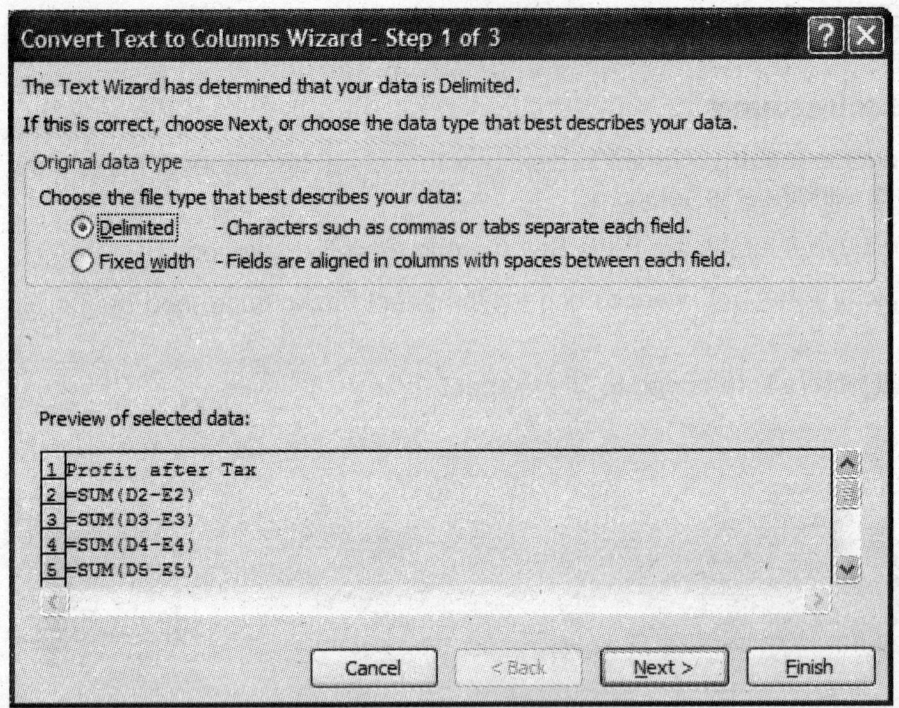
Convert Text to Columns Wizard - Step 1 of 3
The Text Wizard has determined that your data is Delimited.
If this is correct, choose Next, or choose the data type that best describes your data.
Original data type
Choose the file type that best describes your data:
Delimited - Characters such as commas or tabs separate each field.
Fixed width - Fields are aligned in columns with spaces between each field.
Preview of selected data:
1 Profit after Tax
2 =SUM(D2-E2)
3 =SUM(D3-E3)
4 =SUM(D4-E4)
5 =SUM(D5-E5)
Cancel
< Back
Next >
Finish

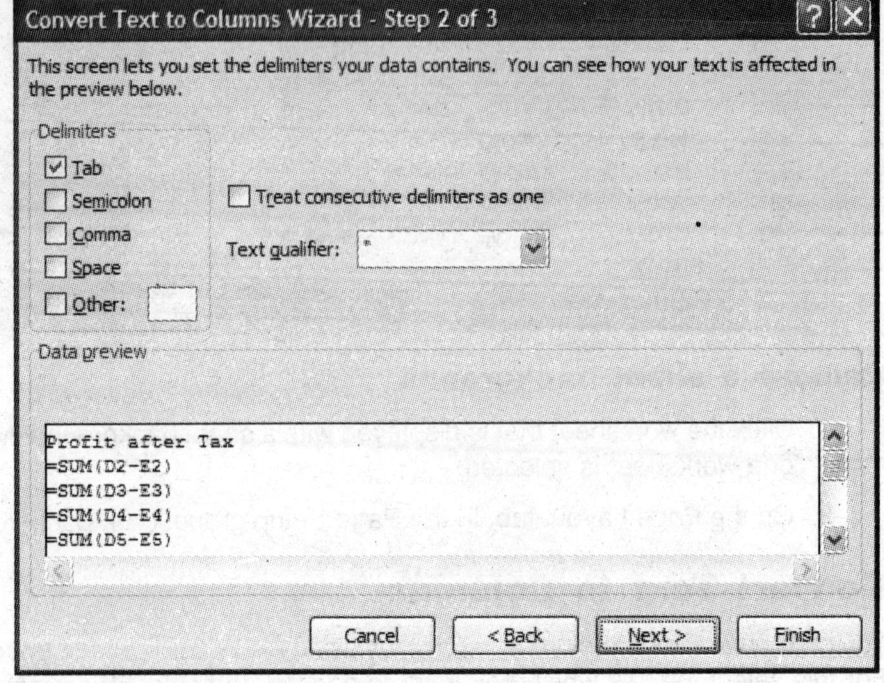
Convert Text to Columns Wizard - Step 2 of 3
This screen lets you set the delimiters your data contains. You can see how your text is affected in the preview below.
Delimiters
Tab
Semicolon
Comma
Space
Other:
Treat consecutive delimiters as one
Text qualifier:
Data preview
Profit after Tax
=SUM(D2-E2)
=SUM(D3-E3)
=SUM(D4-E4)
=SUM(D5-E5)
Cancel
< Back
Next >
Finish

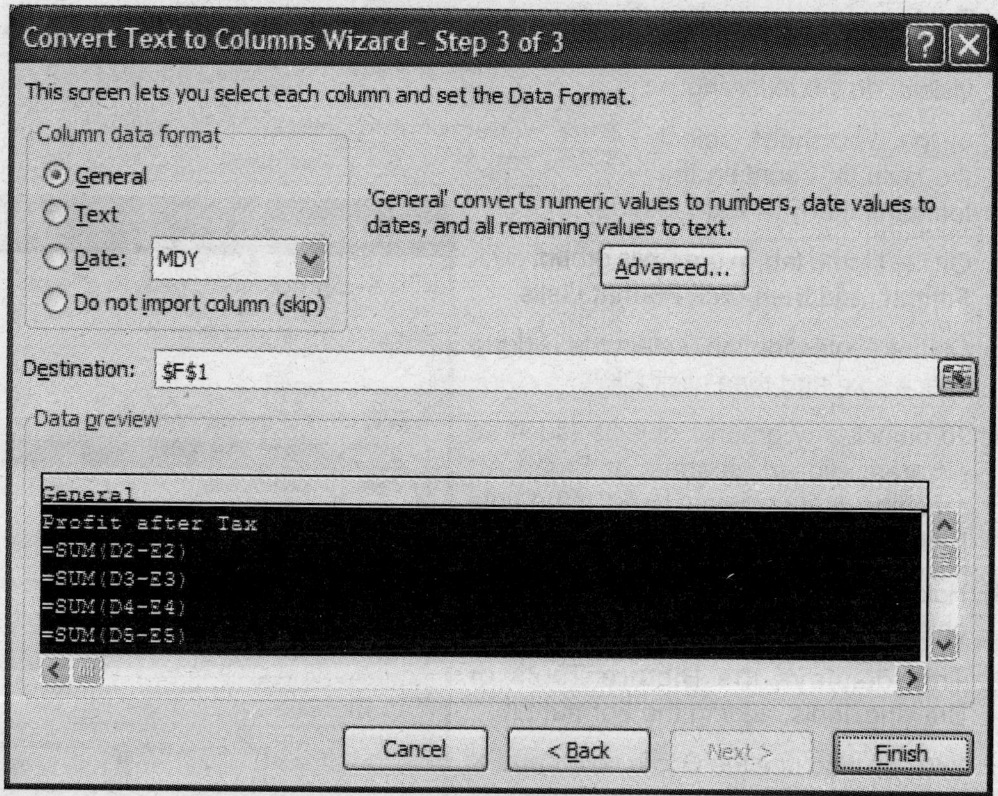

Protect Worksheet or Workbook Elements

To prevent a user from accidentally or deliberately changing, moving, or deleting important data, you can protect certain worksheet (worksheet: The primary document that you use in Excel to store and work with data. Also called a spreadsheet. A worksheet consists of cells that are organized into columns and rows; a worksheet is always stored in a workbook.) or workbook elements, with or without a password.

Workbook and worksheet element protection should not be confused with workbook-level password security. Element protection cannot protect a workbook from users who have malicious intent.

Protect Worksheet Elements

1. Select the worksheet that you want to protect.
2. To unlock any cells or ranges that you want other users to be able to change, do the following:

1. Select each cell or range that you want to unlock.
2. On the Home tab, in the Cells group, click Format, and then click Format Cells.
3. On the Protection tab, clear the Locked check box, and then click OK.

3. To hide any formulas that you don't want to be visible, do the following:

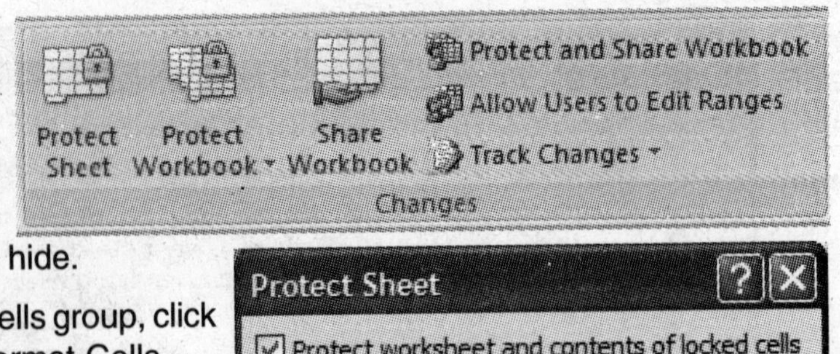

1. In the worksheet, select the cells that contain the formulas that you want to hide.
2. On the Home tab, in the Cells group, click Format, and then click Format Cells.
3. On the Protection tab, select the Hidden check box, and then click OK.
4. To unlock any graphic objects (such as pictures, clip art, shapes, or Smart Art graphics) that you want users to be able to change, do the following:

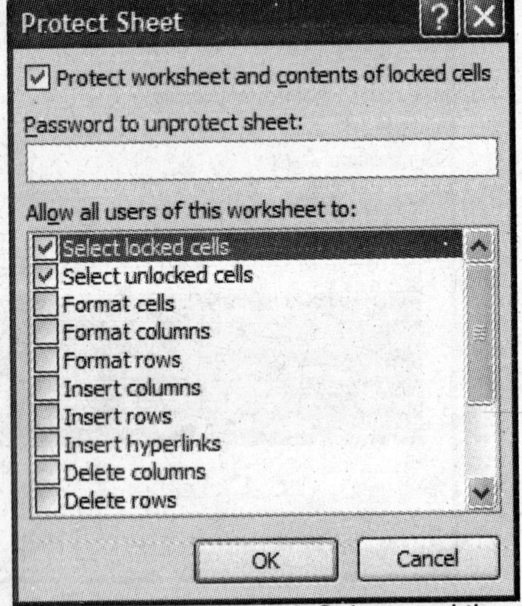

1. Hold down CTRL and click each graphic object that you want to unlock.
2. This displays the Picture Tools or Drawing Tools, adding the Format tab.

   You can also use the Go To command to quickly select all of the graphic objects in a worksheet. On the Home tab, in the Editing group, click Find & Select, and then click Go To. Click Special, and then click Objects.

3. On the Format tab, in the Size group, click the Dialog Box Launcher next to Size.
4. On the Properties tab, clear the Locked check box, and if present, clear the Lock text check box.

   You don't need to unlock buttons or controls for users to be able to click and use them. You can unlock embedded charts, text boxes, and other objects created with the drawing tools that you want users to be able to modify.

5. On the Review tab, in the Changes group, click Protect Sheet.
6. In the Allow all users of this worksheet to list, select the elements that you want users to be able to change.

Worksheet elements

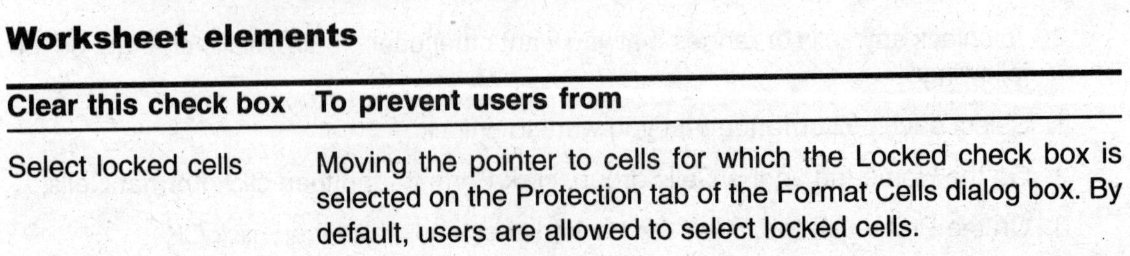

Clear this check box	To prevent users from
Select locked cells	Moving the pointer to cells for which the Locked check box is selected on the Protection tab of the Format Cells dialog box. By default, users are allowed to select locked cells.

Select unlocked cells	Moving the pointer to cells for which the Locked check box is cleared on the Protection tab of the Format Cells dialog box. By default, users are allowed to select unlocked cells, and they can press the TAB key to move between the unlocked cells on a protected worksheet.
Format cells	Changing any of the options in the Format Cells or Conditional Formatting dialog boxes. If you applied conditional formats before you protected the worksheet, the formatting continues to change when a user enters a value that satisfies a different condition.
Format columns	Using any of the column formatting commands, including changing column width or hiding columns (Home tab, Cells group, Format button).
Format rows	Using any of the row formatting commands, including changing row height or hiding rows (Home tab, Cells group, Format button).
Insert columns	Inserting columns.
Insert rows	Inserting rows.
Insert hyperlinks	Inserting new hyperlinks (hyperlink: Colored and underlined text or a graphic that you click to go to a file, a location in a file, a Web page on the World Wide Web, or a Web page on an intranet. Hyperlinks can also go to newsgroups and to Gopher, Telnet, and FTP sites.), even in unlocked cells.
Delete columns	Deleting columns. Note If Delete columns is protected and Insert columns is not also protected, a user can insert columns that he or she cannot delete.
Delete rows	Deleting rows. Note If Delete rows is protected and Insert rows is not also protected, a user can insert rows that he or she cannot delete.
Sort	Using any commands to sort data (Data tab, Sort & Filter group). Note Users can't sort ranges that contain locked cells on a protected worksheet, regardless of this setting.
Use AutoFilter	Using the drop-down arrows to change the filter on ranges when AutoFilters are applied. Note Users cannot apply or remove AutoFilters on a protected worksheet, regardless of this setting.
Use PivotTable reports	Formatting, changing the layout, refreshing, or otherwise modifying PivotTable reports or creating new reports. Edit objects Doing the any of the following: • Making changes to graphic objects—including maps, embedded charts, shapes, text boxes, and controls—that you did not unlock before you protected the worksheet. For example, if a worksheet has a button that runs a macro, you can click the button to run the macro, but you cannot delete the button.

- Making any changes, such as formatting, to an embedded chart. The chart continues to be updated when you change its source data.
- Adding or editing comments.

Edit scenarios — Viewing scenarios that you have hidden, making changes to scenarios that you have prevented changes to, and deleting these scenarios. Users can change the values in the changing cells, if the cells are not protected, and add new scenarios.

Functions in Excel

As mentioned earlier, functions are ready-made formulas which can be recalled and used while working in Excel. Here is the complete list of functions, alongwith some examples.

Financial Functions

DB	Returns the depreciation of an asset for a specified period using the fixed-declining balance method.
DDB	Returns the depreciation of an asset for a specified period using the double-declining balance method or some other method you specify.
FV	Returns the future value of an investment.
IPMT	Returns the interest payment for an investment for a given period.
IRR	Returns the internal rate of return for a series of cash flows.
ISPMT	Returns the straight-loan payment interest.
MIRR	Returns the internal rate of return where positive and negative cash flows are financed at different rates.
NPER	Returns the number of periods for an investment.
NPV	Returns the net present value of an investment based on a series of periodic cash flows and a discount rate.
PMT	Returns the periodic payment for an annuity.
PPMT	Returns the payment on the principal for an investment for a given period.
PV	Returns the present value of an investment.
RATE	Returns the interest rate per period of an annuity.
SLN	Returns the straight-line depreciation of an asset for one period.
SYD	Returns the sum-of-years digits depreciation of an asset for a specified period.
VDB	Returns the depreciation of an asset for a specified or partial period using a declining balance method.

Logical Functions

AND	Returns TRUE if all its arguments are TRUE.
FALSE	Returns the logical value FALSE.
IF	Specifies a logical test to perform.
NOT	Reverses the logic of its argument.

OR	Returns TRUE if any argument is TRUE.
TRUE	Returns the logical value TRUE.

Text Functions

BAHTTEXT	Converts a number to text (bath).
CHAR	Returns the character specified by the code number.
CLEAN	Removes all nonprintable characters from text.
CODE	Returns a numeric code for the first character in a text string.
CONCATENATE	Joins several text items into one text item.
DOLLAR	Converts a number to text, using currency format.
EXACT	Checks to see if two text values are identical.
FIND	Finds one text value within another (case-sensitive).
FIXED	Formats a number as text values are identical.
LEFT	Returns the leftmost characters from a text value.
LEN	Returns the number of characters in a text string.
LOWER	Converts text to lowercase.
MID	Returns a specific number of characters from a text string starting at the position you specify.
PROPER	Capitalizes the first letter in each word of a text value.
REPLACE	Replaces characters within text.
REPT	Repeats text a given number of times.
RIGHT	Returns the rightmost characters from a text value.
SEARCH	Finds one text value within another (not case-sensitive).
SUBSTITUTE	Substitutes new text for old text in a text string.
T	Converts its arguments to text.
TEXT	Formats a number and converts it to text.
TRIM	Removes spaces from text.
UPPER	Converts text to uppercase.
VALUE	Converts a text argument to a number.

Date and Time Functions

DATE	Returns the serial number of a particular date.
DATEVALUE	Converts a date in the form of text to a serial number.
DAY	Converts a serial number to a day of the month.
DAYS360	Calculates the number of days between two dates based on a 360-day year.
HOUR	Converts a serial number to an hour.
MINUTE	Converts a serial number to a minute.
MONTH	Converts a serial number to a month.
NOW	Returns the serial number of the current date and time.
SECOND	Converts a serial number to a second.
TIME	Returns the serial number of a particular time.
TIMEVALUE	Converts a time in the form of text to a serial number.
TODAY	Returns the serial number of today's date.

WEEKDAY Converts a serial number to a number that represents a day of the week.

YEAR Converts a serial number to a year.

Lookup and Reference Functions

ADDRESS Returns the number of areas in a reference.

AREAS Chooses a value from a list of values.

CHOOSE Chooses a value or action to perform from a list of values, based on an index number.

COLUMN Returns data stored in a PivotTable.

COLUMNS Returns the number of columns in an array or reference.

GETPIVOTDATA Extracts data stored in a PivotTable

HLOOKUP Looks in the top row of an array and returns the value of a cell in the same column, in the row that you specify.

HYPERLINK Creates a shortcut or jump that opens a document stored on a network server, an intranet, or the internet.

INDEX Uses an index to choose a value from a reference or array.

INDIRECT Returns a reference indicated by a text value.

LOOKUP Looks up values in a one-row or one-column vector or array.

MATCH Looks up values in a reference or array and returns its relative position in the array.

OFFSET Returns a reference offset from a given reference.

ROW Returns the row number of a reference.

ROWS Returns the number of rows in a reference.

RTD Retrieves real-time data from a program that supports COM automation.

TRANSPOSE Returns the transpose of an array.

VLOOKUP Looks in the first column of an array and moves across the row to return the value of a cell in the column you specify.

Math and Trigonometric Functions

ABS Returns the absolute value of a number.

ACOS Returns the arccosine of a number.

ACOSH Returns the inverse hyperbolic cosine of a number.

ASIN Returns the arcsine of a number.

ASINH Returns the inverse hyperbolic sine of a number.

ATAN Returns the arctangent of a number.

ATAN2 Returns the arctangent from x- and y- coordinates.

ATANH Returns the inverse hyperbolic tangent of a number.

CEILING Rounds a number up to the nearest integer or to the nearest multiple of significance.

COMBIN Returns the number of combinations for a given number of objects.

COS Returns the cosine of a number.

COSH Returns the hyperbolic cosine of a number.

DEGREES Converts radians to degrees.

EVEN	Rounds a number up to the nearest even integer.
EXP	Returns e raised to the power of a given number.
FACT	Returns the factorial of a number.
FLOOR	Rounds a number down, toward zero.
INT	Rounds a number down to the nearest integer.
LN	Returns the natural logarithm of a number.
LOG	Returns the logarithm of a number to a specified base.
LOG10	Returns the base-10 logarithm of a number.
MDETERM	Returns the matrix determinant of an array.
MINVERSE	Returns the matrix inverse of an array.
MMULT	Returns the matrix product of two arrays.
MOD	Returns the remainder from division.
ODD	Rounds a number up to the nearest odd integer.
PI	Returns the value of p (pi) to 15 digits.
POWER	Returns the result of a number raised to a power.
PRODUCT	Multiplies its arguments.
RADIANS	Converts degrees to radians.
RAND	Returns a random number between 0 and 1.
ROMAN	Converts an arabic numeral to roman, as text.
ROUND	Rounds a number to a specified number of digits.
ROUNDDOWN	Rounds a number down, toward zero.
ROUNDUP	Rounds a number up, away from zero.
SIGN	Returns the sign of a number.
SIN	Returns the sine of the given angle.
SINH	Returns the hyperbolic sine of a number.
SQRT	Returns a positive square root.
SUBTOTAL	Returns a subtotal in a list or database.
SUM	Adds its arguments.
SUMIF	Adds the cells specified by a given criteria.
SUMPRODUCT	Returns the sum of the products of corresponding array components.
SUMSQ	Returns the sum of the squares of the arguments.
SUMX2MY2	Returns the sum of the difference of squares of corresponding values in two arrays.
SUMX2PY2	Returns the sum of the sum of squares of corresponding values in two arrays.
SUMXMY2	Returns the sum of squares of differences of corresponding values in two arrays.
TAN	Returns the tangent of a number.
TANH	Returns the hyperbolic tangent of a number.
TRUNC	Truncates a number to an integer.

Statistical Functions

AVEDEV	Returns the average of the absolute deviations of data points from their mean.

AVERAGE	Returns the average of its arguments.
AVERAGEA	Returns the average of its arguments, including numbers, text, and logical values.
BETADIST	Returns the cumulative beta probability density function.
BETAINV	Returns the inverse of the cumulative beta probability density function.
BINOMDIST	Returns the individual term binomial distribution probability.
CHIDIST	Returns the one-tailed probability of the chi-squared distribution.
CHIINV	Returns the inverse of the one-tailed probability of the chi-squared distribution.
CHITEST	Returns the test for independence.
CONFIDENCE	Returns the confidence interval for a population mean.
CORREL	Returns the correlation coefficient between two data sets.
COUNT	Counts how many numbers are in the list of arguments.
COUNTA	Counts how many values are in the list of arguments.
COUNTBLANK	Counts the number of blank cells within a range.
COUNTIF	Counts the number of non blank cells within a range that meet the given criteria.
COVAR	Returns covariance, the average of the products of paired deviations.
CRITBINOM	Returns the smallest value for which the cumulative binomial distribution is less than or equal to a criterion value.
DEVSQ	Returns the sum of squared of deviations.
EXPONDIST	Returns the exponential distribution.
FDIST	Returns the F probability distribution.
FINV	Returns the inverse of the F probability distribution.
FISHER	Returns the Fisher transformation.
FISHERINV	Returns the inverse of the Fisher transformation.
FORECAST	Returns a value along a linear trend.
FREQUENCY	Returns a frequency distribution as a vertical array.
FTEST	Returns the result of an F-test.
GAMMADIST	Returns the gamma distribution.
GAMMAINV	Returns the inverse of the gamma cumulative distribution.
GAMMALN	Returns the natural logarithm of the gamma function, G(x).
GEOMEAN	Returns the geometric mean.
GROWTH	Returns values along an exponential trend.
HARMEAN	Returns the harmonic mean.
HYPGEOMDIST	Returns the hypergeometric distribution.
INTERCEPT	Returns the intercept of the linear regression line.
KURT	Returns the kurtosis of a data set.
LARGE	Returns the kth largest value in a data set.
LINEST	Returns the parameters of a linear trend.
LOGEST	Returns the parameters of an exponential trend.
LOGINV	Returns the inverse of the lognormal distribution.
LOGNORMDIST	Returns the cumulative lognormal distribution.

MAX	Returns the maximum value in a list of arguments.
MAXA	Returns the maximum value in a list of arguments, including numbers, text, and logical values.
MEDIAN	Returns the median of the given numbers.
MIN	Returns the minimum value in a list of arguments.
MINA	Returns the smallest value in a list of arguments, including numbers, text, and logical values.
MODE	Returns the most common value in a data set.
NEGBINOMDIST	Returns the negative binomial distribution.
NORMDIST	Returns the normal cumulative distribution.
NORMSINV	Returns the inverse of the standard normal cumulative distribution.
PEARSON	Returns the Pearson product moment correlation coefficient.
PERCENTILE	Returns the kth percentile of values in a range.
PERCENTRANK	Returns the percentage rank of a value in a data set.
PERMUT	Returns the number of permutations for a given number of objects.
POISSON	Returns the Poisson distribution.
PROB	Returns the probability that values in a range are between two limits.
QUARTILE	Returns the quartile of a data set.
RANK	Returns the rank of a number in a list of numbers.
RSQ	Returns the square of the Pearson product moment correlation coefficient.
SKEW	Returns the skewness of a distribution.
SLOPE	Returns the slope of the linear regression line.
SMALL	Returns the kth smallest value in a data set.
STANDARDIZE	Returns a normalized value.
STDEV	Estimates standard deviation based on a sample.
STDEVA	Estimates standard deviation based on a sample, including numbers, text, and logical values.
STDEVP	Calculates standard deviation based on the entire population.
STDEVPA	Calculates standard deviation based on the entire population, including numbers, text, and logical values.
STEYX	Returns the standard error of the predicted y- value for each x in the regression.
TDIST	Returns the Student's t-distribution.
TINV	Returns the inverse of the Student's t-distribution.
TREND	Returns values along a linear trend.
TRIMMEAN	Returns the mean of the interior of a data set.
TTEST	Returns the probability associated with a Student's t-test.
VAR	Estimates variance based on a sample.
VARA	Estimates variance based on a sample, including numbers, text, and logical values.
VARP	Calculates variance based on the entire population.
VARPA	Calculates variance based on the entire population, including numbers, text, and logical values.

WEIBULL	Returns the Weibull distribution.
ZTEST	Returns the two-tailed P-value of a z-test.

Database Functions

DAVERAGE	Returns the average of selected database entries.
DCOUNT	Counts the cells that contain numbers in a particular field of records that match specified criteria in a database.
DCOUNTA	Counts non blank cells in a particular field of records that match specified criteria in a database.
DGET	Extracts a single record from a database that matches the specified criteria.
DMAX	Returns the maximum value from selected database entries.
DMIN	Returns the minimum value from selected database entries.
DPRODUCT	Multiplies the values in a particular field of records that match the criteria in a database.
DSTDEV	Estimates the standard deviation based on a sample of selected database entries.
DSTDEVP	Calculates the standard deviation based on the entire population of selected database entries.
DSUM	Sums the values in a particular field for all records that match the specified criteria.
DVAR	Estimates variance based on a sample from selected database entries.
DVARP	Calculates variance based on the entire population of selected database entries.

Information Functions

CELL	Returns information about the formatting, location, or contents of a cell.
ERRORTYPE	Returns a number corresponding to an error type.
INFO	Returns information about the current operating environment.
ISBLANK	Returns TRUE if the value is blank.
ISERR	Returns TRUE if the value is any error value expect #N/A.
ISERROR	Returns TRUE if the value is any error value.
ISLOGICAL	Returns TRUE if the value is a logical value.
ISNA	Returns TRUE if the value is the #N/A error value.
ISNONTEXT	Returns TRUE if the value is non text.
ISNUMBER	Returns TRUE if the value is a number.
ISREF	Returns TRUE if the value is reference.
ISTEXT	Returns TRUE if the value is text.
N	Returns a value converted to a number.
NA	Returns the error value #N/A.
TYPE	Returns a number indicating the data type of a value.

4 Introduction to Microsoft PowerPoint 2007

Creating Presentation from Template

Most of the office 2007 software have ready made outputs called Templates. This is true in the case of PowerPoint 2007 too. Let us see how it can be used to create a presentation.

1. Select New from the Office button.
2. Select Installed Themes and then select any one of the available templates. I have chosen Introduction to PowerPoint 2007.
3. Click at Create to start with the presentation.
4. The first slide with the Introduction to PowerPoint 2007 appears on the screen.
5. As you will that on the left panel 18 slides have been created and are thus numbered from 1 to 18.
6. You can see any one of them by just clicking at it. I am showing here the slide numbers 5, 9 and 18.

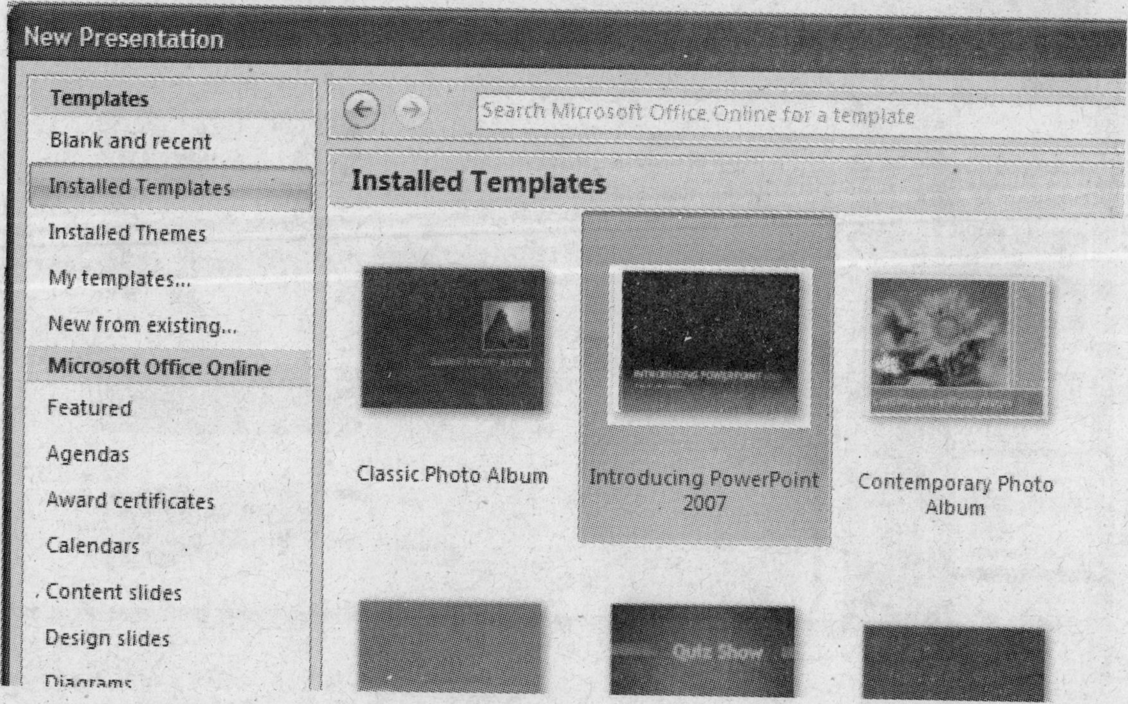

INTRODUCING POWERPOINT 2007
A tour of new features
Slides
Outline
The Power of OfficeArt Graphics
Make a statement with great looking graphics. PowerPoint makes it easy to produce visuals that used to require multiple applications to accomplish. Easily apply soft shadows, reflections, glows, bevels, 3D and more!
Soft Shadow
Reflection
Bevel
3D
Click to add notes
Slide 5 of 18
"IntroducingPowerPoint2007"

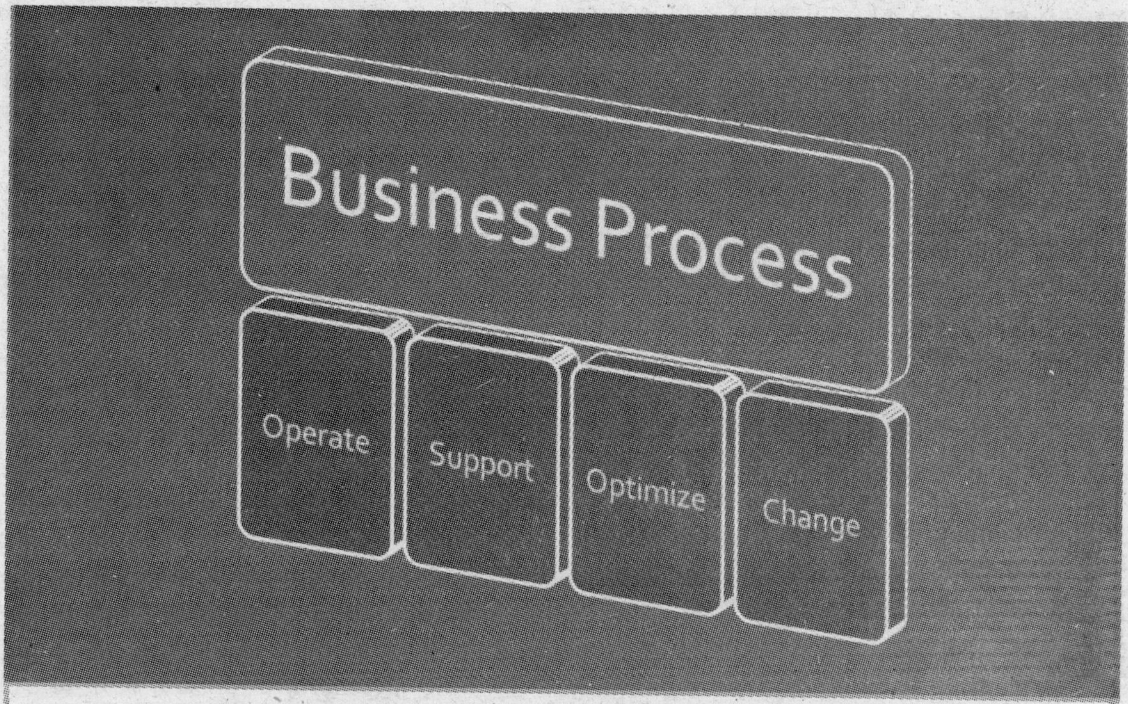

Arrange it Your Way

With custom layouts you design your own slide arrangements. You can create new kinds of documents with PowerPoint. Easily create everything from business pitchbooks to family photo albums.

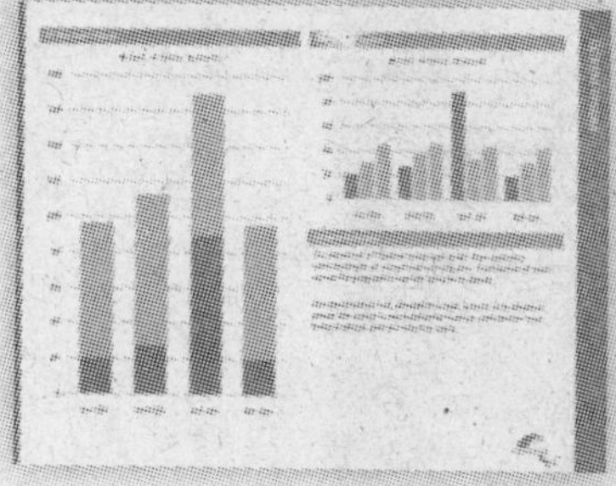

Creating a New Presentation

Another method of creating presentation is by using the option of New presentation using the Blank presentation option. You can select an option of text and graphics to make show on the screen.

1. Select New from the Office button.
2. Select Blank presentation and click Create.

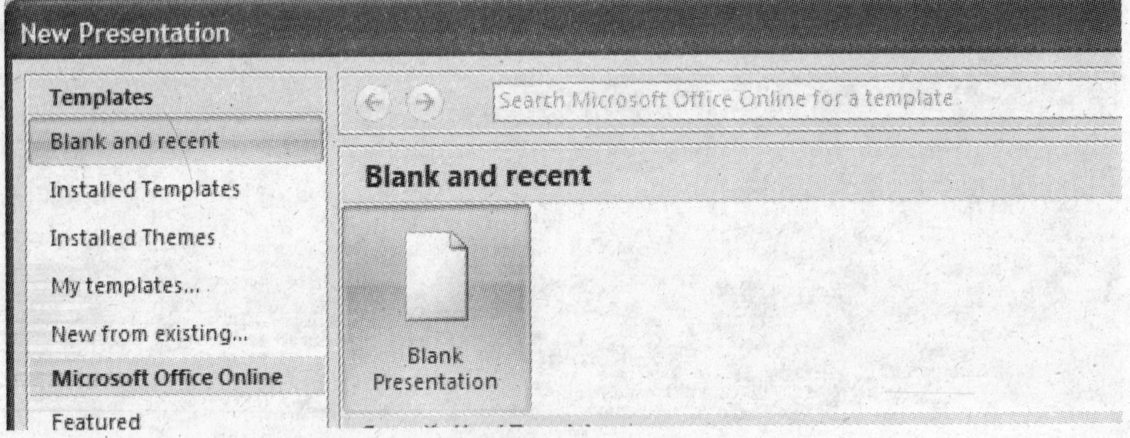

3. A new slide is shown on the screen.

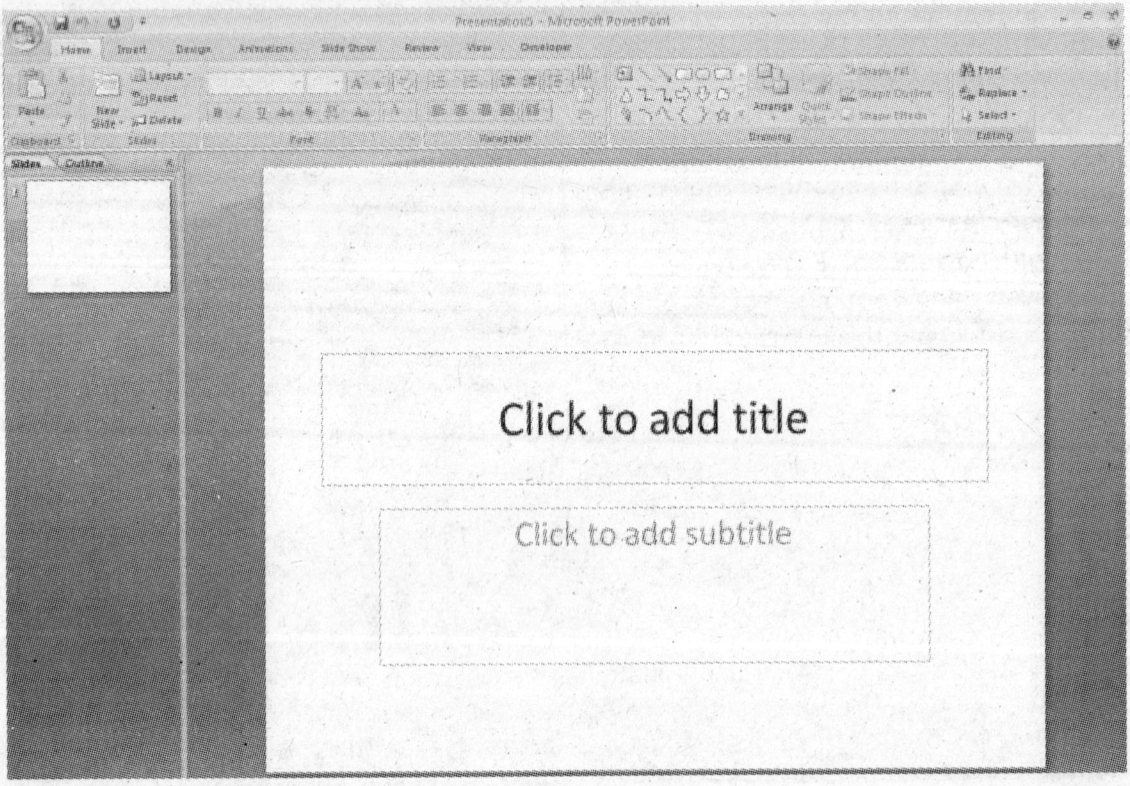

PowerPoint Views

There are different ways of looking at the presentations. These are called the views. There are as many as 5 different views in which you can see your presentation. They are:

Outline view: It displays only the text of the presentation in the outline form, allowing you to work easily with the content.

Normal view: It displays 3 panes that show the outline, the slide, and an area which you can enter speaker's notes.

Slide Sorter view: It displays thumbnail views of your slides so that you can reorganize the slides and change the overall look of the presentation. In this view you can also add and edit the transition effects for the slide show.

Slide Show view: It displays the presentation one slide at a time in sequence as an automatic slide show.

Notes Page view: It is available only from the view menu, lets you enter and edit speaker's notes for the presenter.

Points to Remember

1. Each view shows a different aspect of the same presentation.
2. You can switch from one view to another at any time.
3. Right-click in Slide Sorter view or click the button at lower left corner of the current slide to display the Slide Show shortcut menu.

Entering the Text

Let us create another presentation which has more of text. Here, we will add the text as per the following:

1. Create a new presentation which has only text in the slide.
2. Type the name Adobe Corporation in the title bar.
3. In the next box, type the name of the famous software of the company called PageMaker.
4. Pressing enter would lead you to another sub heading.
5. Type here the next heading, Photoshop CS 2.
6. Similarly press enter and type Illustrator CS 2.
7. Now we come to adding text in between the main headings, i.e., sub-headings.
8. Place your cursor at the end of the first heading, i..e., after PageMaker and press Enter. A new heading with 2 will appear. Just press Tab to get the bulleted text format. Type here the first line of your tabbed matter, which is Version 6.5.

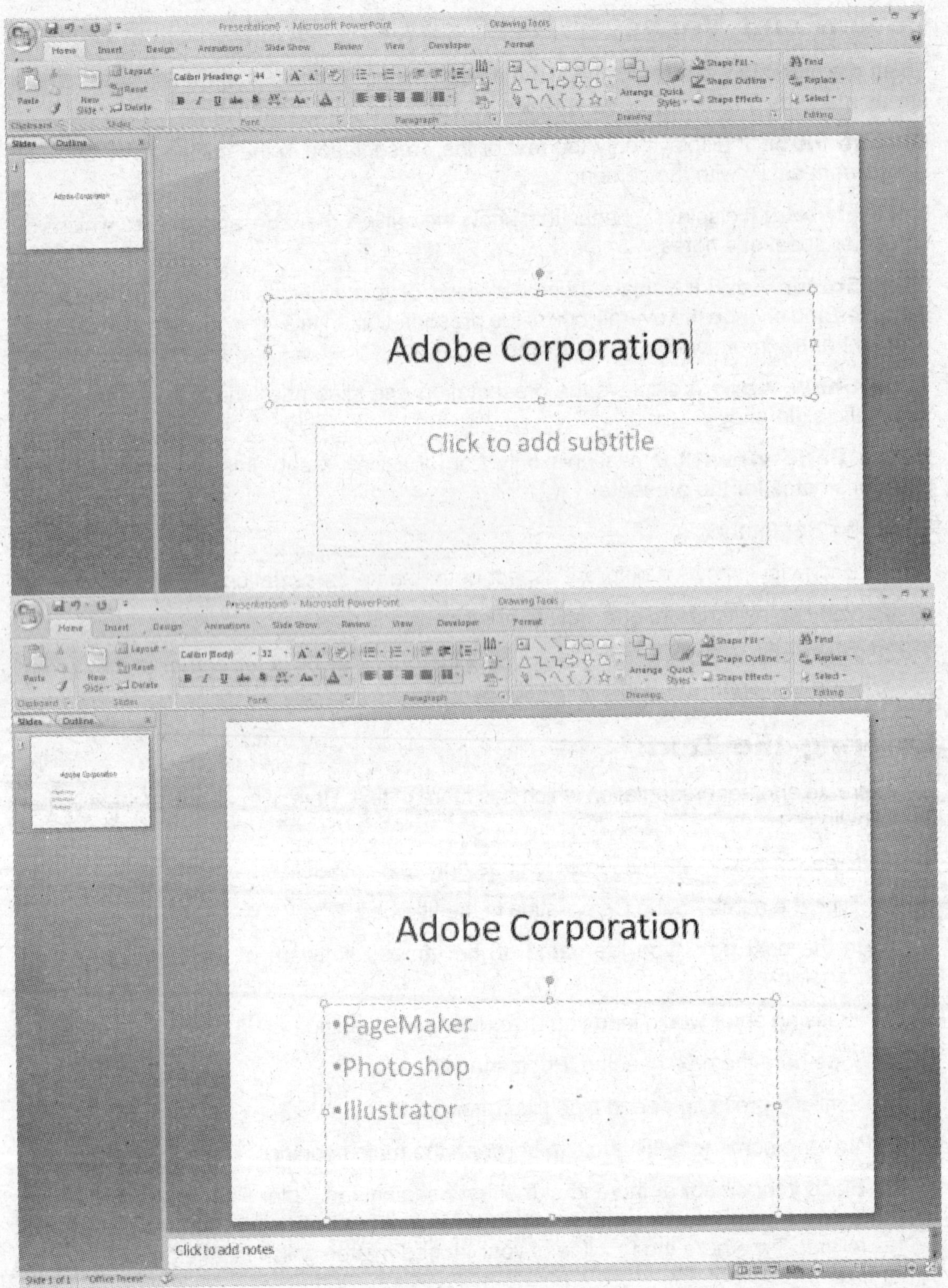
Adobe Corporation
Click to add subtitle
Adobe Corporation
•PageMaker
•Photoshop
•Illustrator
Click to add notes

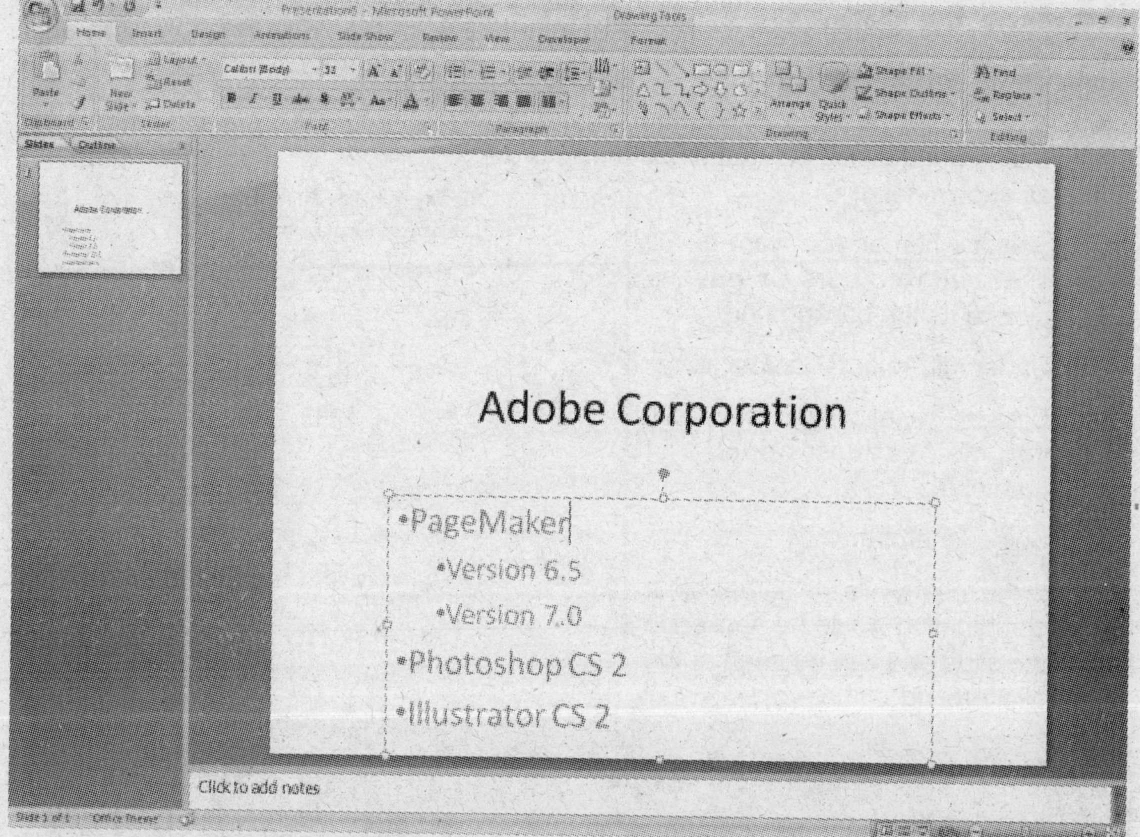

9. Press enter again to get the new line and type version 7.0.
10. You can thus type the date in the steps required by you.
11. All these slides are shown on the next pages.
12. Next obvious step would be change the data, read on.

Moving the Text

You can move up or down a particular heading for reorganizing. For this do the following:

1. Highlight the text you want to move.
2. With text highlighted drag the text up or down.
3. Leave the mouse button at the place where you feel like placing the text.
4. The text will be moved there.

Changing the Colour

The colour schemes are always used to suit the atmosphere. So it depends where the presentation is going to be. Depending upon that the colour of the presentations are selected.

To Change the Colours

1. Select Background Styles from Design menu.
2. Background dialog box appears, as shown next.
3. Select whether you want to Fill slide with colours or have a picture as the background.
4. Under Fill, select Gradient fill.
5. Click at Preset colors, it will show you the various options of gradients.
6. Select one of them.
7. In the meanwhile the same colour combination would be applied to the slide and can be seen at the background.

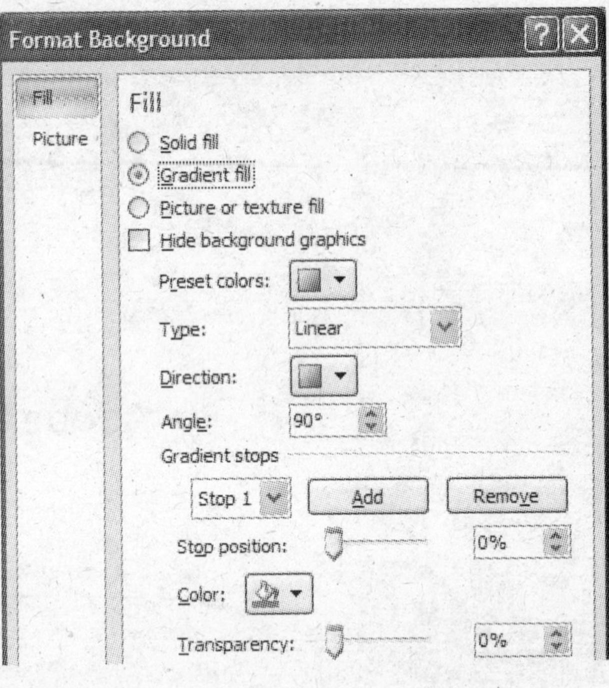

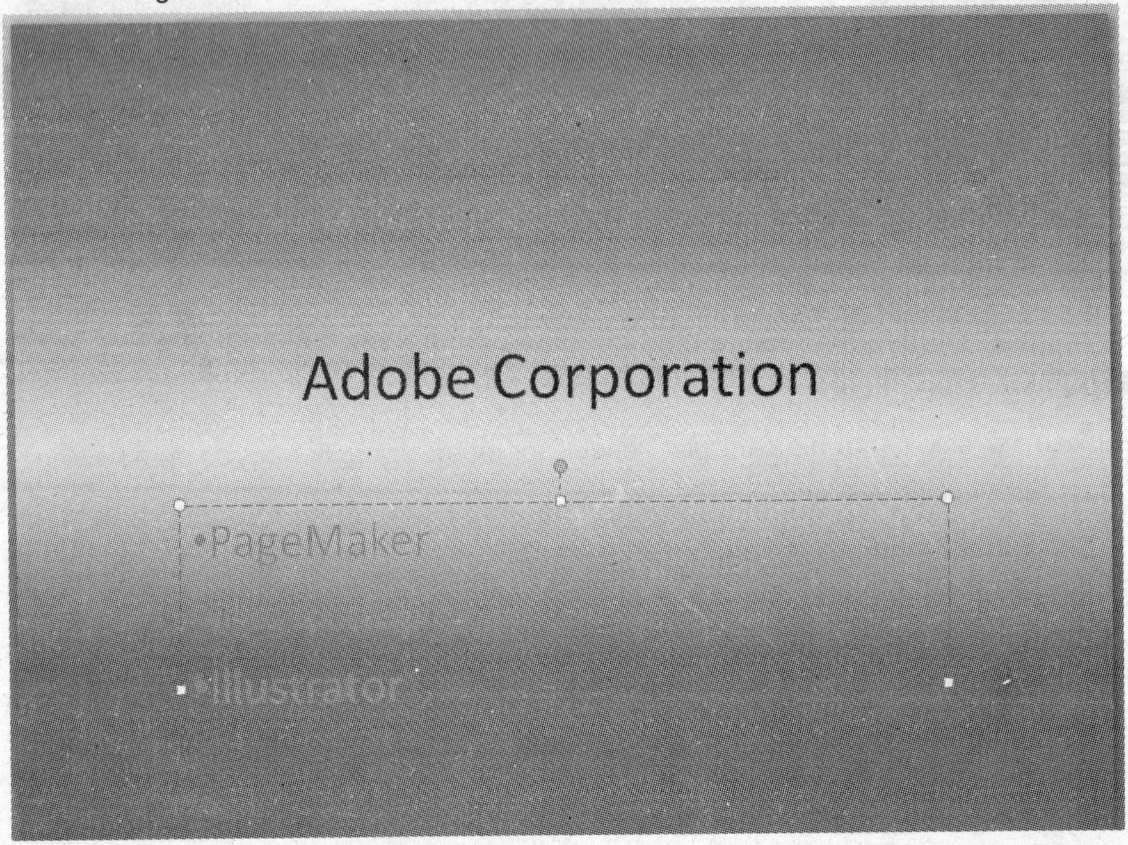

Adobe Corporation

•PageMaker

•Illustrator

8. Click Ok to make the changes in the slide, as shown below.

To change a slide background picture

1. From the Desing menu, choose background styles option.
2. The Format Background dialog box is displayed.
3. Under Picture, select the picture you want to have as background.
4. Click Apply button to apply the change to the current slide or click Apply to All to apply change to all the slides.

Adding Graphics to a Slide

You can add effects to your slide by adding the various types of graphics to it. Such graphics can be informative, such as a chart that displays sales results; or they can be decorative, such as a cartoon smiley face that emphasizes the presentation's good news.

The three common types of graphics you can add to a PowerPoint slide include:

- **Picture files**: Includes clip art images as well as images you may have stored on your hard disk, such as photographs from your digital camera.
- **Charts**: Displays bar, column, line, pie, and other types of charts.
- **WordArt**: Displays text as colourful tex.

Adding Picture to the Presentation

1. Click a slide to which you want to add a picture.
2. Click the Insert tab.
3. Click the Picture icon in the Illustrations group.
4. Click the picture file you want and then click Open.

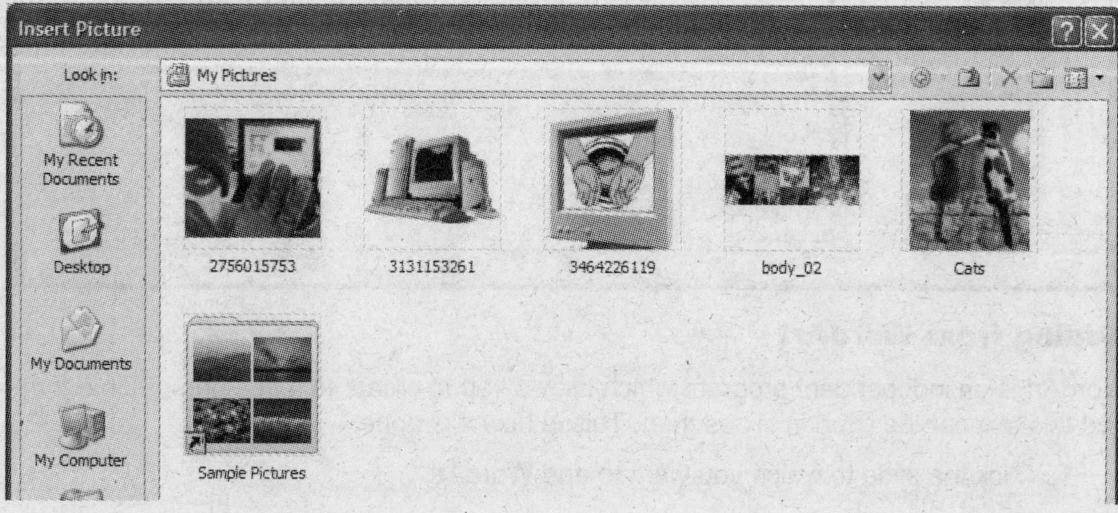

Adding Clip Art on a Slide

Clip Art consists of drawings that come with PowerPoint. To add a clip art image to a slide, follow these steps.:

1. Click a slide to which you want to add a click art.
2. Click the Insert tab.
3. Click the Clip ARt icon in the Illustrations group.
4. Click in the Search For text box and type a word that describes the type of image you want to find.
5. Click Ok.
6. Click the clip art image you want to use.

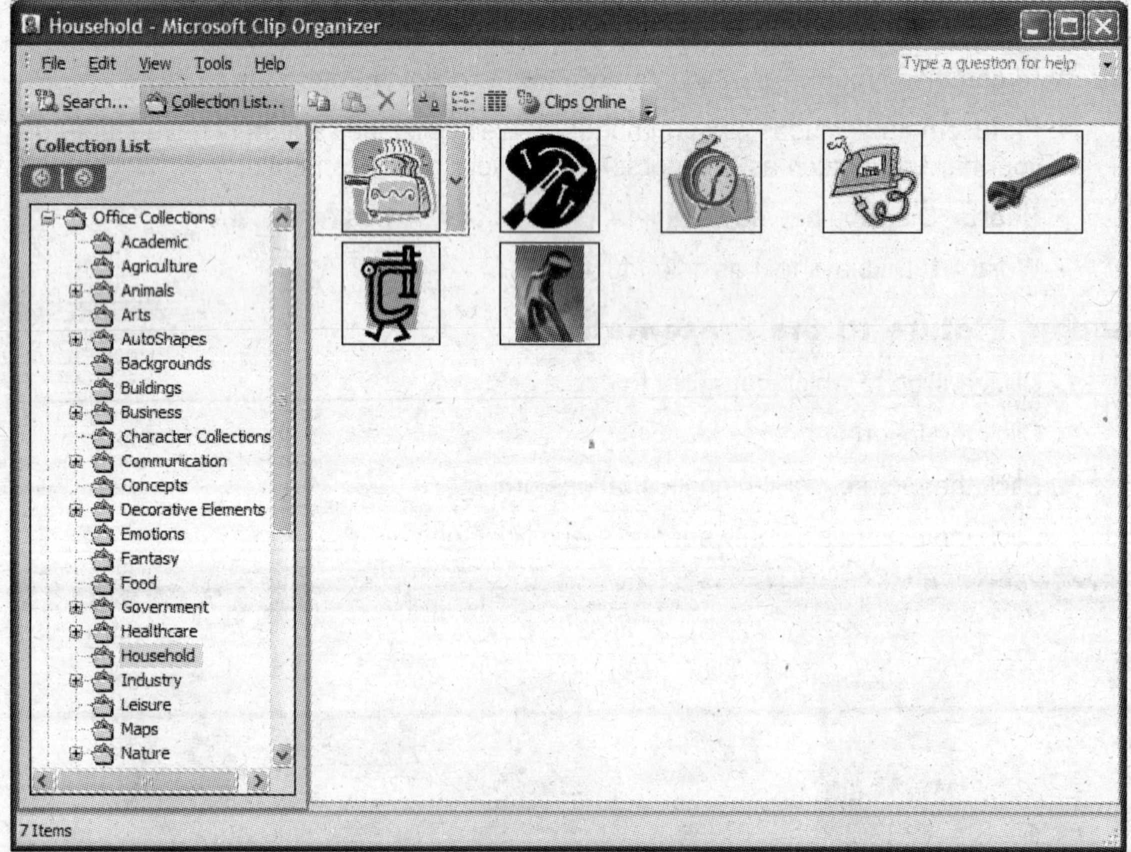

Adding from WordArt

WordArt is an independent program which allows you to create text in a presentable form and this text can be used in slides then. This is how it is done.

1. Click the slide to which you want to add WordArt.

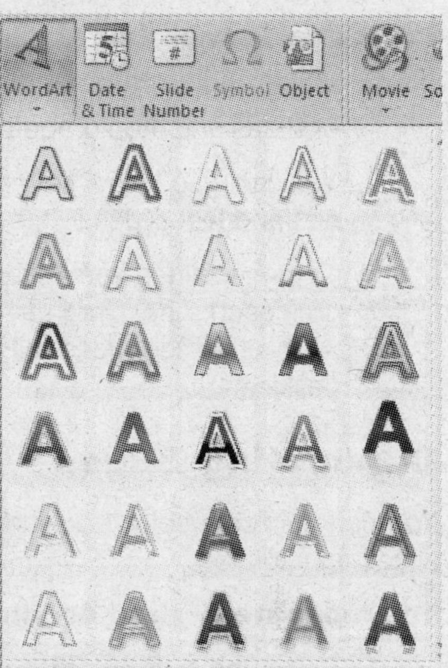

2. Click the Insert Tab.
3. Click the WordArt icon in the Text group.
4. Click a WordArt style to use.
5. Click in the WordArt text box and type text.

Reordering Slides

As you see from the view, each slide is numbered. These number belong to their order of display. This order can be changed at any point of time in the presentation.

To Change the Order of the Slides:

1. Click with the mouse the slide whose position you want to change.
2. Pressing the mouse button drag the slide to a new position.
3. A vertical line appears to indicate where the slide will drop when you release the mouse button.
4. Releasing the mouse button will drop the slide at the right place.
5. In the figure below, you will see that the slide 3 has been placed between the number 1 and 2. The numbering of all the slides has been changed subsequently.
6. Both original and after change figures are shown here.

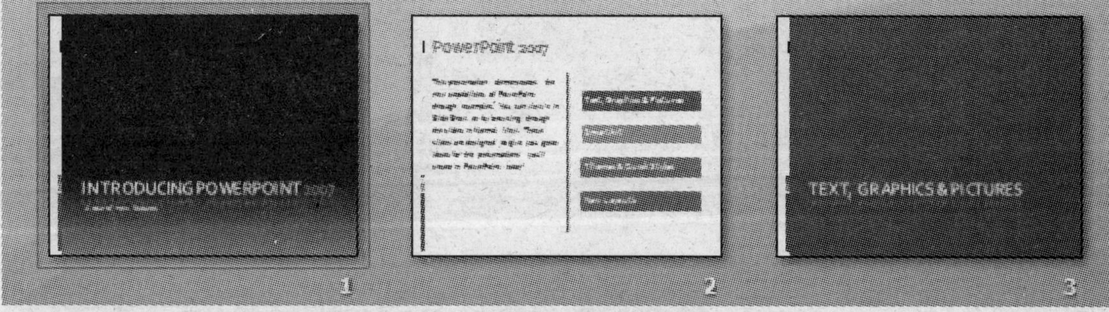

Points to Remember

1. You can select several slides to move by drawing a selection box around the group of slides and then dragging the group to the new position.
2. You can also select several slides by holding down the Shift key and selecting the first and last slides in the series.
3. To gather slides from different parts of a presentation, hold down the Ctrl key as you click each slide. Drag any one slide in the group to a new point in the presentation. All the selected slides will appear in sequence and in the same relative order at new position.

Duplicating Slides

You can duplicate selected slides in Slide Sorter view and see the effect on the flow of slides immediately.

To Duplicate a slide or slides:

1. Select the slide or slides you want to duplicate.
2. Press Ctrl + D to duplicate the slide.
3. Slide would be duplicated.
4. In the following figure slide 18 has been duplicated as slide 19.

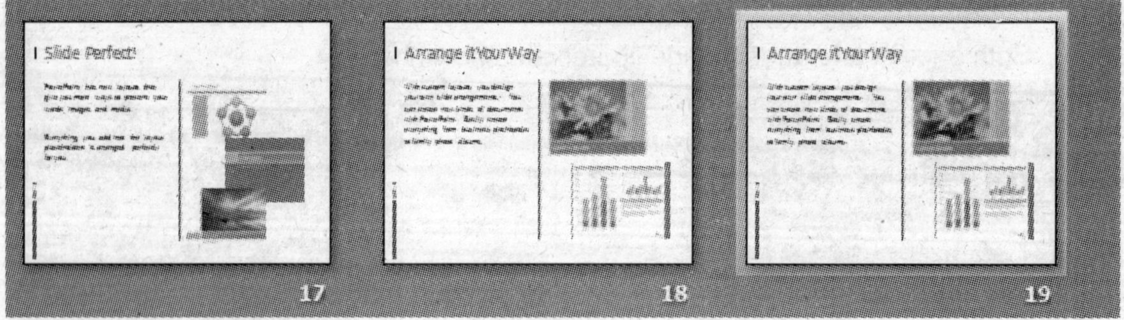

Deleting Slides

You can delete the selected slides in Slide Sorter view and see that the numbering of other slides change immediately.

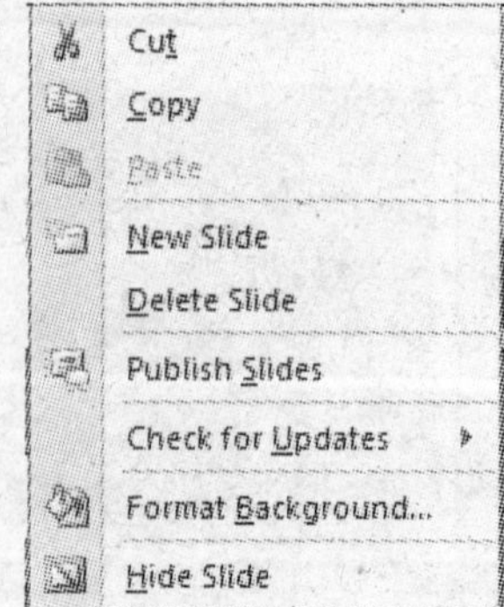

To delete a slide or slides:

1. Select the slide or slides you want to delete.
2. Press right mouse button to get the sub menu.
3. Select Delete slide to delete the slide.

Adding an Animated Cartoon to a Slide

PowerPoint includes a library of simple animated cartoons that you can place on a slide for added visual emphasis. To include one of these animate cartoons on a slide, follow these steps.

1. Click the slide to which you want to add an animated cartoons,
2. Click the Insert tab.
3. Click the downward pointing arrow underneath the Movie icon in the Media Clips group.
4. Choose Movie from Clip Organizer.
5. Click a cartoon.

You won't see the animate cartoon in action until you view your presentation by pressing F5.

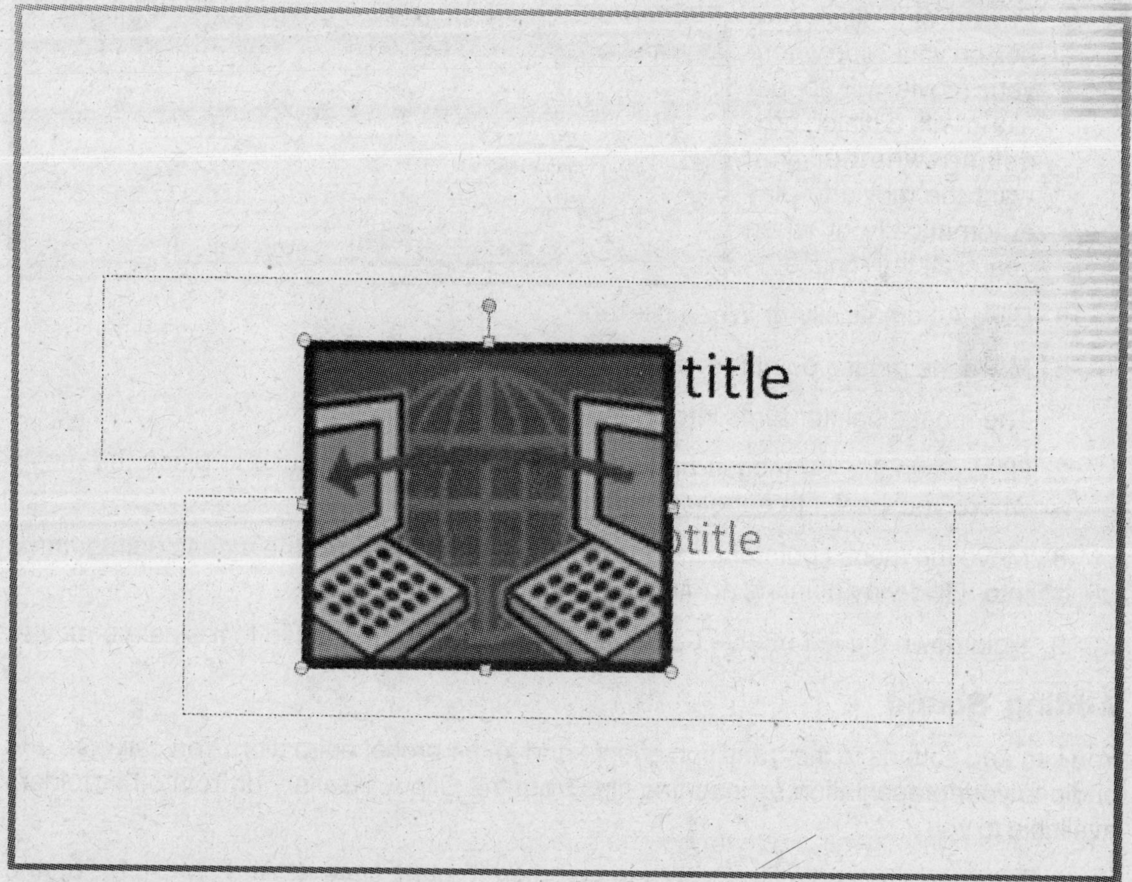

Adding a Movie to a Slide

PowerPoint slides can also display a movie. When you store a movie on a slide, you can resize its size and move it anywhere on your slide. As soon as your slide appears, you hae the option of having the movie play automatically or wait until you click the mouse first.

PowerPoint can use movies stored in common Windows view formats such as AVI, MPEG, ASF (streaming video), and WMV files. If your movie is stored in a different file format, such as QuickTime, you have to convert the file first before you can add it to a PowerPoint presentation.

To add a movie to a slide, follow these steps:

1. Click the slide to which you want to add a movie.
2. Click the Insert tab.
3. Click the Movie icon in the Media Clips group.

   The Insert Movie dialog box appears.
4. Click the movie file you want to add and then click Ok.

   PowerPoint displays a box on your slide where your movie will appear along with a dialog box, asking whether you want the movie to play automatically or when you click the mouse.

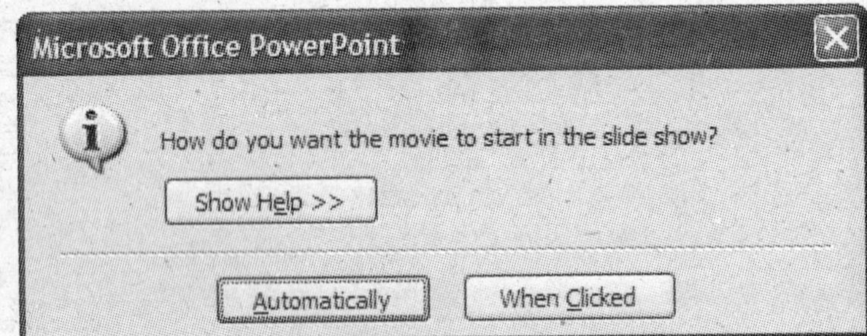

5. Clikc Automatically or When clicked.
6. Move the mouse pointer over the movie.

   The mouse pointer turns into a long-way pointing arrow.
7. Hold down the left mouse button and drap (move) the mouse to place the movie where you want it to appear on the slide.
8. Move the mouse pointer over one corner of the movie until the mouse pointer turns into a two-way pointing arrow.
9. Hold down the left mouse button and drag (move) the mouse to resize the movie.

Adding Sound

You can add sounds to the transition effects and to the preset animation. You can also add audio to your presentation by inserting files from the Clip Art Gallery or from other folders available to you.

PowerPoint can use audio files stored in common formats such as AIFF, MIDI, MP3, and WAV file. If your audio file is stored in a different file format, such as Real Audio, you will have to convert the file first before you can add it to a PowerPoint presentation.

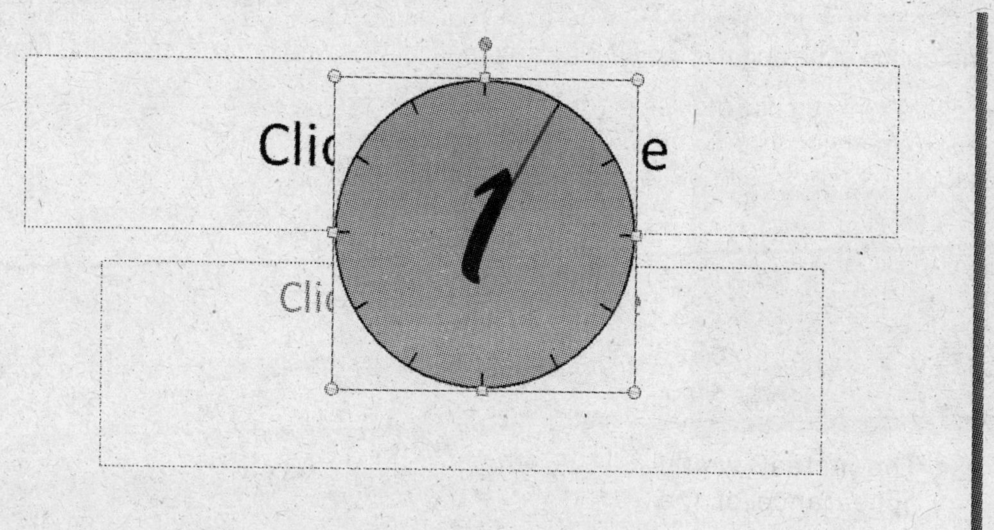

To Add an Audio File

1. Select the slide where you want to put this audio.
2. Click the Insert tab.
3. Click the downward-pointing arrow underneath the Sound icon to the Media Clips group.
4. Choose Sound from File

   The Insert Sound dialog box appears.

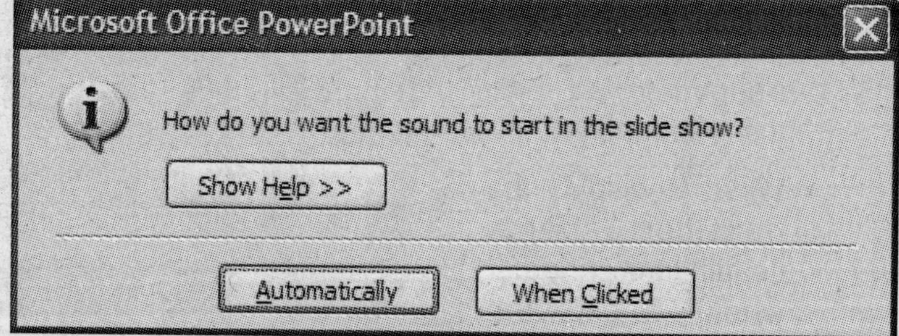

5. Click the audio file you want to add and thne click Ok.

   PowerPoint adds you audio file to the currently displayed slide (reprresent as a horn icon) and displays a dialog box, asking whether you want the sound to play automatically or when you click the mouse.

6. Click Automatically or When Clicked.

   PowerPoint displays your audio file as a sound icon on your slide. You may want to move the sound icon on your slide so it doesn't obscure part of your slide.

Adding Slide Transitions

These effects can be of the form of wipes, splits, dissolves, etc., which you usually see in the film show. For this you have to work in the Slide Sorter view.

When creating a transition, you need to define the following:

- The actual visual appearance of the transition.
- The speed of the transition (Slow, Medium, or Fast).
- Any sound effects you want to play during the transition (these can get really annoying, so use them sparingly)
- When to display the transition (after a certain time period or when you click the mouse).

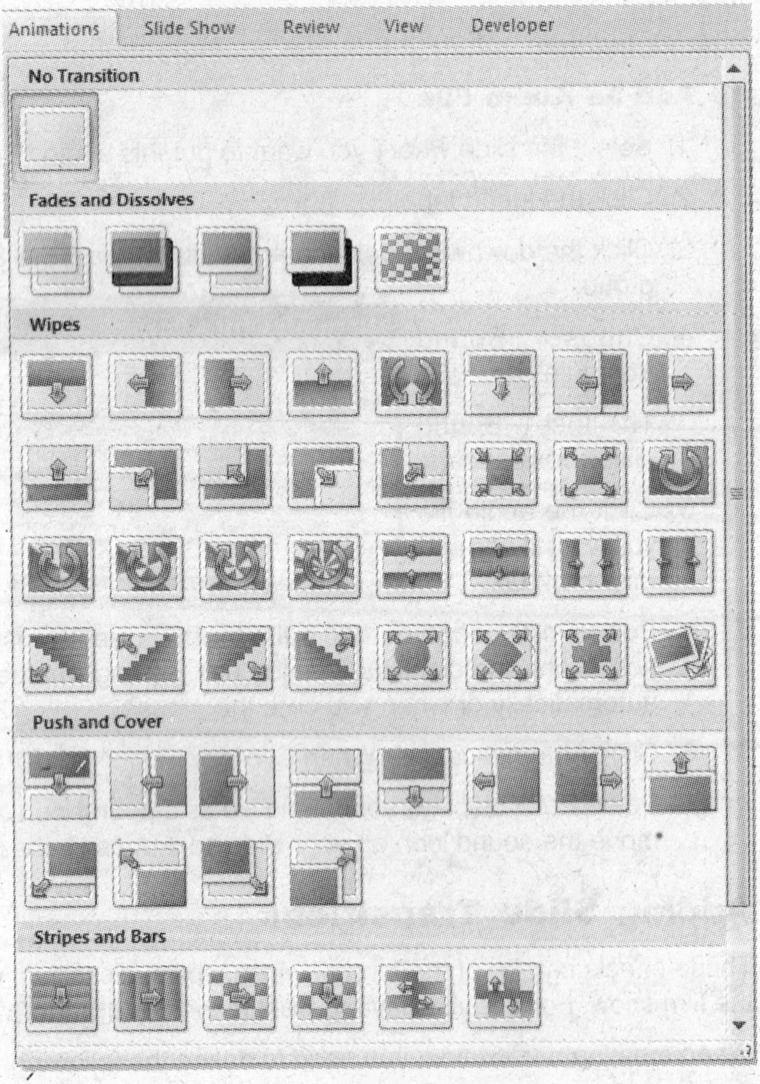

To Add a Transition View

1. Click a slide (in the Slide or Outline view pane).

   Any transition you choose will end by displaying the slide you choose in this step.

2. Click the Animations tab.

   PowerPoint displays the different animation.

3. Click the More button of the Transition To This Slide group.

   A pull-down menu appears listing all the different transitions available. If you move the mouse over the a transition, PowerPoint shows you what that transition will look like on your chosen slide.

4. Click the transition you want.
5. Click in the Transition Sound list box and choose a sound, such as Cash Register or Drum Roll.
6. Click in the Transition Speed list box and choose a speed (Slow, Medium, or Fast).
7. Select the Automatically After or the On Mouse Click check box.

   If you select the Automatically After check box, you have to specify a time in the Automatically After text box for the slide to wait before running the transition.

   You can select both the On Mouse Click and Automatically After check boxes, so the slide transition waits until you click the mouse or until a certain amount of time passes.

8. Click Apply to All to apply your transition to every slide in your presentation.

Adding Text Transitions

Besides animating how your slides appear and disappear you can also add transitions to your text boxes or graphics so they fly or drop into place across a slide.

Use text transitions sparingly becaust eht transitions can get distracting when people just want to read your presentation without having to watch letters zoom around the screen.

To Create a simple text ransition, follow these steps:

1. Click a text box or picture on a slide.

   PowerPoint displays handles around your chosen item.

2. Click the Animations tab.
3. Click the Animate list box in the Animations group.

   A list of different animation schemes appear.

4. Click an animation, such as Fly In or Wipe.

   PowerPoint animates your text so you can see how it looks.

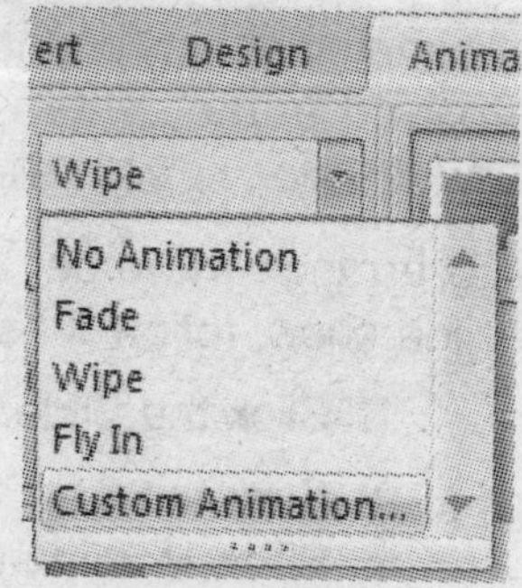

Viewing a Presentation

After you finish arranging your slides, adding transitions, and adding hyper links, you are ready to test how your entire presentation looks. To view your entire presentation, follow these steps:

1. Click the Slide Show tab.
2. Click the From Beginning icon in the Start Slide Show group.

   PowerPoint displays the first slide of your presentation.
3. Choose one of the following:

- Click the mouse or press the spacebar to view the next slide.
- Press Esc to exit your presentation.

If you have a large presentation consisting of 300 slides, you may not want ot view the first 290 slides just to test how your last 10 slides look. To avoid this problem, PowerPoint lets you choose to view your presentation starting with any slide.

To view your presentation starting with a slide other than the first one, follow these steps:

1. Click the Slide Show tab.
2. Click the From Current Slide icon in the Start Slide Show group. PowerPoint displays the currently displayed slide.
3. Choose one of the following:

- Click the mouse or press the spacebar to view the next slide.
- Press Esc to exit your presentation.

Making Slide Shows

This effect shows all the hard work you have put in making the slides. It shows one slide after another, stopping in between for a set time on either the monitor of your screen or on the projector which may have been attached to your computer. It is also possible to add animated effects on the slides and show them in a sophisticated manner. It is also possible to add audio, video, narration, music, etc., to your slides.

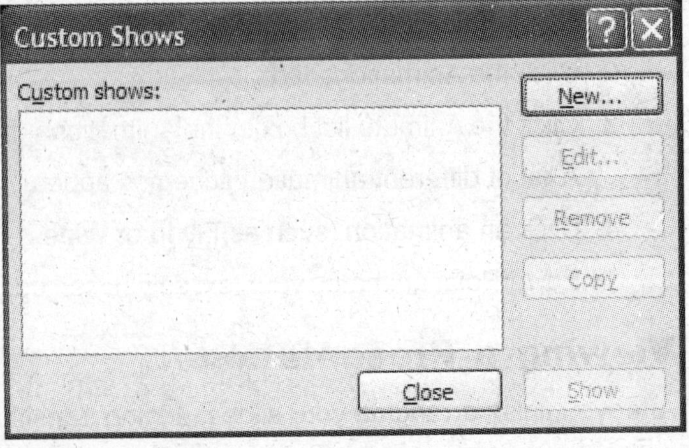

To arrange the order of a custom slide show, follow these steps:

1. Click the Slide Show tab.
2. Click the the Custom Slide Show icon in the Start Slide Show group.

   A pull down menu appears.
3. Choose Custom Shows.

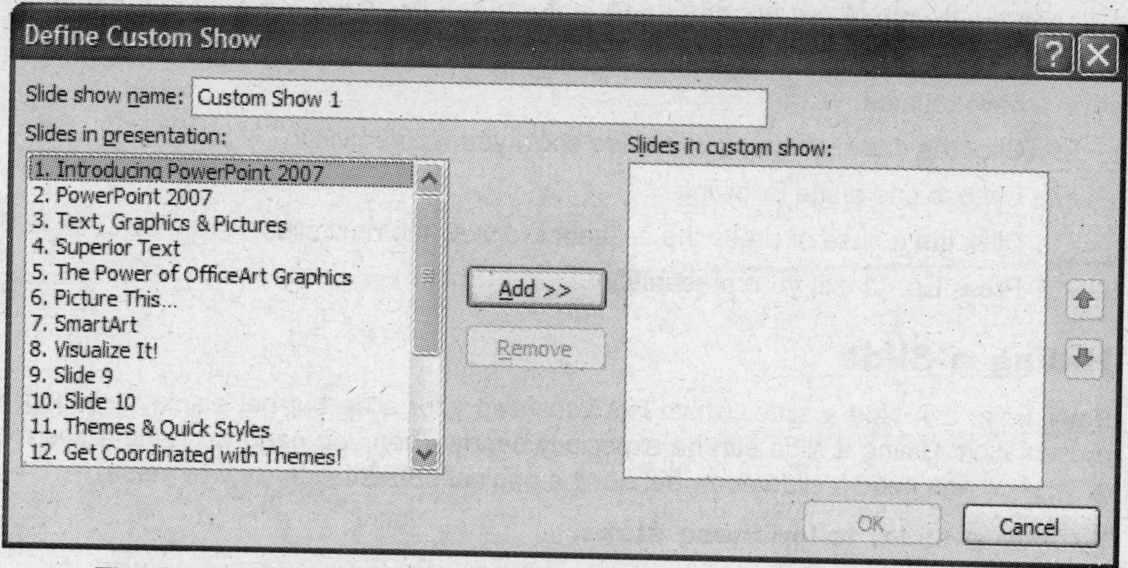

The Custom Shows dialog box appears.

4. Click New.

   The Define Custom Show dialog box appears.

5. Click in the Slide Show Name text box and type a name for your custom slide show.
6. Clcik a slide in the Slides in Presentation list box and then click the Add button.

   This tells PowerPoint which existing slides you want to resuse in your custom slide show.

7. Repeat Step 6 for each slide you want to include in your custom slide show.
8. Click a slide in the Slides in Custom Show list box and click the Up or Down arrow button to rearrange their order.
9. Repeat Step 8 for each slide you want to rearrange in your custom slide show.
10. Click Ok.

    The Custom Shows dialog box appears again.

11. Click the name of your custom slide show and then click Show.

    PowerPoint shows your new, customized presentation.

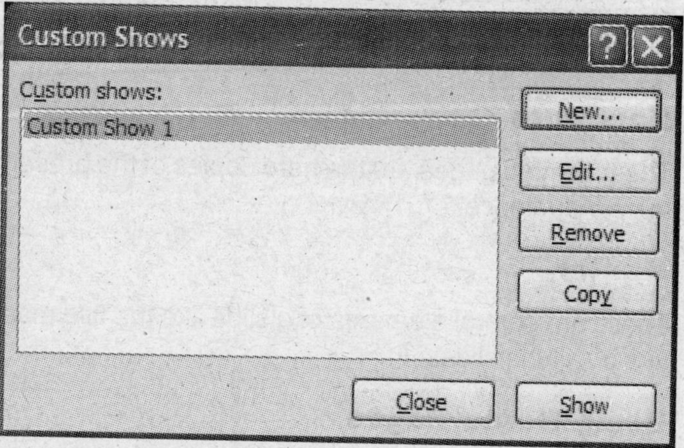

To present a custom slide show, follow these steps:

1. Click the Slide Show tab.

2. Click the Custom Slide Show icon in the Start Slide Show group.

   A pull-down menu appears that lists the names of all the custom slide shows you have created.

3. Click the name of the custom slide show you want to view.
4. Choose one of the following:
   - Click the mouse or press the spacebar to view the next slide.
   - Press Esc to exit your presentation.

Hiding a Slide

PowerPoint can hide a slide, which lets you keep your slide but not display it during a presentation. Hiding a slide can be expecially handy when you need to create a custom slide show and need a slide show but not the original presentation (or vice versa).

To hide a slide, followthese steps:

1. Click the slide that you want to hide (in Slide or Outline view).
2. Click the Slide Show tab.
3. Click the Hide Show icon in the Set Up group.

   PowerPoint dims your selected slide.

   To unhide a slide, just repeat the above three steps.

Notes, Handouts and Masters for Presentation

There are three important tools for your presentation. These tools are:

Notes Pages

These pages are like the script for your presentation. In this script you have an image of slides along with the words you want to deliver for the specific slide.

Handouts

These printed pages are the hard copies of the presentation slides which you can distribute to your audience.

Master

These are control elements of a slide like the title master which controls appearance of the title on all the slides.

Using Notes Pages

Notes Pages act like a cheat sheet for your presentation. You would write the text you want to read without letting the audience know that you are reading during the course of a presentation for each slide.

Printing Handouts

You can print your entire presentation in the form of handouts. These handouts are used to distribute among the audience in advance. You can also print specific slides, notes pages or outline pages.

For this do the following:

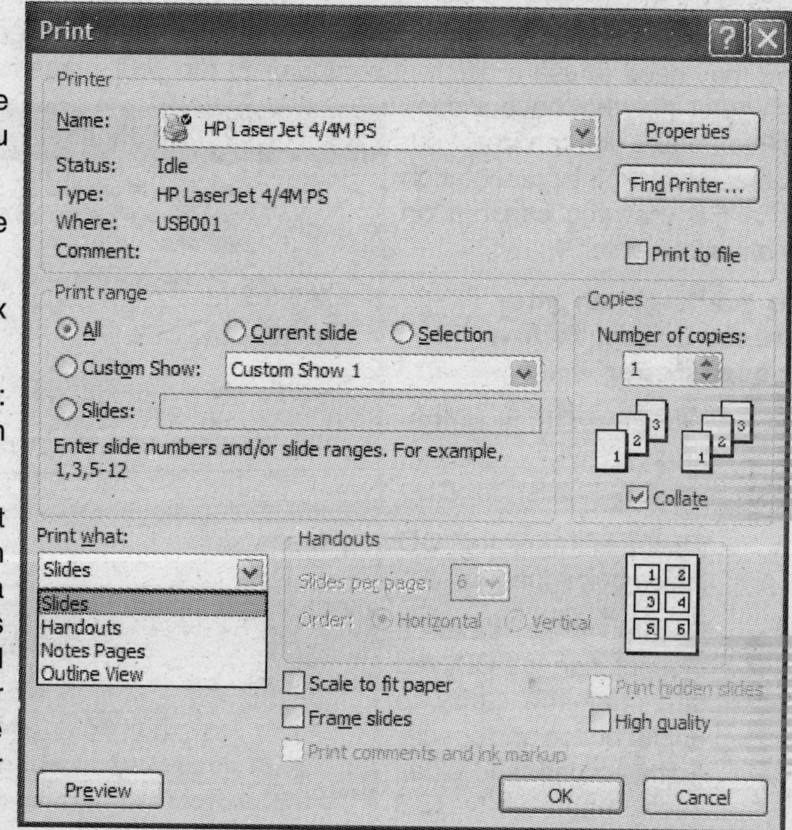

1. Open the presentation you want to print.
2. Click the Office button and Print.
3. The Print dialog box appears.
4. In the Print what: box, click the item you want to print.
5. If you select Handouts, you can then select a number of slides per page and whether the order should be horizontal or vertical,
6. Select any other options you want to apply.
7. After applying the option in the handouts section, click OK.

Handouts Master

The Handouts Master can be used to modify your Handout format.

For this do the following:

1. Click the View menu, highlight Master and choose Handout Master. The Handout Master appears.
2. In the Handout Master view, you can select the two slide per page, three slides per page or the six slides per page formats by clicking on the Handout Master toolbar as shown.
3. To apply any changes to the Handout Master, just follow the procedure as for the Notes master.
4. Save the presentation file to save any changes you make to the Handout Master.

5. You cannot change the position of the slide images on the Handout Master.
6. There is no notes text placeholder on the Handout Master.

Packing Presentations to Go

Many people use their laptops to display their PowerPoint presentations, but occasionally, you may need to use a different computer to run your presentaion. Because that other computer may not have a copy of PowerPoint, you can store your entire PowerPoint presentation on a CD that you can run on another computer.

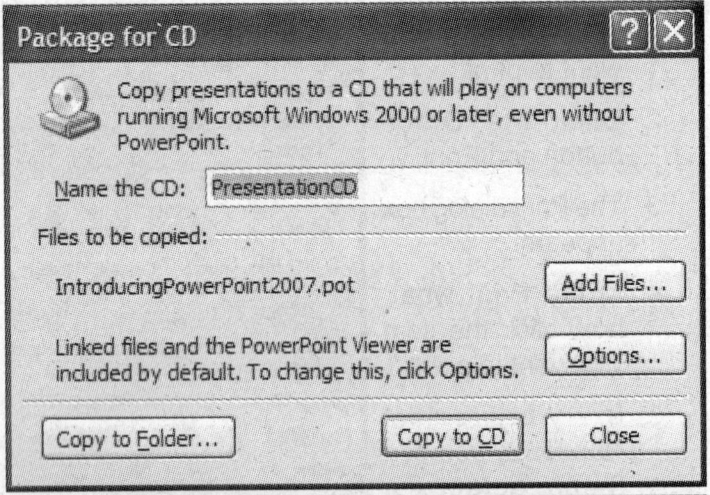

To package up your presentation, follow these steps:

1. Click the Office button and choose Publish<Publish for CD.

   The Package for CD dialog box appears.

   Rather than save a presentation to a CD, you can click the Copy to Folder button and specify a different drive and folder, such as a USB removeable drive.

2. Click in the Name the CD text box and type a descriptive name for your presentation.
3. Insert a blank CD in your rewritable CD drives.
4. Click Copy to CD.

   If your presentation includes hyperlinks to other programs, PowerPoint displays a dialog box to alert you. This dialog box is meant to keep you from accidentally creating a presentation that could spread viruses or Trojan Horses.

5. Click Close.

5 Introduction to Microsoft Access 2007

Creating a Database

Creating database with a Wizard is probably the easiest and fastest method of creating a database where you have to fill up some information and the database is ready for you. It not only creates Tables for you but all the Forms, Reports, etc., connected with it are done too.

Creating Database using the Wizard

Access can create a blank database or a database using one of many templates available from the Microsoft Web site. No matter how you create a database, you will likely need to modify it to customize it for the type of data you want.

To create a blank database, follow these steps:

1. Click the Office button and choose New.

   The Getting Started with Microsoft Access screen appears.

2. Click the Blank Database icon.

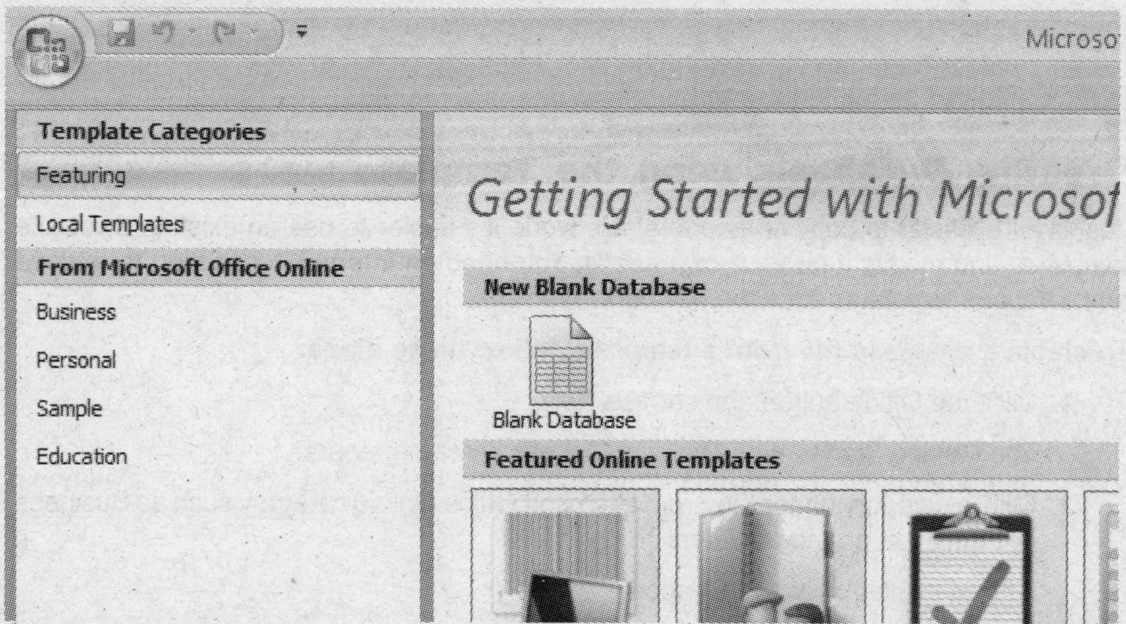

The file name text box appears in the right corner of the screen.

3. Type a descriptive filename for your database.

   You may want to click the Browse icon to specify a different folder or drive to store your database.

4. Click Create.

   Access displays a blank table and an Add New Field text box. Displaying your database in rows and columns in Datasheet view.

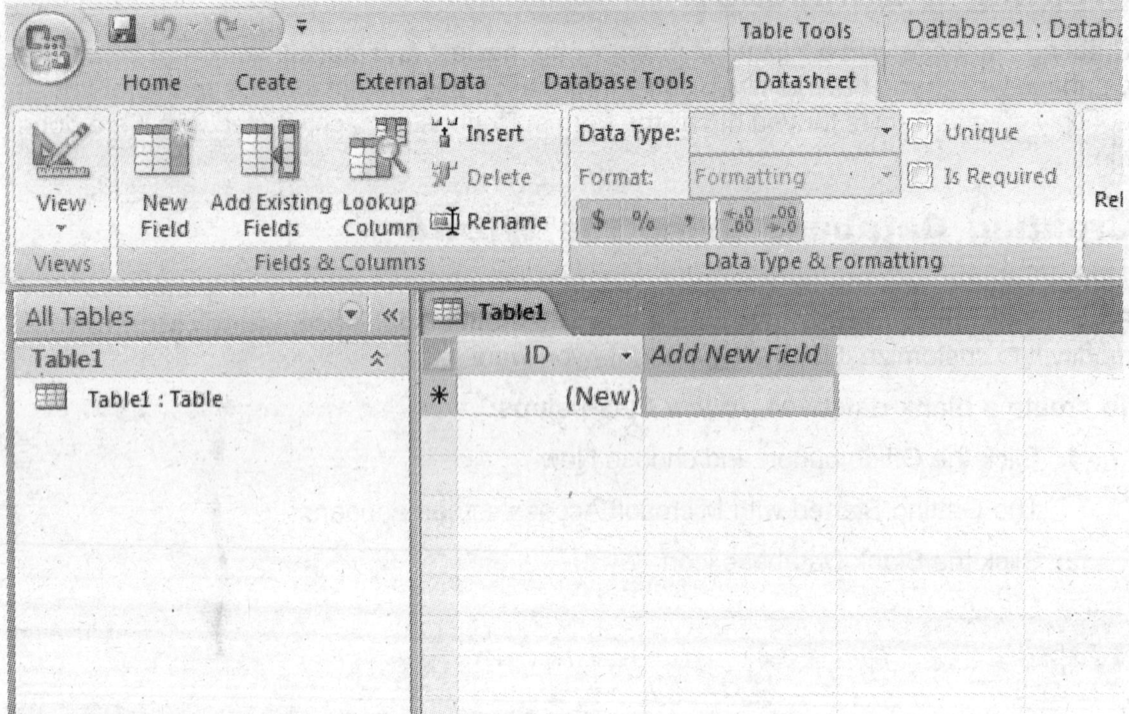

Creating Database using the Template

Just like it's easier to copy someone else's work, it's easier to use an existing database templates and modify it for your own needs. You need an Internet connection to retrieve any database templates from the Microsoft Web site.

To create a database file from a template, follow these steps:

1. Click the Office button and choose New.

   The Getting Started with Microsoft Access screen appears.

2. Click a category under the From Microsoft Office Online categroy such as Business or Education or choose Local Templates.

   A list of available templates appear.

3. Click a template. Access displays a default name in the File Name text box in the bottom right corner of the screen.
4. Type a descriptive name for your database in the File Name text box and then click Create.

   Access displays your database in rows and columns (Datasheet View).

   On the next page, see the database of Marketing Project Home.

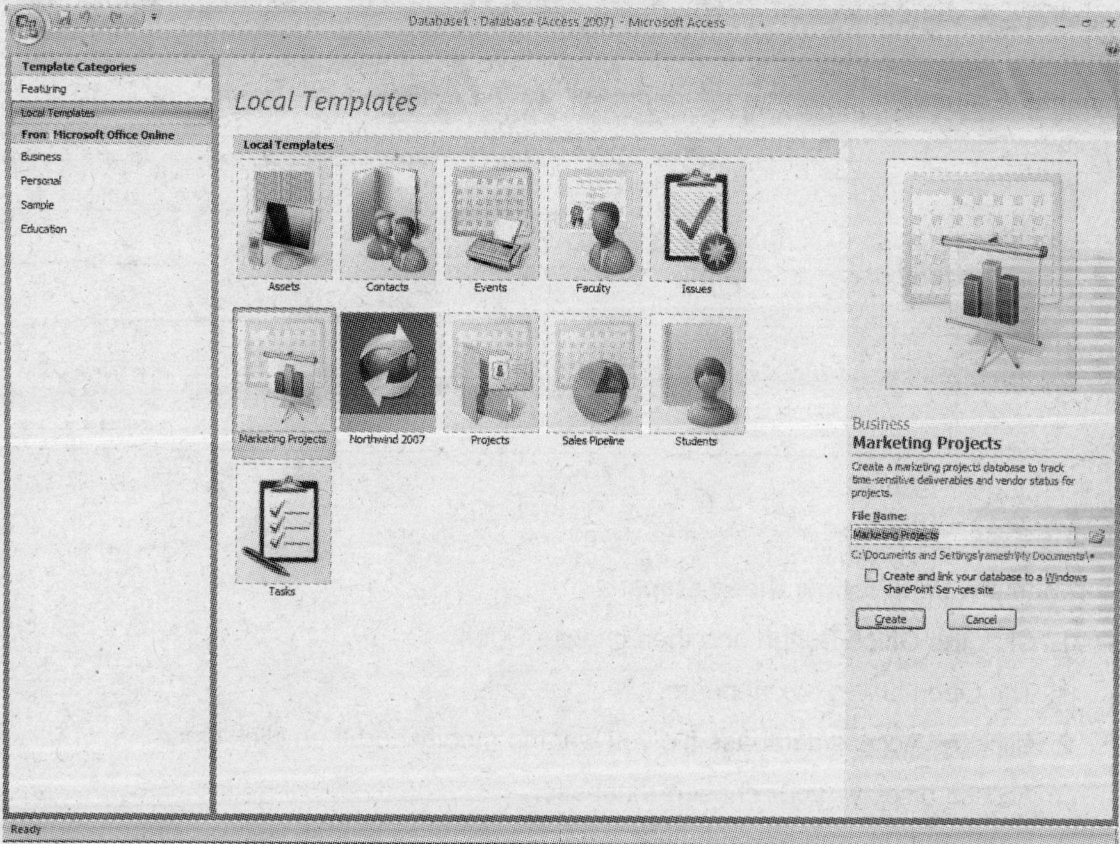

Working with Fields of Database

After you have created a database and it has given you a database in the Datasheet View. It becomes apparent that you add fields, name them and then fill up the data in them (or import it).

Naming a Field

If you create a database from scratch, Access displays generic field names such as Field1. If you create a database from a template, you will see the descriptive field names, but you may still want to rename the fields to something else.

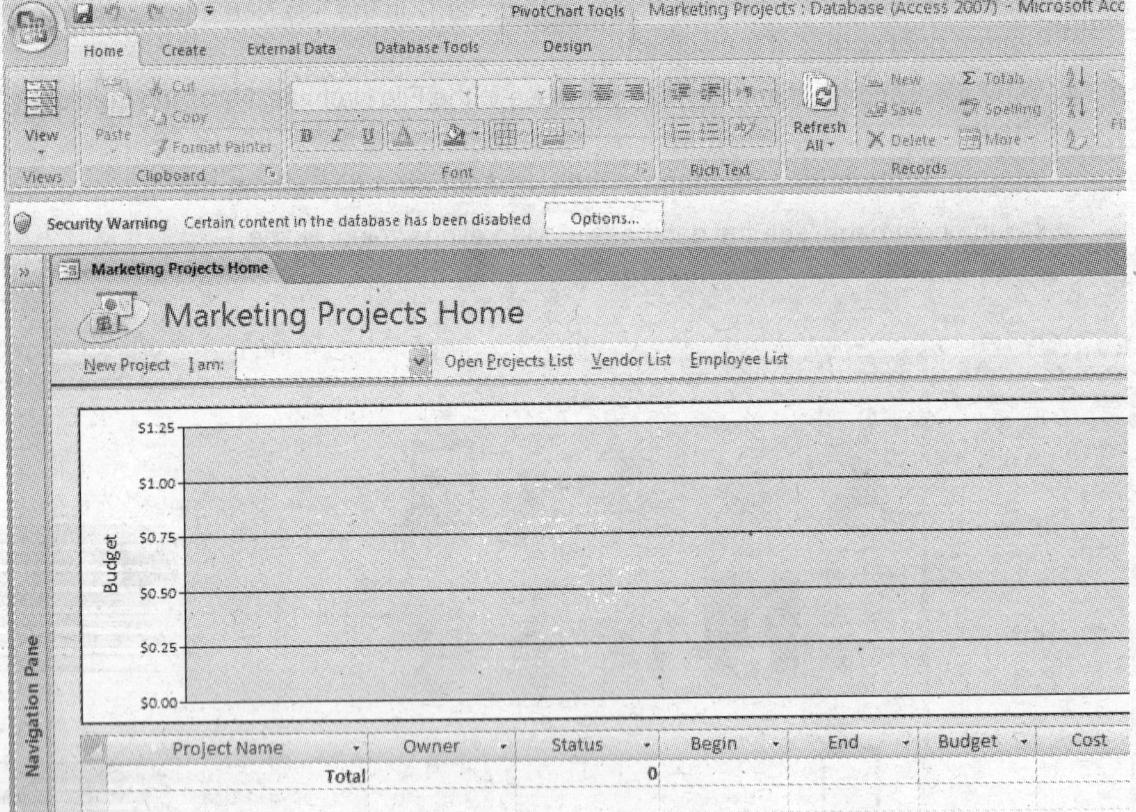

To rename a field, follow these steps:

1. Click the Office Button and then choose Open.

   The Open dialog box appears.

2. Click the Access database file you want to modify and then click Open.

   Access displays your chosen database.

3. In the All Tables pane on the left of the screen, double-click the table that contains the fields you want to rename.

   Access displays the Datasheet view of your database.

4. Click the Datasheet tab.
5. Click the field (column head) that you want to rename.
6. Click the Rename icon in the Fields & Columns group.

   Access highlights the field name.

7. Type a new name for your field and then click outside the field name when you are done.

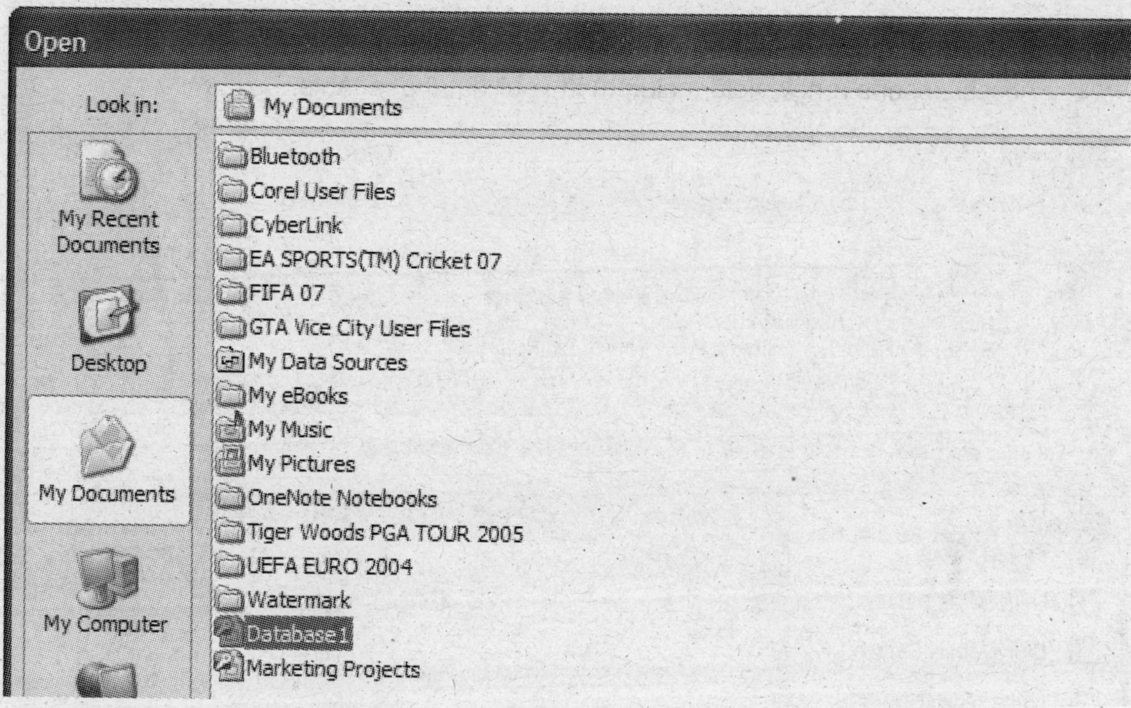

Adding/Deleting a Field

Sometimes you may need to add a field to make room to store new information. Other times, you may want to delete a field that you don't really want after all.

To add a field to a database table, follow these steps:

1. Click an existing field in your database table.
2. Click the Datasheet tab.

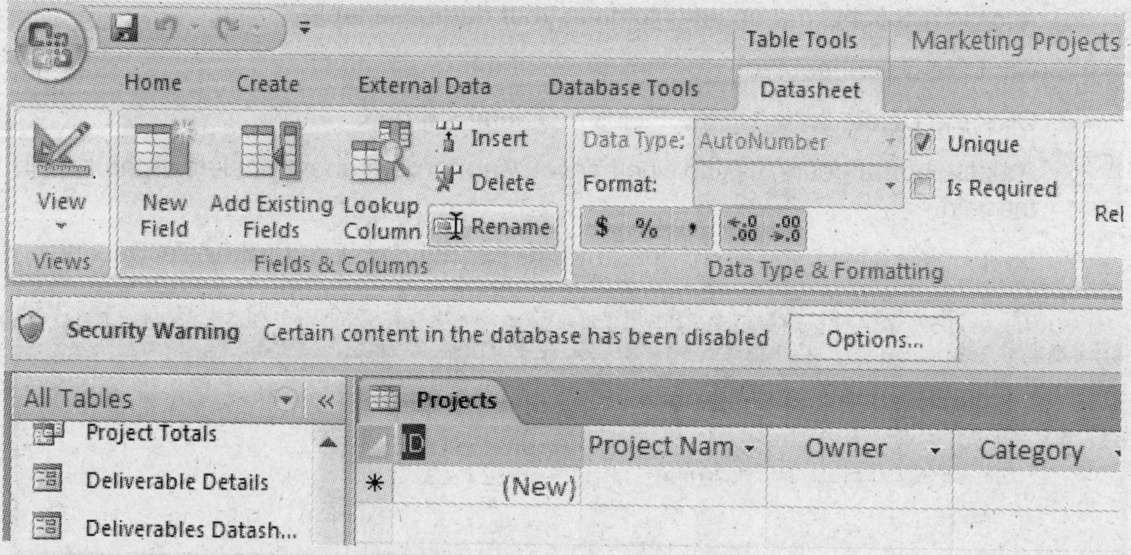

3. Click the Insert button in the Fields & Columns group.

   Access inserts a new field (column) in your database table.

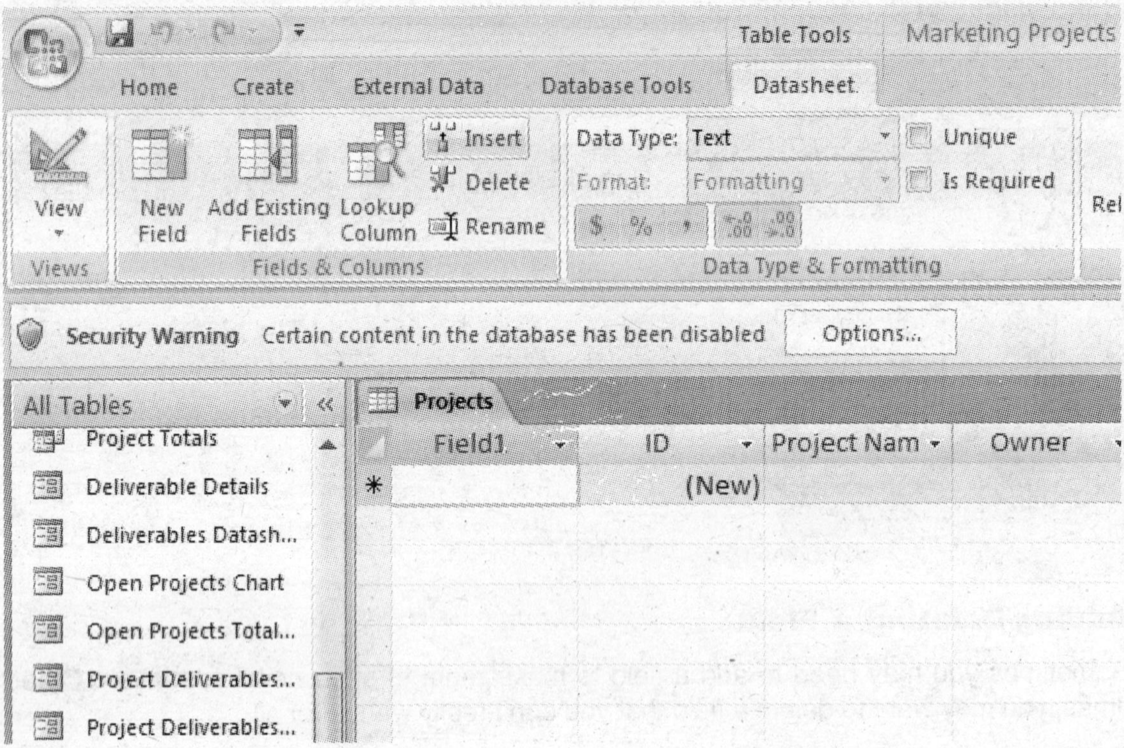

To delete a field from a database table, follow these steps:

1. Click the field you want to delete.

   Access highlights the entire column in your database table.

2. Click the Datasheet tab.

3. Click the Delete button in the Fields & Columns group.

   A dialog box appears, asking whether you want to permanently delete all the data in the field.

   If you delete a field, you also delete any data that may be stored in the field. Depending

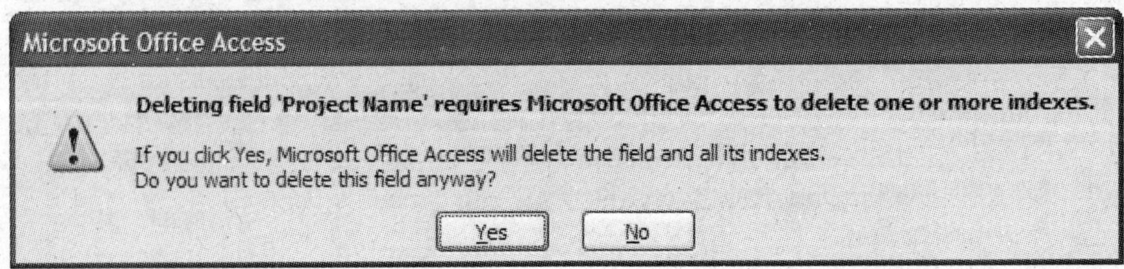

on how much data you have stored, you could wipe out a lot of information by deleting a signle field, so be careful.

4. Click Yest (or No).

   If you click Yes, Access deletes your chosen field.

Setting the Type and Size of a Field

The type of a field defines the type of data the field can hold (numbers, text, dataes, and so on), and the size of a field defines the amount of data the field can hold (no numbers larger than 250 digits, any text string fewer than 120 characters, and so on).

To define the type and amount of a data a field can store, follow these steps:

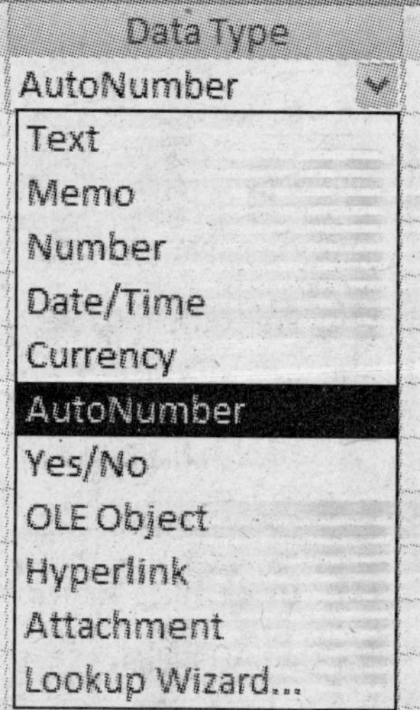

1. Click the Home or Datasheet tab.
2. In the All Tables pane on the left of the screen, double-click the table that contains the fields you want to define.

   Access displays the Datasheet view of your table.
3. Click the downward-pointing arrow underneath the View icon, which appears in the Views group.

   A pull down menu appears.
4. Click Design View.

   Access displays the Design view of your database table.
5. Click in the Field Name column and edit an existing filed name.

   If you click in a blank row, you can add a field to a database table.
6. Click in the Data Type column.

   A downward-pointing arrow appears.
7. Click the downward-pointing arrow.

   A pull-down menu appears, listing all the different types of data you can define to store in a field.
8. Choose a data type, such as Number, Text or Data/Time. Access displays a General tab that contains different options for modifying your chosen data type.
9. Click one of the data type options, such as Format or Input Mask, listed under the General tab.

   Sometimes you have to type a value directly into a data type option. Other time a pull-down menu appears, from which you can choose an option.

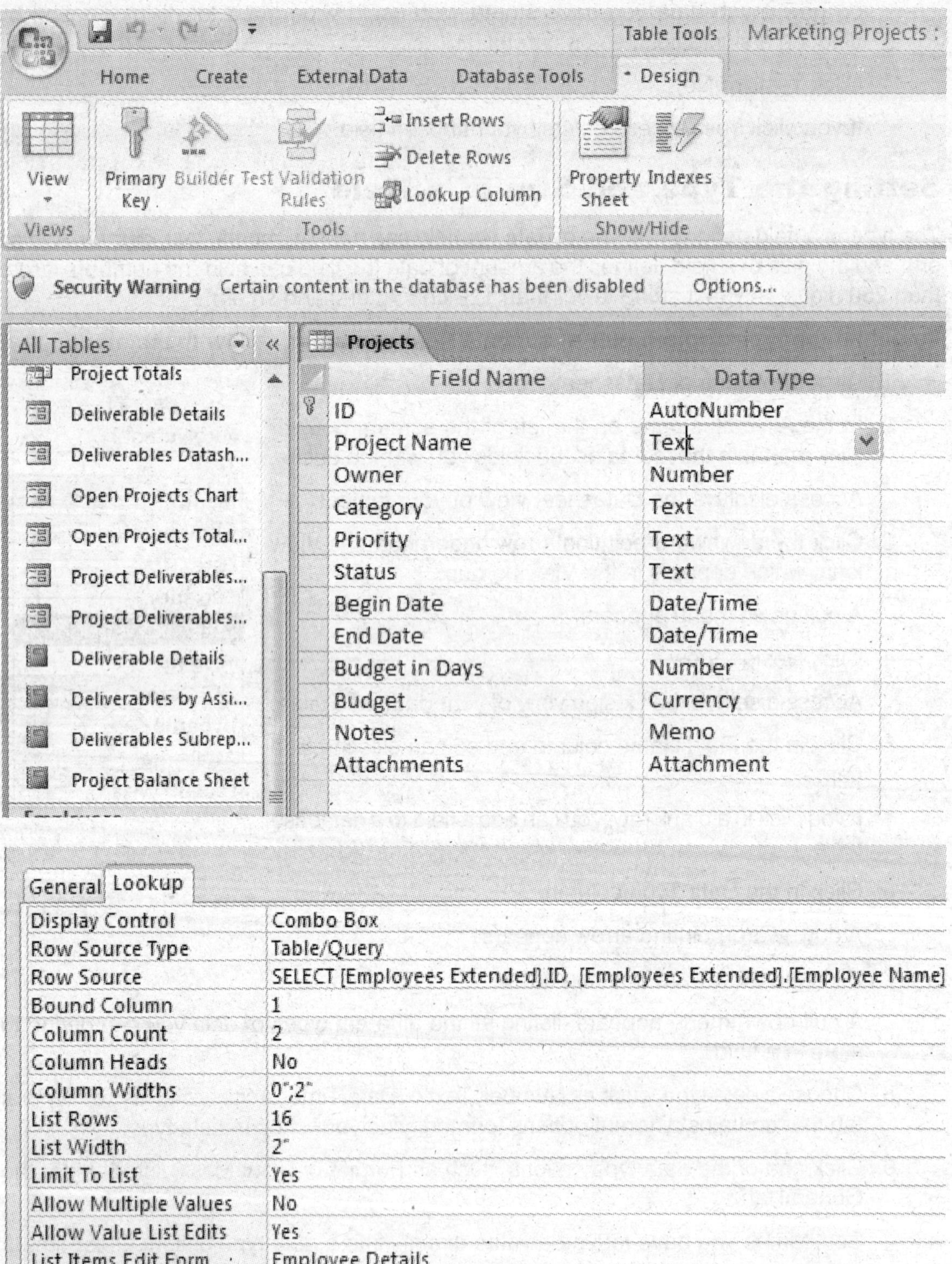
Table Tools
Marketing Projects :
Home
Create
External Data
Database Tools
Design
View
Primary Key
Builder
Test Validation Rules
Insert Rows
Delete Rows
Lookup Column
Property Sheet
Indexes
Views
Tools
Show/Hide
Security Warning
Certain content in the database has been disabled
Options...
All Tables
Project Totals
Deliverable Details
Deliverables Datash...
Open Projects Chart
Open Projects Total...
Project Deliverables...
Project Deliverables...
Deliverable Details
Deliverables by Assi...
Deliverables Subrep...
Project Balance Sheet
Projects
Field Name
Data Type
ID
AutoNumber
Project Name
Text
Owner
Number
Category
Text
Priority
Text
Status
Text
Begin Date
Date/Time
End Date
Date/Time
Budget in Days
Number
Budget
Currency
Notes
Memo
Attachments
Attachment
General
Lookup
Display Control
Combo Box
Row Source Type
Table/Query
Row Source
SELECT [Employees Extended].ID, [Employees Extended].[Employee Name]
Bound Column
1
Column Count
2
Column Heads
No
Column Widths
0";2"
List Rows
16
List Width
2"
Limit To List
Yes
Allow Multiple Values
No
Allow Value List Edits
Yes
List Items Edit Form
Employee Details
Show Only Row Source V
No

10. Repeat Step 9 for each data type option you want to modify.

Creating a Form

The biggest problem with Datasheet view is that it can be confusing to find a field for a specific record. Because most people are familiar with paper forms or index cards that arrange related data (fields) on a page, Access offers you Form view. Form view simply displays the fields of a single record onscreen. To use Form view, you must first create a form and arrange your fields on that form. After you create a form, you can add, edit and view data through that form.

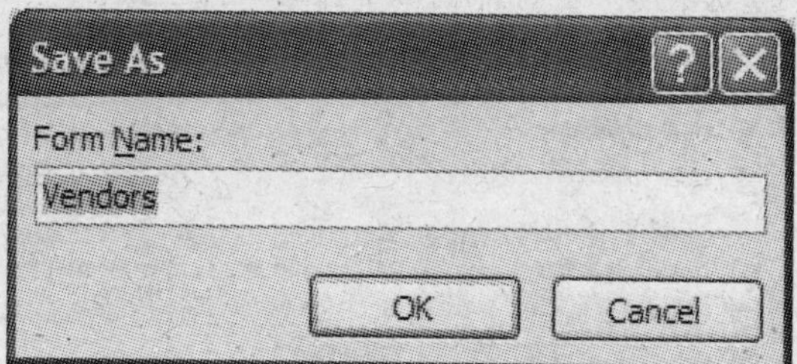

Creating a Form

The simplest way to create a form to let Access desing one for you, which you can modify.

To create a form quickly, follow these steps:

1. Click the Office Button and then choose Open.

   The Open dialog box appears.

2. Click the Access database file you want to add or edit data. Then click Open.

   Access displays your chosen database.

3. In the All Tables pane on the left of the screen, double-click a table.

   Access displays the Datasheet view of your database.

4. Click the Create tab.

5. Click the Form icon in the Forms group.

   Access creates a form. Notice that the form name automatically uses the name of the database table you choose in Step 3.

6. Click the Office Button and then choose Save (or click the Save icon on the Quick Access toolbar).

   The Save As dialog box appears, asking you to type a name for your form.

7. Type a descriptive name for your form in the Form Name text box and then click Ok.

   Acess displays your form's name underneath the All Tables pabe. The next time you open this database and want to view the form, you can double-click the form's name in the left pane.

Searching a Database

The simplest type of search ooks for a specific record. To search for a record, you need to

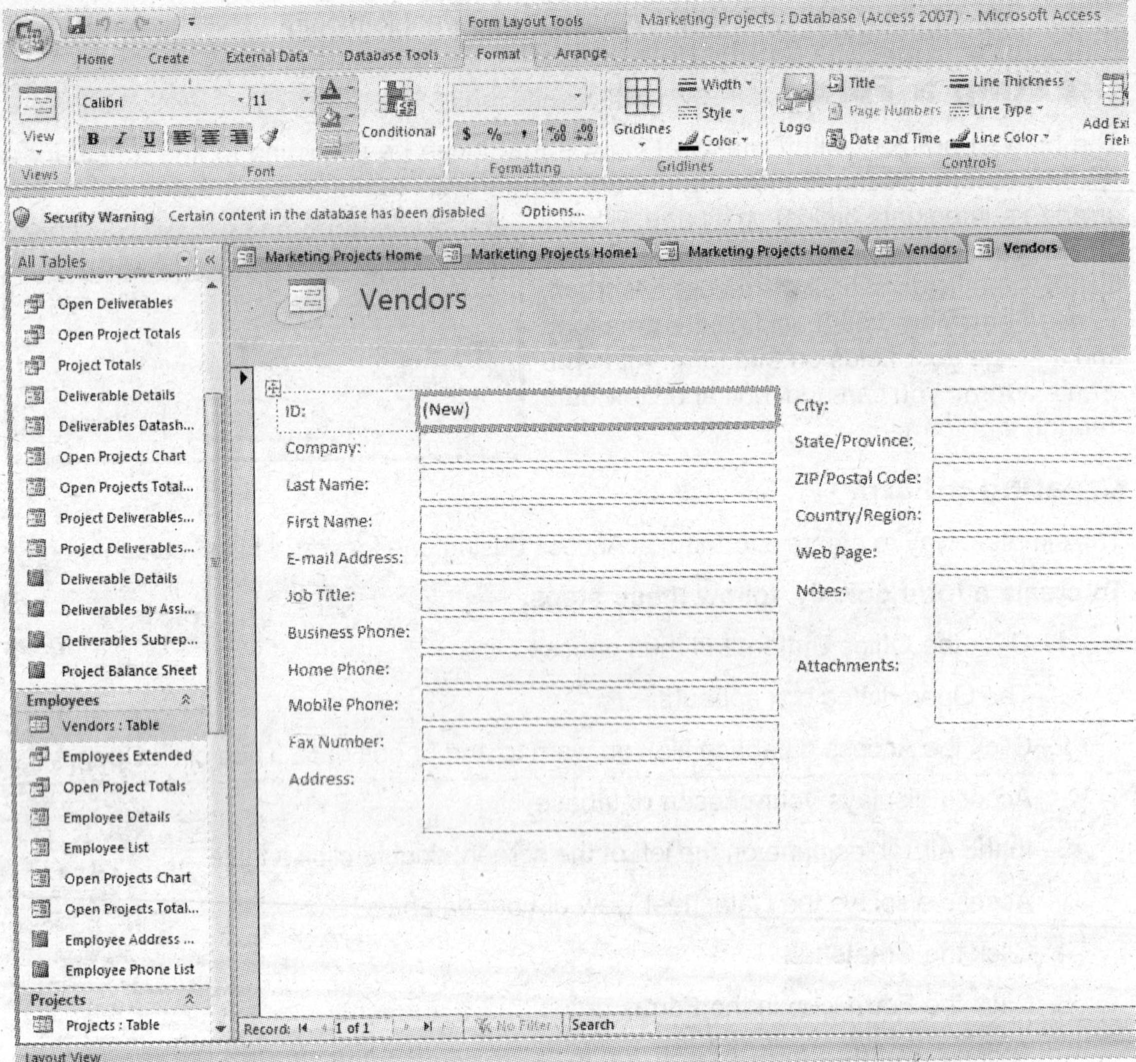

know the data stored in at least one of its fields, such as a phone number and e-mail address. The more information you already know, the more likely Access will find the one record you want. If you search for all records that contain the first name, Access could find dozens of records. But, if you feed in the name and surname, your search would narrow down to just few records.

To search for a specific record in a database table, follow these steps:

1. In the All Tables pane on the left of the screen, double-click the name of the databse table you want to search.

   Access displays the Datasheet view of your database.

2. Click the Home tab.
3. Click the Find icon in the Find group.

The Find and Replace dialog box appears.

4. Click in the Find What text box and type in the data you know is stored in the record in the record you want to find.

   For example, if you want to find the phone number of a person but you know only that person's last name in the Find What text box.

5. Click the Look In list box and choose the name of the entire databse table.
6. Click in the Match list box and choose one of the following:
   - Any Part of Field: The Find What text can appear in any part of a field.
   - Whole Field: The Find What text is the only text stored in a field.
   - Start of Field: The Find What text can be only at the beginning of a field.
7. Click in the Search list box and choose one of the following:.
   - Up: Searches from the record where the cursor appears, up to the beginning of the database table.
   - Down: Searches from the record where the cursor appears, down to the end of the database table.
   - All: Searches the entire database table.
8. Click Find Next.
9. Repeat Step 8 to search for more records that might contain the text you typed in Step 4.
10. Click Cancel or the Close button.

Creating a Query

A query is nothing more than a saved version of your sort or filter criteria. By saving the particular sort or filter criteria as a query, you can select that query by name later.

Creating a Simple Query

If your databse table contains dozens of different fields, you may find it confusing to make sense of all your information. As an aid, a simple query strips away fields so you see only the fields containing data you want to see, such as a person's name and phone number but not her hire date or employee number.

To create a query, follow these steps:

1. Click the Create tab.
2. Click the Query Wizard icon in the Other group.

   The New Query dialog box appears.

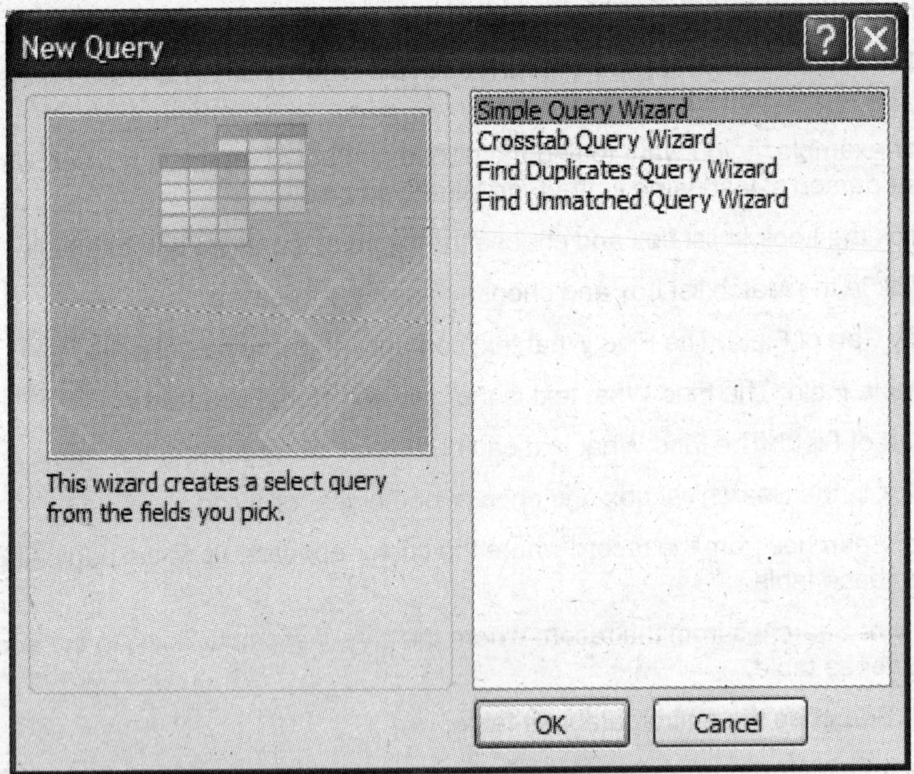

3. Click Simple Query Wizard and then click Ok.

   The Simple Query Wizard dialog box appears.

4. Click a field name listed in the Available Fields box and then click the > button.

   Access displays your chosen filed in the Selected Fields box.

5. Repeat Step 4 for each field you want to use in your query.
6. Click Next.

   Another dialog box appears. This dialog box asks whether you want to display a Detail or Summary (shows numerical information such as the total number of records found, the average value, and the minimum/maximum value) view of your data.

7. Select the Detail or Summary radio button and then click Next.

   Another dialog box appears, asking you to type a descriptive name for your query.

8. Click to the text box, type a descriptive name for your query, and then click Finish.
9. Click the Office Button and then choose Save to save your query.

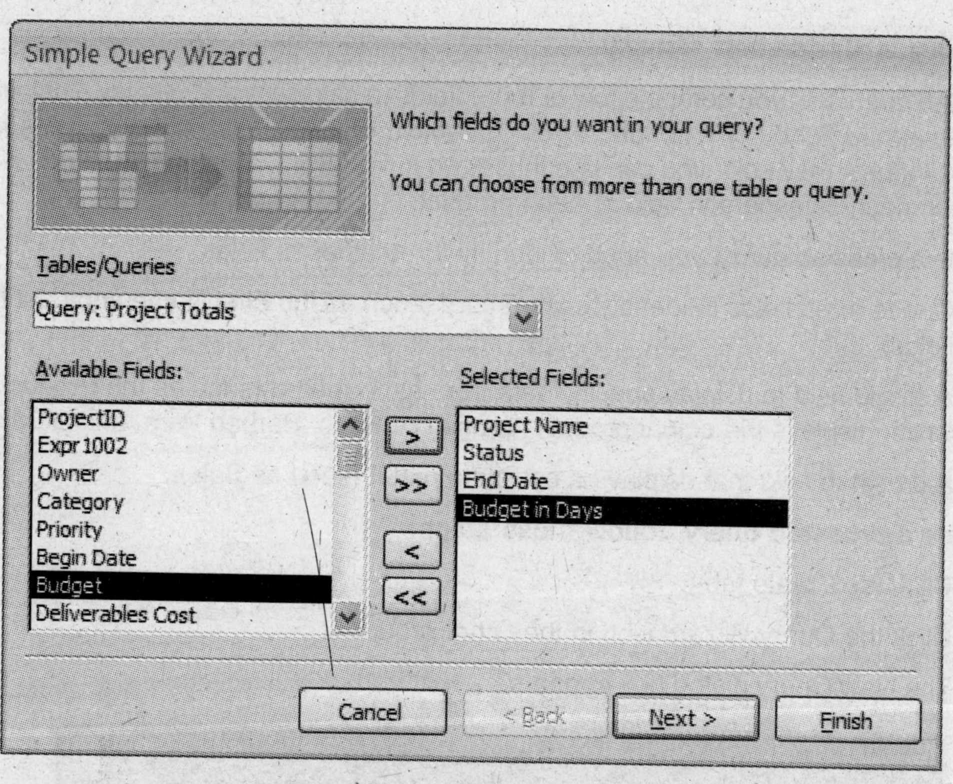
Simple Query Wizard
Which fields do you want in your query?
You can choose from more than one table or query.
Tables/Queries
Query: Project Totals
Available Fields:
ProjectID
Expr1002
Owner
Category
Priority
Begin Date
Budget
Deliverables Cost
Selected Fields:
Project Name
Status
End Date
Budget in Days
>
>>
<
<<
Cancel
< Back
Next >
Finish

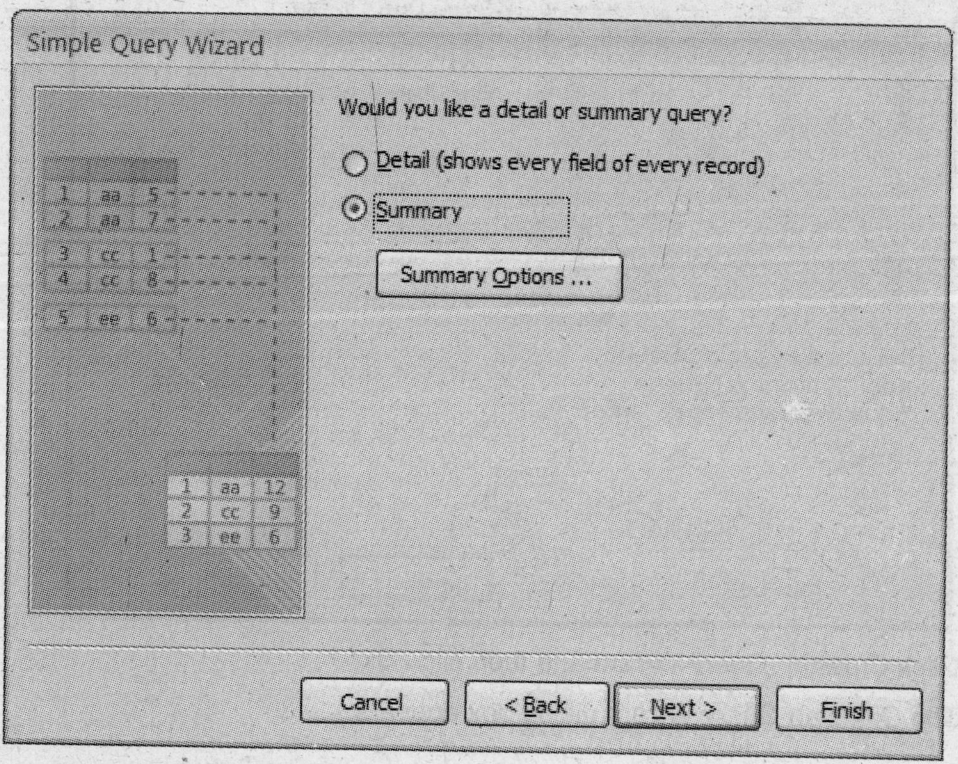
Simple Query Wizard
Would you like a detail or summary query?
Detail (shows every field of every record)
Summary
Summary Options ...
Cancel
< Back
Next >
Finish

Creating a Crosstab Query

A crosstab query lets you combine tow or more fields to calculate and display a calculation based on a third field. For example, if your database contains the names of salespeople and the products they sold, you can use those two fields to create a crosstab that tells you how much each salesperson sold of each product.

To create a crosstab query, you need to identify three types of fields.

- One to three fields to identify each record (such as the First Name and Last Name fields)
- A single field to dsiplay specific data from each record (such as the Product field, which displays the actual product names like Nails, Barbed Wire, and Screws)
- A crosstab field that dsiplays a calculate result (such as Sales)

To create a crosstab query, follow these steps:

1. Click the Create tab.
2. Click the Query Wizard icon in the Other group.

   The New Query dialog box appears.

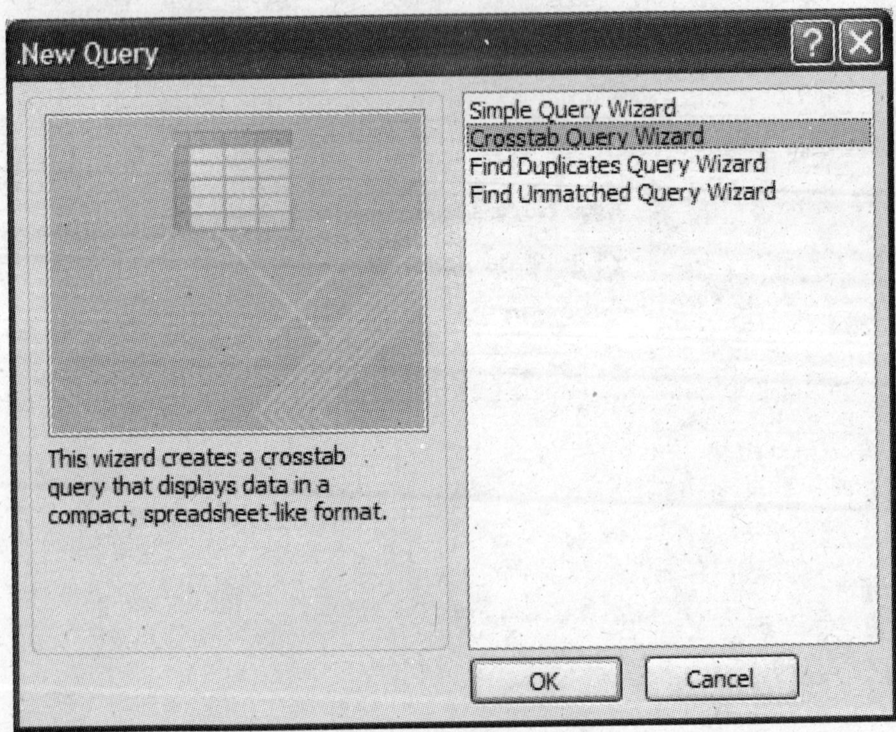

3. Click Crosstab Query Wizard and then click Ok.

   The Crosstab Query Wizard dialog box appears.

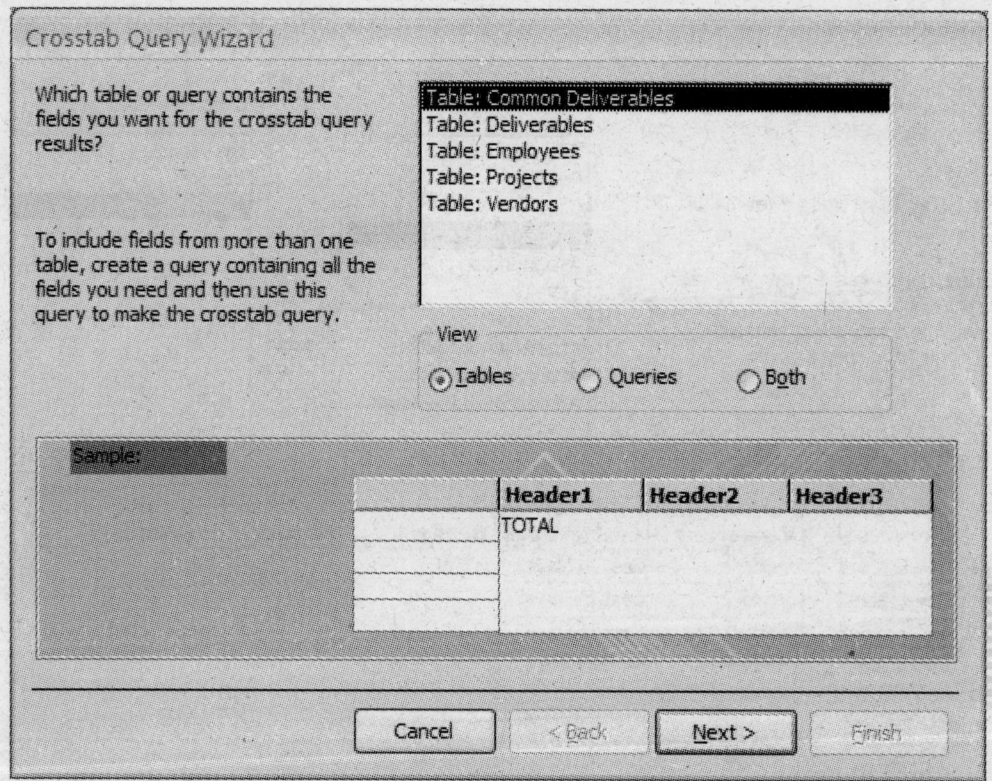

4. Click a database table and then click Next.

   Another Crosstab Query Wizard dialog box appears that asks for between one and three fields to identify each row (record).

5. Click a field in the Available Fields box and then click the > button to move your chosen field to the Selected Fields box.

6. Repeat Step 5 for each additional field you want to include.

7. Click Next.

   Another dialog box appears, asking for a single field to use to crosstabular data with the fields you choose in Steps 5 and 6.

8. Click a field name and then click Next.

9. Click a field that contains numerical data and then click a matematical function that you want Access to calculate, such as Sum, Avg., or Count.

10. Click Next.

    Another dialog box appears.

11. Type a descriptive name for your query in the text box at the top of the dialog box and then click Finish.

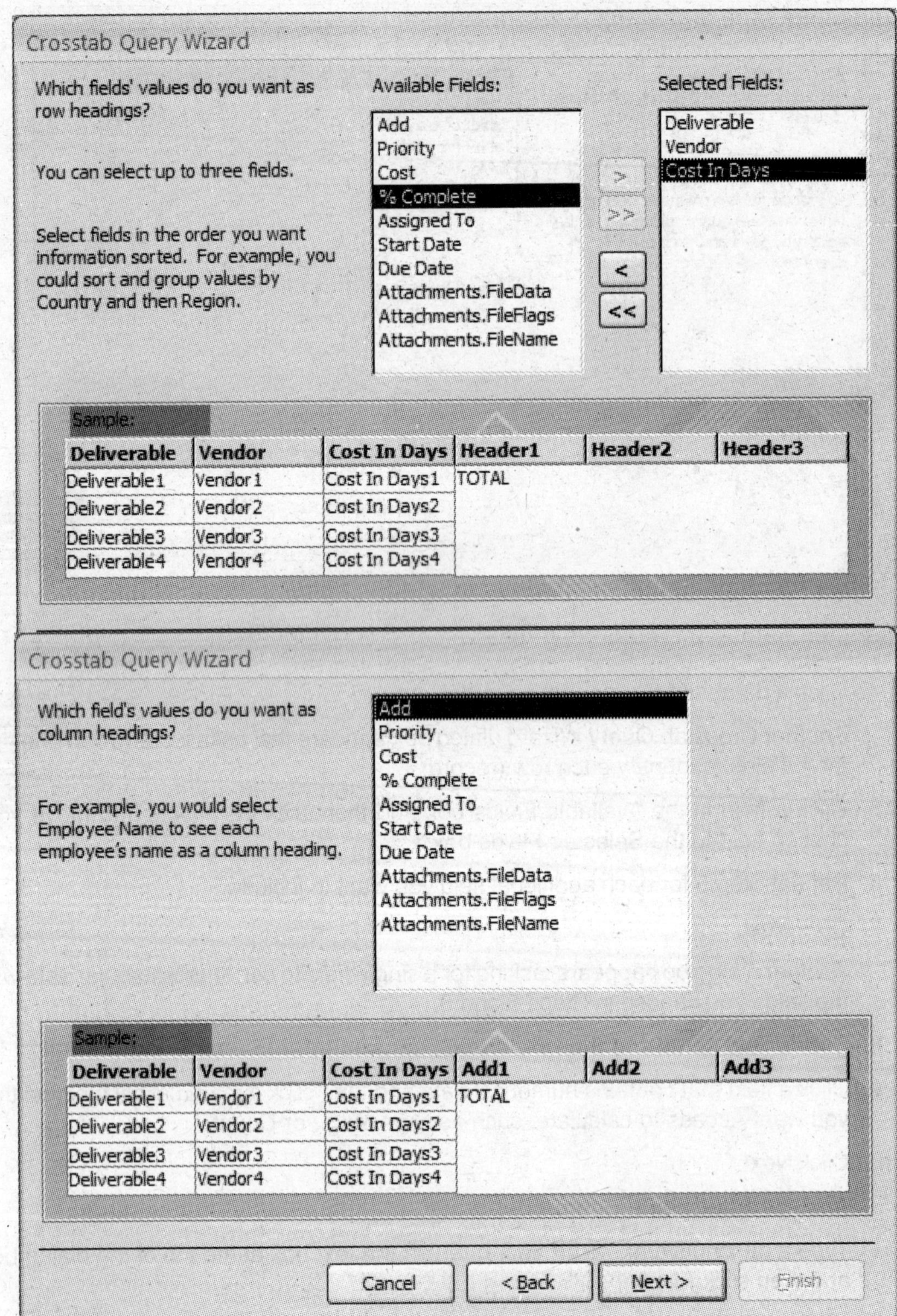

Crosstab Query Wizard
Which fields' values do you want as row headings?
You can select up to three fields.
Select fields in the order you want information sorted. For example, you could sort and group values by Country and then Region.
Available Fields:
Add
Priority
Cost
% Complete
Assigned To
Start Date
Due Date
Attachments.FileData
Attachments.FileFlags
Attachments.FileName
Selected Fields:
Deliverable
Vendor
Cost In Days
Sample:
Deliverable
Vendor
Cost In Days
Header1
Header2
Header3
Deliverable1
Vendor1
Cost In Days1
TOTAL
Deliverable2
Vendor2
Cost In Days2
Deliverable3
Vendor3
Cost In Days3
Deliverable4
Vendor4
Cost In Days4
Crosstab Query Wizard
Which field's values do you want as column headings?
For example, you would select Employee Name to see each employee's name as a column heading.
Add
Priority
Cost
% Complete
Assigned To
Start Date
Due Date
Attachments.FileData
Attachments.FileFlags
Attachments.FileName
Sample:
Deliverable
Vendor
Cost In Days
Add1
Add2
Add3
Deliverable1
Vendor1
Cost In Days1
TOTAL
Deliverable2
Vendor2
Cost In Days2
Deliverable3
Vendor3
Cost In Days3
Deliverable4
Vendor4
Cost In Days4
Cancel
< Back
Next >
Finish

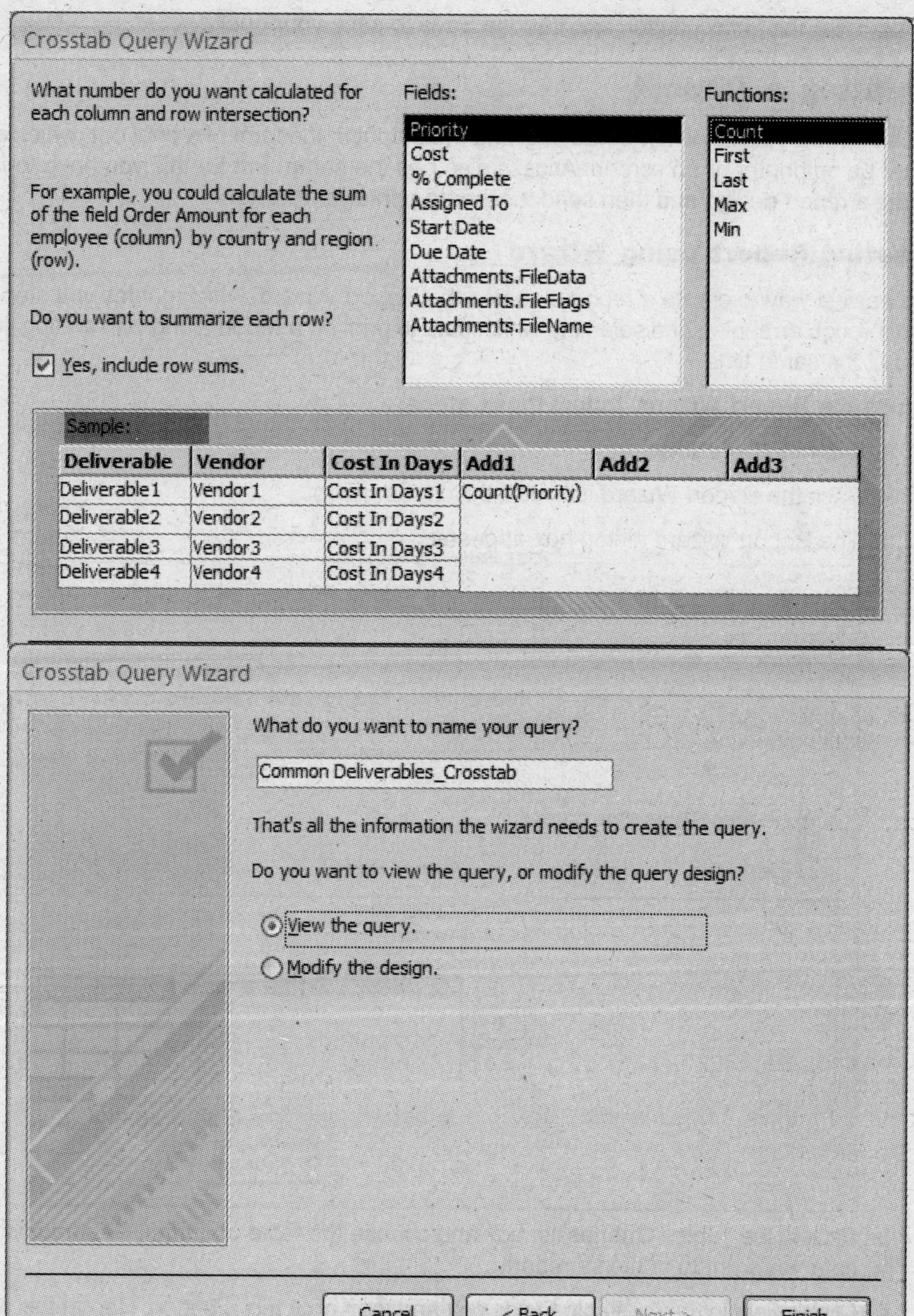

Crosstab Query Wizard
What number do you want calculated for each column and row intersection?
For example, you could calculate the sum of the field Order Amount for each employee (column) by country and region (row).
Do you want to summarize each row?
Yes, include row sums.
Fields:
Priority
Cost
% Complete
Assigned To
Start Date
Due Date
Attachments.FileData
Attachments.FileFlags
Attachments.FileName
Functions:
Count
First
Last
Max
Min
Sample:
Deliverable
Vendor
Cost In Days
Add1
Add2
Add3
Deliverable1
Vendor1
Cost In Days1
Count(Priority)
Deliverable2
Vendor2
Cost In Days2
Deliverable3
Vendor3
Cost In Days3
Deliverable4
Vendor4
Cost In Days4
Crosstab Query Wizard
What do you want to name your query?
Common Deliverables_Crosstab
That's all the information the wizard needs to create the query.
Do you want to view the query, or modify the query design?
View the query.
Modify the design.
Cancel
< Back
Next >
Finish

12. Click the Office Button and choose Save to save your query.

Creating a Report

Each software has its own method of giving the output in the form of a print out, which can either be on printer or on screen. Access also has the same. But for this you have to first create a report design and then send it either to printer or monitor.

Creating Report using Wizard

The easiest way to create a report is to use the Report Wizard, which guides you step by step through arranging and selecting which data to print on a report along with sorting your data at the same time.

To use the Report Wizard, follow these steps:

1. Click the Create tab.
2. Click the Report Wizard icon in the Reports group.

   The Report Wizard dialog box appears.

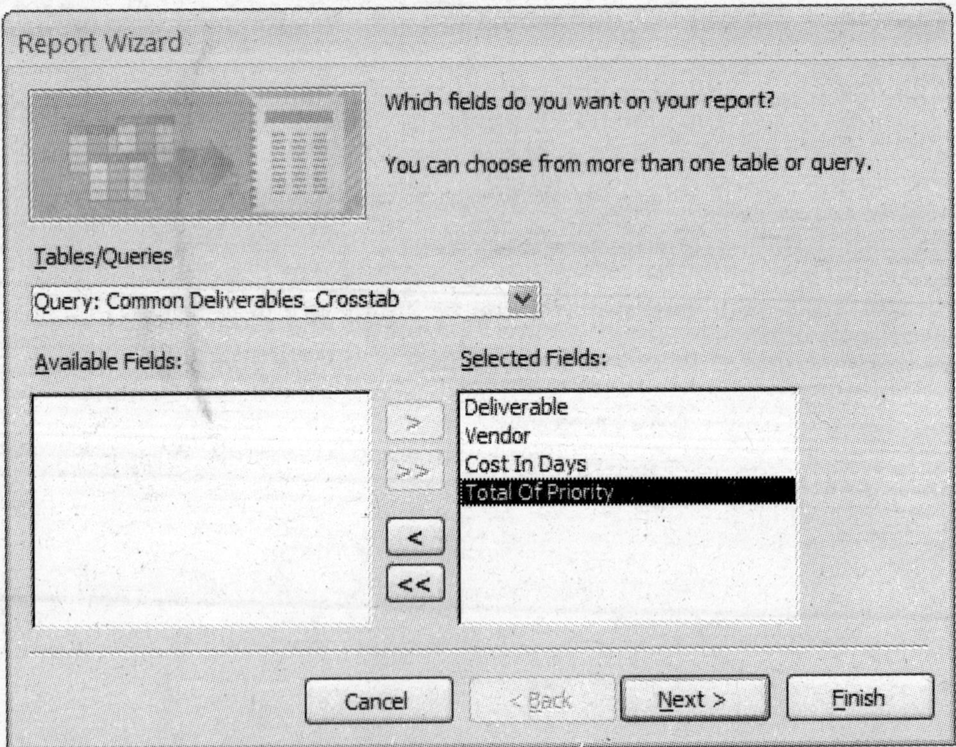

3. Click in the Tables/Queries list box and choose the table or query that contains the data you want to print in a report.
4. Click a field in the Available Fields box and then click this > button. Report this step for each additional field you want to display in your report.

5. Click Next.

   Another dialog box appears, asking whether you want to group your data by a speecific field such as Last Name or Employee Number.

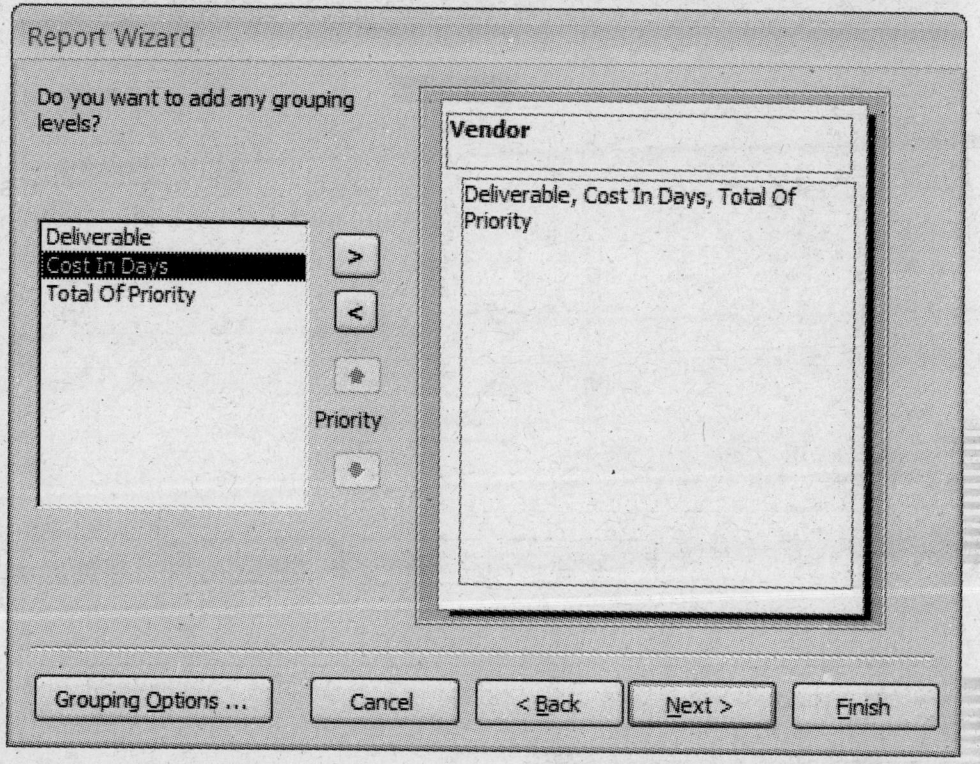

6. Click a field name displayed in the box and then click the > button. Repeat this step for each additional field you want to use to group your data on the report.
7. Click Next.

   Another dialog box appears, asking you to choose up to four fiels to use for sorting your data in your report.
8. Click in a list box and choose a field to sort your data.

   Data will be sorted by the order chosen here for each additional field you sort on.
9. Click the Ascending button to change the soring criteria from Ascending to Descending and vice versa.
10. Click Next.

    Another dialog box appears.
11. Select a radio button under the Layout group, such as Stepped or Outline.
12. Select on a radio button in the Orientation group, such as Portrait or Landscape.

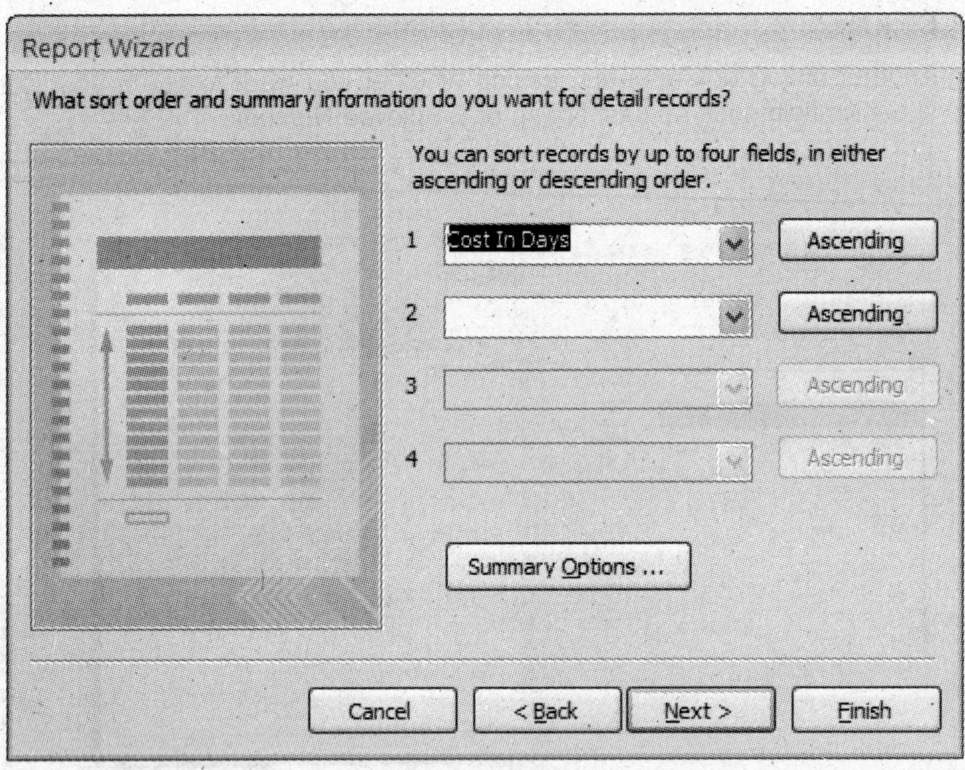
Report Wizard
What sort order and summary information do you want for detail records?
You can sort records by up to four fields, in either ascending or descending order.
1
Cost In Days
Ascending
2
Ascending
3
Ascending
4
Ascending
Summary Options ...
Cancel
< Back
Next >
Finish

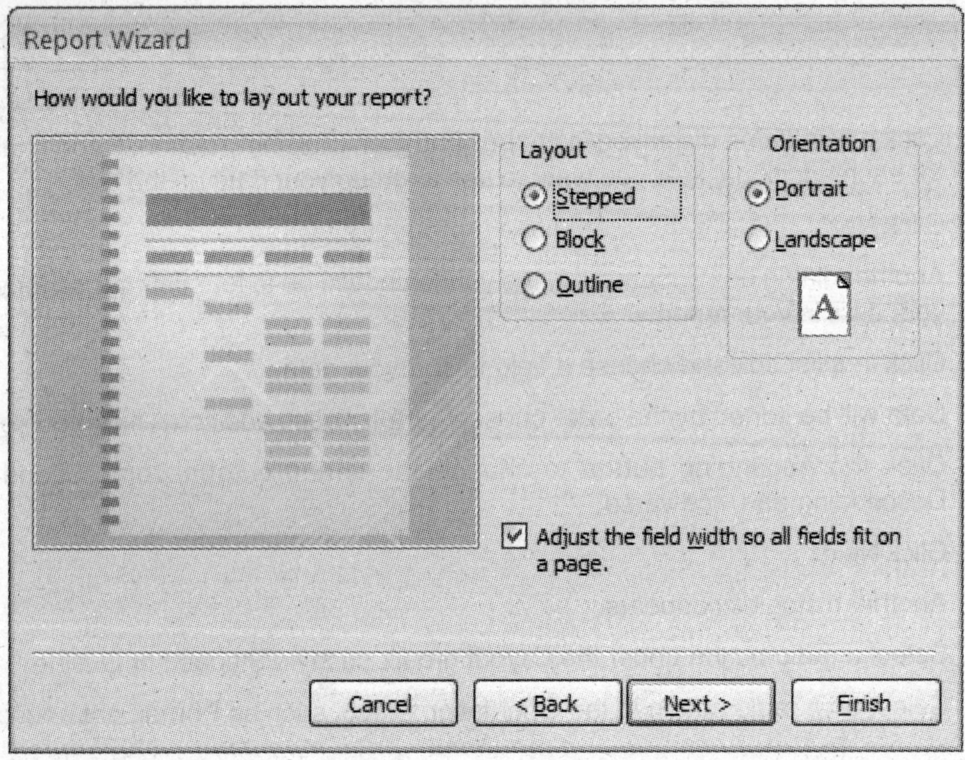
Report Wizard
How would you like to lay out your report?
Layout
Stepped
Block
Outline
Orientation
Portrait
Landscape
A
Adjust the field width so all fields fit on a page.
Cancel
< Back
Next >
Finish

13. Click Next.

    Another dialog box appears, asking you to choose a style for your report. The preview to the left will give you an indication of what the printed report will look like.

14. Click Next.

    Another dialog box appears, asking you for a descriptive name for your report.

15. Type a descriptive name for your report and then click Finish.

    Access displays your report.

16. Right-click the Report tab.

    A pop-up menu appears.

17. Click Close.

    A dialog box appears.

18. Click Yes.

    Access saves your report for future use and removes it from view.

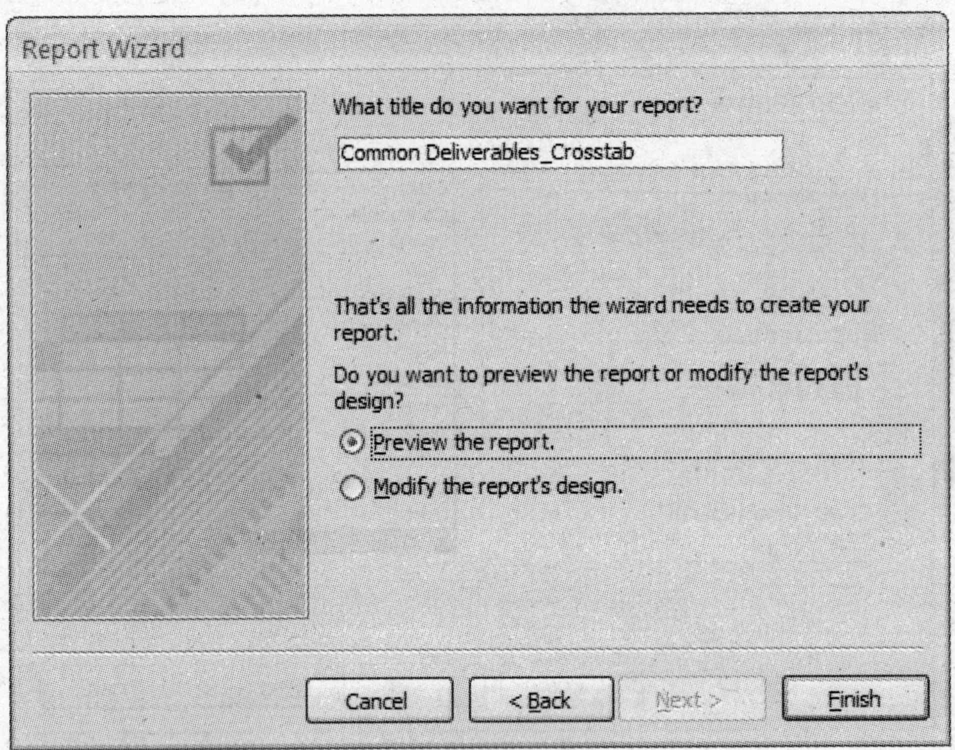
Report Wizard
What title do you want for your report?
Common Deliverables_Crosstab
That's all the information the wizard needs to create your report.
Do you want to preview the report or modify the report's design?
Preview the report.
Modify the report's design.
Cancel
< Back
Next >
Finish

6 Questions

Chapter 1 — Introduction to Windows Vista

1. What is Windows Vista?
2. Describe the various items available on the Desktop of Windows Vista?
3. What is there on the Taskbar?
4. What is the use of Recycle Bin?
5. How would you create a shortcut?
6. Describe the various method of using mouse.
7. Describe the common keyboard commands.
8. How would you access Control Panel of Windows Vista?
9. Write a short note on the following commands of Windows Vista Control Panel.

Add Hardware	Adminstrative Tools
AutoPlay	Backup and Restore Centre
BitLocker Drive Encryption	Color Management
Date and Time	Default Programs
Device Manager	Ease of Access
Folder Options	Fonts
Game Controllers	Indexing Options
Internet Options	iSCSI Initiator
Keyboard	Mail
Mouse	Network and Sharing Centre
Offline Files	Parental Controls
Pen and Input Devices	People Near Me
Performance Information	Personalize
Phone and Modem Options	Power Options

Printers	Problem Reports and Solutions
Programs and Features	Regional and Language Options
Scanners and Cameras	Security Center
Sound	SoundMAX
Speech Recognition	Sync Center
System	Table PC Settings
Taskbar and Start Menu	Text to Speech
User Accounts	Welcom Center
Windows CardSpace	Windows Defender
Windows Firewall	Windows Sidebar Properties
Windows SlideShow	Windows Update

Chapter 2 — Introduction to Microsoft Word 2007

1. Write a short note on the following commands of Microsoft Word.

Applying Fonts	Paragraph Setting
Page Numbering	Change Case
Date and Time	Insert Picture
Sort	Bullets and Numbering
Animate Text	AutoCorrect
AutoFormat	Break, Insert
Columns	Comments, Insert
Table of Contents	Creating a Table
Creating an Index	Drop Cap
File, Insert	Find and Replace
Footnotes and Endnotes	Header and Footer
Hyperlinks	Macro
Protect Document	Reveal Formatting
Send To	Tabs
Tracking the Document Changes	Bookmarks
Versions	Word Count
Zoom	

2. How would you save a document file?
3. Which alignments Word 2007 supports?
4. How would you apply various fonts?
5. Describe the process of Spell Checking in Word 2007.
6. What is Thesaurus?
7. What are Styles?
8. Describe the various Borders in Word 2007.
9. How would you close a document file?
10. Describe the various options of saving the document.
11. How would you print your document?
12. Describe the process of mailmerge in Word 2007.

Chapter 3 — Introduction to Microsoft Excel 2007

1. What conventions are used in Excel 2007?
2. How would you create a worksheet?
3. How would you copy a formula?
4. How are decision making formula used?
5. Write a short note on the following commands of Microsoft Excel.

Styles	Functions
AutoCalculate	Sum Function
Average Function	Creating Charts
Auditing	Comments
Outlines	Fitting on a page
Function wizard	Goal seeking
Scenarios manager	Pivot Table
AutoFill	Formatting Numbers and Labels
Applying Themes	Background Themes
Protecting Worksheets	Functions
Adding/Deleting Rows	Inserting Page Breaks
Convert Text to Columns	

Chapter 4 — Introduction to PowerPoint 2007

1. How would you create presentation from Template?
2. Describe the various PowerPoint views.
3. How would you change the background colour of the presentation?
4. How would you add graphics to the slide?
5. Describe the process of reordering the slides.
6. How would you add an animated cartoon to a slide?
7. What are slide transitions?
8. How would you create a Slide Show?
9. How would you pack the presentation?

Chapter 5 — Introduction to Access 2007

1. How would you create a database?
2. Describe the process of creating a database using the wizard.
3. How would you create a database using template?
4. What is a Form?
5. How would you create a Query?
6. How would you create a Report?